MATTHEW 24 FULFILLED

By Evangelist
John L. Bray

★ ★

Title: MATTHEW 24 FULFILLED

Copyright 1996 by John L. Bray

First edition October 1996, 5,000 copies
Second edition June 1998, 5,000 copies
Third edition June 2000, 5,000 copies

Printed in the United States of America

Library of Congress Catalog Card Number 96-097160

Subjects: 1. The Olivet Discourse. 2. Eschatology. 3. Second Coming of Christ. 4. The Great Tribulation. 5. The Abomination of Desolation. 6. The End of the Age.

Published by:
JOHN L. BRAY MINISTRY, Inc.
P.O. Box 90129
Lakeland, Florida 33804
U.S.A.

★ ★

Table of Contents ●●●●●●●●●●●●●●●●●●●●

Introduction 3

Section 1 - "When Shall These Things Be?" 9

Section 2 - "The Abomination of Desolation" 35

Section 3 - "Then Shall be Great Tribulation" 64

Section 4 - "Immediately After the Tribulation" 106

Section 5 - "The Sign of the Son of Man in Heaven" . 137

Section 6 - "Coming in the Clouds of Heaven" 167

Section 7 - "This Generation Shall Not Pass" 196

Section 8 - "Heaven and Earth Shall Pass Away" 221

Section 9 - "No Man Knows the Day Nor the Hour" .. 256

Section 10 - Conclusion 273

Section 11 - Personal Testimony of the Author 276

Bibliography 286

Introduction ●●●●●●●●●●●●●●●●●●●●●●●

    This book took a few years of research and study and writing before it was finally completed. The various sections of this book were first printed in a series of smaller books and mailed free, as published, beginning in September 1990, and ending in May 1996, to those on our mailing list. The research took me personally to many large theological libraries both in the United States and overseas. The research involved mainly the older authors, preachers and commentaries prior to 1864, before the extremes of both dispensationalism and speculative Biblical criticism had, in their divergent ways, gained their foothold everywhere. I wanted to find out what the "old dusty books" (most of them rare) had to say about **Matthew 24** (as well as the book of Revelation and other New Testament prophecies). I have also gained knowledge of what later writers had to say as well, though their voices these days are not sounding much like the forgotten voices of earlier years. I have read innumerable books on the subject of this book, and I have quoted from over one hundred books, as listed in the bibliography in the back.

    But I must say that all I have read from others has added to my knowledge, though not necessarily met my acceptance. Inclusive in my research and study have been the many books on eschatology in my own library which includes many commentaries and books on the book of Revelation itself, the early church fathers, the Talmud, etc.

    I am not a scholar. It has been said that one of the differences between a student and a scholar is that a scholar has to know Greek and Hebrew. I have to accept the scholar's authority for definition of Bible words. My situation is that of attempting to provide Bible interpretation on the basis of accepting the Bible as it is written, and believing that it means just what it says. Biblical criticism is not my "cup of tea," especially since the critics cannot even agree among themselves, and they only make believe that they know where much of the disputed portions of the Bible came from. I accept the Bible by faith and believe that its inspiration is valid for the Christian faith which is centered in that Bible. Jesus said that His words would never pass away, and I believe that. My approach may be thought academic, but at the same time a lot of excitement is provided as my mind keeps learning things that were not understood before, even though it means a constant upgrading of my theological beliefs. But I will say this: it did not take me just the last few years to arrive at what I have written in this book. I started studying the Bible with an honest heart and an open mind before I was even saved at the age of 15, and when one puts nearly fifty-eight years (my ministry) into constant and diligent Bible study, that ought to be of help for something. Even so, I feel I know even less today than I thought I knew when I was ordained a Baptist pastor in September 1940 at the age of 18 (I started preaching at the age of 16). But tomorrow I will try to learn still something else. I hope this book will open your eyes to new insights as well.

The publication of this book means that for some while now I have not held to the interpretations given previously in earlier books on some matters relating to **Matthew 24** and the book of Revelation and other passages dealing with these things. So I must put a disclaimer here applicable to some of my earlier writings which are in conflict with this book. But read my previous books (those which might be around somewhere out of the more than 2,000,000 published) to see what I used to believe. They are still much closer to the truth than all the dispensational prophecy literature being put out today, and they might help one to "bridge the gap" between dispensational futurism and the teachings that are given here.

In this study it is my desire to give to you all the results of the many months of study and research done on this subject, and with sufficient documentation as to indicate that all I say is not simply the product of my own mind. It would be impossible to even suggest the multitudinous books and writings of others which have been studied and which have helped to formulate my own thinking and to clarify these matters. I say "helped," because in the final analysis this book is the result of the personal struggles in my own mind and soul to arrive at the truth of what Jesus was really saying in His Olivet discourse. As a pastor in Michigan told his congregation, "Brother Bray milks a lot of cows, but he churns his own butter." These struggles have pushed through doubts, discouragement, frustration, late nights of study, constant prayer, unending conversation and discussion both in person and by correspondence with others, travel, days in libraries, much reading and studying and typing and retyping. But these struggles have carried me through and now here is the book. This book was written without secretary, computer or word processor, on manual typewriters. Final preparation of the book was completed during a time while I was having trouble with my eyes. It might be pointed out that it was not written during some absence from my ministry, but was written during a period of many months while traveling and conducting evangelistic and revival campaigns in many countries, sometime while secluded in a hotel or motel room, or while at home in between long trips while carrying on all the details of other work involved in the publishing and distribution of all of our gospel sermons and Bible study literature, plus much correspondence and other activities, along with family life.

To Evelyn, my wife of forty-five years, goes the credit of so very much encouragement, personal help, note-taking, assistance in libraries, etc., as this book developed and finally came to pass. She put up with me and this book-writing for a long time.

Appreciation is here publicly expressed to Mrs. Thomas (Joyce) Martin of Red Bank, New Jersey, for giving of her time and service in proofreading this book in preparation for printing.

Our thanks also go to our many friends whose financial support of our ministry has made possible the publication of this book.

While this book is actually a commentary on the entire 24th chapter of Matthew, the specific purpose of the book is to show that the destruction of Jerusalem and the Temple, the "end of the age," and the *parousia*/coming of the Son of man, all occurred in the first century in A.D. 67-70.

Rather than use footnotes for quotations of other authors, I have simply put the author's name, book title, volume and page number, after each quotation. This seems more practical than footnotes, for my purpose, and also makes for easier reading. You will not have to look all over the book to find out whom I am quoting. The bibliography is not a summary of books which are available on this subject; it would take many, many more pages for that. This bibliography lists **only** those books from which I quote or to which I refer.

If it be said that this book is not of the highest literary or journalistic excellence, my reply is that it is written in such a way that those who read it can understand what I say, which is not always true of many books which seem to be written mostly for theologians and scholars to read. I found some of these very difficult to follow myself.

Now read the book. I trust that through it God will reveal some things to you that have taken many years for me to learn.

John L. Bray
Lakeland, Florida
August 14, 1996

Section 1 ●●●●●●●●●●●●●●●●●●●●●●●●

"WHEN SHALL THESE THINGS BE?"

The entire 24th chapter of Matthew concerns the prophecy of Jesus Christ concerning the coming destruction of Jerusalem and the Temple in the year A.D. 70.

To help us understand fully the teaching and meaning of that chapter, let us go back to chapter 21 of the same book and read a parable that Jesus gave to the chief priests and elders of His day. It is the parable of the householder, in **Matthew 21:33-41:**

"Hear another parable: There was a certain householder, which planted a vineyard, and hedged it round about, and digged a winepress in it, and built a tower, and let it out to husbandmen, and went into a far country:

"And when the time of the fruit drew near, he sent his servants to the husbandmen, that they might receive the fruits of it.

"And the husbandmen took his servants, and beat one, and killed another, and stoned another.

"Again, he sent other servants more than the first: and they did unto them likewise.

"But last of all he sent unto them his son, saying, They will reverence my son.

"But when the husbandmen saw the son, they said among themselves, 'This is the heir; come, let us kill him, and let us seize on his inheritance.

"And they caught him, and cast him out of the vineyard, and slew him.

"When the lord therefore of the vineyard cometh, what will he do unto those husbandmen?

"They say unto him, He will miserably destroy those wicked men, and will let out his vineyard unto other husbandmen, which shall render him the fruits in their seasons."

In this parable Jesus was describing God (pictured as the householder), the Jews (pictured as the husbandmen who should have brought forth fruits for the householder), the prophets and disciples (pictured as the servants who were beaten and slain), and then Himself (pictured as the son who at last was sent). The Jews did not bring forth spiritual fruit for God, but instead persecuted and killed the prophets and later the disciples; so finally God sent His Son into the world, but Him too they killed. And as to what God would do to them because of this was answered by the chief priests and Pharisees themselves when they replied that the householder would destroy those wicked men and turn over the vineyard to other people who would bring forth fruits for the householder.

In verse 42 Jesus plainly indicated He was talking about Himself as He referred to the "stone which the builders rejected," and then He said to them, "Therefore say I unto you, The kingdom of God shall be taken from you, and given to a nation bringing forth the fruits thereof" **(vs. 43)**. Keep this passage in mind, because it relates to the prophecy of Jesus in **Matthew 24**. These wicked chief priests and Pharisees understood perfectly that Jesus was talking about them **(vs. 45)**. It was definitely prophesied by Jesus that the kingdom of God would be taken away from the Jews and given to another nation who would bring forth the fruits thereof (and we know who that new nation was, according to I Peter 2:9). And unknowingly they prophesied their own coming destruction when they said, "He will miserably destroy those wicked men."

In **Isaiah 65:15** there was a prophecy made, "The Lord God shall slay thee, and call his servants by another name."

But let us continue, leading up to Matthew 24. In chapter 23, Jesus pronounces woe after woe upon the scribes and Pharisees. In fact, most of the chapter contains these woes, and He told them they would persecute, scourge and kill the prophets that He sends to them, and that because of this "all the righteous blood shed upon earth . . . All these things shall come upon this generation" **(vss. 34-36)**.

So in this passage He gives the **timetable** as to when the Jewish people would be punished for their rejection of God's servants and of Jesus Christ, and when the kingdom of God would be taken away from them and given to another nation. It would all happen in "THIS GENERATION," He said. That is, it would happen during the generation of those living then.

"And Jesus went out, and departed from the temple: and his disciples came to him for to shew him the buildings of the temple" (Matthew 24:1).

The discussion of Jesus with the scribes and Pharisees had no doubt taken place inside the Temple grounds (see **Matthew 21:23**). Now they depart from the temple, and His disciples begin to point out the various buildings of the temple and no doubt to discuss the magnificence of those buildings.

The stones themselves at these buildings were fabulous in size. Those in the foundations were as much as 60 feet long, and others above as much as 67 feet or more long, 7½ feet high, and 9 feet wide. To the Jewish people, there was nothing like this building in the whole world!

Some are not aware that there were three temples, and that this one in the time of Christ was the third. Solomon's temple was the first one, erected by Solomon in the 10th century, B.C. It was destroyed in 587 or 586 B.C. by Nebuchadnezzar II, the king of Babylon. The second temple was the one which was rebuilt by the Jewish leader Zerubbabel by 516 B.C. at the end of 70 years of Babylonian captivity. It was the second temple that was desecrated by Antiochus Epiphanes, the king of Syria, in 168 B.C. More will be said about this when we study **Matthew 24:15**.

The third temple is the one under discussion, and it was called Herod's temple. It was begun in 19 B.C. by Herod the Great, king of Judaea, and was completed about A.D. 64. Herod had kept 10,000 workmen employed in building this temple for eight successive years. This third temple surpassed the first two in architectural splendor. Herod wanted a temple of far greater beauty than the one that then existed, and so he did this—using the best ornamentation possible in that day. The temple was a source of wonder. The huge blocks were alternately red and white marble. Nine of the gates were overlaid with silver and gold, and one was of solid Corinthian brass. It was a sight to behold for all those in Jesus' day.

What we find spoken by Jesus in **Matthew 24** was spoken about 40 years before the things came to pass which He prophesied, and Matthew wrote his book about 33 years before they happened. Matthew was the first of the four gospels, as claimed by Origen and Eusebius. John is the only one of the writers of the four gospels who does not mention in his gospel the events recorded in Matthew 24. Therefore, these passages telling of these events were PROPHECIES, and not simply records of events already transpired.

Why are there three accounts? How were they written? Well, it is certain they were not verbally dictated from Heaven to these three men—else all three accounts **(Matthew 24, Mark 13,** and **Luke 21)** would be precisely the same in the recorded portions. But these men, who had been with Jesus and heard this discourse, recorded them to the best of their ability (with the help and inspiration of the Holy Spirit, of course) at some later time (even as Luke said in **Luke 1:1-3)**—one writing some things, another some other things, etc., and with some things either different or in addition to what another had written. As for example, Matthew said "abomination of desolation" **(Matthew 24:15),** and Luke said "Jerusalem compassed with armies"

(**Luke 21:20**), etc. Later compilers of our New Testament put the writings of these men into "canon" form, and we have our "books" today. So we need to read and study all three passages (as well as others) to gain the most knowledge of all that was said. After all, we never would know that Jesus said, "It is more blessed to give than to receive," if Paul had not told us so in **Acts 20:35**, for certainly neither Matthew, Mark, Luke nor John told us that Jesus said this; we had to learn from Paul that Jesus said this. And John tells us in **John 21:31**, "And there are also many other things which Jesus did, the which, if they should be written every one, I suppose that even the world itself could not contain the books that should be written."

So inasmuch as we do not have a record of everything that Jesus did and said, we need to study carefully ALL the passages dealing with this very important subject so that we can get the best possible understanding of what He was saying.

It is in the last part of chapter 23 that we find the plaintive heart-cry of Jesus as He thinks of how these people have rejected Him and of their fate awaiting them because of this. He said, "O Jerusalem, Jerusalem, thou that killest the prophets, and stonest them which are sent unto thee, how often would I have gathered thy children together, even as a hen gathereth her chickens under her wings, and ye would not!" (vs. 37).

And then He said, "**Behold, your house is left unto you desolate**" (**vs. 38**).

What? Did not Jesus remember all those marvelous blessings promised to Israel (**Deuteronomy 22**), etc.? Yes, but Jesus was also reminded of the negative aspects of the promises of God too — that not only were blessings promised, based on faithfulness to Him; but curses were promised if they disobeyed. He remembered all the warnings. He knew that God's wrath toward Israel was now filled up and must soon be poured out — and in that generation too!

His statement that their house would be left unto them desolate was His prophecy of the coming destruction of Jerusalem, God's wrath and judgment that would be poured out upon them in A.D. 70, and the utter desolation of both the city and the Temple. These tragic and prophetic words of Jesus were uttered at the end of His ministry, just several days before He was crucified. This was the last time He ever went into the Temple.

Another passage, **Luke 19:41-44**, also tells of the concern of Jesus and His prediction concerning their fate:

"And when he was come near, he beheld the city, and wept over it.

"Saying, If thou hadst known, even thou, at least in this thy day, the things which belong unto thy peace! but now they are hid from thine eyes.

"For the days shall come upon thee, that thine enemies shall cast a trench about thee, and compass thee round, and keep thee in on every side,

"And shall lay thee even with the ground, and thy children within thee; and they shall not leave in thee one stone upon another; because thou knewest not the time of thy visitation."

From the time of Antiochus Epiphanes (185 B.C.) until Jerusalem was destroyed by the Romans in A.D. 70, Israel was a backslidden nation which deserved the wrath of God. The events during the time of Antiochus did not remedy the condition of Israel; and when Jesus came, He came to a group of people to whom He constantly preached repentance and warning of further wrath to come.

John Calvin said:

". . . after his time (Antiochus), the Jewish religion was more and more injured, not only by foreign enemies, but by their own priesthood. Nothing remained unpolluted, since their avarice and ambition had arrived at such a pitch, that they trode under foot the whole glory of God, and the law itself" **(John Calvin's Commentary on Daniel).**

No wonder the scathing denunciations of Christ to the Jewish leaders in Matthew 23 were so harsh as He predicted in the following chapter 24 the judgment and wrath that would come upon them.

Jesus promised that these things would happen, and they did come to pass, and in their generation. This we read about in the 24th chapter of Matthew, which we shall now study verse by verse.

Readers are urged to also read the parallel passages and other verses in the gospels relating to this event. They are: **Mark 13:1-33; Luke 17:20-37; Luke 19:41-44;** and **Luke 21:5-36.**

"And Jesus said unto them, See ye not all these things? verily I say unto you, There shall not be left here one stone upon another, that shall not be thrown down" (Matthew 24:2).

Jesus predicted that all the greatness of this magnificent temple would be utterly destroyed — not one stone left upon another. This came to pass in the year A.D. 70 exactly as Jesus said it would. After the Roman armies had taken Jerusalem, Titus the Roman general gave orders that the soldiers should dig up even the foundation of the temple, and also of the city itself. Titus had not really wanted to destroy the city and the temple, but to preserve them; but circumstances at last caused him to give the order, and Turnus Rufus, who was left in command of the army at Jerusalem, ploughed up the hill of the Sanctuary and tore up the foundation of the Temple. This destruction of the temple and the city to this extent also fulfilled the prophecy of **Micah 3:12**, "Therefore shall Zion for your sake be plowed as a field, and Jerusalem shall become heaps."

Here at the very first of this chapter is an example of non-literal language which suggests that we should be willing to allow the same understanding of some other statements of grandeur or heightened description which we shall come across. It is very obvious to anyone visiting Jerusalem even today that not EVERY stone was literally torn apart from each other, as the wailing wall which is still being used by the Jews for their prayers was one part of the temple in Jesus' day. I have been there and seen it and taken pictures of it. But what His statement suggests is that of utter destruction, and as a matter of fact it was fulfilled in a near-literal way.

"Not leaving one stone upon another . . . is a proverbial and hyperbolical way of speaking to denote very exemplary destruction" **(Thomas Newton)**.

Luke put it in these words:

"For the days shall come upon thee, that thine enemies shall cast a trench about thee, and compass thee round, and keep thee in on every side,

The Wailing Wall is believed to be the remains of the western wall of Herod's Temple. Photo taken by John L. Bray in June 1979.

"And shall lay thee even with the ground, and thy children within thee; and they shall not leave in thee one stone upon another; because thou knewest not the time of thy visitation" (**Luke 19:43-44**).

It is interesting to note in the above passage the REASON which Jesus gave for this utter destruction that came upon the city of Jerusalem: "BECAUSE thou knewest not the time of thy visitation" (**vs. 44**). If the people had not rejected Him as the Messiah, things would have been different. It was as the people said at the time when he was crucified, "Then answered all the people, and said, His blood be on us, and on our children" (**Matthew 27:25**).

Josephus recorded the fulfillment of this prophecy thusly:

"Caesar gave orders that they should now demolish the entire city and temple, but should leave as many of the towers standing as were of the greatest eminency . . . and so much of the wall as enclosed the city on the west side. This wall was spared in order to afford a camp for such as were to lie in garrison; as were the towers also spared, in order to demonstrate to posterity what kind of city it was, and how well fortified, which the Roman valor had subdued; but for all the rest of the wall, it was so thoroughly laid even with the ground by those that dug it up to the foundation, that there was left nothing to make those that came thither believe it had ever been inhabited" (**Josephus**, v. 1, p. 473).

So complete was the destruction of Jerusalem that it was two hundred years or so before people began to do anything much in that area where the city had been.

Dr. F.F. Bruce, theologian and author of Manchester, England, described the last days of the conquest of Jerusalem thusly:

"Accordingly, in April of A.D. 70 Titus invested Jerusalem . . . As the seige wore on, the horrors of famine, and even cannibalism, were added to the hazards of war, but the defenders had no thought of capitulating, least of all when Titus, using Josephus as his interpreter, urged the advantages of timely surrender upon them. On July 24 the Romans captured the fortress of Antonia. Twelve days later the daily sacrifice in the temple was discontinued. On August 27 the temple gates were burnt; two days later, on the anniversary of the destruction of the First Temple by the Babylonians in 587 B.C., the Sanctuary itself was set on fire and destroyed. By September 26 the whole city was in Titus' hands. It was razed to the ground, only three towers of Herod's palace on the western wall being left standing, with part of the western wall itself" (**F.F. Bruce**, p. 223).

"**And as he sat upon the mount of Olives, the disciples came unto him privately, saying, Tell us, when shall these things be? and what** shall be the sign of thy coming, and of the end of the world?" (**Matthew 24:3**).

Jesus and His disciples left the Temple and went over to the Mount of Olives. As He sat there, the disciples approached Him with this threefold question which we are now to discuss. (**Mark 13:3** indicates that it was Peter, James, John and Andrew who came to Him with this question.) No doubt the staggering thought was still lingering in their minds of what Jesus had said about the buildings of the Temple whose stones would all be thrown down, and they rememberd how He had just previously pronounced all those woes on the unbelieving Jews and told them that all those things would come UPON THAT GENERATION (**Matthew 23:36**) and how their "house" would be left desolate (**Matthew 23:38**). Why this would virtually mean the end of the Jewish age itself when all this should happen! Not only so, but they associated such an event with the act of God Himself, in a "coming" of Christ in judgment against those people.

So their question was three-fold: **"When shall these things be? and what shall be the sign of thy coming, and of the end of the world?"**

There is absolutely no reason at all for us to divide this question up into three different time-events. The disciples had only one thing in mind, and that is, when would these things happen that He had been talking about — not, when will three different events take place. Jesus had mentioned only the destruction of the Temple. They had no cause to be thinking of any other events except those centered around the coming destruction of Jerusalem.

We have taken for granted that most all of the New Testament prophecies deal with the future in our time (this age), and have not given enough recognition to the fact that when prophecies or predictions made during the ministry of Christ and the lives of the apostles spoke of the "present" age, or the "end of the age," they were referring to THEIR age, the Jewish age (which came to an end in A.D. 70), and not to our Christian age of today. Many prophecies which we have assigned to a future second coming of Christ, for example, were actually fulfilled at the end of THEIR age, in the destruction of Jerusalem and the Temple. The fact that many Bible expositors do not recognize this difference accounts for the many varied and confused interpretations concerning the prophecy of Matthew 24. I hope that in this book that difference can be plainly shown, so that the Olivet discourse of Jesus can more readily be understood in the way that Jesus meant it to be. The prophetic future of **ISRAEL** was summed up in **Daniel 8:26**, "wherefore shut thou up the vision; for it shall be for many days," the fulfillment of which was brought about at the end of THEIR age. Paul spoke of those in his day as those "upon whom the ends of the world (age) are come" (**I Corinthians 10:11**). This was not OUR end-time, but THEIRS.

There is not the faintest suggestion that this three-fold question of the disciples was a question regarding two or three different events separated by a period of time of many hundreds of years. Their concern was that of what was going to happen at the time of which Jesus spoke, namely, at the time when the Temple would be destroyed. The events of the answer of Jesus in reply to their question referred to events that would occur in "this generation" (**Matthew 24:34**), and not to people in a future age and time who had not even appeared on the scene as yet. This division of time and events is made by interpreters of this passage, but was not made by the disciples themselves (nor Jesus).

First, they asked precisely as to when these things would be.

Second, they associated these things with His coming. The word "coming" is from the Greek word, *"parousia"* which means "arrival," "advent," and "presence." It is translated mostly as "coming" in the New Testament. It signified the arrival and presence of some great person — such as a king.

The reason the disciples associated these things with His presence on the scene, is because of the numerous statements He had made as to His coming in that generation, that is, during the lifetime of those to whom He was talking. And the word *"parousia"* did mean "arrival" and not "return". It did not have to refer to any future return of Christ. To the early disciples the *"parousia"* of the Son of man signified the full manifestation of the Messiahship relative to His first coming, His arrival in personal history after His receiving the kingdom from the Father upon His ascension. And the word has not only the meaning of an event which has happened, but also the meaning of that person who has arrived now **being** with those to whom He came.

The disciples remembered that Jesus said He would "come" in their lifetime. For example, He had said, "Verily I say unto you, There be some standing here, which shall not taste of death, till they see the Son of man coming in his kingdom" (**Matthew 16:28**). And in **Mark 9:1** likewise, "And he said unto them, Verily I say unto you, That there be some of them that stand here, which shall not taste of death, till they have seen the kingdom of God come with power."

Some say that what Jesus was referring to in these verses was what happened six days later when His disciples saw Him in shining white on the mount of Transfiguration. But this would not accord with proper use of language, for why would He have indicated that some of them would **still be living** when He came, if He were only talking about something to happen in **just six days?** They would have needed to be so sick and old and near death that most of them would be dead within six days for His statement to make sense if that is what He was referring to. He was not talking about six days later, but about 40 years later, and in their generation. The disciples evidently understood His coming to be associated with the destruction of Jerusalem.

Notice also that they spoke of the "sign of thy COMING" whereas in **Mark 13:4** they speak of "the sign when all these things shall be fulfilled." They definitely connected these events to His coming. The same thing is asked in **Luke 21:7**, "What sign will there be when THESE THINGS shall come to pass?" We cannot by-pass the connection of these words.

The disciples definitely were not thinking of a future second coming of Christ thousands of years away from those events, but rather they associated those things with an actual coming of Christ in judgment and power at that time. His presence would be acknowledged when He arrived in such judgment. Jesus had told Caiaphas the high priest, "Hereafter shall ye see the Son of man sitting on the right hand of power, and coming in the clouds of heaven" (**Matthew 26:64**).

When the disciples asked, "When shall these things be? and what shall be the SIGN of thy coming . . .?" the parallel reading in **Mark 13:4**, "What shall be the SIGN when all these things shall be fulfilled?" definitely indicates that the disciples considered His "coming" and "these things" to be identical events — that is, the sign of His coming was the same as the sign of those things, and those things were connected with the destruction of Jerusalem in the year A.D. 70. If language means anything at all, there is no way His "coming" (as mentioned here) could refer to an event many hundreds of years ahead still in our own future!

So "THESE THINGS" are connected with His "COMING"!

Third, they also associated "these things" with "the end of the world." But please note here that the word "world" is not from the Greek word *"kosmos"* which means the world and its inhabitants, nor *"oikoumene"* which means inhabited earth; but rather, it is from the Greek word *"aeon"* which simply means "age." Many Bible scholars have overlooked the meaning of this word and associated it instead with the end of the physical world. This was the world of the Jews that the disciples were thinking about — the Jewish age itself. Why should "the end" be thought of as the end of OUR age or the world, rather than the end of THEIR age to whom he was talking?

The disciples were not talking about the end of **OUR** age, nor about the end of time as such; but rather, the end of the world (age) in which they **then** lived. They were not concerend about OUR age, though they may have thought (in their ignorance) that the end of that age would also usher in the end of the whole world too. But we need to understand that their question had to do with **THAT AGE** in which they lived then, and which came to a conclusion when Jerusalem and the Temple were destroyed. (Of course, the Jews did not think the end of their age had come then, but from the Christian perspective we say that it did as we understand the Messiah has already come even though they did not receive Him as such).

The Jewish people recognized two ages — the one in which they then lived (under the law), and the future age of the Messiah. "A common Jewish conception was that the appearing of the Messiah would close 'this age', and introduce 'the coming age' — these phrases often occurring in the Talmud" (**John Broadus**, p. 482). The end of that present age (to them) was the age to which the disciples had reference. They were talking about the end of the age in which THEY lived — the end of the Jewish age. They were speaking of that age that was closing in the LAST DAYS mentioned in **Hebrews 1:2**, "Hath in these LAST DAYS spoken unto us by his Son." Not OUR last days, but the last days of the Jewish age — in the last days during which Jesus Christ came. This is the same age referred to as was mentioned in **Hebrews 9:26**, "Now once IN THE END OF THE WORLD (ages) hath he appeared to put away sin by the sacrifice of himself." The crucifixion of Christ took place as THAT age was coming near a close. Peter said that Christ came "in these last times" (**I Peter 1:20**). Paul, writing elsewhere regarding his contemporaries, said, "upon whom the ends of the world (ages) are come" (**I Corinthians 10:11**). Jesus came during the last days of the age that was then (the Jewish age), which age definitely came to an end with the destruction of Jerusalem and the Temple in A.D. 70. In their question to Jesus, the disciples connected the destruction of the Temple with the end of the age. It was **THEIR** age under discussion — not **OUR** age.

When we consider whether the meaning of "end of the age" refers to the end of OUR age, or to the end of some earlier age, we need only to pay attention to the fact that Jesus connected the "end of the age" with the events involved in the destruction of the Temple and Jerusalem in the year A.D. 70 Thus, the end of the age which Jesus and the disciples anticipated, was the end of the **Jewish age** which took place when the Jewish Temple, rituals, and the capital city were all completely destroyed. This was a coming of Christ in judgment on the Jewish world which finally ended one age and brought another into existence. So when in the New Testament we see the expression, "end of the age," let us remember that that expression **CANNOT** refer to **OUR** age, as applied by so many Bible teachers, but refers to that age which is now past and closed. **ALL of the things prophesied by Jesus in Matthew 24 occurred at the end of THAT age.**

Peter quoted Joel as saying, "And it shall come to pass IN THE LAST DAYS, saith God, I will pour out of my Spirit upon all flesh" (**Acts 2:17**). The Spirit was poured out on the day of Pentecost, and this was in "the last days." Peter said, "But THIS is THAT which was spoken by the prophet Joel" (**Acts 2:16**). He was not talking about the last days of THIS age, but of THEIR age. Why should anyone today confuse this matter by trying to put the pouring out of the Spirit into some latter days in the times in which we live just before a future return of Christ, when this happened in the same age that Jesus Christ was here in those last days (**Hebrews 1:2**)? What happened at Pentecost happened in the last days, and was not a fulfillment of a prophecy which was promised to be fulfilled sometime hundreds of years later.

"And it shall come to pass afterward," says Joel — or "in the last days," as Peter renders the phrase "that I will pour out my spirit upon all flesh . . . And I will show wonders in the heavens and in the earth, blood, and fire, and pillars of smoke. The sun shall be turned into darkness, and the moon into blood, before THE GREAT AND THE TERRIBLE DAY OF THE LORD COME. And it shall come to pass, that whosoever shall call on the name of the Lord shall be delivered" (**Joel 2: 28-32**).

"The Apostle Peter, quoting the whole of this passage, expressly declares that the first and last parts of it were fulfilled at the Pentecostal effusion of the Spirit, and the conversions immediately following it. Evident therefore it is that the '**great and terrible day of the Lord**' — bound up with these events as part of one and the same great chapter of church history — is no other, according to inspiration itself, than **the day of Jerusalem's judicial destruction**" (**David Brown,** p. 438).

Jesus came in the last days (**Hebrews 1:1-2**).

Jesus died at the end of the age (**Hebrews 9:26**), and "in these last times" (**I Peter 1:20**). If "end of the age" meant the end of OUR age, it would be incomprehensible to say that Christ appeared "in the end of the world (age)," for that would not be possible if the end of this age had not yet come!

The Holy Spirit was poured out in the last days (**Acts 2:16-17**).

Paul indicated that those living in his day, prior to the destruction of Jerusalem, were those "upon whom the ends of the world (ages) are come" **(I Corinthians 10:11).**

The last days ended with the end of that age. This is what the disciples asked about — when that age would end and Jesus appear and manifest Himself as the Messiah, or Son of Man. The answer was given by Jesus, Who promised that that age would end during "this generation" (their generation) **(Matthew 23:36, 24:34).**

Because this interpretation of what "last days" and "end of the age" means is not clearly understood by many, is one of the reasons why there has been so much confusion about this 24th chapter of Matthew. We have become mesmerized by those words, "last days"; and all they mean to many of us is the period of time just before Christ returns in our **future.** But this is not correct.

The disciples asked about the end of the world (age). What age? We are accustomed to thinking in terms of "our" age, "this" age, etc., but when we read these expressions in the New Testament we need to think in terms of "their" age, "that" age in which "they" lived, etc. Only in this way will New Testament prophecy make sense. This is why there is so much error in prophecy preaching today, because the teachers want to pull everything over into "our" age, when this is not what was meant at all. If, in **Hebrews 9:26**, it says that Christ came in the "end of the world (age)," which was the end of the Jewish age, then that same expression must mean the same thing in Matthew 24. Can you see how this changes the picture completely different from the way "end time" messages are given over radio and T.V. all the time?

Strong's concordance indicates the word *"aion"* (Greek word for "age") was a Jewish expression signifying the Messianic period (present or future), and not the same as the word *"kosmos"* meaning world and inhabitants.

The question by the disciples as phrased in **Mark 13:4**, "What shall be the sign when all these things shall be fulfilled?" indicated that the disciples understood His "coming" (*parousia*) and "end of the age" to be identified with the time "when all these things shall be fulfilled."

But whether the end of that age would coincide with the end of the world itself was not suggested nor mentioned; and this would only be known in future years by the actual happenings of events themselves. The disciples may have even been under the apprehension that the end of the age (the Temple, etc.) would be the actual end of the world; but Jesus did not say that, nor did He intend that to be so understood. He Himself did not even know the exact day nor the hour of the events He was discussing, so how then could He have known when the end of the world would be?

Many Bible scholars today believe that the disciples in Matthew 24 were asking Jesus what would be the sign of His second coming in our future. But nothing could be further from the truth than this. They did not even believe at that time that Jesus had to die, or was going to die. So how could they have been thinking in terms of a "second" coming in our future if this were true? What they were actually asking Him was what would be the sign of His presence (*"parousia,"* translated "coming" in our New Testament), and they connected this presence (*"parousia"*) with the destruction of Jerusalem about which He had been speaking. This, to them, would be the "end of the world" (or "age"), after which a new age would begin. The Jews thought in terms of the age in which they lived, and in the next age in which Messiah would reign. This is exactly what the disciples had in mind when they asked Jesus these questions. The manifestation of His presence as Messiah would be seen and felt at the destruction of the Temple and Jerusalem; this was all tied together in their question and in the response that Jesus gave to them. They did not have in mind anything at all about a "second coming of Christ" as Christians in general believe today. And that age did end when the entire Jewish economy, both religious and otherwise, came to an end, and the temple and Jerusalem both were made desolate.

When this all happened, the disciples all found themselves in a new age which is the age in which we live today — the age of the Messiah (which the Jews are still looking for, as they are for a coming Messiah yet). But that age is already here, and Jesus is the Messiah and King, and His kingdom has been manifested to them and it is a present reality today. And nothing is taught in the Bible about a coming so-called millennial age after another coming of Christ during which the Jews will all be back in Palestine and Jesus reigning over them there from an earthly temple in an earthly city for a period of a thousand years. This teaching is un-Scriptural nonsense and is part of the futuristic teachings that keep so many Christians from understanding the Bible in the right way.

John Gill, Baptist preacher of many years ago, said:

". . . this coming of his, the sign of which they inquire, is not to be understood of his coming a second time to judge the world, at the last day, but of his coming in his kingdom and glory, which they had observed him some little time before to speak of; declaring that some present should not die, till they saw it . . ." **(John Gill**, vol. 1, on Matthew 24:3).

It has been thought that when Jesus said concerning the "unpardonable sin" that it could not be forgiven in this world (age), nor in the world (age) to come (**Matthew 12:32**), that He was referring to this life and to eternity. But we must keep in mind that the age that was present to Him, was that age which we have been talking about, which ended in the destruction of Jerusalem and the Temple in A.D. 70 The "age to come" referred to that which followed that age, the age in which we now live. Otherwise, one would have Jesus saying that the unpardonable sin could not be forgiven either on earth or in eternity, which really wouldn't make much sense, for sins can only be forgiven in this life alone anyway. We have no promise that ANY sins will ever be forgiven in eternity. Once again we see the meaning of "the age" which the disciples had in mind when they spoke of "the end of the age."

The disciples could not be asking about two different events that would be separated by at least a couple of thousands of years; rather, they associated these things together as connected with each other. This is why some commentaries put part of Matthew 24 events out into our future (another Temple, another abomination of desolation, another tribulation, and yes, even make the *parousia* of Matthew 24 the same as a future second coming of Christ, because they realize the inseparableness of these events from each other). Honest Bible exegesis would seem to require that the events mentioned (including the *"parousia"*) take place at the same immediate time in connection with each other, that is, during that generation, and while some of those who heard Jesus were still living.

The sign of His COMING in **Matthew 24:3** was the same as the sign when THOSE THINGS in **Luke 21:7** would come to pass. These were not separate events, but one and the same.

The coming of the kingdom of God (as mentioned in **Matthew 16:28** and **Mark 9:1** and **Luke 21:31**) was equated in the minds of the disciples with the restoration of the kingdom to Israel, as seen by their question in **Acts 1:6**, "Lord, wilt thou at this time restore again the kingdom to Israel?" They did not at that time understand that the seed of David (Christ) would sit upon his throne by means of His resurrection and ascension, as preached by Peter in **Acts 2:29-36**, and as understood by Peter on the day of Pentecost. In His resurrection and ascension, Christ was now reigning on the Father's right hand (**vss. 34-35**), and the MANIFESTATION of that kingdom would come, or be revealed, when Christ would come in judgment on Jerusalem just 40 years later — in that generation, and while some of those who heard Him would still be living. During THIS age in which we live now, Christ is reigning and His saints are reigning with Him (see **Revelation 20:4**). At the "end," (**I Corin-**

thians 15:23-24) "he shall have delivered up the kingdom to God, even the Father; when he shall have put down all rule and all authority and power. For he must reign, till he hath put all enemies under his feet. The last enemy that shall be destroyed is death" (**I Corinthians 15:24-26**). Then Christ reigns forever and ever along beside God the Father, after having presented His kingdom, His people, to His Father.

Some say that when the disciples asked Jesus the question, "Lord, wilt thou at this time restore again the kingdom to Israel?" (**Acts 1:6**) that the answer Christ gave was answering that question itself as they had asked it, that is, as an earthly kingdom (see the book, **Until the Coming of Messiah and His Kingdom**, for example, by **Robert Shank**). Of course Jesus did not answer concerning something else, and He did answer their question. But He was showing the actual fulfillment of those prophecies dealing with the restoration of the kingdom, and how they were spiritually fulfilled and not in an earthly, materialistic way. He told them all about "the kingdom" as He expounded the Scriptures concerning Himself (**Luke 24:27**) during those few days between His resurrection and ascension. He called them foolish for not believing "all that the prophets have spoken" (**vs. 25**) and then asked, "Ought not Christ to have suffered these things, and to enter into his glory?" (**vs. 26**). His entering into His glory was not something to happen two thousand years later, nor was his kingdom something to be revealed only two thousand or more years later; but His kingdom was something that had not been understood by His disciples any more than His death and resurrection were understood by them. "Then opened he their understanding, that they might understand the scriptures" (**Luke 24:45**). But it was not until after Pentecost that the Holy Spirit really brought these things to their remembrance in such a way that they could preach with authority on these matters. "But the Comforter, which is the Holy Ghost, whom the Father will send in my name, he shall teach you all things, and bring all things to your remembrance, whatsoever I have said unto you" (**John 14:26**).

Read through the book of Acts and notice how Paul in particular went everywhere preaching "the kingdom of God," ending the recorded part of his ministry in these words, "Preaching the kingdom of God, and teaching those things which concern the Lord Jesus Christ" (**Acts 28:31**). Nowhere do we hear him preaching of a future millennial kingdom (one restored to the Jews), but instead, his preaching was that of the kingdom of God as a present reality and one centering around a resurrected and ascended Lord and Savior Jesus Christ.

"**And Jesus answered and said unto them, Take heed that no man deceive you.**

"For many shall come in my name, saying, I am Christ; and shall deceive many" (Matthew 24:4-5).

There are many today who take this passage (as well as the following ones which are connected to it) and apply it to our own day and time, seeking to show the fulfillment in various personages of modern days, as though these present day appearances prove that Jesus is ready to come back again. Even Billy Graham has been guilty of this, as for example in his sermon, "25 Signs of the Second Coming of Christ," which I heard him preach at a Southern Baptist Convention many years ago, and part of which he still preaches. But Jesus was not talking here about the things that would happen in OUR age; rather, He was talking about what would occur BEFORE the coming destruction of Jerusalem and its temple. These things applied to THEIR age, before the "end" of their age would come. And these were "things," not "signs," for He said, "all these things must come to pass, BUT THE END IS NOT YET" **(Matthew 24:6)**. Rather than indicate the immediate nearness of the "end," those things indicated the end was "not yet."

The first thing which Jesus mentioned would occur before the end of their age, was the appearance of false Christs — those who claimed themselves to be the Messiah. Jesus said that **many** would appear on the scene during this time. And they did appear — many of them!

Acts 8:9-10 tells of one of these:

"But there was a certain man, called Simon, which beforetime in the same city used sorcery, and bewitched the people of Samaria, giving out that himself was some great one:

"To whom they all gave heed, from the least to the greatest, saying, This man is the great power of God."

Henry Hammond (1681) even felt that Simon Magus was the man of sin as mentioned in **II Thessalonians 2:3-4**. And Hammond translated Irenaeus (from the Latin) as saying:

"Simon Magus set himself to contend against the Apostles, that he might also appear glorious. He was for his Magick honored with a statue by Claudius Caesar. He was glorified by many as a God, and taught that himself was he that appeared as the Son among the Jews, that in Samaria he descended as the Father, and in other nations came as the Holy Ghost. That he was the most sublime virtue, that is, he which was the Father over all, and that he was content to be called by the highest titles that any man did call him" **(Henry Hammond, p. 272)**.

"The chief representatives of early Gnosticism were Simon Magus and his pupil Menander. There can be no reasonable doubt that Simon endeavoured to be a rival of Christ, and that he came to teach in Rome. He represented himself as God and the Word of God" **(Leighton Pullan, p. 223).**

A number of the early church fathers wrote about Simon Magus. For example, **Eusebius** quoted **Justin Martyr** as saying:

"After the Lord was taken up into heaven the demons put forth a number of men who claimed to be gods. These not only escaped being persecuted by you, but were actually the objects of worship — for example Simon, a Samaritan from a village called Gittho, who in Claudius Caesar's time, thanks to the art of the demons who posssessed him, worked wonders of magic, and in your imperial city of Rome was regarded as a god, and like a god was honoured by you with a statue in the River Tiber between the two bridges. It bears this inscription in Latin, SIMONI DEO SANCTO. Almost all Samaritans, and a few from other nations too, acknowledge him as their principal god, and worship him" **(Eusebius, p. 86).**

This statue, which translated said, "to Simon the Holy God," was also affirmed by **Tertullian.**

Then there was Dositheus the Samaritan, who claimed to be the Messiah predicted by Moses.

A few years later, during the reign of Nero, these false prophets became so numerous that many of them were apprehended and killed every day.

Jesus warned His disciples that these men would be showing up, and they were not to be deceived by them.

Josephus told of one by the name of Theudas, 12 years after the death of Christ, who claimed to be a great prophet and deceived a great multitude into believing he could divide the River Jordan for their passage.

This is recorded for us in **Acts 5:36** as Gamaliel told of Theudas: "For before these days rose up Theudas, boasting himself to be somebody; to whom a number of men, about four hundred, joined themselves: who was slain; and all, as many as obeyed him, were scattered, and brought to nought."

Eusebius told about this Theudas in these words:

"When Fadus was procurator of Judea, an impostor called Theudas persuaded a vast crowd to take their belongings and follow him to the River Jordan; for he claimed to be a prophet, and promised to divide the river by his command and provide them with an easy crossing. A great many people were deceived by this talk. Fadus however did not allow them to enjoy their folly, but sent a troop of cavalry against them. These attacked them without warning, killed many, and took many alive, capturing Theudas himself, whose head they cut off and conveyed to Jerusalem" (**Eusebius**, pp. 84-85).

Eusebius also told about an Egyptian (mentioned in **Acts 21:38**) who must have gathered up quite a following:
"A greater blow than this was inflicted on the Jews by the Egyptian false prophet. Arriving in the country this man, a fraud who posed as a seer, collected about 30,000 dupes, led them round by the wild country to the Mount of Olives, and from there was ready to force an entry into Jerusalem, overwhelm the Roman garrison, and seize supreme power, with his fellow-raiders as bodyguard. But Felix anticipated his attempt by meeting him with the Roman heavy infantry, the whole population rallying to the defence, so that when the clash occurred the Egyptian fled with a handful of men and most of his followers were killed or captured" (**Eusebius**, pp. 96-97).

Gamaliel also told of another: "After this man rose up Judas of Galilee in the days of the taxing, and drew away much people after him: he also perished; and all, even as many as obeyed him, were dispersed" (**Acts 5:37**).

I John 2:18 says:
"Little children, it is the last time: and as ye have heard that antichrist shall come, even now are there many antichrists; whereby we know that it is the last time." When John said this, he seemed to be referring to the approaching end of the Jewish age, and also the prophecies of Christ relating to the false prophets who were to appear before the end of that age when Jerusalem fell.

"**And ye shall hear of wars and rumours of wars: see that ye be not troubled: for all these things must come to pass, but the end is not yet.**

"**For nation shall rise against nation, and kingdom against kingdom: and there shall be famines, and pestilences, and earthquakes, in divers places**" (**Matthew 24:6-7**).

Wars and rumors of wars **must** come to pass — not only in the sense of being prior to "the end," but "must" in the sense of inevitability. In the very nature of things there would be wars and rumors of wars. They are in the ordinary course of events. But those things are not the sign nor signs of the end. The disciples were not to be deceived by these things when they heard of them. Wars and rumors of wars would be inevitable, but "the end is not yet."

Jesus did not want the disciples to think that any of these wars would signal the end. He would tell them shortly of one which would really count.

In spite of what Jesus was really saying here, many today take this passage out of context and say that a sign of the soon-coming of Christ in our time is the multiplied numbers of wars going on in the world. No, this is not true. There have always been wars and rumors of wars, and this is no sign of "the end" to which Jesus referred, nor to the end of our age either.

Men of all ages have looked on various earthly calamities as signs of an approaching end of the world, etc., including those in our own day and time. What Jesus is here calling to the attention of the disciples is that these things are NOT signs of any end, but rather events which have no particular significance so far as helping them to arrive at an answer to their question as to what would be the sign of His coming and those things which He said would happen.

Jesus wanted to show them the **false**, before He gave them the **true** sign. Many use these so-called "signs" to predict a soon-coming of Christ in our time, when Jesus actually meant the exact opposite in regards to what He was talking about.

There were wars in the tributaries of Rome and all over Palestine, Galilee, and Samaria in A.D. 66, preceding the destruction of Jerusalem.

They heard of wars! In A.D. 40 there was a disturbance at Mesopotamia which (**Josephus** says) caused the deaths of more than 50,000 people. In A.D. 49 a tumult at Jerusalem at the time of the Passover resulted in 10,000 to 20,000 deaths. At Caesarea contentions between Jewish people and other inhabitants resulted in over 20,000 Jews being killed. As Jews moved elsewhere, over 20,000 were destroyed by Syrians. At Scythopolis, over 13,000 Jews were killed. Thousands were killed in other places, and at Alexandria 50,000 were killed. At Damascus, 10,000 were killed in an hour's time.

These were not wars of a world-wide scope as we know the world today. They were in Galilee, and in Syria, and in the areas east and south of Judaea. And Judaea was in revolt against Rome, "while the armies of Spain, and Gaul and Germany, Illyricum and Syria, converged upon Italy, to decide who should succeed to Nero's purple."

"There shall be famines" (vs. 7). **Acts 11:28** says, "And there stood up one of them named Agabus, and signified by the Spirit that there should be great dearth throughout all the world: which came to pass in the days of Claudius Caesar." Many died in this famine.

This famine was mentioned by Josephus and Eusebius. **Eusebius** said that right after the imposter Theudas was killed "that the great famine took place in Judaea, in which Queen Helen at great expense bought corn from Egypt and distributed it among those in want" (**Eusebius**, p. 85).

There was also a famine in Rome and parts of Italy, which began the first year of the reign of Claudius and lasted until the next. Another famine in the same region was mentioned by Tacitus and Eusebius in the 10th or 11th year of Claudius. "Without taking into account the great scarcity which prevailed under Claudius, food in the year 68 was extremely dear" (**Renan,** p. 194).

"**. . . and pestilences**" (vs. 7). In A.D. 40 there was a pestilence at Babylon, in which Jews suffered. In A.D. 60 there was much death at Rome on account of a pestilence.

Josephus told about Niger being killed by the Jewish zealots and how "famine and pestilence upon them" was brought about (**Newton,** p. 378).

"**. . . and earthquakes in divers places**" (vs. 7). Earthquakes did occur at Crete, at Smyrna, at Miletus, at Chios, at Asmos, at Rome, at Apamea (same region), at Laodicea (in the reign of Nero) "which city was overthrown, as were likewise Hierapolis and Colosse" (**Newton**), at Campania in the year 62 or 63, and at Rome and Judaea. These earthquakes did not prove the "end" was imminent; contrariwise, as Jesus said, all of those things proved that "the end is not yet" (**vs. 6**). Modern-day prophets ought to keep this in mind too, as they keep on talking about how many more earthquakes there are and how much more destructive they are, etc., as though all this proves it cannot be long now until Jesus comes. What Jesus was trying to say is that these things "must" be, and do not prove a thing so far as indicating "the end" was at hand. But preaching and teaching about earthquakes being another sign of the soon-coming of Christ makes for "good" preaching, and tickles people's ears, even though it does not prove one thing so far as God's word is concerned in the matter of prophecy.

"**All these are the beginning of sorrows**" (**Matthew 24:8**).

All of these things that Jesus mentioned were not to upset the disciples and cause them to think the end had come. They were only the beginning, the same as birth pangs come before the actual hard labor of a woman waiting to be delivered of her child. They were nothing compared to what would happen to the Jews later. Jesus said plainly, "All these are the beginning of sorrows." They were not signs of "the end" then, and neither are they today.

"**Then shall they deliver you up to be afflicted, and shall kill you: and ye shall be hated of all nations for my name's sake**" (**24:9**).

The disciples of Jesus would suffer and be killed wherever they were. The book of Acts tells us of case after case where they were brought before councils and before rulers and kings (**Acts 4, 6, 16, 18, 24, 25**). But wherever they were, in "all nations", they would be hated for the name of Jesus. The coming persecution would be from two sources — from the Jewish leaders, and then from Rome itself.

Persecution against Christians actually began not long after Jesus went back to Heaven. Stephen became the first martyr (**Acts 7:59-60**). Acts 8:1 says, "And at that time there was a GREAT PERSECUTION against the church which was at Jerusalem." This persecution included Saul making "havock of the church, entering into every house, and haling men and women committed them to prison" (**vs. 3**). The word "persecution" used in **Acts 11:19** is the Greek word *"thlipsis"* and is the same word translated as "tribulation" in both **Matthew 24:21, 29** and **Revelation 7:14**. So, by **Acts 8:1** the church was already in great tribulation.

The parallel reading of **Matthew 24:9** in Mark says, "they shall deliver you up to councils; and in the synagogues ye shall be beaten: and ye shall be brought before rulers and kings for my sake, for a testimony against them" (**Mark 13:9**). The word "councils" refers to the local Jewish tribunals which were in the Jewish cities, which were patterned after the Sanhedrin, the great council of Jerusalem. The use of this word shows the context of the Jewish situation, as also does the mention of the disciples being beaten "in the synagogues." Paul the apostle was an example of this. He said, "Of the Jews five times received I forty stripes save one" (**II Corinthians 11:24**). These actions would be applicable so far as this prophecy is concerned in these things that were going to happen to the disciples themselves in the coming days before their persecutors would face judgment in the catastrophe of A.D. 67-70. They would also be brought before "rulers and kings" — the Gentile rulers in Palestine. "The reference to 'rulers and kings' does not demand a situation outside Palestine. Pilate and Herod Antipas would be good examples" (**Jerome's Commentary** on Mark 13:9, p. 624).

But persecution of the Christians actually extended further than just the environs of Palestine itself. The persecution of Christians under Nero took place shortly before the fall of Jerusalem. (Nero ruled from Rome for fourteen years, 54-68, and during the last three and one half years of this time, 64-68, brought untold persecution upon the Christians.) Philip Schaff (**History of the Christian Church**) gives us plain language of the awful persecution of the Christians which was brought about by Nero (the Beast) during this time:

"A 'vast multitude' of Christians was put to death in the most shocking manner. Some were crucified, probably in mockery of the punishment of Christ, some sewed up in the skins of wild beasts and exposed to the voracity of mad dogs in the arena. The satanic tragedy reached its climax at night in the imperial gardens on the slope of the Vatican (which embraced, it is supposed, the present site of the place and church of St. Peter): Christian men and women, covered with pitch or oil or resin, and nailed to posts of pine, were lighted and burned as torches for the amusement of the mob; while Nero, in fantastical dress, figured in a horse race, and displayed his art as a charioteer. Burning alive was the ordinary punishment of incendiaries; but only the cruel ingenuity of this imperial monster, under the inspiration of the devil, could invent such a horrible system of illumination" **(Philip Schaff, pp. 381-382).**

It was during this time, no doubt, that John was sentenced to exile on the island of Patmos, and wrote: "I John, who also am your brother, and companion in TRIBULATION, and in the kingdom and patience of Jesus Christ, was in the isle that is called Patmos, for the word of God, and for the testimony of Jesus Christ" **(Revelation 1:9).**

"And then shall many be offended, and shall betray one another, and shall hate one another" (Matthew 24:10).

When persecution comes, it is easier for Christians to give in to temptation. **II Timothy 1:15** and **4:10** are examples of this. And Jesus said they would even "betray one another"; that is, they would yield to pressure of authorities to reveal information about one another. All of this would cause many to hate one another. In those days many Christians were convicted and executed because of others who were caught and confessed.

"And many false prophets shall rise, and shall deceive many" (Matthew 24:11).

Paul spoke of these in **II Corinthians 11:13** and **II Timothy 2:17-18**. **Acts 13:6** mentions "a certain sorcerer, a false prophet, a Jew, whose name was Bar-jesus" who "withstood them, seeking to turn away the deputy from the faith" **(vs. 8)**. And Paul said, "But evil men and seducers shall wax worse and worse, deceiving, and being deceived" **(II Timothy 3:13).**

"And because iniquity shall abound, the love of many shall wax cold" (Matthew 24:12).

Paul the apostle mentioned that perilous times were coming upon them "in the last days" **(II Timothy 3:1-9)**, and he also pointed out that "all that will live godly in Christ Jesus shall suffer persecution" **(vs. 12).**

"But he that shall endure unto the end, the same shall be saved" (Matthew 24:13).

It is most interesting to know that none of the Christians perished during the final siege and destruction of Jerusalem. When Titus the Roman general finally came into the city, he did not find a single Christian there. Of course, they had all fled the city upon the instruction of Jesus when they first saw the armies surrounding the city (see **vss. 16-20**).

But if this passage is to be applied spiritually, it would mean that those who were finally saved were those who had persevered and who were not false professors.

"And this gospel of the kingdom shall be preached in all the world for a witness unto all nations; and then shall the end come" (Matthew 24:14).

Once again, as we read this ("the end") we need to understand it is the same "end of the world (age)" that the disciples asked Jesus about in verse 3 — that is, the end of that age in which they lived — the end of the Jewish age. This is not a passage of Scripture to be applied to a time just before some future second coming of Christ, as though what we are now waiting on is for the last soul on the face of the earth to have the gospel preached to him or to have the Bible translated into the last language or dialect not yet so done, so that Jesus can return. Jesus was talking about what would be done in **that** age, before the end would come.

Paul very plainly said that what Jesus predicted had actually come to pass in his own day. Writing in A.D. 64 he mentioned "the gospel, which ye have heard, and WHICH WAS PREACHED TO EVERY CREATURE WHICH IS UNDER HEAVEN" **(Colossians 1:23)**. He had just mentioned "the gospel; Which is come unto you, as it is in ALL THE WORLD" **(Colossians 1:5-6)**. This has been done already, in his own lifetime, he said!

Paul said to the Romans that "your faith is spoken of throughout the whole world" **(Romans 1:8)**.

Paul said in **Romans 10:18**, "But I say, Have they not heard? Yes verily, their sound went into all the earth, and their words unto the ends of the world."

Paul said in **Romans 16:25-26**, ". . . my gospel, and the preaching of Jesus Christ . . . now is made manifest, and . . . made known to ALL NATIONS for the obedience of faith."

Preaching "for a witness" **(Matthew 24:14)** meant to present the message and proof (with signs) that Jesus was the promised Messiah. "Unto all nations" was the extent to which this witness should go. In the Great Commission of **Matthew 28:19**, Jesus said again, "ALL NATIONS." In **Mark 16:15** it reads, "ALL THE WORLD." The word "world" is from the Greek word *"oikoumene"* which meant the inhabited world as they knew it in their day and time. But usage of the word in that day meant different things to different peoples. To the Romans, it was the Roman Empire. To the Greeks, it meant all the countries where their language was spoken. But to the Jew, it meant primarily the land of Palestine with all of its tribes, and then later inclusive of all areas where their peoples were scattered.

In **Luke 2:1** it says, "And it came to pass in those days, that there went out a decree from Caesar Augustus, that ALL THE WORLD should be taxed." Surely this referred to the Roman Empire at that time; they taxed only their own empire. In **Acts 11:28** a prophecy was made "that there should be great dearth throughout ALL THE WORLD." This was probably a large area of the Roman Empire.

What did this expression as to all nations mean in **Acts 2:5**? There it says, "And there were dwelling at Jerusalem Jews, devout men, out of EVERY NATION UNDER HEAVEN." Then in **verses 9-11** these people are described as being:

"Parthians, and Medes, and Elamites, and the dwellers in Mesopotamia, and in Judaea, and Cappadocia, in Pontus, and Asia, Phrygia, and Pamphylia, in Egypt, and in the parts of Libya about Cyrene, and strangers of Rome, Jews and proselytes, Cretes and Arabians . . ."

As can be seen, these were people from the known parts of the world as recognized by the Jews at that time. The idea was not present concerning many nations in the world today; in fact, many of the nations of the world today were not even in existence at that time. But the people mentioned in this passage came from the known "world" of that day. This is the world that Jesus told His disciples to reach with the gospel message, and then said that when that witness had been made in all nations the end would come. During the lifetime of Paul this had been accomplished.

Doddridge is quoted by Rev. Henry Cowles as saying:

"It appears from credible records that the gospel was preached in Idumea, Syria and Mesopotamia, by Jude; in Ethiopia by Candace's eunuch, and Matthias; in Pontus, Galatia and the neighboring parts of Asia, by Peter; in the territories of the seven Asiatic churches, by John; in Parthia, by Matthew; in Scythia, by Philip and Andrew; in the northern and western parts of Asia, by Bartholomew; in Persia, by Simon and Jude; in Media, Carmania and several eastern parts, by Thomas; through the vast tract from Jerusalem round about unto Illyricum, by Paul, as also in Italy and probably in Spain and Gaul; in most of which places Christian churches were planted in less than thirty years after the death of Christ — i.e., before the destruction of Jerusalem" **(Henry Cowles,** p. 208).

" 'And this gospel of the kingdom shall be preached in all the world for a witness unto all nations; and then shall the end come' could be regarded as a hyperbolical prediction of what was fulfilled before the destruction of Jerusalem, even as Paul wrote to the Colossians (about A.D. 63), concerning 'the gospel which ye heard, which was preached in all creation under heaven.' (Col. 1:23, Rev. Ver.) It will evidently be fulfilled much more thoroughly before the second coming of Christ; yet Paul's phrase, and the primary reference here to A.D. 70 as 'the end,' should restrain theorizers from insisting that the second coming of Christ cannot take place until this has been fulfilled with literal completeness" **(John A. Broadus,** p. 485).

And if today it be objected that literally every last person in the world would have to hear the gospel before Jesus will come again, then Christ could never come, for there is always someone somewhere who has not heard the gospel, and always will be.

It is certain that this prophecy of Jesus was fulfilled before the destruction of Jerusalem. Jesus said, "and then shall the end come." Not the end of the physical natural world, nor the end of our own present age, but the end of that age they were talking about — the end of the Jewish age — the end of Jerusalem and the Temple, and all that went along with those things.

This does not mean that the gospel was not to continue being preached after the "end" had come. In fact, there would be greater opportunities for the preaching of the gospel and the salvation of multitudes. In the parable of the wedding feast in **Matthew 22:1-14,** Jesus told how that "he sent forth his armies, and destroyed those murderers, and burned up their city" **(vs. 7),** and after that He said:

"Go ye therefore into the highways, and as many as ye shall find, bid to the marriage. So those servants went out into the highways, and gathered together all as many as they found, both bad and good: and the wedding was furnished with guests" **(vss. 9-10).**

Notice that the wedding feast was not complete until there had been further invitations going out to everybody AFTER THE CITY WAS DESTROYED. This parable goes right along with the parable of the householder in **Matthew 21:33-45** where the murderers who killed the householder's son were to be destroyed, and Jesus saying that "the kingdom of God shall be taken from you, and given to a nation bringing forth the fruits thereof" **(vs. 43).** The chief priests and Pharisees knew that Jesus was talking about THEM **(vs. 45).** The destruction of Jerusalem brought about a tremendous advantage for the propagation of the gospel into all of the Gentile world.

Section 2 ●●●●●●●●●●●●●●●●●●●●●●●●●

"THE ABOMINATION OF DESOLATION"

"When ye therefore shall see the abomination of desolation, spoken of by Daniel the prophet, stand in the holy place, (whoso readeth, let him understand:)" (Matthew 24:15).

Sometime in our future, according to the modern prophecy end-time experts, the Jews are going to build a new temple in Jerusalem. Then there is going to arise from the east a man who is going to rule the world — the Antichrist, the Man of sin, the Beast of Revelation 13. This world dictator will then, during a "great tribulation" period, enter into this temple at Jerusalem and proclaim himself to be God. He will then put, or have put, into the temple a statue of himself which (these modern interpreters say) will be "the abomination of desolation."

Now is this what the Bible teaches will come to pass? Indeed it is not. The Bible says nothing about the Jews building a temple in Jerusalem in our day nor in the future. And it certainly says nothing about a statue being placed in such a temple. Jesus was talking about something that would happen, and did happen, in His generation.

Read what **Dr. J. R. Boyd** of Canada said recently concerning those who are making predictions based on prophecies which have already been fulfilled:

"What would your reactions be toward a modern prophet who would come in the name of the Lord insisting that Genesis 6:5-7 and verses 11-21 is about to be fulfilled? Even Hal Lindsey's sensationalism would pale into drabness in contrast with the pictures such a preacher could paint. He could assure you that he was giving the Word of God, and you would have to agree that technically he was right, though, at the same time you would insist that his message had absolutely no validity to it. If he were of the Hal Lindsey type, he would ignore your protests and would go right on depicting the indescribable scenes of cities, towns, valleys, mountains and continents being inundated as the ceaseless rain pours down day after day and earthquakes, tidal waves and tempests relentlessly deluge the whole world. No modern device or structure will withstand the force of that assault as wreckage and carnage are hurled into heaps and shattered again into miles of shambles. That preacher could stir as Orsen Wells never dreamed of doing with his moving pictures of on-rushing doom, but no one would take him seriously, because his basic Scriptures have been completely fulfilled long ago and God has pledged that there will never be another flood that will reduce this world's population to eight survivors. Yet, that in principle is exactly what preachers and schools are doing today. They are forecasting repetitions of fulfilled prophecies that will never again be repeated" (**J. R. Boyd**, p. 9).

What, then, does the Bible say about "the abomination of desolation?" When Jesus talked to His disciples about the coming destruction of Jerusalem and the end of the age, he told them that THEY (the disciples to whom He was talking) would see this event — "the abomination of desolation." And it would be a sign to them (in fact, THE sign) that they had better be ready to get out of Jerusalem and Judaea when they saw it, for "great tribulation" would begin to fall upon that area immediately thereafter. We need to understand that "the abomination of desolation" is a thing of the past, and not predicted as something to occur again in our future. The foolishness of such modern-day speculation of so-called end-time events is brought about by preachers lifting prophecies out of context and relating them to our future when they have already been fulfilled long ago.

Let us see what Jesus was talking about in this passage.

The Jewish Abomination of Desolation

In Jewish terminology, an "abomination" was anything that involved the worship of false gods in sacred places.

For example, **I Kings 11:7** says, "Then did Solomon build an high place for Chemosh, the abomination of Moab, in the hill that is before Jerusalem, and for Molech, the abomination of the children of Ammon." During Josiah's reformation, these places of abomination were defiled by the king (**II Kings 23:13**).

Years later, in **Jeremiah 4:1** the Lord told Israel to put away her abominations so she would not be removed. In **Jeremiah 13:27** He warned them that He had seen their "abominations on the hills in the fields."

Then later, in **Ezekiel 5:11** God told them that because they had defiled even His sanctuary with all their abominations, that He would not spare them nor have pity on them. And as we know, they were finally taken away into Babylonian captivity.

The Jewish people understood clearly the meaning of the word "abomination" and especially as it pertained to the holy city and the Temple. When Antiochus Epiphanes in December of 168 B.C. profaned the Temple with his pagan actions and caused a pig to be barbecued in sacrifice to Zeus, the Jews understood full well that something like this was the meaning of what Daniel had said would happen when he prophesied of a coming "abomination of desolation." And Jesus pointed back to this when talking to His disciples, and told them that similar things would take place in Jerusalem and the Temple in their own generation, and that when they saw the beginning of it all (the placing of the Roman armies with their pagan banners surrounding the city), they were to immediately get out of the city and not return to it (**Matthew 24:16-20**). For then, Jesus said, "great tribulation" such as never had been seen would take place (**Matthew 24:21**).

The Reference in Daniel

When Jesus referred to "the abomination of desolation" in verse 15, He said that it had been "spoken of by Daniel the prophet." What did He mean by this?

Jesus was referring to **Daniel 9:26-27, 11:31,** and **12:11.**

In **Daniel 9:26-27** it says, ". . . and the people of the prince that shall come shall destroy the city and the sanctuary; and the end thereof shall be with a flood, and unto the end of the war desolations are determined . . . and for the overspreading of abominations he shall make it desolate, even until the consummation, and that determined shall be poured upon the desolate."

In **Daniel 11:31** it says, "And arms shall stand on his part, and they shall pollute the sanctuary of strength, and shall take away the daily sacrifice, and they shall place the abomination that maketh desolate."

In **Daniel 12:11** it says, "And from the time that the daily sacrifice shall be taken away, and the abomination that maketh desolate set up, there shall be a thousand two hundred and ninety days."

Antiochus Epiphanes and His Abomination

According to Jewish history recorded in the **Apocrypha,** these passages in Daniel were fulfilled in the inter-Biblical period (the time between the Old and the New Testaments). It is recorded for us in the apocryphal book of **I Maccabees.** This book records how Antiochus Epiphanes (who ruled Syria from 174 to 164 B.C.) came against Jerusalem and what he did that the Jews called "the abomination of desolation."

While not included in any canon of Scriptures, except the Catholic Bible, and therefore not looked on as inspired, yet these apocryphal books (such as Maccabees) can be read to give us historical insight into some of the things that happened in the inter-Biblical period between Malachi and Matthew. In the **Apocrypha** we read:

"And entered proudly into the sanctuary, and took away the golden altar, and the candlestick of light, and all the vessels thereof" (**I Maccabees 1:21**).

"Now the fifteenth day of the month Casleu, in the hundred forty and fifth year, they set up the abomination of desolation upon the altar, and builded idol altars throughout the cities of Juda on every side" (**I Maccabees 1:54**).

"Now the five and twentieth day of the month they did sacrifice upon the idol altar, which was upon the altar of God" (**I Maccabees 1:59**).

Antiochus, king of Syria, had surnamed himself Epiphanes, which means "the God Made Manifest." He had as his goal not only to put down Jewish resistance, but also to stamp out the Jewish religion. He even turned priests' rooms and the Temple chambers into public brothels. In December 168 B.C. the Temple was dedicated to Zeus, and over the altar was placed a statue of Zeus which resembled Antiochus. A pig was sacrificed on the altar itself! This was a filthy abomination in the sight of the Jews.

Antiochus Epiphanes the Syrian ruler had Menelaus appointed as high priest. Menelaus was not in sympathy with Jewish traditions. He was not even a member of the family of priests — a man who only wanted power. The "Hellenizers" in Jerusalem had complete control of Judaea's government. Menelaus collaborated with Antiochus Epiphanes. He promised money from the Temple treasury to Antiochus, and was therefore appointed as high priest. Antiochus also promised to give Jerusalem a Greek constitution and the right to coin their own money.

"The 'Desolating Abomination' — To Antiochus the unwillingness of the Jews to be Hellenized was stiff-necked nonsense. If Judaism stood in his way, so much the worse for Judaism. He gave orders that Judaism be destroyed.

"A part of the Syrian army marched into Jerusalem to support Menelaus and his policy. Many of the inhabitants of the city were killed; others escaped to the hills. Only the known Hellenists remained. Orders were given prohibiting the observance of the Sabbath, the Holidays and circumcision. In the Temple above the altar was placed a statue of Jupiter bearing an obvious resemblance to Antiochus. Over such a Temple Menelaus consented to remain as high priest. To that statue were brought as sacrifices the animal most detested by the Jews, the pig. An abominable act had been perpetrated on that 25th day of Isley in the year 168 B.C.E. and, to use the descriptive expression of the Book of Maccabees, it left the Jewish people desolate" (**Solomon Grayzel**, pp. 55-56).

As to the statue placed in the Temple, the Book of Maccabees says it was that of Zeus, and here Grayzel says it was Jupiter. However, **Funk and Wagnall's New Encyclopedia**, vol. 25, p. 452, says that "The

Romans identified Jupiter with Zeus." So they were the same.

The Scofield Reference Bible says (p. 915, 1917 edition) that only Daniel 11:31 referred to Antiochus Epiphanes, while Daniel 9:27 and 12:11 refer to a still yet future "Beast." But Josephus the Jewish historian indicates that Daniel 12:11 referred to Antiochus Epiphanes as well.

Josephus said, as he told of the activities of Antiochus Epiphanes, "He also spoiled the temple, and put a stop to the constant practice of offering a daily sacrifice of expiation for three years and six months . . . he compelled the Jews to dissolve the laws of their country, and to keep their infants uncircumcised, and to sacrifice swine's flesh upon the altar" **(Josephus,** vol. 1, pp. 10-11).

In the book, **A History of the Jewish People,** by **Max L. Margolis** and **Alexander Marx,** there is an account given of the profanation and desecration of the Temple caused by Antiochus Epiphanes in the year 168 B.C.:

"The King ordered Apollonius to advance upon Jerusalem. He entered the city on a sabbath. The unresisting inhabitants were butchered; the soldiers pillaged at will and carried off women and children to be sold as slaves. The walls of the city were razed; the citadel south of the Temple hill was fortified, and there the apostate Jews, who were friendly to the king's cause, were quartered together with non-Jewish residents.

"A royal edict was proclaimed suspending the practice of the Jewish religion on pain of death. The rescript was couched in general terms commanding the fusion of all nationalities in the realm into one people and the acceptance of the Greek religion by all; but that was only a blind. The force of the proclamation was directed against the Jews and the Samaritans. Accordingly the Temple in Jerusalem was converted into a sanctuary of Jupiter the Olympian, while that on Mount Gerizim was dedicated to Jupiter Xenius (the Defender of Visitors). On the fifteenth day of Chislev, 168, a statue of the god was set up on the altar, the image of the 'lord of heaven,' which the pious Jews spoke of as 'the abominable thing causing horror'; on the twenty-fifth day of the month heathen sacrifices were offered on what had been the altar of God. The Temple was filled with riots and revelings; within the sacred precincts men dallied with harlots; swine's blood was poured upon the altar" **(Max L. Margolis** and **Alexander Marx,** pp. 137-138).

". . . for so it was, that the temple was made desolate by Antiochus, and so continued for three years. This desolation happened to the temple in the hundred forty and fifth year . . . And this desolation came to pass according to the prophecy of Daniel, which was given four hundred and eight years before" **(Josephus,** vol. 3, p. 191).

To show what an antagonist of the Jews and their religion Antiochus Epiphanes was, **Robert Dick Wilson** said:

"The blood-thirsty tyrant executed his threats of death upon all who opposed his will. Men, women, and children were ruthlessly slaughtered. Whole families were extirpated for the guilt of one of their number. The chosen people were on the point of being annihilated and the promises and the hopes of the covenant of being annulled for ever . . . Now, under Epiphanes, was attempted what had never been proposed by Babylonian conqueror or Persian friends, the entire destruction of peoples, and religion at one fell blow" **(Robert Dick Wilson,** second section, p. 274).

Other good source material on Antiochus Epiphanes and the abomination of desolation can be found in the **International Bible Encyclopedia,** c. 1939, vol. 1, p. 16.

Later Attempts to Paganize the Temple

Even after the time of Christ and before the events of A.D. 70, there were other attempts to paganize the Jewish Temple, by the Romans.

1. Herod "the king had put up a golden eagle over the great gate of the temple." **(Josephus,** vol. 1, p. 122). When some Jews brought it down, Herod caused them to be burnt alive. But he himself was later eaten of worms and died.

2. Then Josephus told of Pilate: "Pilate, who was sent as procurator into Judea by Tiberius, sent by night those images of Caesar that are called Ensigns, into Jerusalem" **(Josephus,** vol. 1, p. 152). The Jews made such an outcry against this that he finally relented.

3. Then Josephus told of Caligula (Caius Caligula Caesar), who has been called by some "the Anti-Christ." "Caius Caesar did so grossly abuse the fortune he had arrived at, as to take himself to be a god, and to desire to be so called also . . . He also extended his impiety as far as the Jews. Accordingly, he sent Petronius with an army to Jerusalem, to place his statues in the temple, and commanded him that, in case the Jews would not admit of them, he should slay those that opposed it, and carry all the rest of the nation into captivity; but God concerned himself with these his commands" **(Josephus,** vol. 1, p. 154).

The Jews got together in great numbers and prevailed on Petronius so that he left his army and the statues at Ptolemais, even though he reminded them that "all the nations in subjection to them had placed the images of Caesar in their several cities, among the rest of their gods" **(Josephus,** vol. 1, p. 155). The Jews insisted they would sacrifice their whole nation, including their wives and children, before they would allow the images to be placed among them. Petronius then "took the army out of Ptolemais, and returned to Antioch" (**Josephus,** vol. 1, p. 156), and Caius Caesar died before Petronius could be punished for his giving in to the Jews.

The images never were set up, according to Josephus. However, **Eusebius** the early church historian, tells us:

"Philo has given us an account, in five books, of the misfortunes of the Jews under Caius. He accounts at the same time the madness of Caius: how he called himself a god, and performed as emperor innumerable acts of tyranny; and he describes further the miseries of the Jews under him . . . For while all other subjects of Rome erected altars and temples to Caius, and in all other respects treated him just as they did the gods, they alone considered it disgraceful to honor him with statues and to swear by his name . . ."

Then **Eusebius** continues:

"After the death of Tiberius, Caius received the empire, and, besides innumerable other acts of tyranny against many people, he greatly afflicted especially the whole nation of the Jews. These things we may learn briefly from the words of Philo, who writes as follows: 'So great was the caprice of Caius in his conduct toward all, and especially toward the nation of the Jews. The latter he so bitterly hated that he appropriated to himself their places of worship in the other cities, and beginning with Alexandria he filled them with images and statues of himself (for in permitting others to erect them he really erected them himself). The temple in the holy city, which had hitherto been left untouched, and had been regarded as an inviolable asylum, he altered and transformed into a temple of his own, that it might be called the temple of the visible Jupiter, the younger Caius' " (**Eusebius,** pp. 108-109, **The Nicene and Post-Nicene Fathers,** Second Series).

Many perhaps thought that Caligula would be the fulfillment of this part of Jesus' prophecy. It probably intensified their anticipation that the end was near. But the disciples had been told to wait until they saw the armies surrounding the city.

These events indicate the increasing pressures that were being brought to bear on the Jews at Jerusalem to have the Roman emperor's image set up in Jerusalem itself, even in the holy Temple. The power of the Roman empire wanted to "sit" in the very Temple of God itself proclaiming Caesar as God. Before the year A.D. 70 would end, this would come about, when the soldiers would take their ensigns and place them before the eastern wall at the Temple and worship and sacrifice before them and proclaim Titus "Imperator."

The Interpretation of Matthew 24:15

But in A.D. 66-70 a similar situation to that of Antiochus Epiphanes was to occur in Judaea and Jerusalem in particular, and Jesus knew this. It would occur when the pagan Roman armies would surround, then besiege Jerusalem. Awful abominations would take place inside the Temple by some of the Jews themselves. The holy vessels would be melted by a wicked Jew. The priests, including the high priest, would all be killed. An ignorant man who knew nothing of priestly affairs would be chosen to be high priest. The daily sacrifices would cease on account of there being no priest to offer them. Drunkenness would occur in the Temple. Thousands of Jews would die by the hands of other Jews. Finally the Roman armies would break into the city, and the city and the Temple would be destroyed. The Temple would be burned and the pagan soldiers and Titus the Roman general would enter the Temple itself. Then the soldiers would place the images (ensigns) of Caesar up against the eastern wall and worship them, calling Titus "Imperator". Such would be the total "overspreading of abominations" that would occur at Jerusalem in A.D. 66-70 And it was of this time that Jesus spoke when He said, "When ye therefore shall see the abomination of desolation, spoken of by Daniel the prophet, stand in the holy place, (whoso readeth, let him understand:)" **(Matthew 24:15)**.

The parallel passage to this is found in **Luke 21:20-21**, where Jesus told the disciples,

"And when YE SHALL SEE JERUSALEM COMPASSED WITH ARMIES, then know that the desolation thereof is nigh."

"Then let them which are in Judaea flee to the mountains . . ."

This was "the abomination of desolation" — the pagan armies surrounding the city. And this was only the beginning of abominations that occurred later in the Temple itself. And as to the soldiers themselves, later, after the city was taken, Josephus tells us that the Romans "brought their ensigns to the temple, and set them over-against its eastern gate; and there did they offer sacrifices to them" **(Josephus,** vol. 1, pp. 456-457).

Joseph Ernest Renan said, "The Romans planted their standards in the place where the sanctuary had stood, and, as was their custom, offered them worship" **(Renan,** p. 260).

So there certainly should be no place in our interpretation of this prophecy for extending its fulfillment out into the distant future of our times to occur when some futuristic antichrist places some image in some re-built temple of the Jews, as taught by some of the dispensationalists. The predicted "abomination of desolation" mentioned by Jesus in **Matthew 24:15** is a thing of the past, fulfilled during the events of A.D. 66-70.

The Armies Themselves Were the Abomination of Desolation

And notice in considering the parallel passage in **Luke 21:20** that in this verse Jesus connected the Roman armies which surrounded the city with the "desolation" of that city, indicating that Jesus Himself regarded those pagan armies as the "abomination of desolation," or the "abomination that makes desolate." This is the very event which was the signal for the disciples to flee the city (**vs. 21**) even as in **Matthew 24:15-16** He told them that when they saw the "abomination of desolation" they were to flee into the mountains.

Some have thought that in Matthew Jesus had in mind some sacrilege inside the Temple itself, but such could not have been a signal to the disciples elsewhere in Judaea **outside** the city, and Jesus did specifically warn those also to flee (see **Matthew 24:16**). Jesus did not say that just those in Jerusalem only were to flee, but those "in Judaea" (vs. 16) all over the land were to flee. Luke put it this way: "And let them which are in the midst of it depart out; and let not them that are in the countries enter thereinto." (**Luke 21:21**). When the armies were known to be surrounding Jerusalem, this was the signal to get out of the entire country as soon as possible.

Eusebius said:

"The calamities which at that time overwhelmed the whole nation in every part of the world; the process by which the inhabitants of Judaea were driven to the limits of disaster; the thousands and thousands of men of every age who together with women and children perished by the sword, by starvation, and by countless other forms of death; the number of Jewish cities besieged and the horrors they endured — especially the terrible and worse than terrible sights that met the eyes of those who sought refuge in Jerusalem itself as an impregnable fortress; the character of the whole war and the detailed events at all its stages; the last scene of all when the Abomination of Desolation announced by the prophets was set up in the very Temple of God, once world-renowned, when it underwent utter destruction and final dissolution by fire — all this anyone who wishes can gather in precise detail from the pages of Josephus's history. I must draw particular attention to his statement that the people who flocked together from all Judaea at the time of the Passover Feast and — to use his own words — were shut up in Jerusalem as if in a prison, totaled nearly three million. It was indeed proper that in the very week in which they had brought the Saviour and Benefactor of mankind, God's Christ, to His Passion, they should be shut up as if in a prison and suffer the destruction that came upon them by the judgement of God" (**Eusebius, p. 112, The History of the Church**).

(There is a different translation of this same passage in **The Nicene and Post-Nicene Fathers,** vol. 1, p. 138).

Please note that **Eusebius** said, ". . . the last scene of all when the Abomination of Desolation announced by the prophets was set up in the very Temple of God, once world-renowned, when it underwent utter destruction and final dissolution by fire . . ." It is interesting that we have the record of Caesar's image being placed right inside the temple itself, though it was not necessary for the fulfilment of prophecy. And Jesus may have known this would happen, but He did not say so, and He did not say for the disciples to wait on that; it was sufficient (and necessary) that they move quickly whenever they saw the armies surrounding the city.

So, then, the prophecy of the abomination of desolation spoken of by Jesus was actually fulfilled in the Temple at Jerusalem by the time that Jerusalem was destroyed in A.D. 70. But the Christians had been instructed to flee the place when they first saw the soldiers advancing around the city and not to wait further for this. This is not some event that is supposed to happen in our future during a Tribulation period either just before or after a future Rapture. To handle the teachings of Jesus in this way is to eliminate what He was actually saying to His disciples in answer to their question as to when the Temple would be destroyed. This happened, already, and there is no prediction of any future either re-building of a Temple nor any abomination of desolation in such a Temple. This sort of teaching is simply dispensational, futuristic, and un-Scriptural nonsense.

Dr. B. H. Carroll, founder and first president of the Southwestern Baptist Theological Seminary in Fort Worth, Texas, tells us this, as he mentions one of the attempts to paganize the Jewish Temple:

". . . This same Pilate, at that time Roman Procurator, sent from Caesarea, the seaport of that country on the Mediterranean Sea, a legion of Roman soldiers and had them secretly introduced into the city and sheltered in the tower of Antonio overlooking the Temple, and these soldiers brought with them their ensigns. The Roman ensign was a straight staff, capped with a metallic eagle, and right under the eagle was a graven image of Caesar. Caesar claimed to be divine. Caesar exacted divine worship, and every evening when those standards were placed, the Roman legion got down and worshipped the image of Caesar thereon, and every morning at the roll call a part of the parade was for the whole legion to prostrate themselves before that graven image and worship it. The Jews were so horrified when they saw that image and the consequent worship, they went to Pilate, who was at that time living in Caesarea, and prostrated themselves before him and said, 'Kill us, if you will, but take that abomination of desolation out of our Holy City and from the neighborhood of our holy temple.' While that was an abomination, Jerusalem was not encompassed with armies. 'When ye shall see the abomination which makes desolation spoken of by Daniel, the prophet, set up where it ought not to be, and see Jerusalem encompassed by armies,' that is the sign of the destruction of Jerusalem. The greatest desolation ever wrought in the world on a people, was made under that standard and by the Roman power. Therefore, it was the abomination that maketh desolation" (**B. H. Carroll**, pp. 263-264.)

That Jesus by-passed any declared fulfillment in Antiochus Epiphanes as understood by the Jews of the inter-Biblical period, and that He interpreted that prophecy as relating directly to the events at the destruction of Jerusalem in A.D. 70 which He was predicting, seems very evident.

Dr. John A. Broadus said, "It is evident that our Lord interprets the prediction in Daniel as referring to the Messiah, and to that destruction of the city and temple which he is now foretelling; and his interpretation is authoritative for us" (**John A. Broadus**, vol. 1, p. 486).

The Disciples Would See the Abomination of Desolation

To whom was Jesus referring when He said, "ye" (vs. 15)? It was His disciples to whom He was talking on the mount of Olives (vs. 3); not to the Jews in general even of His day, nor yet of the Jews of some future time generations of time away from the time of that discussion. A student of prophecy recently told me that this verse applies to the Jews during the time of a tribulation period in **our** future day and time, and he was very adamant and dogmatic about this and refused to acknowledge that here Jesus was talking to His disciples and that, therefore, the "ye" applied to them! This man's trouble was that he was so brainwashed by modern futuristic interpretation of "the abomination of desolation" that he could not see it any other way. This kind of folks gets to believing some things so strongly that they actually come to believe that the Bible teaches it even though they cannot prove it from the Bible.

To illustrate this kind of thinking still further, this man said that "the abomination of desolation" would be a statue set up in a future rebuilt temple at Jerusalem (haven't you heard that somewhere before, too?). I questioned him as to where he found this, and he stated, unequivocally and dogmatically, that Revelation 13 states that the image of the Beast was put inside the temple. And then, even in the presence of several others, this man refused to acknowledge his error when it was emphatically pointed out that Revelation 13 says nothing of an image being brought into a temple. I think I lost a friend that day because pride would not give in and acknowledge error. But I had to remind this man that not Revelation 13, and neither the book of Daniel (anywhere), nor Matthew 24, say that a statue will be placed inside a temple, anytime or anywhere! (Even though such did happen back then, no prediction was made beyond that for the future.

So who says "the abomination of desolation" means a statue in the temple, anyway (either past or future)? Jesus reminded his disciples of "the abomination of desolation, spoken of by Daniel the prophet" (**Matthew 24:15**), and indicated that when such a situation arose it would then be time to flee from Jerusalem. The disciples clearly remembered, no doubt (as is taught in the book of I Maccabees in the Apocrypha to which we have previously referred), that such a thing had occurred before under Antiochus Epiphanes in 168 B.C. It is true that Antiochus Epiphanes did indeed have a statue of Jupiter put into the temple at that time.

But the statue or image in the Temple in 168 B.C. would not have to be repeated in order to fulfill any prophecy. That very presence of the offending pagans in the holy place **WAS** the "abomination", and that is why Jesus in **Luke 21:20-21** spoke of the Roman armies around the city as being the signal to flee after mentioning in **Matthew 24:15** that they were to flee at the sign of the "abomination". **THIS** was the "abomination of desolation"; not a statue, but the pagan armies themselves. And it was those armies that made Jerusalem "desolate", fulfilling "the abomination that makes desolate."

The thought in Jesus' statement was: "When **YOU** see the abomination of desolation . . ." No matter about those in the days when Antiochus Epiphanes set up his statue of Jupiter in the Temple in 168 B.C. and according to the Jews actually caused a fulfillment of Daniel's prophecies. Jesus was concerned about the present (HIS present time), and he said, "When **YOU** see this abomination . . .". And keep in mind He must have had in mind especially **Daniel 9:27** concerning the time of the fulfillment of Daniel's 70th week prophecy. The tragedy that happened in 168 B.C. would happen again, and when the disciples saw the unmistakable signs of it in the surrounding of Jerusalem by the armies, they were to get out of the city and Judaea as fast as possible.

Certain it is that **Luke** (in **21:20**) understood the "abomination of desolation" to be the armies surrounding Jerusalem, or He would not have used the expression about the armies in the same context and place where Jesus said "abomination of desolation" in **Matthew 24:15**.

Why should a statue being placed in a temple be considered "the abomination of desolation" which necessitated the disciples by the thousands to flee the city in such great haste? We can understand the reason for such great haste if the signal was that of the armies suddenly being seen surrounding the city. But the city and the Temple were practically all but demolished before any ensign (statue) of Caesar the Roman emperor was carried into the Temple, and the disciples had long gone before them. The conclusion is that "the abomination of desolation" of which Jesus spoke was not a statue in a Temple, whether then or later, but was the presence of the armies who were to invade the city. And this is what Jesus said, according to **Luke 21:20**.

There was a wide-spread belief among the Jews that the prophecy of **Daniel 9:24-27** was soon to be fulfilled, and that the 490 years mentioned would soon be at an end. With this in mind, we know that Jesus Himself was now teaching that this prophecy was soon to be fulfilled.

"Furthermore, there were many in Israel who believed that Antiochus Epiphanes had not completely fulfilled the visions of **Daniel 8, 9, 11** and **12**. That book had promised the advent of the kingdom of God after the profanation of the sanctuary by the wilful king. But certainly the kingdom had not come with the rededicated sanctuary of 165 B.C. Therefore, they reasoned, the woes under Antiochus must have been pre-figurative of worse woes to come." (**Desmond Ford**, p. 157).

The abomination of desolation (the Roman armies surrounding the city, **Luke 21:20**) was to be the signal for the disciples to flee from Jerusalem and Judaea (**vs. 16**). They were not to be concerned about wars and rumors of wars in general (**Matthew 24:6**), but when the situation developed so that the Roman armies stood where they ought not (at Jerusalem, the holy place), this then was the sign for the disciples to depart as quickly as they could.

Of the "abomination of desolation," **Albert Barnes' Commentary** says: "This is a Hebrew expression, meaning an abominable or hateful destroyer. The Gentiles were all held in abomination by the Jews. Ac. x. 28. The abomination of desolation means the Roman army, and is so explained by Lu, xxi. 20. The Roman army is further called the **abomination** on account of the images of the emperor, and the eagles, carried in front of the legions, and regarded by the Romans with divine honours" (**Barnes**, p. 254.)

When all is considered, it is evident that Jesus, in referring to the prophecy in Daniel about the "abomination of desolation," certainly applied that prophecy to that which happened at Jerusalem when the Roman armies came and besieged the city. Writing of the parallel passage in **Mark 13, G. C. Berkouwer** said: "What is noteworthy is that Christ does not speak about this horror as about an event in some ancient past. There is a particularly prominent actuality about what He says. A very relevant admonition is evident: 'when **you** see the desolating sacrilege set up . . .' (**Mark 13:14**). Christ is not referring back to the tribulations of Israel during the time of Antiochus Epiphanes, but to today and tomorrow. When the desolating sacrilege comes, Christ proclaims, 'then let those who are in Judaea flee to the mountains.' Daniel's words are assumed into a relevant proclamation dealing with a grave crisis affecting Judaea and putting its inhabitants to flight. There is widespread uncertainty as to the precise meaning of this 'desolating sacrilege,' but this much is clear: it constitutes an admonition reinterpreting Daniel's vision. What Daniel says is applied to the imminent destruction of the temple in Jerusalem." (**Berkouwer,** pp. 275-276).

Cecil Sanders, Professor of Bible at Free Will Baptist College in Moore, Oklahoma, in a recent book has well said, "When reporting on the Olivet prophecy, Luke did let us know who the abomination of desolation was. He said, 'And when ye shall see Jerusalem compassed with armies, then know that the desolation thereof is nigh' (Lk. 21:20). By reading the surrounding verses one cannot deny that this is a parallel account to Matthew's Olivet Discourse found in chapter 24. Parallel accounts cannot have a different meaning. By combining Luke's statement with secular history it is clear that Titus and his Roman army were the abomination of desolation. It was fulfilled in A.D. 70 when the Romans desecrated and destroyed the Temple and Jerusalem. **Matthew 24:15** and **Luke 21:20** are parallel accounts speaking of the same event." (**Cecil Sanders,** p. 68).

F.F. Bruce, theologian of Manchester, England, described the abomination of desolation under Antiochus Epiphanes in these words: "Orders were given that the temple ritual must be suspended, that the sacred scriptures be destroyed, that the sabbath and other festival days be no longer observed, that the strict food-laws be abolished, and that the rite of circumscism (to the Jews the sign of the covenant made by God with their ancestor Abraham) be discontinued. These steps were taken towards the end of 167, and the culminating attack on the Jewish worship came in December of that year, when a new and smaller altar was erected upon the altar of burnt offering in the the temple court, and solemnly dedicated to the worship of Olympian Zeus, the deity of whom Antiochus claimed to be a manifestation." (F.F. Bruce, p. 145).

Then on page 224 of the same book, Dr. Bruce described the abomination of desolation that was set up in the Jewish Temple when the Romans conquered the city in A.D. 70: "When the temple area was taken by the Romans, and the sanctuary itself was still burning, the soldiers brought their legionary standards into the sacred precincts, set them up opposite the eastern gate, and offered sacrifice to them there, acclaiming Titus as **imperator** (victorious commander) as they did so. The Roman custom of offering sacrifice to their standards had already been commented on by a Jewish writer as a symptom of their pagan arrogance, but the offering of such sacrifice in the temple court was the supreme insult to the God of Israel. This action, following as it did the cessation of the daily sacrifice three weeks earlier, must have sensed to many Jews, as it evidently did to Josephus, a new and final fulfillment of Daniel's vision of a time when the continual burnt offering would be taken away and the abomination of desolation set up" (F.F. Bruce, p. 224).

The "abomination of desolation" was the ungodly intruders who desecrated the holy place and caused its desolation.

"**The abomination of desolation** — The abomination of profanation was followed by the abomination of desolation. Such is the name given to the Roman army, gathered from all nations; whose military standards the Jews held in abomination as idols, since the Romans attributed divinity to them." (**John Albert Bengel, p. 270**).

"By **the abomination of desolation,** or **the abomination that maketh desolate,** therefore is intended the Roman armies, with their ensigns. As the Roman ensigns, especially the eagle, which was carried at the head of every legion, were objects of worship; they are, according to usual title of scripture, called **an abomination." (Lardner,** p. 49).

". . . the **abomination of desolation** standing in the Holy Place at **Jerusalem** (a prophecy which doubtless had reference to the time of the consummated iniquity of the Christ-rejecting Jerusalem, and of the Roman besieging army with its idolatrous stands gathering into the sacred precincts of the Jewish city . . ." (**E.B. Elliott,** vol. 4, p. 617).

". . . the **Apalling Horror** spoken of by the prophet Daniel shall stand erect **in the holy place,** apparently a reference to the presence of Roman armies round Jerusalem, and so rightly interpreted by Luke" (**Theodore Robinson,** p. 198).

The **Jamieson, Fausset and Brown Commentary,** on the parallel passage in **Mark 13:14,** says:

"That the abomination of desolation here alluded to was intended to point to the Roman ensigns, as the symbols of an idolatrous, and so unclean Pagan power, may be gathered by comparing what Luke says in the corresponding verse (xxi. 20); and the commentators are agreed on it. It is worthy of notice, as confirming this interpretation, that in I Macc. i. 54 — which though Apocryphal **Scripture**, is authentic **history** — the expression of Daniel is applied to the idolatrous profanation of the Jewish altar by Antiochus Epiphanes." **(Jamieson, Fausset and Brown,** vol. 3, p. 192).

If I have seemed to labor on this point under discussion at long length, it is both deliberate and purposeful. The weight of the united testimony of interpretation of these varied commentators perhaps will help to offset some of the influence of the more modern futuristic concepts of what the "abomination of desolation" was meant to signify. I do not think it would be easy to overlook the consensus of interpretation of these outstanding men of scholarship.

Early Church Fathers Who Said the Abomination of Desolation Was in the Past

What about the early church fathers? What did they believe about this?

Clement of Alexandria, one of the early church fathers (born A.D. 153), said, "For he said that there were two thousand three hundred days from the time that the abomination of Nero stood in the holy city, till its destruction . . . These two thousand three hundred days, make six years four months, during the half of which Nero held sway" **(Clement,** vol. 2, p. 334).

While Clement can get one's head spinning in trying to follow all his calculations of time in all he said in the context, what I wanted to show here is that in the days of early Christianity this Christian leader said that Nero held sway over Jerusalem for more than three years, and that "the abomination of Nero stood in the holy place." This early Christian interpretation was that Nero the Roman emperor was the abomination even though he himself was not actually physically present at Jerusalem itself.

Chrysostom (born 347 at Antioch, capital of Syria) said, "For this it seems to me that **the abomination of desolation** means the army by which the holy city of Jerusalem was made desolate."

Chrysostom also said, "Or because he who had desolated the city and the temple, placed his statue within the temple."

St. Augustine (born 354 in North Africa) said, "Luke to show that the abomination spoken of by Daniel will take place when Jerusalem is captured, recalls these words of the Lord in the same context: **When**

you shall see Jerusalem compassed about with an army, then know that the desolation thereof is at hand (xxi. 20)."

St. Augustine also said, "For Luke very clearly bears witness that the prophecy of Daniel was fulfilled when Jerusalem was overthrown." In a section dealing with the harmony of the gospels, St. Augustine said, "In like manner, what Matthew states thus, 'When ye therefore shall see the abomination of desolation, spoken of by Daniel the prophet, stand in the holy place, whoso readeth, let him understand,' is put in the following form by Mark: 'But when ye shall see the abomination of desolation standing where it ought not, let him that readeth understand.' But though the phrase is thus altered, the sense conveyed is the same. For the point of the clause 'where it ought not,' is that the abomination of desolation ought not to be in the holy place. Luke's method of putting it, again, is neither, 'And when ye shall see the abomination of desolation stand in the holy place,' nor 'where it ought not,' but 'And when ye shall see Jerusalem compassed with an army, then know that the desolation thereof is nigh.' At that time, therefore, will the abomination of desolation be in the holy place." (**St. Augustine,** vol. 6, p. 170).

Seemingly, this view of St. Augustine was either that when the armies surround the city, this will be proof that the abomination is already in the Temple; or else, he possibly could have meant that the armies surrounding the city was the same as the abomination being in the holy place. In either case, St. Augustine's view was that the abomination of desolation had already occurred and was not a prediction of some still future event from his time.

But **Abbot Sulpitius Severus** (born A.D. 363) came along with his "double sense" idea. He proposed that the prophecy had been fulfilled, but that if it was not opposed to the faith to believe so, it could also be interpreted to mean that it would happen again at some future time. He said:

"For sometimes when a difference of opinion is expressed on one and the same subject, either view may be considered reasonable and be held without injury to the faith either firmly, or doubtfully, i.e., in such a way that neither is full belief nor absolute rejection accorded to it, and the second view need not interfere with the former, if neither of them is found to be opposed to the faith: as in this case: where Elias came in the person of John, and is again to be the precursor of the Lord's Advent: . . . and in the matter of the 'Abomination of desolation' which 'stood in the holy place,' by means of that idol of Jupiter which, as we read, was placed in the temple in Jerusalem, and which is again to stand in the Church through the coming of Antichrist, and all those things which follow in the gospel, which we take as having been fulfilled before the captivity of Jerusalem and still to be fulfilled at the end of this world. In which matter neither view is opposed to the other, nor does the first interpretation interfere with the second." **(Sulpitius Severus,** vol. 11, p. 377).

Whether Severus was the one who started this "double sense" fulfilment type of interpretation or not, I do not know; but it is certain that some modern dispensationalist futurists have adopted this kind of Bible interpretation and made this prophecy to have a "double-reference" if not a "double-sense" to it.

If it happened, it happened; and there is no just cause for believing it will necessarily happen again. To believe so is just speculation. And speculation is what much of today's end-time prophecy fulfillment is based upon.

We do not consider the writings of the early church fathers as inspired, yet they offer us valuable insight into matters of history long since past. Neither do we believe all that they said, but some of their writings do tell us of things of which we would have no knowledge otherwise. In one of these earliest writings, Peter is quoted as having said,

" 'For we,' said I, 'have ascertained beyond doubt that God is much rather displeased with the sacrifices which you offer, and the time of sacrifices having now passed away; and because ye will not acknowledge that the time for offering victories is now past, therefore the temple shall be destroyed, and the abomination of desolation shall stand in the holy place; and then the Gospel shall be preached to the Gentiles for a testimony against you' " **(The Ante-Nicene Fathers,** vol. 8, p. 94).

Other Abominations Inside the Temple

Concerning the event of which Jesus spoke to His disciples, and leading up to the time when the Roman soldiers finally came into the Temple itself, the priesthood was completely demoralized. Up until this time nothing secular nor unholy was allowed in the Temple, but now the Jews who were rebelling against Rome and creating so much havoc by their actions came right on into the Temple itself and stayed there.

"Now, however, Zelotes and brigands dwelt pellmell within the sacred building, all the rules of legal parity seemed forgotten, the courts were stained with blood that defiled the feet of those who walked therein. In the eyes of the priests there was no crime more horrible. To many devotees this was the 'abomination' predicted by Daniel as destined to take place on the eve of the supreme days" **(Joseph Ernest Renan,** p. 143).

Renan, the French historian and philosopher, further tells us that these fanatics paid no attention to the traditional way of selecting a high priest, but drew lots to secure a new one. "Drawing lots naturally brought about absurd results; the office fell to a rustic who had to be dragged to Jerusalem and invested, in spite of himself, with the sacred robes. The High Priesthood was profaned with carnival scenes . . ." **(Renan,** p. 143). They let Idumaean bandits into the city and a massacre followed, during which "all the members of the priestly caste who could be found were slain" **(Renan,** p. 143).

But Jesus warned His disciples not to wait until the final stages of this "abomination of desolation," but rather just as soon as they saw Jerusalem compassed with armies, they would know that the desolation was near and all of them in Judaea were to flee to the mountains, and those inside Jerusalem were to leave immediately, and not any of them were to come inside the city **(Luke 21:20-21).** This was the beginning of the abomination of desolation, and even those outside of Jerusalem ("them which are in Judaea") would be able to see these armies and know that the destruction and desolation of the city was imminent.

So this was the "abomination of desolation, spoken of by Daniel the prophet," to which Jesus referred. He said that when the disciples saw it, they were to flee. That sounds like Jesus understood that Daniel's prophecy had not yet been fulfilled, does it not? The Jews during the inter-Biblical period did feel that Antiochus Epiphanes was the fulfillment of Daniel's prophecy. Possibly Jesus was saying, "The same thing is going to happen again, so keep your eyes open and be ready to flee." But more than likely, Jesus was by-passing any fulfillment in Antiochus Epiphanes, and applying the fulfillment directly to what would happen in a few years when the Roman soldiers came against Jerusalem. He said that what they saw would be that which was spoken of by the prophet Daniel. So I think we can accept that, just like He said it. He did not say that the abomination of desolation was something that had already passed; He said, "When **YE** therefore shall see the abomination of desolation." It was to be fulfilled in their time. Therefore, we can also say that it was not a prophecy to be fulfilled in our own day and time or later. It has already been fulfilled nearly 2,000 years ago when Jerusalem was destroyed.

But someone says that the prophecy says "armies" — not "army." Exactly so; and reading the historical accounts of what happened, one can easily understand that it was plural — "armies."

Titus only had about 25,000 soldiers of his own, but he conscripted perhaps more than that from Syria (who didn't like the Jews much anyway), and others, until there were in the neighborhood of 54,000 soldiers in the combined armies that came against Jerusalem. In preparation for the war on Jerusalem, Nero sent Vespasian into Syria to take command of the armies there, and Vespasian sent his son Titus to Alexandria to bring back the 5th and 10th legions, while he himself gathered together the Roman forces in Syria "with a considerable number of auxiliaries from the kings in that neighborhood" (**Josephus,** vol. 1, p. 222). Arabia sent 6,000 soldiers. Titus' "whole army, including the auxiliaries sent by the kings, amounted to sixty thousand," plus others who were not the fighting men. F. W. **Farrar** said that Titus had a force of 80,000 legionaires and auxiliaries. (**Farrar,** p. 487). It was like the multi-national coalition armies gathered in Saudi-Arabia recently under the leadership of the United States as confrontation was made with Iraq, except that at Jerusalem Rome was in total control.

"Holy Place" Not Necessarily the Holy of Holies in the Temple

If it be objected that "the holy place" meant the temple and not the city, it might be pointed out that in the Apocrypha (inter-Biblical writings) "the holy place" meant the whole area of the "holy land." In **II Maccabees 2** it said, "As he promised in the law, will shortly have mercy upon us, and gather us together out of every land under heaven into the holy place." So the Jews considered the entire land as the holy place. This included the city and the temple, all of which were looked on as "holy." The land was called "holy" (**II Maccabees 1:7**), and the city was called holy (**II Maccabees 3:1**).

Meyer's Commentary on the New Testament, on Matthew 24:15 says, "**Others,** and among them de Wette and Baumgarten-Crusius (comp. Weiss on Mark), understand the words as referring to **Palestine,** especially to the **neighborhood of Jerusalem** (Schott, Wiesler), or to the Mount of Olives (Bengel), because it is supposed that it would have been too late to seek escape after the temple had been captured, and so the flight of the Christians to Pella took place as soon as the war began." (**Meyer,** vol. 1, pp. 414-415).

"By **standing in the holy place,** or **where it ought not,** needs not to be understood the temple only, but Jerusalem also, and, any part of the land of Israel" (**Lardner,** p. 49).

Followed Daniel's Prophetic "70th Week"

Daniel 9:27 referred to the abomination that caused desolation which came sometime after the 70th week of Daniel was fulfilled (about 37-40 years after Christ gave His prophecy according to Matthew 24). The prophecy of the 70th week of Daniel was fulfilled during 3½ years before the death of Christ, in the middle of the 7 years, and 3½ years after His death. He was "cut off" (crucified) in the middle of the 70th week. It does not say exactly how much later the "abominations" would be, but they would be next in chronological order so far as the prophecy was concerned. It was about 37 years later after His death. In the previous verse 26 it was stated that "the people of the prince that shall come [the Roman armies] shall destroy the city and the sanctuary." That was predicted to take place **after** Messiah was cut off, but it did not say how much later after Messiah was cut off that this would take place. It did say that it would continue until the consummation (the end) when what was determined would be poured upon the desolate (the final end of the city and Temple in A.D. 70).

Modern-day dispensationalists take that prophecy of Daniel's 70th week (**Daniel 9:24-27**) and stretch it like a rubber band away from the 69th week, and keep stretching it until they get it way out into the future, and then make of it a 7 years tribulation period between the "Rapture" and the "Revelation" of Christ. And incidentally, the seven years of this prophecy is the **ONLY** place in the entire Bible where dispensationalists get that exact period of time for their so-called seven years of tribulation in OUR future; and that ONE reference certainly does not refer to anything in our future. It was sometime later, after that 70th week of Daniel was fulfilled, that the destruction of Jerusalem and the Temple took place — about 40 years later to be exact; and that prophecy cannot have meaning for some end-time event in our own future.

Philip Schaff's Description of the End

Before leaving verse 15 and the abomination of desolation, let me give the vivid wording of **Philip Schaff** in his **History of the Christian Church** concerning the final destruction of the Temple and the worship of Caesar which occurred in that "holy" place:

"Titus (according to Josephus) intended at first to save that magnificent work of architecture, as a trophy of victory, and perhaps from some superstitious fear; and when the flames threatened to reach the Holy of Holies he forced his way through the flame and smoke, over the dead and dying, to arrest the fire. But the destruction was determined by a higher decree. His own soldiers, roused to madness by the stubborn resistance, and greedy of the golden treasures, could not be restrained from the work of destruction. At first the halls around the temple were set on fire. Then a firebrand was hurled through the golden gate. When the flames arose the Jews raised a hideous yell and tried to put out the fire; while others, clinging with a last convulsive grasp to their Messianic hopes, rested in the declaration of a false prophet, that God in the midst of the conflagration of the Temple would give a signal for the deliverance of his people. The legions vied with each other in feeding the flames, and made the unhappy people feel the full force of their unchained rage. Soon the whole prodigious structure was in a blaze and illuminated the skies. It was burned on the tenth of August, A.D. 70, the same day of the year on which, according to tradition, the first temple was destroyed by Nebuchadnezzar. 'No one,' says Josephus, 'can conceive a louder, more terrible shriek than arose from all sides during the burning of the temple. The shout of victory and the jubilee of the legions sounded through the wailings of the people, now surrounded with fire and sword, even to Peraea (?), increased the deafening roar. Yet the misery itself was more terrible than this disorder. The hill on which the temple stood was seething hot, but seemed enveloped to its base in one sheet of flame. The blood was larger in quantity than the fire, and those that were slain more in number than those that slew them. The ground was nowhere visible. All was covered with corpses; over these heaps the soldiers pursued the fugitives.'

"The Romans planted their eagles on the shapeless ruins over against the eastern gate, offered their sacrifices to them, and proclaimed Titus **Imperator** with the greatest acclamation of joy. Thus was fulfilled the prophecy concerning the abomination of desolation standing in the holy place." **(Philip Schaff,** vol. 1, pp. 397-398).

In summary of Matthew 24:15 concerning the abomination of desolation, there are four things to be said:

1. The "abomination of desolation" is not something that will occur in our future, nor in our present time.

2. The "abomination of desolation" is a past event, fulfilled in a series of events beginning with the pagan soldiers camping around the holy place (city of Jerusalem) in A.D. 66-70.

3. This event fulfilled the prophecies of Daniel concerning the "abomination of desolation" as said by Jesus in **Matthew 24:15** — "spoken of by Daniel the prophet."

4. The "abomination of desolation" was a signal for the disciples to leave Jerusalem and Judaea to insure their safety from the coming great tribulation upon the Jewish people.

"Then let them which be in Judaea flee into the mountains" (Matthew 24:16).

Jesus told His disciples to get out of Jerusalem as fast as they could when they saw the beginning of the abomination of desolation and before "the great tribulation" (vs. 21) came upon that city. These disciples did what Jesus told them to do and thereby escaped the awful onslaughts and horrors that befell the inhabitants and others in Jerusalem.

Josephus (pp. 200-206) tells us how that when the Roman army first came against Jerusalem, led by Cestius Gallus the general, "had he but at this very time attempted to get within the walls by force, he had won the city presently" (p. 203). But because he did not immediately do what needed to be done to conquer the city, this became the reason the war lasted so long and the Jews went through such dire calamities. Some of the principal men invited Cestius to enter the city and almost opened the gates for him, but he was skeptical of their offer, and so again delayed any aggression against the city. Afterwards they attacked the walls for five days but to no avail. But then a fear came on the people, and if Cestius had continued his attack a little longer he could have taken the city. Instead, "he retired from the city, without any reason in the world" (p. 204). Then the Jews became courageous and chased after Cestius and his army, and before it was over "had slain of the Romans five thousand and three hundred footmen, and three hundred and eighty horsemen." **(Josephus, p. 206)**. This was in the 12th year of the reign of Nero.

A footnote on page 204 by the translator of **Josephus**, says, "There may another very important, and very providential reason be here assigned for this strange and foolish retreat of Cestius; which, if Josephus had been now a Christian, he might probably have taken notice of also; and that is, the affording the Jewish Christians in the city an opportunity of calling to mind the prediction and caution given them by Christ about thirty-three years and a half before, that 'when they should see the abomination of desolation' (The idolatrous Roman armies, with the images of their idols in their ensigns, ready to lay Jerusalem desolate,) 'stand where it ought not;' or, 'in the holy place,' or, 'when they should see Jerusalem encompassed with armies,' they should then 'flee to the mountains.' By complying with which those Jewish Christians fled to the mountains of Perea, and escaped this destruction."

Josephus himself, who concerned himself with history of Jews only with no regard for Christians, simply related, "After this calamity had befallen Cestius, many of the eminent of the Jews swam away from the city, as from a ship when it was going to sink" **(Josephus, vol. 1, p. 206)**.

Eusebius, early church father (A.D. 263-339) who wrote the only surviving account of the Church during its crucial first 300 years, gives us these words about the flight of the Christians from Jerusalem and Judaea before the awful destruction of Jerusalem and its attendant great tribulation took place:

"Furthermore, the members of the Jerusalem church, by means of an oracle given by revelation to acceptable persons there, were ordered to leave the City before the war began and settle in a town in Peraea called Pella. To Pella those who believed in Christ migrated from Jerusalem; and as if holy men had utterly abandoned the royal metropolis of the Jews and the entire Jewish land, the judgement of God at last overtook them for their abominable crimes against Christ and His apostles, completely blotting out that wicked generation from among men." **(Eusebius, The History of the Church, p. 111).**

In October 1987, while looking through a book shop in London, I came across an old book written by **Ernest Renan** (1823-92), French historian and philosopher, entitled, **Renan's Antichrist.** I paid a nice little price to secure this book, but I believe it was worth it. In this book there is included a detailed description of the flight of the Christians from Jerusalem and a description of where they went and settled in order to escape all of those things. I quote this at length from pages 150-152:

"The departure seems to have been decided on in the early part of 68. To give more authority to this resolution the rumour was spread that the heads of the community had received a revelation in the matter; according to some, this revelation had been granted through the ministry of an angel. It is probable that all responded to the chief's appeal, and that none of the brethren remained in the city which, a very just instinct told them, was doomed to extermination.

"There are indications inclining one to believe that the flight of the peaceful band was not performed without risk. Apparently the Jews pursued it; as a matter of fact the terrorists exercised a vigilant watch over the roads, and slew as traitors all those who sought to escape, unless they could pay a high ransom. A circumstance, to which we only have a veiled allusion, saved the fugitives:

" **'And the serpent cast out of his mouth after the woman (the Church of Jerusalem) water as a river, that he might cause her to be carried away by the stream. And the earth helped the woman, and the earth opened her mouth, and swallowed up the river which the dragon cast out of his mouth. And the dragon waxed wroth with the woman.' (Revelation 12:15-17).**

"Perhaps the Zelotes tried to drive the holy band into the Jordan, and the latter succeeded in crossing the river at a place where the water was shallow; it may be that the troop sent in pursuit went astray, and thus lost the traces of those whom it was chasing.

"The place selected by the heads of the community to serve as the principal asylum for the fugitive Church was Pella, one of the towns of Decapolis, situated near the left bank of the Jordan in an admirable position, overlooking on one side the whole plain of Ghor, and having on the other precipitous cliffs, at the foot of which runs a torrent. No wiser choice could have been made. Judaea, Idumaea, Peraea, and Galilee were in insurrection; Samaria and the coast were in a very unsettled state owing to the war. Thus Scythopolis and Pella were the nearest neutral cities to Jerusalem. Pella, by its position beyond the Jordan, must have offered much more tranquillity than Scythopolis, which had become one of the Roman strongholds. Pella was a free city like the other towns of Decapolis, but apparently it had given allegiance to Agrippa II. To take refuge there was openly to avow horror of the revolt. The importance of the town dated from the Macedonian conquest. A colony of Alexander's veterans had taken up their quarters there, and changed the Semitic name of the place into another, which recalled their native land to the old soldiers. Pella was captured by Alexander Jannaeus, and the Greek inhabitants, who refused to be circumcised, suffered much from Jewish fanaticism. The pagan population doubtless took new root, for, in the massacres of 66, Pella was considered a Syrian town, and was once more sacked by the Jews. It was in this anti-Jewish town that the Church of Jerusalem found refuge during the horrors of the seige. Here it was at ease, and looked on its tranquil abode as a sure place, a desert prepared by God, where, far from man's tumultuous strife, the hour of the coming of Jesus might be awaited in peace. The community lived on their savings; it was believed that God himself took it upon him to feed them, and many saw in such a lot, so different from that of the Jews, a miracle predicted by the prophets. No doubt the Galilean Christians had for their part betaken themselves to the east of the Jordan and the lake into Batanaea and Gaulonitis. The territories of Agrippa II, thus formed an adoptive country for the Judeo-Christians of Palestine." **(Renan, pp. 150-152).**

"It is a remarkable but historical fact that Cestius Gallus, the Roman general, for some unknown reason, retired when they first marched against the city, suspended the siege, ceased the attack and withdrew his armies for an interval of time after the Romans had occupied the temple, thus giving every believing Jew the opportunity to obey the Lord's instruction to flee the city. Josephus the eyewitness, himself an unbeliever, chronicles this fact, and admitted his inability to account for the cessation of the fighting at this time, after a siege had begun. Can we account for it? We can. The Lord was fighting against Jerusalem — Zechariah 14:2: 'For I will gather all nations against Jerusalem to battle; and the city shall be taken, and the houses rifled, and the women ravished; and half of the city shall go forth into captivity, and the residue of the people shall not be cut off from the city.' The Lord was besieging that city. God was bringing these things to pass against the Jewish state and nation. Therefore, the opportunity was offered for the disciples to escape the siege, as Jesus had forewarned, and the disciples took it. So said Daniel; so said Jesus; so said Luke, so said Josephus'' **(Foy E. Wallace, Jr., p. 352).**

"But the faithful followers of Jesus, were steadie to their profession, and attended to his predictions concerning coming calamities, and observed the signs of their near approach, escaped, and obtained safety, with only the lesser difficulties of a flight, which was necessarie in the time of a general calamitie." **(Lardner, p. 76).**

". . . it is remarked by several interpreters, and which Josephus takes notice of with surprise, that Cestius Gallus having advanced with his army to Jerusalem, and besieged it, on a sudden without any cause, raised the siege, and withdrew his army, when the city might have been easily taken; by which means a signal was made, and an opportunity given to the Christians, to make their escape: which they accordingly did, and went over to Jordan, as Eusebius says, to a place called Pella; so that when Titus came a few months after, there was not a Christian in the city . . ." **(John Gill,** on Matthew 24:16).

Henry Hammond, in commenting on verse 16, said, "How exactly the several passages of story in Josephus agree with these predictions will easily be discerned by comparing them, particularly that which belongs to this place of their **flying to the mountains, &c.** For when Gallus besieged Jerusalem, and without any visible cause, on a sudden raised the siege, what an act of God's special providence was this, thus to order it, that the believers of Christian Jews being warned by this siege, and let loose (set at liberty again) might **fly to the mountains,** that is, get out of Judea to some other place! Which that they did accordingly appears by this, that when Titus came some months after and besieged the city, there was not one Christian remaining in it" **(H. Hammond,** vol. 3, p. 160).

"When Christ came to destroy the Jews, he came to redeem the Christians that were persecuted and oppressed by them." **(Matthew Henry Commentary,** vol. 5, p. 805, on Luke 21:28).

"**Let him which is on the housetop not come down to take any thing out of his house:**

"**Neither let him which is in the field return back to take his clothes.**

"**And woe unto them that are with child, and to them that give suck in those days!**

"**But pray ye that your flight be not in winter, neither on the sabbath day**" (Matthew 24:17-20).

In these verses Jesus was telling His disciples of the haste that would be necessary when they fled the city. When my wife and I visited Jerusalem (on our own — not with a tour group) we saw those flat-topped houses adjoining one another in old Jerusalem; in fact, I talked Evelyn into climbing to the top of one of them and then walking along the tops of them with me. Jesus was saying that when the armies were seen surrounding the city, if they were up on a roof, they were not even to take time to come down inside the house, but should "scoot" along the roofs to where they could get outside the city just as soon as they could.

Likewise, anyone in the field should not take time to go back to get his clothing, but leave just like he was in order to save time and escape before danger overtook him. It was like the instructions given to Lot many years before, "Escape for thy life; look not behind thee, neither stay thou in all the plain; escape to the mountain, lest thou be consumed" **(Genesis 19:17)**. And concerning this, Jesus said, "But the same day that Lot went out of Sodom it rained fire and brimstone from heaven, and destroyed them all. Even thus shall it be in the day when the Son of man is revealed" **(Luke 17:29-30)**.

And now I know what it was that Jesus meant by that statement, "Remember Lot's wife" **(Luke 17:32)**. After God had told Lot and his wife to escape to the mountain from Sodom and Gomorrah, Lot's wife looked back and she was turned into a pillar of salt **(Genesis 19:26)**. Jesus was instructing His disciples to get out of Jerusalem and Judaea as quickly as possible and head to the mountains, else they would be overtaken in the awful tribulation and destruction which was to be poured out on that place. This statement has nothing to do with a future second coming of Christ, as thought by some.

Christian women who were pregnant would have an unusually difficult time of it, as well as those with nursing babies.

Jesus indicated to His disciples that if they had to flee in the winter, or upon a Sabbath day, it would be bad for them. In the winter the roads would be bad, the days would be short, and it would not be the best time to travel. And as all these disciples were Jews, the Jewish regulation of not traveling on the Sabbath except for a Sabbath day's journey could create some problems. So the disciples were encouraged to hope and pray that their flight from Jerusalem would not be on the Sabbath day. In **Acts 1:12** we read, "Then returned they unto Jerusalem from the mount called Olivet, which is from Jerusalem a sabbath day's journey." This gives us something of the distance that could be travelled on the Sabbath day. This tradition was based on the ordinance given in **Exodus 16:29**: "See, for that the LORD hath given you the sabbath, therefore he giveth you on the sixth day the bread of two days; abide ye every man in his place, let no man go out of his place on the seventh day. So the people rested on the seventh day." Of course the rabbis interpreted the ordinance to suit themselves, and allowed that 2,000 yards would be all right to travel, even though the ordinance had said, "Abide ye every man in his place." Even though Christians were not bound by this ordinance, they could have faced difficulties because of it.

But regardless of the problems, they were to make haste to get out of the city as soon as they saw the armies surrounding it. One main reason for this was that if they did not do so quickly, they would not be able to do so at all later. In **Luke 19:43** Jesus said, "For the days shall come upon thee, that thine enemies shall cast a trench about thee, and compass thee round, and KEEP THEE IN on every side."

Were this speaking of some future second coming of Christ, whether it were summer or winter would not matter at all (vs. 20). Nor would it matter whether it were the Sabbath or not (vs. 20), nor whether a woman were pregnant or not (19), nor whether a man had all his clothes or not (vs. 18), nor whether someone was on a housetop or not (vs. 17). These instructions can only apply to the situation involving the "tribulation of those days" prior to the destruction of Jerusalem — not a future tribulation period prior to a second coming of Christ as taught by the dispensationalists. This sort of far-fetched teaching results from "futurizing" these events of Matthew 24. The interpretation that puts these events out into our future instead of back there in A.D. 66-70, is a modern one and was not held in general by Bible scholars of years ago.

"So it is not surprising that the dispensational identification of v.v. 15-18 **exclusively** with the Great Tribulation after the Rapture of the church, whether revealed or unrevealed, finds no exponent till the nineteenth century" (**D. A. Carson**, vol. 8, p. 495).

"It is said that there is reason to believe that not one Christian perished in the destruction of that city, God having in various ways secured their escape, so that they fled to Pella, where they dwelt when the city was destroyed" (**Albert Barnes Commentary** on **Matthew 24:31**).

Of the pull-back of Cestius Gallus from Jerusalem after first attacking it, and thereby giving the Christians opportunity to escape from the city, I shall have more to say later in this series when I tell of the total war itself that took place in those days.

The 144,000 of Revelation 7:1-8

Right here would be a good place to say just a word about the 144,000 of Revelation 7:1-8. I now believe that the book of Revelation was written before the fall of Jerusalem when God's wrath came on that land in A.D. 66-70. And the book was written to encourage the Christians of that day in spite of all that the Jews had done against them, and that Rome (Nero) had done against them, and to show the ultimate triumph of the gospel and Christ's kingdom. God promised to preserve His Christians from the wrath and slaughter that was to come on the land. Jesus told them that "he that shall endure unto the end, the same shall be saved" (**Matthew 24:13**). This was not talking about spiritual salvation, but of physical deliverance; and this is why right after that Jesus told them to flee into the mountains at the proper time (**vs. 16**). God's protecting care is pictured for us in His command to the four angels, "Hurt not the earth, neither the sea, nor the trees, till we have sealed the servants of our God in their foreheads" (**Revelation 7:3**). These were the 12 tribes of 12,000 each from Israel, a total of 144,000 — a figurative number denoting completeness or fulness. In **Revelation 14:4** it is said that "These were redeemed from among men, being the first fruits unto God and to the Lamb." It is a known fact that practically all the converts in those first few years of Christianity in Palestine were Jews. But these are the "redeemed" Jews, who were the "firstfruits" unto God; that is, they were the first ones to be converted and redeemed from among men out of all the Jews. They were the ones to be delivered from the coming holocaust. These were the Jewish Christians who escaped out of Palestine before the fires of God's judgment covered that place. The wrath that was to come would cause men to hide "themselves in the dens and in the rocks of the mountains: And said to the mountains and rocks, Fall on us, and hide us from the face of him that sitteth on the throne, and from the wrath of the Lamb" (**Revelation 6:16**). These were the same words Jesus used to describe what would happen at the time of the destruction and fall of Jerusalem in A.D. 70, as He told the crying mothers, "Weep not for me, but weep for yourselves, and for your children . . . Then shall they begin to say to the mountains, Fall on us; and to the hills, Cover us" (**Luke 23:28, 30**).

But God's "sealed" people, the Jewish Christians, managed to escape that wrath (**Revelation 6:16** and **I Thessalonians 2:16**), and it was said that not a single Christian was in Jerusalem when Titus the Roman general finally led his men into the city. They had all fled to Pella over in Trans-Jordan and escaped the wrath which fell upon all the Jewish people.

Section 3 ••••••••••••••••••••••••••

"THEN SHALL BE GREAT TRIBULATION"

"For then shall be great tribulation, such as was not since the beginning of the world to this time, no, nor ever shall be" (Matthew 24:21).

The most tragic time in the history of the nation of Israel was in A.D. 67-70, during the siege and destruction of the city of Jerusalem by the Roman armies. Jesus said it would be a time of **great tribulation** such as never had been before, nor ever would be again. This was the reason that Jesus had warned His disciples to get out of the city and to head for the mountains just as soon as possible when they saw the armies surrounding the city. This was the abomination of desolation, as discussed in our previous section, and was the sign for the disciples to flee.

Please note that Jesus said, "**THEN** shall be great tribulation" — not many hundreds or thousands of years or more in the future. The GREAT TRIBULATION talked about in **Matthew 24:21** took place during the days of the siege of Jerusalem in A.D. 67-70 and was a tribulation on the Jewish people and not on the Christian people. It is pointless to separate this tribulation mentioned here from its contemporary setting and move it out of place to a time either just before or just after a future second coming of Christ, as many do. This great tribulation is an actual historical fact, and we need not try to make anything else out of it. The Great Tribulation is not a period of time in **our** future. It already happened years ago.

"FOR then shall be great tribulation." The word "for" gives the reason for the flight of the disciples. This was a local matter with them, in Jerusalem and Judaea, and not something that applies to people in our future.

In **Luke 21:22-23** Jesus said concerning that awful time of tribulation, "For these be the days of vengeance, that all things which are written may be fulfilled. But woe unto them that are with child, and to them that give suck, in those days! for there shall be great distress in the land, and wrath upon this people." This would be the time when God's wrath was finally poured out on Israel, as was said also by Paul in **I Thessalonians 2:16**, "for the wrath is come upon them to the uttermost." That day would be just around the corner after the Christians got out of the city and left Judaea for the mountains and safety elsewhere. The wrath was to be upon "THIS PEOPLE;" that is, Israel — not the Christians. The Christians had, and would have, their tribulation, from both the Jews and the Romans; but the tribulation that would fall upon Jerusalem and Judaea would be the wrath of God. God would "recompense tribulation to them that trouble you" **(II Thessalonians 1:6)**.

God preserved His people from the days of "great tribulation" which came upon the land of Israel and on Jerusalem in particular in A.D. 67-70. By following Jesus' instructions to get out of the city and country when they saw the armies surrounding the city of Jerusalem, they thereby secured for themselves safety and security during that awful time of Tribulation.

When they were taking Jesus away to be crucified, Jesus told the daughters of Jerusalem not to weep for Him, but for themselves and their children. He said:

"Daughters of Jerusalem, weep not for me, but weep for yourselves, and for your children.

"For, behold, the days are coming, in the which they shall say, Blessed are the barren, and the wombs that never bare, and the paps which never gave suck.

"Then shall they begin to say to the mountains, Fall on us; and to the hills, Cover us" **(Luke 23:28-30)**.

This cannot refer to a final day of judgment in our future nor to some future tribulation period after the Rapture, but to that great day of His wrath against Jerusalem, etc. It was directed to them and to their children.

This expression of crying for the mountains and hills to fall on them is used concerning man's reaction and response to the wrath of God, as for example, in **Hosea 10:8** when God was predicting His judgment upon Israel. It was predicted there that "they shall say to the mountains, Cover us; and to the hills, Fall on us." These cries from the lost came from Israel, not from Gentile nations.

William Kimball, who has more on The Great Tribulation of Matthew 24 than in any book I have seen said:

"It should be noted that Luke flatly states that: 'These be the days of vengeance, THAT ALL THINGS WHICH ARE WRITTEN MAY BE FULFILLED' **(Luke 21:22)**. Knowing that these events described by Luke apply to Jerusalem's tragic destruction in 70 A.D., we can safely conclude that it was those awesome events which marked the fulfillment of all the previous prophetic statements concerning the eventual judgment which was destined to befall Israel. History overwhelmingly corroborates the fulfillment of all the tragic events prophesied concerning the fall of Jerusalem and the ensuing dispersion of the surviving remnant. The numerous prophecies spoken by Moses, Daniel, Jeremiah, and even Christ found their fulfillment in 70 A.D.

This period of **great tribulation** is not an event which the entire world is yet awaiting, but a past historic event of unparalled concentrated severity specifically afflicting the Jewish nation in 70 A.D." (**William R. Kimball, What the Bible Says About the Great Tribulation**, pp. 88-89).

Eusebius of Caesarea (exact date of birth unknown, but he lived in the 3rd and 4th century) believed that the flight of the Christians, the abomination of desolation, and the great tribulation, were all connected with the events leading up to the destruction of Jerusalem in A.D. 70. (See **The Nicene and Post-Nicene Fathers**, vol. 1, pp. 138, 141). Eusebius was a preterist in his interpretation of these events.

But keep in mind that the great tribulation was not the time when the Romans finally came into the city, etc. By then, the tribulation was practically near the end. The great tribulation was the entire 3½ years of suffering, and hunger, and famine, and murder, and desecration, and death, which were all taking place in those last several years of the history of Jerusalem. Much of it (or even most of it) was brought upon themselves by what went on inside the city. Of these things I shall speak more later.

Background and Cause of the War

Rome did not initiate the war against Jerusalem. Jerusalem was under the authority and control of Rome. Headstrong men in Jerusalem itself, greedy of gain, kept irritating the people and inciting them to rebel against Rome. The people quit paying their taxes and removed the connecting "cloisters" from between the Temple and the tower of Antonia where Roman soldiers were stationed. This would have been sufficient in itself to cause Rome to go against Jerusalem. Feelings kept building up until King Agrippa himself called the multitude together in a large gallery and pled with them, on the basis of the immense power of the Romans in the world, not to do such a foolish thing as to go to war against Rome for their liberty, for, he said, it would amount to their complete destruction. He said:

"But certainly no one can imagine that you can enter into a war as by an agreement, or that when the Romans have got you under their power they will use you with moderation, or will not rather, for an example to other nations, burn your holy city, and utterly destroy your whole nation; for those of you who shall survive the war will not be able to find a place whither to flee, since all men have the Romans for their lords already, or are afraid they shall have hereafter. Nay, indeed, the danger concerns not those Jews that dwell here only, but those of them who dwell in other cities also; for there is no people upon the habitable earth which have not some portion of you among them, whom your enemies will slay, in case you go to war, and on that account also; and so every city which hath Jews in it will be filled with slaughter for the sake only of a few men . . ." **(Josephus,** vol. 1, p. 185).

Agrippa appealed to them to be mindful of the fact that such a great multitude of nations in the world already were under authority of Rome, and living peaceably with no intention of rebellion; and should Jerusalem, for its just one nation, take up arms against the mighty Roman Empire? Agrippa temporarily stopped the war that was threatened, and the people started paying their taxes and began rebuilding the cloisters. But time would provide a fulfilment of what Agrippa had warned them about. Feelings kept building up. And the true beginning of the war with the Romans (according to **Josephus,** vol. 1, p. 187) was when they refused to offer up any sacrifice of Caesar, which was customary to be done for their princes. Eleazar, son of Ananias the high priest, and governor of the Temple, persuaded the officials of the religious services not to receive any gift or sacrifice for any foreigner **(Josephus,** vol. 1, p. 187). Leading men remonstrated with the Temple officials, but to no avail. A great conflict and slaughter broke out between these opposing forces, and the tower of Antonia was stormed. But all this was the beginning of the war that at last saw Rome's power come down on Israel, and the ultimate destruction of both city and Temple, with the entire country devastated. This account is given that you might better understand something of the historical background of what led up to the great tribulation upon the Jews and the desolation of their land and city and Temple.

The Great Tribulation Period

In dealing with this entire matter of "the great tribulation" of **Matthew 24:21,** it might be well to summarize all the main events from the time of the escape of the Christians from the city, up to the time that the Roman general Titus camped his armies outside Jerusalem, and also what happened during the entire war and then the final destruction of the Temple and the city itself. Other commentaries on this subject have not given us all these details. **Most of what I say is culled from the Jewish historian Josephus' account of these things.** Josephus was a Jew who was actually present himself in those days, and you can read the entire account in **The Works of Josephus,** vol. 1, **The War of the Jews.** I shall give you the page numbers. It would pay you to get a copy of this volume, reprinted by Baker Book House in 1979, and read in detail the awful, horrible, gruesome, sickening things that went on in Jerusalem in those days of "great tribulation." Other sources are also cited.

The Jewish revolt against Rome began in A.D. 65. **F. W. Farrar** said, "But though the Jews and the Romans felt for each other a profound hatred, there was no overt rebellion till the days of Gessius Florus, who was appointed Procurator in A.D. 65" **(Farrar, p. 415)**.

Though this probably had nothing at all to do with the war against Jerusalem, it might be of passing interest here to mention at this point, that it was in A.D. 64 that Nero began his persecution of Christians from Rome. The approximate 3½ years of persecution on the Christians during A.D. 64-68 would almost fit into the same time slot as the approximate 3½ years of tribulation upon the Jewish people in Jerusalem from A.D. 67-70, with some months separating the two periods. Of course, if the Christians had not fled from Judaea and Jerusalem after Cestius Gallus' withdrawal from the city, they too would have suffered the awful consequences of what happened in those days. And when Titus finally came against the city, he felt that by destroying the Jews he would thereby get rid of the Christians as well. But when he did come into the city, he did not find any Christians there, for they had fled many months before.

I shall not guarantee the accuracy of each and every date mentioned on these pages, for in our total research on these matters we have found some variations and inconsistencies in the accounts by different authors. But as a whole, I would hope that the dates are fairly accurate and consistent. I have tried to record all the proper dates with the various events that took place, and in chronological order.

The first stage of the war against Jerusalem itself was by Cestius Gallus October 15-22, A.D. 66. The "war" group (the Zealots) were in control of the city by this time. The Roman army pitched close to Jerusalem on Mount Scopus. On November 17 Cestius led his troops into Jerusalem. They soon lost this battle against the Jews and withdrew and fled.

Jesus had told His disciples to get out of Jerusalem and Judaea as fast as they could when they first saw the armies surrounding the city **(Luke 21:20-21)**, for those would be "the days of vengeance that all things which are written may be fulfilled." (vs. 22). And "then shall be great tribulation, such as was not since the beginning of the world to this time, no, nor ever shall be" **(Matthew 24:21)**. The Christians took advantage of this "lull" in the war, and escaped from the city and fled to Pella, as mentioned previously.

The next year Nero sent Vespasian to Judaea to stop the rebellion. His commission from Nero was in A.D. 67, and the declaration of war against Judaea occurred in the early part of February of that year. (It was three years and six months later, on August 10, A.D. 70, that Jerusalem was destroyed. This is the 42 months during which the holy city was to be given to the Gentiles to tread under foot, according to **Revelation 11:2**.) Much of all of Judaea was devastated before Jerusalem was ever reached.

In **The History of the Jewish People, Max L. Margolis** and **Alexander Marx**, said, "The Nazarenes, that is, those who accepted Jesus of Nazareth as the Messiah, indifferent to the national cause, sought safety in flight from Jerusalem; the small community settled in Pella beyond Jordan" **(Margolis, pp. 199-200)**.

After Cestius Gallus retreated, and following which all the Christian Jews fled from the city and went to Pella (later called Petra) in Perea, the Roman Emperor Nero (who reigned thirteen years and eight months, October 13, 54 — June 9, A.D. 68) determined to send armies and destroy Jerusalem **(Josephus, p. 221f)**.

In February A.D. 67 Nero put Vespasian in charge of plans for real war. Vespasian's son Titus helped. "Vespasian, in the spring of A.D. 67, advanced against the rebels" **(Josephus, foreword)**. They had 60,000 soldiers. Gadara was the first target. They took it. "He came then into it, and slew all the youth, the Romans having no mercy on any age whatsoever; and this was done out of the hatred they bore the nation" **(Josephus, p. 236)**.

Jotapata was next, then Japaha where 15,000 were destroyed and 2,130 made captives. It took longer to take Jotapata.

Then Mt. Gerizzim (the Samaritans had assembled there). 11,600 were slain.

Taricheae was next. 6,500 were killed on land and in the sea.

Gamala was next. 4,000 were slain, while 5,000 killed themselves by throwing themselves over precipices.

Then there was the small city of Gischala. There they slew 6,000 women and children when many of the men fled and went to Jerusalem. Included in those who escaped was John Levi, who played a big part in the coming destruction of Jerusalem. John Levi persuaded the people of Jerusalem to go to war with the Romans instead of submitting to them, deceiving them as to the power of the Roman armies **(Josephus, p. 291)**.

Vespasian and Titus also took other cities, and there were "disorders and civil wars in every city" also **(Josephus, p. 292)**.

Conditions Within the City

Jerusalem was now without a governor. (Josephus, who had served as governor, was taken in the battle at Jotapata, then gave himself up to the Romans. He predicted that Vespasian and Titus would become emperor of Rome after Nero. Vespasian took a liking to him, and Josephus later became a translator for Titus. After the war, he spent five years writing his history of the Jewish people.) So without a governor, so much wickedness was going on in the city that robbers themselves appointed high priests of "unknown and ignoble persons" who would cooperate with them in their wickedness **(Josephus, p. 294)**. By casting lots, they chose Eniachim for the high-priesthood who was "not only unworthy of the high priesthood, but that did not well know what the high-priesthood was" **(Josephus, p. 295)**. One of the best-esteemed of the regular high-priests, Ananus, said, "Certainly, it had been good for me to die before I had seen the house of God full of so many abominations" **(Josephus, p. 296)**. He said, "They have seized upon the strongest place of the whole city; you may call it the temple, if you please, though it be like a citadel or fortress" **(Josephus, p. 297)**. He accused the people of allowing all this to happen, and exhorted them to overthrow those robbers and Zealots who wanted to go to war against Rome. Ananus chose 6,000 armed men as the wicked men had gone into the holy part of the Temple and secured themselves there, staining that sanctuary with their own blood **(Josephus, p. 300)**. They even got drunk in the sanctuary **(Josephus, p. 305)**. The zealots who were in control sent messengers to the Idumeans to come and help them **(Josephus, pp. 303-304)**, and 20,000 of them came to Jerusalem **(Josephus, p. 304)** for this purpose. The gates were closed to the Idumeans by Ananus, but men from the Temple went with saws and opened the gates and let the Idumeans in **(Josephus, p. 311)**. They succeeded in coming into the city at night during a heavy downpour of rain, and they began murdering and looting. 8,500 people were slain **(Josephus, p. 313)**. The Idumeans plundered every house, and killed the high priests, including Ananus.

Josephus said, "I shall not mistake if I said that the death of Ananus was the beginning of the destruction of the city, and that from this very day may be dated the overthrow of her walls, and the ruin of her affairs" **(Josephus, p. 313)**. Josephus also added, "and I cannot but think that it was because God had doomed this city to destruction, as a polluted city, and was resolved to purge his sanctuary by fire, that he cut off these their great defenders and wellwishers" **(Josephus, p. 314)**.

The Idumeans then slaughtered people to the extent of 12,000 **(Josephus, p. 315)**. After the Idumeans left, the Zealots killed more of the people. All this caused Vespasian to bide his time in coming and attacking Jerusalem "while their enemies are destroying each other with their own hands" **(Josephus, p. 319)**. "Vast numbers of dead bodies lay in heaps," and the Zealots would not allow them to be buried **(Josephus, p. 320)**.

Vespasian in the meantime took Gadara (15,000 plus slain), and then laid waste other cities which were revolting from Nero (**Josephus, pp. 326-327**).

The people of Jerusalem were kept sealed in the city by the Zealots (**Josephus, p. 332**). When Vespasian finally decided to march against Jerusalem, he heard that Nero was dead (A.D. 68). The empire passed to Galba, who reigned 7 months and 7 days, and was slain; then to Otho, who killed himself after reigning 3 months and 2 days. Then Vitellius held the government 8 months and 5 days.

More warring broke out by another faction led by a Simon with 20,000 armed men who ravaged cities and villages as he planned to go on to Jerusalem and take it.

At this time **John Levi** was in control at Jerusalem. More will be said about this man later. The high priests and people decided to admit Simon and his army into the city to put down John and the Zealots (**Josephus, p. 339**). Simon then gained possession of Jerusalem (**Josephus, p. 340**).

After Nero's death, Vespasian hastened back to Rome for the purpose of becoming emperor. He was proclaimed emperor in July A.D. 69. The people were already celebrating "sacrifices and oblations" when they heard this news (**Josephus, p. 345**). So Vespasian "sent his son Titus, with a select party of his army, to destroy Jerusalem" (**Josephus, p. 349**).

Much fighting broke out inside the city between the warring factions. The factions of John and Simon were fighting each other, and the areas around the Temple were burned down (**Josephus, p. 354**). The innocent were killed. Nothing was done for the wounded. Dead bodies lay unburied. The soldiers fought on top of dead bodies. John Levi had already "set on fire those houses that were full of corn, and of all other provisions. The same thing was done by Simon . . . almost all the corn was burnt, which would have been sufficient for a siege of many years" (**Josephus, p. 354**). This "was the direct occasion of that terrible famine, which consumed incredible numbers of the Jews in Jerusalem during its siege" (**Josephus, p. 345, footnote**).

In Jerusalem, all who were opposed to the rebellion against Rome were imprisoned and killed by the Zealots.

Truly, this time for Jerusalem was "great tribulation."

Titus in the meanwhile had gotten his armies together at Caesarea, ordering other armies to meet him at Jerusalem, and he marched to Jerusalem. He had armies from Italy, Syria, Egypt and Greece (**Josephus, p. 356**). Titus pitched camp at Scopus near Jerusalem. The siege began April 14, A.D. 70.

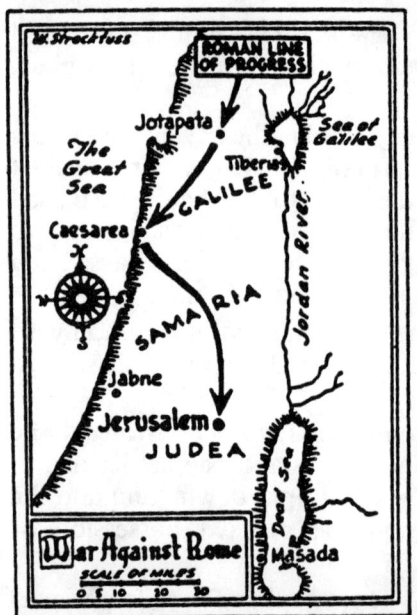 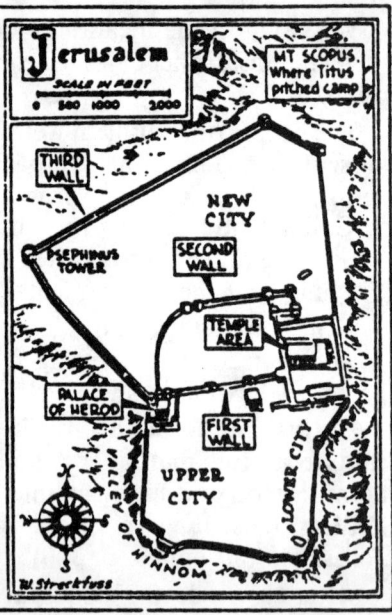

Pictures from *A History of the Jews,* by Solomon Grayzel. By courtesy of The Jewish Publication Society of America, Philadelphia, Pennsylvania.

During the War Against Jerusalem

While Titus encamped at Scopus, other legions encamped at the Mount of Olives (**Josephus**, p. 359). Much planning and preparation was done on account of the strong fortification of the city. Trees around the city were cut down for visibility, and the timber was used to build banks, or ramps, up to the walls. The engines of war threw javelins, and darts, and stones, while those inside the walls did the same to them. The Romans erected high towers to more easily reach those on the walls. On the fifteenth day of the siege, Titus got possession of the first wall and "demolished a great part of it." Titus went inside the city, and John Levi and his faction fought them from the tower of Antonia and Simon's army from another area (**Josephus**, p. 386). Five days later the Romans took the second wall and entered with a thousand of his men. They were driven out, but they took it again. Inside the city many were dying for lack of necessities (**Josephus**, p. 391). Titus kept trying to get the Jews to surrender so all would not be slain and so the city and their religion would be preserved, but the Zealots were adamant.

The famine inside the city was such "that children pulled the very morsels that their fathers were eating out of their very mouths, and, what was still more to be pitied, so did the mothers do as to their infants; and when those that were most dear were perishing under their hands, they were not ashamed to take from them the very last drops that might preserve their lives . . . The seditious everywhere came upon them immediately, and snatched away from them what they had gotten from others **(Josephus, p. 402)**.

"They also invented terrible methods of torment to discover where any food was, and they were these: to stop up the passages of the privy parts of the miserable wretches, and to drive sharp stakes up their fundaments!" **(Josephus, p. 403)**.

Josephus said, "That neither did any other city ever suffer such miseries, nor did any age ever breed a generation more fruitful in wickedness than this was, from the beginning of the world" **(Josephus, p. 404)**.

The Romans tortured those who ventured out of the city to escape the tortures of the Zealots inside. ". . . they were first whipped, and then tormented with all sorts of tortures before they died, and were then crucified before the wall of the city. This miserable procedure made Titus greatly to pity them, while they caught every day five hundred Jews; nay, some days they caught more . . . So the soldiers out of the wrath and hatred they bore the Jews, nailed those they caught, one after one way, and another after another, to the crosses, by way of jest; when their multitude was so great, that room was wanting for the crosses, and crosses wanting for the bodies" **(Josephus, p. 405)**.

The translator's footnote says, " . . . they had brought this judgment on themselves by the crucifixion of their Messiah" **(Josephus, p. 405)**.

Titus built a wall clear around the city so that none could escape, and then the famine began to consume the people by whole houses and families **(Josephus, p. 410)**.

Renan said, "From this time forth, hunger, rage, despair, and madness dwelt in Jerusalem. It was a cage of furious maniacs, a city resounding with howling and inhabited by cannibals, a very hell. Titus, for his part, was atrociously vindictive; every day five hundred unfortunates were crucified in sight of the city with hateful refinements of cruelty or sufficient ground whereon to erect them" **(Renan, p. 254)**.

Jesus had predicted:
"For the days shall come upon thee, that thine enemies shall cast a trench about thee, and compass thee round, and keep thee in on every side,

"And shall lay thee even with the ground, and thy children within thee; and they shall not leave in thee one stone upon another; because thou knewest not the time of thy visitation" **(Luke 19:43-44)**.

When the dead inside the city could not be buried, and the stench of their dead bodies could not be endured, "they had them cast down from the walls into the valleys beneath" **(Josephus, p. 413)**.

When others deserted the city, they swallowed gold pieces for their later use, but "the Arabians, with the Syrians, cut up those that came as supplicants, and searched their bellies. Nor does it seem to me that any misery befell the Jews that was more terrible than this, since in one night's time about two thousand of these deserters were thus dissected" **(Josephus, p. 417)**.

When Titus learned of this, he threatened the Arabian and Syrian soldiers with death, and his own soldiers as well, but some still secretly carried on these tragic acts.

Then "John, when he could no longer plunder the people, he betook himself to sacrilege, and melted down many of the sacred utensils, which had been given to the temple." **Josephus** said:

"I suppose, that had the Romans made any longer delay in coming against these villains, the city would either have been swallowed up by the ground opening upon them, or been overflowed by water, or else been destroyed by such thunder as the country of Sodom perished by, for it had brought forth a generation of men much more atheistical than were those that suffered such punishments; for by their madness it was that all the people came to be destroyed" **(Josephus, p. 418)**.

As time went on, the miseries of the Jews grew worse, and finally the Romans made an assault on the tower of Antonia **(Josephus, p. 420)**. This assault was made on July 17, A.D. 70. The same day that orders were given to demolish the tower, "on that very day, which was the seventeenth day of Panemus (Tamuz), the sacrifice called 'the Daily Sacrifice' had failed, and had not been offered to God for want of men to offer it" **(Josephus, p. 430)**.

"The daily sacrifice ceased July 17th, because the hands were all needed for defense. The last and the bloodiest sacrifice at the altar of burnt offerings was the slaughter of thousands of Jews who had crowded around it" **(Philip Schaff**, vol. 1, p. 397).

From the time that Vespasian declared war on Judaea (Spring of A.D. 67) until cessation of sacrifices in the Temple (July 17, A.D. 70), was approximately 3½ years. During all of the war, the morning and evening sacrifices in the Temple had been offered daily up until this time.

In **"Sacred History"** of **Sulpitius Severus (363-420)**, a contemporary of St. Jerome and St. Augustine, a history of the world from creation to A.D. 400 is given. Of this dreadful tribulation period of the Jews in A.D. 70 he wrote:

"The Jews, meanwhile, being closely besieged, as no chance either or peace of surrender was allowed them, were at length perishing from famine, and the streets began everywhere to be filled with dead bodies, for the duty of burying them could no longer be performed. Moreover, they ventured on eating all things of the most abominable nature, and did not even abstain from human bodies, except those which putrefaction had already laid hold of and thus excluded from use as food. The Romans, accordingly, rushed in upon the exhausted defenders of the city. And it so happened that the whole multitude from the country, and from other towns of Judaea, had then assembled for the day of Passover: doubtless, because it pleased God that the impious race should be given over to destruction at the very time of the year at which they had crucified the Lord. The Pharisees for a time maintained their ground most boldly in defense of the Temple, and at length, with minds obstinately bent on death, they, of their own accord, committed themselves to the flames. The number of those who suffered death is related to have been eleven hundred thousand, and one hundred thousand were taken captive and sold" (**Sulpitius Severus,** p. 111).

The Romans once again urged the Zealots to surrender so that their religious laws and sacrifices could continue, and once again were ignored. Josephus himself, acting as translator for Titus, said, "It is God therefore, it is God himself who is bringing on this fire, to purge that city and temple by means of the Romans, and is going to pluck up this city, which is full of your pollutions" (**Josephus,** p. 432).

One woman who had lost everything but her baby to these bloodthirsty Jews, then killed her baby son, "and then roasted him, and ate the one half of him, and kept the other half by her concealed." When the seditious men smelled "the horrid scent of this food, they threatened her, that they would cut her throat immediately if she did not show them what food she had gotten ready. She replied, that she had saved a very fine portion of it for them; and withal uncovered what was left of her son. Hereupon they were seized with a horror and amazement of mind, and stood astonished at the sight; when she said to them, 'This is mine own son; and what hath been done was mine own doing! Come, eat of this food; for I have eaten of it myself!' The men left, trembling and frightened. The whole city was overcome by distress when they heard of such a thing" (**Josephus,** pp. 443-444).

This kind of thing was the sort of curse that God had promised would come upon Israel as He told them of the conditions that would bring chastisement in the land. See **Deuteronomy 28**, and especially verse **53**.

Titus finally gave orders to set fire to the gates of the Temple (**Josephus, p. 445**). He wanted to save the most holy place, but furious soldiers without orders to do so set fire to a window which opened a passage leading to the rooms of the holy place, which greatly enraged the Jews. But so it was, the "holy house" burned up, even though Titus disapproved of what was done (**Josephus, pp. 448-450**).

On August 9, A.D. 70, Titus entered the Temple. The next day, August 10th, was the same day 600 years before when Nebuchadnezzar had destroyed the first Temple.

Solomon Grayzel, in the book **A History of the Jews**, said:

"As soon as he saw the Temple in flames Titus dashed within. Like all pagans, he was anxious to find out whether the Jews were telling the truth in saying that theirs was a religion without images. Like Pompey more than a century before, Titus went to the Holy of Holies and pulled the curtain aside. Was he impressed or disappointed to find only a small, bare room? Whatever the effect upon him, his sacrilegious act so offended the Jews that they placed him forever alongside Nebuchadnezzar, Haman and Antiochus, in the gallery of their enemies . . . among the Jews he has been known as 'Titus the Wicked' " (**Solomon Grayzel, pp. 171-172**).

Grayzel also said that when the soldiers marched in, "The slaughter which then commenced is beyond description" (p.171).

"While the holy house was on fire, everything was plundered that came to hand, and ten thousand of those that were caught were slain; nor was there a commiseration of any age, or any reverence of gravity; but children and old men, and profane persons, and priests, were all slain in the same manner" (**Josephus, p. 451**).

"And now the Romans, upon the flight of the seditious into the city, and upon the burning of the holy house itself, and of all the buildings round about it, brought their ensigns to the temple, and set them over-against its eastern gate; and there did they offer sacrifices to them, and there did they make Titus imperator" (**Josephus, pp. 456-457**).

Titus then had his men build ramps to the upper city. They brought his machines of war, and they stormed that part of the city. They killed those who resisted, and those not killed were sold as slaves; but 40,000 of the regular people were saved and let go (**Josephus, pp. 463-465**).

The city was taken on September 8, A.D. 70, after the last siege had lasted about five months (April 14 to September 8, A.D. 70). When the city was completely taken, the Roman soldiers "slew those whom they overtook, without mercy, and set fire to the houses whither the Jews were fled, and burnt every soul in them, and laid waste a great many of the rest; and when they were come to the houses to plunder them, they found in them entire families of dead men, and the upper rooms full of dead corpses, that is of such as died by the famine; they then stood in a horror at this sight, and went out without touching anything" (**Josephus**, p. 467).

At the conclusion of the war, when so much killing had been done, the soldiers were weary of killing, Titus gave orders that only those in arms were to be killed, and the rest taken alive. But they slew the aged and the infirm, and then kept the youths. The tallest and most beautiful were reserved for the triumphal march of Titus, while the rest of the multitude over seventeen years of age he sent to Egyptian mines. He sent a great number to various provinces to be destroyed in their arenas by the sword and wild beasts. Those under seventeen were sold for slaves. While everyone's fate was being determined, 11,000 perished for lack of food (**Josephus**, pp. 468-469).

Josephus said, "Accordingly the multitude of those that therein perished exceeded all the destructions that either men or God ever brought upon the world" (**Josephus**, p. 470).

John Levi was condemned to perpetual imprisonment (**Josephus**, p. 471). Simon "was brought to Caesar in bonds, when he was come back to Cesarea which was on the seaside; who gave orders that he should be kept against that triumph which he was to celebrate at Rome upon this occasion" (**Josephus**, p. 477).

At Cesarea, in honor of his brother Domitian's birthday, Titus punished many of the captive Jews, making a total of those who died fighting the beasts and who were burned, to be over 2,500. The same thing was done at Berytus, in honor of his father's birthday (**Josephus**, p. 478).

And so ended the war against the Jews. And all the golden vessels and instruments that were taken out of the Temple, and the Law, and the purple veils of the holy place, were taken to Rome. The great nation of Israel and the entire religious system were now gone. They had suffered "great tribulation."

Vespasian was emperor by the time Jerusalem fell (Nero having committed suicide in A.D. 68. Other Caesars followed Nero — Galba, Otho, Vitellius — for insignificant periods of time). When Jerusalem fell, Vespasian was emperor, but his son Titus was the Roman general who finished things off in the destruction of Jerusalem and the

Temple. Later, Titus became Caesar.

Concerning the historian Josephus, upon whose testimony much of what we know about the Jewish/Roman war rests, and from whom Eusebius the church historian, and others, gained most of their information, **Dr. Thomas Newton** said "that these accounts are transmitted to us by a Jew, and by a Jew who was himself an eye-witness to most of the things which he relates. As a general in the wars he must have had an exact knowledge of all transactions, and a Jewish priest he would not relate them with any favour of partiality to the Christian cause. His history was approved by Vespasian and Titus (who ordered it to be published) and by King Agrippa and many others, both Jews and Romans, who were present in those wars. He had likewise many enemies, who would readily have convicted him of any falsification, if he had been guilty of any. He designed nothing less, and yet as if he had designed nothing more, his history of the Jewish wars may serve as a larger comment on our Saviour's prophecies of the destruction of Jerusalem" **(Newton, p. 433)**.

It was Jesus Christ who gave the city of Jerusalem over into the hands of the Roman armies, even though they were the ones who accomplished the task of bringing about the destruction of the place. It is like God said concerning Jacob, "Who gave Jacob for a spoil, and Israel to the robbers? did not the LORD, he against whom we have sinned? for they would not walk in his ways, neither were they obedient unto his law" **(Isaiah 42:24)**. And it is like when God delivered the king of Judah into the hands of Nebuchadnezzar: "And the Lord gave Jehoiakim king of Judah into his hand" **(Daniel 1:2)**. Though it was the Roman soldiers who destroyed Jerusalem, yet it was God who brought this judgment upon the land. God used human instrumentalities in the Old Testament to accomplish His purposes, as we well know. So it was here.

Even Titus, the Roman general, acknowledged that God's hand was in this. When Titus was viewing the fortifications after the city was taken he could not help ascribing his success to God. He said, "We have certainly had God for our assistant in this war, and it was no other than God who ejected the Jews out of these fortifications; for what could the hands of men, or any machines, do towards overthrowing these towers!" **(Josephus, p. 468)**.

F. W. Farrar's Account

I must give you here also a summary of the siege and destruction of Jerusalem as written by **F. W. Farrar** in **The Early Days of Christianity** (1882). Farrar was "Late Fellow of Trinity College, Cambridge; Canon of Westminster; and Chaplain in Ordinary to the Queen." He said:

"In April, A.D. 70, Titus, with a force of 80,000 legionaires and auxiliaries, pitched his camp on Scopus, to the north of the city. Besides the 2,400 trained Jewish warriors who defended the walls, the city was thronged with an incredible number of Passover pilgrims, and of fugitives from other parts of Judaea. Feats of heroic valour were performed on both sides, and the skill of the besiegers was often checked by the almost insane fury of the besieged. Fanatically relying on the visible manifestation of Jehovah, while they were infamously violating all His laws, the Zealots rejected with insult every offer of terms. At last Titus drew a line of circumvallation round the doomed city, and began to crucify all the deserters who fled to him. The incidents of the famine which then fell on the besieged are among the most horrible in human literature. The corpses bred a pestilence. Whole houses were filled with unburied families of the dead. Mothers slew and devoured their own children. Hunger, rage, despair, and madness seized the city. It became a cage of furious madmen, a city of howling wild beasts, and of cannibals — a hell! For the first time for five centuries, on July 17, A.D. 70, the daily sacrifices of the Temple ceased for want of priests to offer them. Disease and slaughter ruthlessly accomplished their work. At last, amid shrieks and flames, and suicide and massacre, the Temple was taken and reduced to ashes. The great altar of sacrifice was heaped with the slain. The courts of the Temple swam deep in blood. Six thousand miserable women and children sank with a wild cry of terror amid the blazing ruins of the cloisters. Romans adored the insignia of their legions on the place where the Holiest had stood. As soon as they became masters of the Upper City they only ceased to slay when they were too weary to slay any longer. According to Josephus, it had been the earnest desire of Titus to preserve the Temple, but his commands were disobeyed by his soldiers in the fury of the struggle. According to Sulpitius Severus, on the other hand, who is probably quoting the very words of Tacitus, Titus formed the deliberate purpose to destroy Christianity and Judaism in one blow, believing that if the Jewish root were torn up the Christian branch would soon perish. The tallest and most beautiful youths were reserved for the conqueror's triumph. Of those above seventeen years of age multitudes were doomed to work in chains in the Egyptian mines. Others were sent as presents to various towns to be slain by wild beasts or gladiators, or by each other's swords in the provincial amphitheatres. The young of both sexes were sold as slaves. Even during the days on which these arrangements were being made, 11,000 perished for want of food; some because their guards would not give it to them, others because they would not accept it. Josephus reckons the number of captives taken during the war at 97,000 and the number of those who perished during the siege at 1,100,000. The numbers who perished in the whole war are reckoned at the awful total of 1,337,490, and the number of prisoners at 101,700; but even these estimates do not include all the items of many skirmishes and battles, nor do they take into account the multitudes who, throughout the whole country, perished of misery, famine and disease. It may well be said that the nation seemed to have given itself 'a rendezvous of extermination.' Two thousand putrefying bodies were found even in the subterranean vaults of the city. During the siege all the trees of the environs had been cut down, and hence the whole appearance of the place, with its charred and bloodstained ruins, was so completely altered, that one who was suddenly brought to it would not (we are told) have recognized where he was. And yet the site had been so apparently impregnable, with its massive and unequalled fortifications, that Titus freely declared that he saw in his victory the hand of God" (**F.W. Farrar**, pp. 487-489).

This was THE GREAT TRIBULATION which Jesus prophesied would come upon the Jews, remarkably fulfilled exactly as He had predicted. The "great tribulation" is not the same future demonstration of God's wrath on an unsaved world, as claimed by so many dispensationalists, but it was an actual occurrence that came about exactly as Jesus said it would, upon the land of Israel. Who can imagine such horrors of that awful time!

I have used a number of old historical books from my own personal library to gather the facts about the actual Jewish/Roman war and the destruction of Jerusalem and the Temple. Some of them are: **Josephus**, the Jewish historian; **Eusebius**, the early church historian; **Sulpitius Severus** in **The Nicene and Post-Nicene Fathers**; **Philip Schaff** in the **History of the Christian Church**; **Tacitus** in **The Annals of Imperial Rome**; **Renan's Antichrist**; **F.W. Farrar** in **The Early Days of Christianity**, etc.

But many years ago it was my favorite commentary, **Albert Barnes' Notes on the Old and New Testaments**, which helped me to understand that the events of Matthew 24 concerning "the great tribulation" were events of the past, and not prophecies for our own future. If you have this commentary available, you will see that his comments are a condensation of these events under consideration, and I simply mention this rather than quoting him as well.

The Vast Extent of This Devastation

We need to realize the vast scope of this great tribulation upon the people of Israel. It was not just Jerusalem, but all over Palestine that the whole country felt this awful catastrophe which happened to them.

Relying on **Josephus** for his information, and his speaking of "the time when the beginning of the war blazed up in the twelfth year of Nero's reign," **Eusebius** said "that throughout Palestine the revolt of the Jews was followed by hopeless confusion, and that on every side the members of the nation were mercilessly destroyed, as if they were enemies, by the inhabitants of the various cities:

"The cities could be seen full of unburied corpses, the dead bodies of the aged flung down alongside those of infants, women without a rag to conceal their nakedness, and the whole province full of indescribable horrors. Even worse than the atrocities continually committed were the threats of terror to come" **(Eusebius, The History of the Church, pp. 105-106).**

Not only did destruction fall on the cities of Judaea, but even in other countries the Jews found themselves under terrible tribulation. **Josephus** said, "There was not any Syrian city which did not slay their Jewish inhabitants, and were more bitter enemies to us than were the Romans themselves."

Jesus had said, "... for there shall be great distress in the land, and wrath upon this people" (Luke 21:23). This "great distress" and "wrath" was the "great tribulation" of **Matthew 24:21.** It involved "great distress in **THE LAND,** and wrath upon this people" **(Luke 21:23).**

Adam Clarke's Commentary tells us of the geographical extent of this "distress in the land," and the extent of the captivity of thousands of the Jews. These comments sum up the extent of the whole war.

"To St. Matthew's account, St. Luke adds, chap. xxi. 24, **They shall fall by the edge of the sword, and shall be led away captive into all nations; and Jerusalem shall be trodden down by the Gentiles, till the times of the Gentiles be fulfilled.** The number of those who fell by the sword was very great. ELEVEN HUNDRED THOUSAND perished during the siege. Many were slain at other places, and other times. By the commandment of **Florus,** the first author of the war, there were slain at Jerusalem 3,600, JOS. WAR, b. ii, c. 14. By the inhabitants of **Caesarea,** above 20,000. At **Scythopolis,** above 13,000. At **Ascalon,** 2,500. At **Ptolemais,** 2,000. At **Alexandria,** 50,000. At **Joppa,** when taken by **Cestius Gallus,** 8,400. In a mountain called **Asamon,** 10,000. In an **ambuscade** near the **same place,** 8,000. At **Japha,** 15,000. Of the **Samaritans,** on Mount **Gerizim,** 11,600. At **Jotapa,** 40,000. At **Joppa,** when taken by **Vespasian,** 4,200. At **Tarechea,** 6,500. And **after** the **city** was **taken,** 1,200. At **Gamala,** 4,000, besides 5,000 who threw themselves down a **precipice.** Of those who fled with **John** of **Gischala,** 6,000. Of the **Gadarenes,** 15,000 slain, besides **countless** multitudes **drowned.** In the village of **Idumea,** above 10,000 slain. At **Gerasa**, 1,000. At **Machaerus**, 1,700. In the wood of **Jardes**, 3,000. In the castle of **Masada**, 960. In **Cyrene**, by **Catullus** the governor, 3,000. Besides those many of every **age, sex,** and **condition**, were slain in the war, who are not reckoned; but, of those who are reckoned, the number amounts to upwards of 1,357,000, which would have appeared incredible, if their own historian had not so particularly enumerated them. See Josephus, WAR, book ii. c. 18, 20; book iii. c. 2,7,8,9; book iv. c. 1,2,7,8,9; book vii. c. 6,9,11; and Bp. Newton, vol.ii. p. 288-290.

"Many were also **lead away captives into all nations**. There were taken at **Jotapa**, 1,200. At **Tarichea**, 6,000 chosen young men, who were sent to Nero; others sold to the number of 39,400, besides those who were **given** to Agrippa. Of the **Gadarenes** were **taken** 2,200. In **Idumea** above 1,000. Many besides these were taken in **Jerusalem**; so that, as Josephus says, the number of the **captives** taken in the whole war amounted to 97,000. Josephus says, the number of captives taken in the whole war amounted to 97,000. Those above **seventeen** years of age were sent to the **works in Egypt**; but most were distributed through the Roman provinces, to be destroyed in their **theatres** by the **sword,** and by the **wild beasts;** and those under **seventeen** years of age were sold for **slaves.** Eleven thousand in one place perished for **want.** At **Caesarea**, Titus, like a thorough-paced infernal savage, murdered 2,500 Jews, in honour of his brother's birthday; and a greater number at **Berytus** in honor of his father's. See Josephus, WAR, b. vii. c. 3. 3. 1. Some he caused to kill each other; some were thrown to the wild beasts; and others burnt alive. And all this was done by a man who was styled, **The darling of mankind!** Thus were the Jews miserably tormented, and distributed over the Roman provinces; and continued to be distressed and dispersed over all the nations of the world to this present day. Jerusalem also was, according to the prediction of our Lord, to be **trodden down by the Gentiles**" (**Adam Clarke**, pp. 232-233).

"It is doubtful if anything before or since has equaled it for ruthless slaughter and merciless destruction. From the locality of these churches in Asia Minor to the borders of Egypt the land was a slaughterhouse. City after city was wrecked, sacked, and burned; till it was recorded that cities were left without an inhabitant" (**David Clark**, p.55)

Jesus said, "Daughters of Jerusalem, weep not for me, but weep for yourselves, and for your children" (**Luke 23:28**). He had known what was ahead.

But apart from this, we need to think in terms of the **nature** of that tribulation, and not just the quantity. That is, we need to realize the importance of what happened from the **nature** of it, and not just with reference to the number of people killed. From the Jewish standpoint, when their city and Temple were destroyed, and their entire land devastated, along with their religious sacrifices and ritualism, for them **there could never be anything so tragic as that.** Even their genealogies were lost, so that today Jewish people cannot trace their ancestries back.

And it occurs to me, that for anyone to glibly say that this tribulation in A.D. 67-70 could not be as great as some supposed future tribulation on the Jews, such a person evidently has not read in detail the full account of those gruesome things that went on in Jerusalem during the tribulation of those days. It is one thing to be killed; but it is another thing to suffer as horribly as those people did. When one takes into account all the various kinds of suffering and torture that went on, one can easily believe that Jesus meant exactly what He said when He said there never had been a time like that, and never would be again.

But even so, we can grant that apart from the passage used by Jesus describing the severity of this time of tribulation on Israel, a number of other Scriptures in other circumstances were used in the Bible that are the same kind of language, indicating the possibility that the language is of a symbolic nature, that is, a hyperbole. A hyperbole is a form of exaggerated expression especially understood and used by the Hebrew people, as indicating the direst or the greatness or the vastness of something. It was this kind of expression used by Jesus in **Matthew 24:2** when He said, "There shall not be left here one stone upon another, that shall not be thrown down." We know that Titus actually did leave some of the walls standing. But the language described the utter devastation of the place.

As we think of those words, "such as was not since the beginning of the world to this time, no, nor ever shall be" **(Matthew 24:21)**, let us review some other places in the Bible where this kind of language is used, to help us understand the hyperbolical nature of these expressions:

Exodus 10:14: ". . . before them there were no such locusts as they, neither after them shall be such."

Exodus 11:6: "And there shall be a great cry throughout all the land of Egypt, such as there was none like it, nor shall be like it any more."

I Kings 3:12 (of Solomon): ". . . so that there was none like thee before thee, neither after thee shall any arise like unto thee." But later it was said, "A greater than Solomon is here" **(Matthew 12:42)**.

II Kings 18:5 (of Hezekiah): " . . . so that after him was none like him among all the kings of Judah, nor any that were before him."

II Kings 23:25 (of Josiah): "And like unto him was there no king before him . . . neither after him arose there any like him." (The same thing had already been said about Hezekiah.)

Ezekiel 5:9 (concerning Jerusalem): "And I will do in thee that which I have not done, and whereunto I will not do any more the like, because of all thine abominations." (But the same language was used again by Jesus concerning Jerusalem in His generation.)

Daniel 9:12 (concerning Jerusalem): " . . . for under the whole heaven hath not been done as hath been done upon Jerusalem."

Joel 2:2 (concerning Jerusalem): ". . . there hath not been ever the like, neither shall be any more after it, even to the years of many generations."

Even **Josephus** the Jewish historian himself said, in similar language concerning Israel's tribulation of A.D. 67-70, "Accordingly it appears to me, that the misfortunes of all men, from the beginning of the world, if they be compared to these of the Jews, are not so considerable as they were" **(Josephus,** vol. 1, p. 5).

So we can easily see that Jesus was using the same kind of language as used by the prophets of old in describing how great something was or was to be. It was not necessarily to be taken as being fulfilled in a precise, exact, and restricted manner exactly like prescribed by the expression. Some flexibility can be given to the statements. At the same time, there is nothing to say that this time of tribulation for Israel was not the worst for them that they would ever see again — literally!

Whether this 3½-year period of tribulation upon Israel and Jerusalem was LITERALLY and PRECISELY worse than ever had been or would be in the future, or if this statement was one of hyperbole, does not really matter so much when we realize that ACTUALLY and LITERALLY, no other event in the whole world ever did or ever could equal in importance what happened to the Jewish nation in A.D. 67-70. Their Temple, their nation, their cities, their worship, their rituals, their geneologies, their everything, and almost their race, were GONE, with no promise of ever being in existence again! Nothing like it had ever happened before, and never will again. To them, it was worse than ANYTHING that could ever happen to them.

The result of all the devastation in this great tribulation that occurred to those people in A.D. 67-70 was similar to what had been said many years before, in the time of Isaiah, "Thy holy cities are a wilderness, Zion is a wilderness, Jerusalem a desolation. Our holy and our beautiful house, where our fathers praised thee, is burned up with fire: and all our pleasant things are laid waste" **(Isaiah 64:10-11).**

And it was as God had said concerning them at another time, "The LORD shall bring a nation against thee from far, from the end of the earth, as swift as the eagle flieth; a nation whose tongue thou shalt not understand" **(Deuteronomy 28:49)**.

Strong language is uttered by the Lord as to His fury and His anger at His people when they become wicked and go astray:

"Therefore, behold, I, even I, will utterly forget you, and I will forsake you, and the city that I gave you and your fathers, and cast you out of my presence:

"And I will bring an everlasting reproach upon you, and a perpetual shame, which shall not be forgotten" **(Jeremiah 23:39-40)**.

And this tribulation upon the nation of Israel was a fulfillment of **Isaiah 66:15-16**:

"For, behold, the LORD will come with fire, and with his chariots like a whirlwind, to render his anger with fury, and his rebuke with flames of fire.

"For by fire and by his sword will the LORD plead with all flesh: and the slain of the LORD shall be many."

This Tribulation Not In Our Future

It was tribulation upon the Jewish people in "THOSE DAYS" **(vs. 22)** as foretold by Jesus Christ, all of which took place in the 3½ years from April A.D. 67 to September 26, A.D. 70, when Jerusalem went up in flames.

Some Bible teachers who do NOT hold to a pre-tribulation rapture, base their view on this passage **(vss. 21, 29-30)**, because of the teaching that AFTER the tribulation of those days would appear the sign of the Son of Man in Heaven. They say this proves a "post-tribulation" rapture. But as we have already discussed, this passage is not dealing with a future second coming of Christ thousands of years ahead at the end of our Christian age, but it deals with the coming of Christ in judgment on Jerusalem back in A.D. 70. So this passage helps neither the pre-tribulation nor the post-tribulation rapture teachers.

Some may say that while this passage does deal directly with the events of A.D. 70, there is also a "double fulfillment" which means that this will also happen in our future. But who says so? Who gives us the authority to say that there is to be another fulfillment beyond what Jesus said would take place back in His generation? These verses cannot be used to prove what will happen in our future at any future coming of Christ.

Someone says, "The book of Revelation tells us of these same things that will happen in our future." But who says they are to happen in our future? Why say they do not refer to the same historical fulfillment of the past? Especially since John in **Revelation 1:1** said that he was showing "his servants things which must shortly come to pass"? And then again in **vs. 3**, "for the time is at hand." The things recorded in the book of Revelation were things predicted to come to pass very soon (very soon to them, not to us).

Notice that when Jesus was telling the women of Jerusalem not to weep for Him, but to weep for themselves and their children, He said, "For, behold, the days are coming, in the which they shall say, Blessed are the barren, and the wombs that never bare, and the paps which never gave suck. Then shall they begin to say to the mountains, Fall on us; and to the hills, Cover us" **(Luke 23:28-30)**. He was prophesying something to happen in their generation. And this was the same kind of language later used by John the Revelator in describing those things which he said "must shortly come to pass." He said that people "hid themselves in the dens and in the rocks of the mountains; And said to the mountains and rocks, Fall on us, and hide us from the face of him that sitteth on the throne, and from the wrath of the Lamb: For the great day of his wrath is come; and who shall be able to stand?" **(Revelation 6:15-17)**.

Looking ahead to that day, Paul said, "for the wrath is come upon them to the uttermost" **(I Thessalonians 2:16)**.

Failure to understand the time factor involved in the "great tribulation" of **Matthew 24:21** has been the chief cause for modern-day dispensationalists' putting the Rapture ahead of the tribulation. If Christians are to be "delivered from the wrath to come," they feel, then the natural thinking is that the Rapture takes place first—that is, IF "the wrath" is the same as the "great tribulation." At least this is what a pastor in Germany once told me when I asked him what was the strongest passage he could use from the New Testament proving a pre-tribulation Rapture. He said, "And to wait for his Son from heaven, whom he raised from the dead, even Jesus, which delivered us from the wrath to come." **(I Thessalonians 1:10)**. This does seem logical, doesn't it? But if "the wrath" mentioned is something that **already** occurred, then it is not logical after all.

What "wrath" was predicted which was to come upon the land?

Jesus predicted, "But woe unto them that are with child, and to them that give suck, in those days! for there shall be great distress in the land, and WRATH upon this people" **(Luke 21:23)**. He was speaking, of course, of the coming tribulation upon the nation of Israel during His generation.

Right after Paul mentioned that Jesus had "delivered us from the wrath to come" **(I Thessalonians 1:10)**, he went on in the next chapter to say that "the WRATH is come upon them to the uttermost" (I Thessalonians 2:16). Here he was speaking, of course, of the wrath of God which was in just a few years to fall upon the Jewish people.

In a number of places in the book of Revelation, John spoke of the "wrath" of God which was to fall upon the land. Those were references to that time of "great tribulation" which came upon the land of Israel in those 3½ years leading up to the destruction of that holy place.

Christians were delivered from that wrath. They followed the instructions of Jesus and got out of Jerusalem and Judaea before the time of tribulation occurred.

Most dispensationalists believe that there will be a future seven years of tribulation period after the Rapture and before Jesus comes to the earth, a concept that was unheard of before the early 1800s. In fact, the idea of such a tribulation period consisting of seven years has only one source in the Bible, and that is the prophecy of Daniel's 70 weeks in **Daniel 9:23-24**, and that passage says **nothing** in the world about a Rapture, a future second coming of Christ, or even a tribulation period in our future. Everything predicted in Daniel **9:23-24** came to completion by the time of the destruction of Jerusalem in A.D. 70, as can plainly be seen by anyone reading the passage with an unprejudiced mind. There is just no way it can be made to apply to a situation many hundreds and even thousands of years away from that time, for that would do away with the very idea of God's prediction of how long it would take for those things to occur. The exact time was spelled out.

So far as we can discover, the teaching of a pre-tribulation Rapture with a stated period of time between two phases of a future second coming of Christ, was first published in **1788** by **Morgan Edwards**, a Baptist minister in Philadelphia, Pennsylvania. Edwards was born in Wales, and actually wrote the book while he attended the Bristol Academy in England (1742-1744), but he did not publish the book until after he had been pastor of the Baptist church in Philadelphia. The book was entitled, **Two Academical Exercises on Subjects Bearing the Following Titles; Millennium, and Last-Novelties.**

I discovered the book at the library of the Southern Baptist Theological Seminary in Louisville, Kentucky, in March of 1995. A pastor friend in Mississippi showed me a book on **The Life and Works of Morgan Edwards** which suggested that Edwards taught the pre-tribulation Rapture among other things. I made a special effort to locate this book which Edwards wrote.

I obtained photostat copies of this book which taught that when

Christ appears in the air, He would resurrect the dead Christians, transform the living ones, and take all of them to Paradise where they would be judged for 3½ years. During this 3½ years Antichrist would be on the earth. After the 3½ years, Christ would descend to the earth with the Christians and set up His millennial kingdom.

(Edwards also believed that the Millennium would begin in 1996, 3½ years after the Rapture! He also believed that the lake of fire and brimstone was on the moon! His book was a **"novelty"** and **"perhaps nonsense"** as he himself suggested to his tutor.)

Unfortunately, so many of my Southern Baptist friends (as well as the independent Baptists) still believe in this ridiculous unScriptural teaching of a pre-tribulation rapture.

George E. Ladd, a premillennialist, recognized the origin of the futuristic antichrist and tribulation period teaching among Protestants (though not the **pre-tribulation** rapture teaching) as being with Ribera, a Catholic Jesuit priest in 1590. He said:

"It will probably come as a shock to many modern futurists to be told that the first scholar in relatively modern times who returned to the patristic interpretation was a Spanish Jesuit named Ribera. In 1590, Ribera published a commentary which identified the Papacy with the Antichrist. Ribera applied all of Revelation but the earliest chapters to the end time rather than to the history of the Church. Antichrist would be a single person who would be received by the Jews and would rebuild Jerusalem, abolish Christianity, deny Christ, persecute the Church and rule the world for three and a half years. . . .

"This futuristic interpretation with its personal Antichrist and three and a half year period of tribulation did not take root in the Protestant Church until the early nineteenth century. The first Protestant to adopt it was S. R. Maitland" **(George E. Ladd,** pp. 37-38).

But the "great tribulation" of **Matthew 24:21** was definitely a thing of the past, as we have seen. It occurred as it did upon the Jewish people in those 3½ years from A.D. 67-70. Jesus said, "For **THEN** shall be great tribulation" (vs. 21), referring, of course, to that **immediate** time after the "abomination of desolation" which caused the Christians to flee from Judaea.

When I first published two little books, **The Coming of Christ in I and II Thessalonians** and **The Great Tribulation ?** (both now out of print), back in 1981 and 1982, **Dave MacPherson**, author of **The Incredible Hoax,** wrote, asking if I would now classify myself as a post-tribulation rapturist. I replied that while I did not believe in a pre-tribulation Rapture, neither was I a traditional "post-tribulation rapturist."

Also a few years back, I was invited by Dr. Ray Brubaker of the **Good News Behind the News** Broadcast in St. Petersburg, Florida, to be involved in a debate at their February Bible conference, to present the "post-tribulation Rapture" view as opposed to the "pre-tribulation Rapture" view. While feeling highly honored at being invited to such a debate, because of some outstanding men who were going to be there, I declined the invitation, and I remember saying to him that my view was not that of the classical post-tribulation rapture teachers.

The great tribulation and *parousia* of Christ of **Matthew 24:21, 29-30**, do not relate to OUR end-time, but both those events related to the events at the destruction of Jerusalem in A.D. 70 (at the end of THEIR AGE, NOT OURS). The great tribulation and the *parousia* of Matthew 24 have nothing to do with a future tribulation and second coming of Christ at the end of our church age. Years ago I first discovered that the "tribulation" of **Matthew 24:21** did not apply to our future, but precisely to the events that ended with the destruction of Jerusalem in A.D. 70. This was the "key" that started unlocking a lot of problems in my mind about the generally accepted view. When I came to also see that the *"parousia"* (coming) of Christ in Matthew 24 was LIKEWISE part of the same events happening back in A.D. 70 and therefore not a prophecy concerning a future second coming of Christ in our time or later, much more began to clear up in my mind relative to some of these things. If we ever quit learning, our **minds** have stagnated in that they refuse ever to budge on anything they have ever believed or taught on these matters, no matter how much evidence is produced to show that it is not always exactly what we have been "brainwashed" through the years to believe.

And this interpretation now being offered is nothing new. For example, read the book, **The Prophecy of Matthew 24**, by **Thomas Newton** (he was even a pre-millennialist), first published as part of a larger book in 1754—long before such teachings as a pre-tribulation Rapture were ever taught by anyone. Dr. Newton taught that the Abomination of Desolation, the Great Tribulation, the Destruction of Jerusalem, the Coming (**Parousia**) of Christ in judgment on Israel, were all fulfilled in A.D. 67-70.

There are those who believe in a double-fulfillment of many prophecies in the Bible. For example, with reference to this particular verse, they would acknowledge that Jesus referred primarily to the events of A.S. 67-70. But, they say, these events will be duplicated again at some time in our future (the dispensationalists say it will be after the Rapture). Where they find proof for this is something else, but it fits in with their futuristic interpretation of these prophecies.

If the great tribulation which Jesus mentioned nearly 2,000 years ago is still in our future, why did Jesus say, "then shall be great tribulation, such as was not since the beginning of the world TO THIS TIME, no, nor ever shall be" (**Matthew 24:21**)? Why did He not rather say, "then shall be great tribulation, such as was not since the beginning of the world TO THAT TIME, nor ever shall be"? Could it be that it was because He anticipated the great tribulation to be in "THIS" time and not in "THAT" time of some future 2,000 years or so? Just a thought. Think it through! Language is very important.

As **Joseph R. Balyeat** also so clearly pointed out in his book, **Babylon, The Great City of Revelation:**

"Obviously, Jesus would not have said 'until now' if He really meant 'until then', 2,000 years hence. Additionally it would have made no sense for Him to say the Tribulation would never be equaled again in history if the Tribulation of which He spoke was to happen 2,000 years later, **at the end of history.** The plain meaning indicates a Great Tribulation in the middle of history, not a tribulation occurring unto centuries later in a fairy-tale 'generation of the fig tree' " (**Balyeat,** pp. 63-64).

As **William R. Kimball** summed it up:

"The landscape of prophetic interpretation has been cluttered with the verbal litter of dispensationalism in recent years. This dispensationalist school of prophetic interpretation refuses to accept the blatant reality that significant portions of Jesus' Olivet discourse were directly related to the destruction of Jerusalem in 70 A.D. I take issue with this common tendency and join the ranks of those who have pointed out that when Christ warned His disciples of the 'great tribulation' (**Matthew 24:21**), 'the days of vengeance' (**Luke 21:22**), and the 'days of affliction' (**Mark 13:19**) that were to come, He was referring to the approaching destruction of Jerusalem in A.D. 70, and not to a highly speculative, end-time tribulation preceding the second coming" (**William R. Kimball,** p. 13, **What the Bible Says About the Great Tribulation**).

"The 'great tribulation' of Matthew 24:21, however, does not refer to a final worldwide, violent persecution immediately prior to the second advent, but rather to God's judgment in Jerusalem in A.D. 70" (**John Jefferson Davis,** p. 114).

And **Dr. John Broadus,** one-time president of Southern Baptist Theological Seminary, said: "We cannot say that v. 15-22 does not at all refer to the times just preceding our Lord's **final** coming; but no such reference shows itself" (**John Broadus,** p. 488).

Dr. Richard L. Mayhue, assistant professor of Greek and New Testament at Grace Theological Seminary, Winona Lake, Indiana, in a 16-page book defending the pre-tribulation Rapture belief, said,

"Neither a pre-tribulation rapture nor a post-tribulation rapture has found full acceptance with Bible scholars" **(Richard L. Mayhue, p. 15).**

So perhaps the Bible scholars should investigate an alternative and consider the possibility that one does not need to accept either pre- or post-tribulation viewpoint, for THE NEW TESTAMENT DOES SPEAK OTHERWISE.

As previously pointed out, **Eusebius,** the early church historian, taught that these things happened back in the generation of the disciples (**Eusebius, The Nicene and Post-Nicene Fathers**, vol. 1, pp. 138, 141). They were not things to happen in **our** future either before or after the Rapture.

All Prophecy Relative to Israel Fulfilled by 70 A.D.

In the events of the great tribulation which Jesus Christ predicted for the nation of Israel, would be the summed up fulfillment of all prophecies remaining to be fulfilled concerning the Jewish people. In **Luke 21:22** Jesus said, "For these be the days of vengeance, that all things which are written may be fulfilled." Notice that He said "ALL" — not "some." Everything concerning the Jewish people which had been prophesied and not yet been fulfilled, would be fulfilled in those closing days of the history of their nation.

Out of twenty-nine different translations of the New Testament in my library, I am taking just several of the versions for this one verse from **Luke 21:22**, to indicate exactly what this verse does mean, as viewed by more than just one translator or group of translators:

Greek Interlinear: "for days of avenging these are, that may be accomplished all things that have been written."

Today's English Version: "For these are 'The Days of Punishment,' to make come true all that the Scriptures say."

Jerusalem Bible: "For this is the time of vengeance when all that scripture says must be fulfilled."

Phillips Modern English: "For these are the days of vengeance, when all that the scriptures have said will come true."

New English Bible: "because this is the time of retribution, when all that stands written is to be fulfilled."

Revised Standard Version: "for these are days of vengeance, to fulfill all that is written."

And I could go on and on, but you can see the plain evident meaning of this verse. Those things of which Jesus spoke which were to happen during this time of great tribulation upon the Jewish people, would fulfill all that the Scriptures had ever foretold would happen to them.

And if this be true, how is it that some still say that things happening in the land of Israel today is a fulfillment of Bible prophecy? Nowhere in the New Testament do we find a single iota of a promise given concerning any future regathering, conversion, or anything else concerning the Jewish people. (There is a big "if" in Romans 11 concerning unbelieving Israel, but it is an "if" and not a promise nor prediction.)

In **Luke 21:22**, right after Jesus told His disciples to flee Jerusalem and Judaea, He stated, "For these be the days of vegeance, that all things which are written may be fulfilled." Here Jesus was saying that all these things must happen at Jerusalem so that ALL things written might be fulfilled. He did not mean, necessarily, that NOTHING else was predicted to happen, and that this event concluded ALL prophecy. It did conclude all prophecy which had been written concerning the final end of Jerusalem and the Jewish nation in A.D. 70 according to **Daniel 9:24-27**. And we know of no other prophecy concerning the future of Israel yet to be fulfilled. If you think otherwise, please read my book, **Israel in Bible Prophecy**.

This statement of Jesus was like one He made in **Luke 18:31**, "Behold, we go up to Jerusalem, and all things that are written by the prophets concerning the Son of man shall be accomplished" (see also **Luke 24:44** and **Acts 3:18**). This did not mean that what happened in A.D. 33 at Calvary was ALL that was predicted concerning the Son of man, for He Himself had predicted His *parousia* to be at a later date. But it simply means that all that transpired at Calvary **had** to happen in order that **everything** predicted concerning the Son of man could come to pass.

So when Jesus said in **Luke 21:22** that the events of A.D. 67-70 would happen that "ALL things which are written may be fulfilled," He was not saying that this would conclude ALL PROPHETIC EVENTS to be fulfilled, as some say. He was simply saying that those things had to happen so that all prophecy could be fulfilled.

But the statement that "Jerusalem shall be trodden down of the Gentiles, until the times of the Gentiles be fulfilled" **(Luke 21:24)** does not give any promise of restoration to Israel even after the times of the Gentiles be fulfilled. Some think that the creation of Israel as a nation in 1948 was a fulfillment of Bible prophecy and that the times of the Gentiles ended then. But the vast majority of so-called Jews are not of Jewish ancestry at all, and the remainder are mixed in their blood with other races, as the **Encyclopedia Brittanica** says, "There is no Jewish race" (vol. 12, p. 1054, 1973 ed.).

Jerusalem had been under the captivity and dominion of foreign powers (Gentiles) ever since the time of Nebuchadnezzar, and these times of the Gentiles are still in effect. Jesus said, "And they shall fall by the edge of the sword, and shall be led away captive into all nations: and Jerusalem shall be trodden down of the Gentiles, until the times of the Gentiles be fulfilled." (**Luke 21:24**). A 1948 declaration concerning Israel as a nation does nothing to change the races of those who make up Jerusalem today. (Once again, I would urge you to read my book, **Israel in Bible Prophecy**.) Jerusalem today is a **mixture** of races, and neither does the observance of Judaism alone create a Jewish race in Israel today.

"Modern Israel is an ordinary secular state, just one more of the 'nations' which will trample Jerusalem under foot" (**Adrio Konig**, p. 171).

One of the officials of Israel recently expressed concern about the future status of the people with so many Jews coming in from Russia after Russia opened the doors for them to leave. 200,000 have arrived so far, 3,000 of them in one month. 35% of them are not Jews at all, but Gentiles who married among the Jews, plus no telling how many are of Gentile Khazar background.

Incidentally, the expression, "the times of the Gentiles" of **Luke 21:24**, does not have the same meaning as, "the fulness of the Gentiles" found in **Romans 11:25**, though some Bible expositors have tried to make these two the same. One expression speaks about the "TIMES" of the Gentiles, and the other talks about the "FULNESS" of the Gentiles. One is talking about the duration of time during which Gentiles have control of Jerusalem; the other is talking about the performance and completion of what God is doing for the Gentiles spiritually. These are two separate things altogether.

But 3½ years of this "times of the Gentiles" occurred in A.D. 67-70, and during this time the city of Jerusalem was "trodden down of the Gentiles" in a special way, fulfilling prophecy from both the Old and New Testament. In **Revelation 11:2** it was predicted, "it is given unto the Gentiles: and the holy city shall they tread under foot forty and two months."

The amount of time involved in the siege and destruction of Jerusalem was 3½ years, and as **Moses Stuart** said, "in Rev.11:2, the time during which the Romans are to tread down the holy city, (in this case the capital is, as usual in the Jewish Scripture, the representation of the country), is said to be forty-two months = three and a half years. The active invasion of Judea continued almost exactly this length of time, being at the most only a few days more; so few that they need not, and would not, enter into a symbolic computation of time" (**Stuart**, p. 279).

Meyers Commentary says, "... **till the times of the Gentiles shall be fulfilled**, i.e., till the time that the periods which are appointed to the Gentile nations for the completion of divine judgments (not the **period of grace** for the Gentiles...) **shall have run out.** Comp. Rev. xi. 2. Such times of the Gentiles are ended in the case in question by the **Parousia** (vv. 25 f., 27), which is to occur during the lifetime of the hearers (ver. 28) ... hence those ... are in no way to be regarded as of longer duration" (**Meyer**, pp. 530-531).

"We know that the great tribulation of A.D. 70 brought the Jewish state to its complete and final end" (**William E. Cox**, p. 103).

"The terrible devastation which was unleashed on the city of Jerusalem could have been avoided if the nation Israel had turned to the Lord and accepted the sacrifice of His Son. Instead, they refused to repent of murdering the prophets who were sent to them, and of their idolatries and their violations of the covenant. God had to utterly destroy the temple, the genealogical records which qualified descendants of Aaron to serve as priests, and the city of Jerusalem; He had to scatter the people and make it impossible for them to continue their futile and fruitless sacrifices, in order to demonstrate His repudiation of Judaism as a religious system. Jesus said that no man comes to the Father except through Him (**John 14:6**). God verified Jesus' statement when He forcibly put an end to Israel's attempt to relate to the Father apart from the Son" (**J. E. Leonard**, p. 70).

★★★★★★★★★★★★★★

The Great Tribulation of Christians Under Nero

When Jesus spoke of "great tribulation" in **Matthew 24:21**, He was referring to the awful horrors and tragic events of those days on the **Jewish** people back in A.D. 67-70, in Jerusalem and Judaea. When John the Revelator spoke of "the great tribulation" in **Revelation 7:14** he was referring primarily to the awful persecutions being brought upon the **Christian** people of his day, mainly at the instigation of the Roman Emperor Nero but including the tribulation and persecutions they were having under the Jewish leaders. The tribulation under Nero lasted approximately 3½ years, from A.D. 64 until A.D. 68 when Nero committed suicide. This period of time is mentioned several times in the book of Revelation. John called himself their "brother and companion in tribulation" (**Revelation 1:9**), for it was during those approximate days which we have been discussing that those early Christians themselves had been undergoing tremendous tribulation and persecution by Nero the Emperor of Rome. Nero began to reign October 13, 54 A.D. "It was not till A.D. 64, when Nero had been nearly ten years on the throne, that the slow light of History fully revealed to the Church of Christ what this more than monster was" (**Farrar**, p. 13).

Eusebius Pamphilus, early church historian, said:
"When Nero's power was now firmly established he gave himself up to unholy practices and took up arms against the God of the universe. To describe the monster of depravity that he became lies outside the scope of the present work. Many writers have recorded the facts about him in minute detail, enabling anyone who wishes to get a complete picture of his perverse and extraordinary madness, which led him the senseless destruction of innumerable lives, and drove him in the end to such a lust for blood that he did not spare even his nearest and dearest but employed a variety of methods to do away with mother, brothers, and wife alike, to say nothing of countless other members of his family, as if they were personal and public enemies. All this left one crime still to be added to his account—he was the first of the emperors to be declared the enemy of the worship of the almighty God" (**Eusebius, The History of the Church**, p. 104).

About the time that Luke stopped writing the book of Acts, a conflagration of fire broke out in Rome (on July 19, A.D. 64, in the 10th year of Nero's reign). For nine days the fire raged, destroying much of the entire city of Rome. **Edward Gibbon** (1737-1794), in **The Decline and Fall of the Roman Empire**, described the devastating effects of this fire. He said:

"In the tenth year of the reign of Nero the capital of the empire was afflicted by a fire which raged beyond the memory or example of former years. The monuments of Grecian art and of Roman virtue, the trophies of the Punic and Gallic wars, the most holy temples, and the most splendid palaces were involved in one common destruction" (**Gibbon**, p. 456).

F. W. Farrar, in his book, **The Early Days of Christianity**, tells us about how this spectacular event led to the great tribulation inflicted on the Christians in Rome by Nero as a result of that fire. Up until then there had been no persecution of the Christians at Rome, though, "they were sufficiently numerous to be formidable" (**Farrar**, p. 35). There was some question as to how the fire started, but some historians were unanimous in their writings that Nero himself started the fire. After such a magnitude of destruction, and when fingers of guilt began to point to him, Nero put the blame on the Christians.

It is not difficult to understand this Beastly nature when one knows the history of this man and some of the things of which he was capable. He was only seventeen years old when his mother Agrippina murdered her husband Claudius Caesar so that her darling son could become emperor (October 13, A.D. 54). Later on, Nero murdered his own mother; and as though that were not enough, murdered his brother Britannicus to make sure the throne would remain his. He kicked his wife Poppaea, whom he had taken from his friend Otho, to death. This murderous beastly nature kept growing inside of him to the end. **Farrar** said:

"The depths into which he sank are too abysmal for utterance. Even Pagan historians could not without a blush hold up a torch to those crypts of shame . . . The seeds of innumerable vices were latent in the soil of his disposition, and the hot-bed of absolutism forced them into rank growth" (**F.W. Farrar, p. 28).**

One needs to read this **entire** page from Farrar's account drawn from various historical sources to see something of the utter and absolute depravity of this pagan Beast whom the early Christians came to know as Antichrist. To him, the Christians became playthings in his murderous hands to satisfy his insatiable desire for excitement and blood. "Tertullian says that 'Nero was the first who raged with the sword of Caesar against this sect, which was then specially rising at Rome' (Apol. 5)" **(Farrar, p. 38 footnote).**

Tacitus, the Roman historian (A.D. 55-117), in his last and greatest work, **The Annals of Imperial Rome,** wrote:

"But neither human resources, nor imperial munificence, nor the appeasement of the gods, eliminated sinister suspicions that the fire had been instigated. To suppress this rumour, Nero fabricated scapegoats — and punished with every refinement the notoriously depraved Christians (as they were popularly called). Their originator, Christ, had been executed in Tiberius' reign by the governor of Judaea, Pontius Pilatus. But in spite of this temporary setback the deadly superstition had broken out afresh, not only in Judaea (where the mischief had started) but even in Rome. All degraded and shameful practices collect and flourish in the capital.

"First, Nero had self-acknowledged Christians arrested. Then, on their information, large numbers of others were condemned—not so much for incendiarism as for their anti-social tendencies. Their deaths were made farcical. Dressed in wild animals' skins, they were torn to pieces by dogs, or crucified, or made into torches to be ignited after dark as substitutes for daylight. Nero provided his Gardens for the spectacle, and exhibited displays in the Circus, at which he mingled with the crowd—or stood in a chariot, dressed as a charioteer. Despite their guilt as Christians, and the ruthless punishment it deserved, the victims were pitied. For it was felt that they were being sacrificed to one man's brutality rather than to the national interest **(Tacitus,** pp. 365-366).

Philip Schaff said of Tacitus' account of these atrocities, "This is the account of the greatest heathen historian, the fullest we have—as the best description of the destruction of Jerusalem is from the pen of the learned Jewish historian" **(Philip Schaff, vol. 1, p. 382).**

F.W. Farrar, thinking of this account by Tacitus, said: "Imagine that awful scene, once witnessed by the silent obelisk in the square before St. Peter's at Rome! Imagine it, that we may realize how vast is the change which Christianity has wrought in the feelings of mankind! There, where the vast dome now rises, were once the gardens of Nero. They were thronged with gay crowds, among the Emperor in his frivolous degradation—and on every side were men dying slowly on their cross of shame. Along the paths of those gardens on the autumn nights were ghastly torches, blackening the ground beneath them with streams of sulphurous pitch, and each of those living torches was a martyr in his shirt of fire. And in the amphitheater nearby, in sight of twenty thousand spectators famished dogs were tearing to pieces some of the best and purest men and women, hideously disguised in the skins of bears and wolves. Thus did Nero baptize in the blood of martyrs the city which was to be for ages the capital of the world!" **(Farrar, p. 39).**

Farrar went on to say:

"No wonder that Nero became to Christian imagination the very incarnation of evil; the Antichrist; the Wild Beast from the abyss; the delegate of the great red Dragon, with a diadem and a name of blasphemy upon his brow . . . . Even when the infamies of a Petronius had been superseded by the murderous orgies of Gigellinus, Nero was still every where welcome with shouts as a god on earth, and saluted on coins as Apollo, as Hercules, as 'THE SAVIOUR OF THE WORLD' . . . . And yet, though all bad men — who were the majority — admired and even loved him, he died the death of a dog . . . . For retribution did not linger, and the vengeance fell at once on the guilty emperor and the guilty city" **(Farrar, p. 41).**

And even as there would be many signs and wonders seen at Jerusalem before that city was completely destroyed, so also at Rome before Nero died there were many such things that happened. Drawing mostly from Tacitus the historian, **Farrar** said:

"The air was full of prodigies. There were terrible storms, the plague wrought fearful ravages. Rumours spread from lip to lip. Men spoke of monstrous births; of deaths by lightning under strange circumstances; of a brazen statue of Nero melted by the flash; of places struck by the brand of heaven in fourteen regions of the city; of sudden darkenings of the sun. A hurricane devastated Campania; comets blazed in the heavens; earthquakes shook the ground. On all sides were the traces of uneasiness and superstitious terror. To all these portents, which were accepted as true by Christians as well as by Pagans, the Christians would give a specially terrible significance. They strengthened their conviction that the coming of the Lord drew nigh. They convinced the better sort of Pagans that the hour of their deliverance from a tyranny so monstrous and so disgraceful was near at hand" (**Farrar**, p. 42).

I shall not write in detail of the death of that Beast Nero. But when Nero heard in June A.D. 68 that Gaul and Germany and Spain were rebelling agains his government, he underwent an emotional siege; and then when he learned that the Senate was going to punish him by his being "stripped naked and scourged to death with rods, with his head thrust into a fork," he took a dagger and had one of his slaves help him to plunge it into his throat and thereby died a horrible suicide death. (He died on June 9, A.D. 68, at the age of 31.) "So died the last of the Caesars!" (**Farrar**, pp. 42-44). Such was the fate of this one who had brought 3½ years of tribulation upon the Christian people. And the Jewish rulers in Jerusalem would soon be next to go!

It has been thought by many that Domitian, who later followed Nero as emperor, brought much greater persecution upon the Christians than did Nero. And from this thought comes much of the interpretation of the book of Revelation. (Added to this, of course, has been the belief that the book of Revelation was written during the reign of Domitian, though scholars lately have questioned that late date). Though contrary to traditional thinking as it might seem, perhaps it would be well to investigate the historical sources and determine if Domitian ever was such a persecutor of Christians as he has been thought to be. What persecutions he was guilty of were mainly from political motivations, including those of his own relatives.

Edward Gibbon in his **The Decline and Fall of the Roman Empire** gives us his estimate of the extent of the persecution of Christians under Domitian. Domitian banished to exile several of his relatives and others whom he thought might aspire to his throne. Gibbon said:

"Domitilla was banished to a desolate island on the Coast of Campania; and sentences either of death or of confiscation were pronounced against a great number of persons who were involved in the same accusation. The guilt imputed to their charge was that of **Atheism and Jewish manners**; a singular association of ideas, which cannot with any propriety be applied except to the Christians, as they were obscurely and imperfectly viewed by the magistrates and by the writers of that period. On the strength of so probable an interpretation, and too eagerly admitting the suspicions of a tyrant as an evidence of their honourable crime, the church has placed both Clemens and Domitilla among its first martyrs, and has branded the cruelty of Domitian with the name of the second persecution. But this persecution (if it deserves that epithet) was of no long duration. A few months after the death of Clemens and the banishment of Domitilla, Stephen, a freedman belonging to the latter, who had enjoyed the favour, but who had not surely embraced the faith of his mistress, assassinated the emperor in his palace. The memory of Domitian was condemned by the senate; his acts were rescinded; his exiles recalled; and under the Gentile administration of Nerva, while the innocent were restored to their rank and fortunes, even the most guilty obtained pardon or escaped punishment" **(Gibbon, p. 462-463).**

If we are to believe this account, it is difficult to imagine that any persecution of Christians by Domitian was to any great degree.

Eusebius the early church historian tells us that when some descendents of Jude (the brother of Jesus) had accusation brought against them, they were brought before Domitian. Actually, this was "on the ground that they were of the lineage of David and were related to Christ himself" and "Domitian feared the coming of the Christ as Herod also had feared it." But when Domitian interrogated them, he learned that they were just poor Christians who worked hard, and that their view of Christ and His kingdom was that of a spiritual one and not an earthly one, and that it "would appear at the end of the world, when he should come in glory to judge the quick and the dead."

Then **Eusebius** went on to say: "Upon hearing this, Domitian did not pass judgment against them, but, despising them as of no account, he let them go, and by a decree put a stop to the persecution of the Church."

Then in the next paragraph **Eusebius** continued:

"Tertullian also has mentioned Domitian in the following words: 'Domitian also, who possessed a share of Nero's cruelty, attempted once to do the same thing that the latter did. But because he had, I suppose, some intelligence, he very soon ceased, and even recalled those whom he had banished' " **(Eusebius, The Nicene and Post-Nicene Fathers,** Second Series, vol. 1, pp. 148-149).

Even from this brief account, it would seem that Domitian's treatment of Christians had to be mild and not pronounced such as was Nero's.

These facts might have strong implications for those who have taught that the book of Revelation was written during the reign of Domitian, who was considered to be the "Beast" of Revelation and who brought great tribulation upon the Christians. He was nothing to compare with Nero!

★★★★★★★★★★★★★

"And except those days should be shortened, there should no flesh be saved: but for the elect's sake those days shall be shortened" (Matthew 24:22).

The days it would have taken for the complete destruction of the city were shortened, first because of the Roman general Titus wanting to get the siege over with as soon as possible; and secondly, because of the internal strife and warring among the factions of the Jews themselves, by their killing one another, by their burning their provisions and the ensuing famine as a result, and by their disregarding their fortifications so they were easily taken. Jesus said that if those days were not shortened, absolutely no one could have survived, so terrible was the situation. The opinion of Titus was that God had shortened the days.

The word "saved" with its different meanings must always be explained in line with the context. Here it seems to be talking about physical safety (He said "flesh"), and how if the war had been prolonged even the elect would not have been saved (physically, that is; not spiritually). It was for the elect's sake (whether **yet** spiritually converted or not) that the days were shortened.

Even Sodom and Gomorrah would have been spared if there had been just ten righteous people there (**Genesis 18:32**).

In speaking of "no flesh" being saved, Jesus was not here referring to the total world. He was speaking about "no flesh" of the Jewish nation, upon whom those dire calamities would be coming. This verse does not pertain to a dispensational futuristic time, but to those events of the judgment upon Israel. The "those days" of verse 22 are the same as "those days" of the "great tribulation" of that same verse which occurred "then" (**vs. 21**) "when" the abomination of desolation of verse 15 was seen.

The word "flesh" as used here would have the same meaning as the word "flesh" as found in **Isaiah 66:15-16** where it said, "For, behold, the LORD will come with fire, and with his chariots like a whirlwind, to render his anger with fury, and his rebuke with flames of fire.

"For by fire and by his sword will the LORD plead with ALL FLESH: and the slain of the LORD shall be many."

Concerning this passage in Isaiah, **Edwin J. Young** says:

"**All flesh** is here not to be taken in a universal sense, as, for example, Smart does, but is defined by the following verse. It stands for those of the Jewish nation, the great majority, who have abandoned the Lord for the service of idols. The verse pictures the judgment to all upon the Jewish nation at the time of Christ, with all the actual tragic consequences of that judgment in the sufferings that befell the Jews until the destruction of the Temple in A.D. 70. It is this of which our Lord speaks in Matthew 24:22 (note His usage of the words . . . **all flesh**)" **(Edward J. Young**, p. 530).

"**Elect**" — "The word means **Christians** — the chosen of God. If this refers to the destruction of Jerusalem, it means, whatever he may choose to employ for that purpose; signs, wonders, human messengers, or the angels themselves — and gather Christians into a place of safety so that they shall not be destroyed with the Jews" (**Albert Barnes** on Matthew 24:22).

It is very possible that the shortening of days which Jesus mentioned could have been referring to the days during the siege of Cestius Gallus, for it was when his siege was shortened and he withdrew that the Christians were able to escape.

★★★★★★★★★★★★★★

"**Then if any man shall say unto you, Lo, here is Christ, or there; believe it not.**

"**For there shall arise false Christs, and false prophets, and shall shew great signs and wonders; insomuch that, if it were possible, they shall deceive the very elect (Matthew 24:23-34).**

Jesus is talking about false Messiahs who would appear on the scene during the time when Jerusalem was being besieged by the armies. And many false Messiahs did appear on the scene about that time, promising deliverance to the people so that they would not give in to the pressures of Rome. But for these men to actually appear as Messiahs, it was necessary they demonstrate their authority by different signs and wonders. This they did, in various ways, in order to deceive the people.

Several of these men attempted to lead the people out into the desert where they proposed to show such signs that would prove that God would deliver them. But the Roman soldiers came, nevertheless, and the siege began.

Then later, others proposed to lead the people to certain secluded areas so they could be delivered.

Jesus told His disciples that any such kind of talk or promises should be disregarded; those kinds of situations were not to be the method by which He revealed his presence, nor by which they would be saved.

A **false** Christ is different from an **anti**-Christ. One claims to be Christ, while the other is **against** Christ. An anti-Christ is also anti-God. (Think of the "man of sin" of **II Thessalonians 2:3** who "opposeth and exalteth himself above all that is called God, or that is worshipped; so that he as God sitteth in the temple of God, shewing himself that he is God" vs. 4.)

Why should people want to adhere to new Messiahs, when Christ had already come? Because they were still looking for the Messiah to come **the first time.** But he had already come, though His kingdom had not been manifested yet in full power. This would shortly be done, in that generation; but in the meantime imposters would seek to deceive the people, even the elect, if possible. And when Christ did manifest his kingdom in power in the events of A.D. 67-70, this was part of His eschatological coming to the world as Messiah. He would reveal His presence (*parousia*) in the judgments on Israel and in the deliverance of His people, and in the ushering in of His kingdom, now taken from the Jews and given to a nation that would bring forth the fruits thereof **(Matthew 21:43)**.

Josephus mentions one false prophet who urged the people to get up on the Temple and to await signs of deliverance. He said:

"A false prophet was the occasion of these people's destruction, who had made a public proclamation in the city that very day, that God commanded them to get upon the temple, and that there they should receive miraculous signs of their deliverance. Now, there was then a great number of false prophets suborned by the tyrants to impose upon the people, who denounced this to them, that they should wait for deliverance from God . . ." **(Josephus, p. 453).**

Before Christ came, there were no false Christs. No one else had appeared on the scene claiming to be the Messiah. After His ministry, others began to proclaim that they were the Messiah. But when Jerusalem was destroyed, the final verdict was in—proof was there— that Jesus was the Messiah. That event in A.D. 70 forever settled the matter as to Christ's being the Messiah.

". . . from the death of Herod the Great . . . to the destruction of the Temple, the Jewish History is filled with the names of false Christs and false Prophets who deceived both the Jews and Samaritans. None appeared **before** this period, and not more than one for five or six centuries after it" (quoted from **Kett's History, the Interpreter of Prophecy,** 3rd. Edit. vol. I, o. 168, by **N. Nisbett).**

John said, "many false prophets are gone out into the world" **(I John 4:1).** And then he went on to explain what the word "antichrist" meant in their day. He said, "And every spirit that confesseth not that Jesus Christ is come in the flesh is not of God: and this is that **spirit** of antichrist, whereof ye have heard that it should come; and even now already is it in the world" **(I John 4:3).** He had said in chapter 2, "Little children, it is THE LAST TIME: and as ye have heard that antichrist shall come, even now are there many antichrists; whereby we know that it is THE LAST TIME" (**I John 2:18**). According to verse 19, these "antichrists" had been among them, but fell away from them — "went out from us, but they were not of us." Jesus had prophesied that all of this would come about. And when John emphasized "the last time," he evidently believed that the people were on a very fringe of an impending crisis.

It was only natural that in those days leading up to the final dissolution of the Jewish empire, there would appear false prophets who would attempt to deceive the people into following them in the hope of their finding release from the bondage of the Roman government's power over them. The waiting disciples remembered the words of Jesus and refused to be deceived by these false leaders; they were waiting instead for Christ to manifest His power and kingdom as He had promised. **Renan** said:

"The extraordinary events of which Jerusalem was the scene, impressed the Christians indeed in the highest degree. The peaceful disciples of Jesus, deprived of their leader, James, brother of the Lord, at first continued to lead their ascetic life in the Holy City, and, huddled around the Temple, to await the great coming. They had with them the remaining survivors of the family of Jesus, the sons of Cleopas, who were regarded even by the Jews, with the highest veneration. All that was going on must have seemed to them an evident confirmation of the words of Jesus. What could these convulsions be if not the beginning of what was called 'the travail of the Messiah,' preluding the Messianic birth? It was held as certain that the triumphant coming of Christ would be preceded by the appearance of a great number of false prophets. In the eyes of the Christian community's chiefs, these false prophets were the leaders of the Zelotes" (**Renan**, pp. 147-148).

The expectation of the coming of the Messiah, about the time that Jesus came, was everywhere evident, even though the people rejected Jesus as the Messiah. But this expectation was a main reason that the Jewish people were excited into the war with the Romans, thinking that they would soon have deliverance from the Romans through the Messiah. It therefore became an easy matter for false Christs (Messiahs) and false prophets to appear on the scene and to deceive many.

★ ★ ★ ★ ★ ★ ★ ★ ★ ★ ★ ★ ★

"Behold, I have told you before" (Matthew 24:25).

It is most likely here that Jesus is reminding His disciples that He has told them before about false Christs and false prophets who would arise and seek to deceive the people. But it is also true that He had told them before about the coming desolation upon the people of Israel. God always warned people of times of trouble that would be sent their way.

When God planned to destroy the world by a flood, not only was Noah himself a warning to the people, but Enoch's son was born and his name given was "Methusaleh" which means, "at his death it shall be sent."

When God planned to destroy Sodom and Gomorrah, He told Abraham, and then sent angels to take Lot out of the city.

When God planned to slay the first-born children of Egypt, it cannot be said that Pharaoh had not been warned, again and again.

When Jerusalem was to be overthrown by Nebuchadnezzar, Ezekiel prophesied of those things to come.

So Jesus here gives clear warning of that tribulation which is going to fall on Jerusalem and the environs. It cannot be said that He had not warned the people again and again.

★ ★ ★ ★ ★ ★ ★ ★ ★ ★ ★ ★ ★ ★ ★

"**Wherefore if they shall say unto you, Behold, he is in the desert; go not forth: behold, he is in the secret chambers; believe it not" (Matthew 24:26).**

Commenting on this verse, **John Gill** said:

"It was usual for these imposters to lead their followers into deserts, pretending to work wonders in such solitary places: so during the siege, Simon, the son of Giora, collected together many thousands in the mountains and desert parts of Judaea; and the above-mentioned Jonathan, after the destruction of the city, lead great multitudes into the desert: **behold, he is in the secret chambers, believe it not**; or should others say, behold, or for certain, the Messiah is in some one of the secret and fortified places of the temple; where, during some time of the siege, were John and Eleazar, the heads of the zealots; do not believe them. Some reference may be had to the chamber of secrets, which was in the temple; 'for in the sanctuary there were two chambers; one was called . . . **the chamber of secrets**, and the other the chamber of vessels' " **(John Gill**, on Matthew 24:26).

The translator of Josephus said, "The Jews of later times agree with Josephus, that there were hiding-places or secret chambers about the holy house" (**Josephus,** footnote p. 457).

So if the Messiah were not to appear in any fashion as described by any of these false prophets, then how was He to appear? This we shall deal with in our next section in this series entitled, **Immediately After The Tribulation**. "For as the lightning cometh out of the east, and shineth even unto the west; so shall also the coming of the Son of man be" **(Matthew 24:27).**

Section 4 ••••••••••••••••••••••••••

"IMMEDIATELY AFTER THE TRIBULATION"

"For as the lightning cometh out of the east, and shineth even unto the west; so shall also the coming of the Son of man be.

"For wheresoever the carcase is, there will the eagles be gathered together.

"Immediately after the tribulation of those days shall the sun be darkened, and the moon shall not give her light, and the stars shall fall from heaven, and the powers of the heavens shall be shaken" (**Matthew 24:27-29**).

The great tribulation upon the Jewish people at Jerusalem and in Judaea during the years A.D. 67-70 was such as never had been before, nor would ever be again (**Matthew 24:21**). It was so horrible that if those days had gone much longer, no one would have survived (**vs. 22**).

In an old book (1838) entitled **The Pilgrim Soul**, by John Philip Schabalie, translated from the Dutch to German and then to English, are these descriptive words about part of that great tribulation upon the Jews:

"Though corpses lay so thick in the street, the besieged had for some time thrown them over the walls in such numbers, as filled the ditches, to breed a pestilence in the Roman army. From the commencement of the siege, that is, from the 14th of April to the 1st of July, out of only one gate were carried a hundred and fifteen thousand eight hundred and eighty corpses, exclusive of those thrown over the walls, of which every day saw a great number, that the troops on both sides, in their motions, trampled over dead bodies; as shocking circumstance to those who were not quite divested of humanity!"

During that time there arose false prophets and false Christs who promised victory to the Jews if only they would follow them. There would come those who claimed to be the Messiah (false Christs). If it were publicized that the Messiah was in the desert, or in the secret chambers underneath the Temple at Jerusalem, the people were not to believe any such reports (**vs. 26**). This was not the way that the true Messiah would make His appearance. His coming would not be localized.

In this section we shall see how Christ, the true Messiah, would make His appearance.

"**For as the lightning cometh out of the east, and shineth even unto the west; so shall also the coming of the Son of man be**" (**Matthew 24:27**).

The false Christs were to be numerous, but their appearances during those days were to be disregarded. The people were to see something much greater in scope happening than some pseudo-Messiahs doing some magic and promising deliverance to the people. The real Christ would appear, and in a way unexpected. His presence would be likened to the lightning coming out of the east and shining to the west.

Someone has said that the word "lightning" means "great light" which in turn would refer to the sun which does actually come up in the east and go down in the west. However, this does not seem to be the best interpretation when one examines the other places in the New Testament where this same word is used.

Another suggested that here Jesus points out the very march of the Roman armies, which, as Josephus the historian tells us, entered the land of Judaea from the east and continued their way westward across the country. While this may be true, it seems more likely that Jesus was simply using apocalyptic language in the style of the Old Testament prophets. But be that as it may, He is definitely saying that His coming would not be a secret thing, but rather, would be as noteworthy and climactic as lightning flashing in the sky. He would not be found somewhere like in the desert or in the secret chambers of the Temple or some other physical place like that (not even on the Mount of Olives!).

Nevertheless, the point is that the presence of Christ will not be localized as with these false Messiahs; His presence will cover all the known area; it will be universal — from the east to the west. And the expression probably could also refer to the suddenness and the swiftness of the event when it occurs.

The section we are now about to study is one which many scholars have puzzled over. And in our studies on Matthew 24 in relation to the coming of the Son of man, this particular section is where "the water hits the wheel." Without an adequate understanding of what these celestial happenings mean, of the timing involved in what happens, and the meaning of both the "sign of the Son of man in heaven" and "the coming of the Son of man," we shall certainly find it easy to be led astray in our interpretation of this passage. There are numerous interpretations. The interpretation which is shared with you in these pages will cause a lot of things to fall in place which have puzzled many.

From this author's perspective, the five verses of **Matthew 24:27-31** (as well as other preceding verses already studied in this series) are the prediction of Jesus concerning His coming in judgment on Israel in A.D. 67-70. It is not a future event to us. It happened just 40 years after Jesus made the prediction — in that same generation in which He said "all these things" would be fulfilled (**Matthew 24:34**). This is known as the "preterist" interpretation of Matthew 24, because it teaches a "preterite" (past) fulfillment of these things. Our interpretation sees only past events in this passage. There is no double-fulfillment. There is no double-reference. There are no mixed-up passages which change the time factor. There is no "transition" verse separating the destruction of Jerusalem from another event 2,000 years or so in the future. Whatever passages elsewhere in the New Testament may teach a final coming of our Lord in resurrection and judgment power for all the world, they are not to be found in this chapter. Because Christians have not understood this, more error has been taught in eschatology based on a misunderstanding of this passage than possibly on any other passage in the New Testament.

This passage has also caused more perplexity among Bible students than possibly any other prophetic passage in the New Testament. Commenting on verses **29-31, W. Robertson Nicoll** said, "What is said thereon is so perplexing as to tempt a modern expositor to wish it had not been there, or to have recourse to critical expedients to eliminate it from the text" (**W. Robertson Nicoll**, p. 294).

Those of us who write on this subject certainly ought to acknowledge that **none** of us knows it all, and at best we are only giving our own enlightened opinions and interpretations. But human nature being as it is, I suppose many of us are like the little boy who was drawing a picture. His father asked him what he was drawing, and he replied, "I am drawing a picture of God." His father said, "Son, nobody knows what God looks like." "Well," said the son, "they will when I get through with this picture!" So with the humility of this little boy, we are writing our books explaining these "perplexing" passages! It remains to be seen as to whether or not you will agree with our interpretation. But be that as it may, I think one would have a most difficult time in knocking down the arguments we propose in our interpretation — and an interpretation, by the way, which was held pretty much as a consensus 100-150 years or so ago, before dispensationalism began to be promoted.

Commenting on verses 26 and 27, **John Calvin** had this to say:

"The meaning therefore is, that every one who collects his forces into a secret place, in order to regain the freedom of the nation by arms, falsely pretends to be **the Christ**; for the Redeemer is sent to diffuse his grace suddenly and unexpectedly through every quarter of the world. But these two things are quite contrary, to shut up redemption within some corner, and to spread it through the whole world. The disciples were thus reminded that they must no longer seek a Redeemer within the small enclosure of Judea, because he will suddenly extend the limits of his kingdom to the uttermost ends of the world. And, indeed, this astonishing rapidity, with which the gospel flew through every part of the world, was a manifest testimony of divine power. For it could not be the result of human industry, that the light of the gospel, as soon as it appeared, darted from one side of the world to the opposite side **like lightning**; and therefore it is not without reason that Christ introduces this circumstance for demonstrating and magnifying his heavenly glory. Besides, by holding out this vast extent of his kingdom, he intended to show that the desolation of Judea would not hinder him from reigning" **(John Calvin**, vol. xvii, p. 142-143).

The coming of the Son of man was here equated by John Calvin with the coming of the kingdom of God, similar to the way lightning shines from the east to the west. It would be rapid and would affect the entire world.

When Jesus used the picture of lightning to represent His coming, it reminds one of God's words concerning the punishment that came upon Assyria:

"Behold, the name of the LORD cometh from far, burning with his anger, and the burden thereof is heavy: his lips are full of indignation, and his tongue as a devouring fire: . . . And the LORD shall cause his glorious voice to be heard, and shall shew the lighting down of his arm, with the indignation of his anger, and with the flame of a devouring fire, with scattering, and tempest, and hailstones" **(Isaiah 30:27, 30).**

We are also reminded of **Zechariah 9:14**: "And the LORD shall be seen over them, and his arrow shall go forth as the lightning: and the Lord GOD shall blow the trumpet, and shall go with whirlwinds of the south."

Highly apocalyptic language is used to describe God's judgments against peoples. So is the description of the coming of the Son of man in judgment upon Israel.

" . . . the 'lightning' image is used by the prophets, Is 30:27 ff.; Zech 9:14, of divine judgements in the course and not at the end of history. The 'coming' . . . of the Son of Man is therefore not necessarily a coming for the final and universal judgement; it may be his coming for the judgement upon Israel" **(A Catholic Commentary on Holy Scripture**, Matthew 24:27, p. 895).

John Gill (1720-1771), one of the predecessors of Charles H. Spurgeon and dedicated student of the word of God, said:

" . . . **so shall also the coming of the Son of man be**; which must be understood not of his last coming to judgment, though that will be sudden, visible, and universal . . . but of his coming in his wrath and vengeance to destroy that people, their nation, city, and temple: so that after this to look for the Messiah in a desert, or secret chamber, must argue great stupidity and blindness; when his coming was as sudden, visible, powerful, and general, to the destruction of that nation, as the lightning that comes from the east, and, in a moment, shines to the west" (**John Gill**, on **Matthew 24:27**).

". . . so shall also the coming of the Son of man be" (**Matthew 24:27**).

In this verse, Jesus refers to Himself as "the Son of man." Back in **Daniel 7:13** the prophet said that he saw in a vision "one like the Son of man came with the clouds of heaven." This referred to the Son of man coming to the Ancient of days to be given a kingdom over all peoples. Now here in **Matthew 24** this same title is used concerning Christ and His coming, and then in verse 30 the very same expression is used concerning "the Son of man coming in the clouds of heaven." Jesus took this title to Himself, and this is apocalyptic language which He was using. In Daniel the coming of the Son of man was to the Ancient of days. In **Matthew 24** the coming of the Son of man is at the manifestation of that kingdom which He received. In between the time He received the kingdom and manifested it, Stephen, as he preached to the Jewish high priest and the council, looked up into heaven and said, "Behold, I see the heavens opened, and the Son of man standing on the right hand of God" (**Acts 7:56**). This was the only time this title was applied to Christ by any of His disciples. No wonder that the Jewish persecutors cast Stephen out of the city and stoned him until he died. They recognized that in the use of that title "Son of man," Stephen was acclaiming Christ to be the Messiah who was promised in the Old Testament to receive the kingdom. But now in this passage in **Matthew 24**, we come to the time when Jesus is to manifest the power of the kingdom, and His coming is portrayed in an apocalyptic way.

Of this verse **27**, but applicable to verses **27-30**, **John Lightfoot** (1859) said, "That Christ's taking vengeance of that exceeding wicked nation is called Christ's 'coming in glory,' and his 'coming in the clouds,' Dan. vii. It is also called, 'the day of the Lord.' See Psalm i.4; Mal. iii. I, 2, & c; Joel ii.31; Matt. xvi.28; Rev. i.7, &c." (**John Lightfoot**, vol. 2, p. 319).

As God came down to bring judgment on the Egyptians many years ago (**Exodus 3:8**: "I am COME DOWN to deliver them out of the hand of the Egyptians"), so Jesus came to bring judgment on those to whom the early Christians had been in bondage.

The word "coming" as found in **Matthew 24:30** ("they shall see the Son of man coming") and **Matthew 24:48**, ("My lord delayeth his coming") is from the Greek word *erchomai*, and is the verb form. It refers to the same thing.

We have earlier seen that the word *"parousia"* (the Greek word, noun form, for "coming" in this passage) means "arrival" and "presence," though not usually both meanings in the same instance. The word involves an "event," and it involves an idea of **duration**, but not usually in the same instance. Concerning a person, it means that that person has arrived. It can also mean that the person is now here with us. (For passages where this word means "presence," see for example **I Corinthians 16:17; II Corinthians 7:6,7, Philippians 1:26** and **2:12**.) But the word does not necessarily signify a bodily physical presence, especially here in Matthew 24. So Jesus is here definitely speaking of His coming as the manifestation of Himself as the Messiah. Let us keep in mind that He is still answering the disciples' question, "When shall these things be? and what shall be the sign of thy coming, and of the end of the world?" (vs. 3). "These things" referred, of course, to the destruction of the Temple in particular (involved in their questions); and in their minds the "sign of His coming" and "the end of the world (age)" would be connected. They were right about this, and Jesus did not correct them. And in just a moment He is going to tell them that **IMMEDIATELY** after the tribulation of those days He had been telling them about, there would be "the coming of the Son of man." And that coming would be described in such apocalyptic language as had been used in the Old Testament to describe those events when God came in judgment on nations and manifested His presence in that way. Only this time it would be Christ, not God, for all judgment had now been given over to the Son (**John 5:22**).

Interestingly, Matthew is the only gospel writer who uses the word *"parousia*/coming," so it is unique to him. So it is evident that at least Matthew connected the *"parousia"* with the other events mentioned, i.e., the destruction of the Temple and the end of the age. Also interesting is the fact that only Matthew of the gospel writers used the expression "end of the age." We understand better about this when we realize, as many Bible scholars agree, that Matthew was writing primarily to Jewish people. The expression, "end of the world (age)," would certainly convey to them the idea of the end of their age, which to them would end with the coming of the Messiah. We need to see these words through their eyes. The *parousia* (the arrival and/or presence) of the Messiah would occur at the end of that age.

"It is of prime importance for the student of this subject to understand — so often is the case stated otherwise — that Parousia is the

New Testament answer to two distinct words, **arrival** and **presence**, usually the former; that in most instances these meanings are not interchangeable, but that one or the other is required, according to the context; for example, the former in I Cor. 16:17, and the latter in Phil. 2:12" **(William Arnold Stevens, p. 63)**.

It has been very difficult for some to believe that the "coming of the Son of man" here mentioned can be anything else but a future (to us) coming of the Son of God from Heaven to earth in a physical, bodily, personal appearance. But let us remember that great spiritual events occurring in this "dispensation of the fulness of times" on numerous occasions has been called "comings" of Christ. His first appearing in the flesh **(Hebrews 9:26)**, His presence on the Mount of Transfiguration **(II Peter 1:16)**, His ascension **(Daniel 7:13)**, the coming of the Holy Spirit **(John 14:18)**, and the judgment on Israel in A.D. 70 **(Matthew 24)** are all designated as "comings" of Christ.

Ezra P. Gould, professor of New Testament Literature and Language, Divinity School of the Protestant Episcopal Church in Philadelphia, said (1896):

"There have been, up to recent times, two interpretations of this discourse. Both of them separate it into two principal parts: the prediction of the destruction of Jerusalem, and the prophecy of the consummation of all things with the advent of the Messiah in glory. But one of them, the traditional interpretation, postpones the latter part indefinitely, and is still looking for the world-catastrophe which its advocates suppose to be predicted here. The difficulties in the way of this interpretation are grave and insuperable. It ignores the coupling together of the two parts in the discourse, as belonging to one great event. Mt. vs. 29, says that they will follow each other immediately. Mk., that they belong to the same general period. It passes over also, or attempts to explain away, the obvious notes of time. All of the accounts wait until they have come to the end of the prophecy, including both parts, before they introduce the statement of the time of all these events, and the statement itself is, that that generation was not to pass away till all these things came to pass."

Then, after giving the second interpretation (a liberal view), Gould said:

"A third interpretation, the one adopted here, holds that the event predicted in the second part did take place in that generation, and in connection with the destruction of Jerusalem. The event itself, and the signs of it, it interprets according to the analogy of prophecy, figuratively. It finds numerous instances of such use in O.T. prophecy. God coming in the clouds of heaven with his angels, and preceded or announced by disturbances in the heavenly bodies, is the ordinary prophetic manner of describing any special Divine interference in the affairs of nations" (**Gould**, p. 240-241).

". . . the destruction of Jerusalem is described as **his** coming . . ." (**Albert Barnes Commentary** on Matthew 24:27).

When Caiaphas the high priest asked Jesus if He were Christ, the Son of God, "Jesus saith unto him, Thou hast said: nevertheless I say unto you, Hereafter shall ye see the Son of man sitting on the right hand of power, and coming in the clouds of heaven" (**Matthew 26:64**). Jesus was saying, "**From now on** you are going to see my authority manifested and my claim vindicated." And they did see it. They saw it in the earthquake at His death. They saw it in the blackness at midday when He was dying (Pliny the historian, living in Egypt at that time, said, "Either today the world is coming to an end, or else God is dying.") They saw it in the resurrection of the bodies in the cemetery which came to life and entered into the city. They saw it on the day of Pentecost. They saw it in the destruction of Jerusalem and the Temple in A.D. 67-70. They saw His authority and kingdom. They saw His presence in all these things. In symbolical language, it was said that He would be sitting at the place of authority and coming in the clouds of Heaven. This was apocalyptic language that the Jewish leaders well understood.

It has been said, "Jesus did not come as mentioned in **Matthew 24:27-30**, so we know that this Scripture was not fulfilled in 70 A.D. and therefore has to be in our future." Do you know why this statement is made? It is because that ALREADY in the mind of the one who makes this statement there is a PRECONCEIVED notion of what the "coming" of Christ in that chapter HAS to be. Their only notion of a coming of Christ beyond the first coming is in our future — in spite of the fact that God is depicted as coming down from heaven again and again in the Old Testament, but not in a bodily and physical form which could be seen by mortal eyes. Why cannot we accept the fact that Jesus here in **Matthew 24** used highly symbolical language, the same as had been used elsewhere in the Bible, to portray this great event of His coming in judgment on Israel and manifesting His own glory and kingdom through the events that took place?

Does Christ have to be SEEN in order to APPEAR?

Christ can "come," and "appear," and yet not be seen by the physical eyes. When Ananias went to talk to Saul after Saul's conversion, he said to Saul, " . . . the Lord, even Jesus, that APPEARED unto thee in the way as thou camest . . . " (**Acts 9:17**). The word "appeared" is from the same Greek word (*optomai*) as in **Hebrews 9:28** where it says, "unto them that look for him shall he APPEAR the second time . . . ."

So Jesus came (appeared) to Saul on the road to Damascus, the same as he could come (appear) at the judgment on Israel in A.D. 70. But the Bible states that when Christ appeared (**Acts 9:1-7**), none of the men saw him. "And the men which journeyed with him stood speechless, hearing a voice, but SEEING NO MAN" (**Acts 9:7**). This was at the APPEARANCE of Christ to Saul. He appeared, but was not physically seen. The same word used in **Hebrews 9:28** ("shall he APPEAR") does not mean that He would be physically seen.

On the matter of the "coming of the Son of man," much, much more will be said when we come to verse **30**.

★★★★★★★★★★★★★★★★

"**For wheresoever the carcase is, there will the eagles be gathered together**" (**Matthew 24:28**).

Luke puts this statement right after the section where Christ likened His coming to the destruction of the world in Noah's day and the destruction of Sodom and Gomorrah in Lot's day, and after He had said to the disciples that one would be taken and another left (see **Luke 17:37**). Here, we have the saying connected with "the coming of the Son of man" as lightning comes out of the east and shines to the west. As birds of prey flying up in the sky are waiting for some carcase to light upon, so the coming of the Son of man will be to that area where the "carcase" will be found. The Jewish nation, and more specifically the city of Jerusalem, was the carcase which the Romans (eagles) descended upon to devour.

The Persian and Syriac versions translate the word for "eagles" as "vultures."

God used the same kind of language in the Old Testament when referring to the Chaldeans coming against Israel: "For, lo, I raise up the Chaldeans . . . their horsemen shall come from far; they shall fly as the eagle that hasteth to eat" (**Habakkuk 1:6, 8**).

And in **Isaiah 46:10-11**, reference was made to Cyrus as being a bird of prey: ". . . I will do all my pleasure: Calling a ravenous bird from the east, the man that executeth my counsel from a far country."

John Peter Lange said, "As the carcase every where attracts the carrion-eaters, so do moral corruption and ripened guilt everywhere demand the judgment." Here, Jerusalem and the Jews are the carcase, attracting the Roman armies like dead animals attract the vultures.

It is more than likely that Jesus had in mind some of these Old Testament passages of metaphorical style which he drew from in His teachings. He may have thought of **Jeremiah 7:33-34**: "And the carcases of this people shall be meat for the fowls of the heaven, and for the beasts of the earth . . . for the land shall be desolate."

Or, He may have been thinking of **Jeremiah 19:3, 7:** "Hear ye the word of the Lord . . . Behold, I will bring evil upon this place . . . And I will make void the counsel of Judah and Jerusalem in this place; and I will cause them to fall by the sword before their enemies, and by the hands of them that seek their lives: and their carcases will I give to be meat for the fowls of the heaven, and for the beasts of the earth."

Commenting on this verse, **Albert Barnes** said:

"This verse is connected with the preceding by the word 'for,' implying that this is a reason for what is said there—that the Son of man would **certainly** come to destroy the city, and that he would come **suddenly**. The meaning is that he would come, by means of the Roman armies, as certainly, as suddenly, and as unexpectedly as whole flocks of vultures and eagles, though unseen before, see their prey at a great distance and suddenly gather in multitudes around it . . . So keen is their vision as aptly to represent the Roman armies, though at an immense distance, spying, as it were, Jerusalem, a putrid carcass, and hastening in multitudes to destroy it" **(Albert Barnes Commentary on Matthew 24:28).**

John Broadus said, "The meaning of the saying as here applied seems to be, that things will come to pass when the occasion for them exists. When Jerusalem is ready for destruction, the Roman armies will gather and destroy it" **(John Broadus, p. 489).**

Wherever a dead carcase is, there will the eagles (vultures?) be gathered. Wherever the Jews are, there will the Roman soldiers be. The soldiers did not confine themselves to Jerusalem alone, and there was no part of all of Judaea which did not suffer under their conquest. They spread out all over Judaea and the entire Jewish world felt the effects of their conquest.

John Lightfoot (1859) said of this verse:

"for wheresoever the carcase is, &c. I wonder any can understand these words of pious men flying to Christ, when the discourse here is of quite a different thing: they are thus connected to the foregoing: Christ shall be revealed with a sudden vengeance; for when God shall cast off the city and people, grown ripe for destruction, like a carcase thrown out, the Roman soldiers, like eagles, shall straight fly to it with their eagles (ensigns) to tear and devour it. And to this also agrees the answer of Christ, Luke xvii. 37; when, after the same words that are spoken here in this chapter, it was inquired, 'Where, Lord?' he answered, 'Wheresoever the body is,' &c.; silently hinting thus much, that Jerusalem, and that wicked nation which he described through the whole chapter, would be the carcase, to which the greedy and devouring eagles would fly to prey upon it" **(John Lightfoot, vol. 2, p. 319).**

The whole Jewish system, and the lives of the people, were deteriorating into a rotten mess, and it was only inevitable that sooner than later the result would be the judgment of God upon it all. Jesus clearly saw this and predicted it. And it happened as the Roman armies swooped down upon the land, then Jerusalem itself, as vultures looking for a dead carcase to pounce upon. Divine principles were at work.

Possibly Jesus also had in mind **Hosea 8:1** when He made His statement about the eagles and the carcase. Hosea recorded, "Set the trumpet to thy mouth. He shall COME as an EAGLE against the HOUSE OF THE LORD, because they have transgressed my covenant, and trespassed against my law."

It is a well-known fact of history that the Roman army's standards had the ensign of an eagle upon them. Not that this matters so far as the interpretation of the passage goes, but it is an interesting thought with reference to the eagles.

God sent **Nebuchadnezzar** against the land many years ago:

"Behold, I will send and take all the families of the north, saith the LORD, and Nebuchadrezzar the king of Babylon, my servant, and will bring them against this land, and against the inhabitants thereof, and against all these nations round about, and will utterly destroy them, and make them an astonishment, and an hissing, and perpetual desolations" **(Jeremiah 25:9)**. Notice God even called Nebuchadnezzar "my servant."

God sent the **Chaldeans** against the land: "For, lo, I raise up the Chaldeans, that bitter and hasty nation, which shall march through the breadth of the land, to possess the dwelling-places that are not theirs" **(Habakkuk 1:6)**.

And in **Zechariah 14:2** God said He would "gather all nations against Jerusalem to battle." And this is certainly what He did in the area of time we are discussing here. The Roman army was gathered from all nations. And God used the Roman armies to punish Israel, even as He had used the Assyrians many years prior to this to do the same. The Assyrian was "the rod of mine anger, and the staff in their hand is mine indignation" **(Isaiah 10:5)**.

★★★★★★★★★★★★

"**Immediately after the tribulation of those days shall the sun be darkened, and the moon shall not give her light, and the stars shall fall from heaven, and the powers of the heavens shall be shaken**" **(Matthew 24:29)**.

Note several things here. First, Jesus is talking about the tribulation of "THOSE DAYS" (that is, of the very days during which the

Jews were undergoing this terrible tribulation from A.D. 67-70). "Those days" definitely determines the time which is under discussion. Which means, of course, that He is not talking about some "tribulation" during a later course of events in the world, nor a "tribulation" which is to take place either 3½ years or 7 years either prior to or subsequent to the Rapture of Christians at a future (to us) coming of Christ. This is not some future event (to us) as dwelt upon so much by the dispensationalists and futurists. It was "the tribulation of THOSE DAYS" which was mentioned here — the days He had already discussed.

Please let this register in your mind: "**THOSE DAYS**."

Second, what He was talking about was to happen "IMMEDIATELY after the tribulation of those days." The word "immediately" is from the Greek word **eutheos** which means "at once, or soon, as soon as, forthwith, shortly, straight way." It certainly would not portray a time frame of 2,000 years or so later.

This is the one word that really "stumped" me some years ago after I had come to the understanding that the tribulation Jesus was talking about was what happened in "those days" to the Jewish people undergoing the siege of the Roman armies, etc. I really felt then that what followed (the celestial events) was somehow connected to a "second coming" of Christ in our future. And the way that I handled this in a little book I wrote on **The Great Tribulation?** (now out of print), was to project the idea that certainly Jesus was talking about that specific tribulation in those days, but that the tribulation would **extend itself** for many centuries up to the time of the "second coming" of Christ, so that immediately after the final ending of that tribulation would come about these heavenly portents, etc. And I learned that a number of Bible expositors believed this way also. I reasoned this way because of **Luke 21:23-24** which said:

"for there shall be great distress in the land, and wrath upon this people. And they shall fall by the edge of the sword, and shall be led away captive into all nations: and Jerusalem shall be trodden down of the Gentiles, until the times of the Gentiles be fulfilled."

I felt the tribulation would be extended thusly for all these centuries, and then the end would come. But I received a letter from someone who asked me if I did not think this interpretation was a little "strained." The more I thought about it, the more I felt that this was true — I was pushing that interpretation too far in order to accommodate the idea of all this happening just before a final "second coming" of Christ in our future. Since that time, I have come to the conclusion that Jesus meant exactly what He said in the way He said it — that those celestial happenings would occur

IMMEDIATELY after the tribulation of THOSE DAYS. It should be difficult for anyone to get around this and still be honest with this passage of Scripture.

I think our whole problem in this matter has been in wanting to equate "the coming of the Son of man" with something out in our own future, instead of understanding that Jesus was talking about His revealed presence in the judgments that came on Israel back in those days. I shall go further into this at verse 30.

There can be no question about the tribulation of **verse 29** being the same "great tribulation" to which Jesus referred in **verse 21**. In **verse 21** He said, "For THEN shall be great tribulation." It was **THEN**, not later. That great tribulation occurred in connection with the siege and destruction of Jerusalem and the Temple as Jesus plainly said would take place. Therefore, the "tribulation" of **verse 29 CANNOT** refer to some **OTHER** tribulation supposedly to occur many hundreds of years later. It all occurred in A.D. 67-70. And what Jesus said was to happen next ("IMMEDIATELY") had to have happened at that time, or the words of Jesus could be called into question.

Third, Jesus said that "immediately after the tribulation of those days" there would be tremendous celestial happenings. This is in connection with that great tribulation of A.D. 67-70, but **immediately** following it. And this word "immediately" indicates to us that He could not be talking about some far-off distant event some 2,000 years or so away. These celestial things happened at the closing of the great tribulation period of years ago. The sun and the moon were darkened, the stars fell from heaven, and the powers of the heavens were shaken. It is this kind of language which Jesus used to which we shall now give our attention.

Same Kind of Language Used in the Old Testament

We must understand the use of symbolical language by the writers of the Bible (and Jesus), especially when the references were to prophetic events and more especially to times of God's judgments upon peoples and nations. It is language that uses words and ideas of grandeur, of fantastic proportions, of celestial significance. It is not language that signifies an absolutely literal, materialistic, or natural fulfillment, as can be discovered by anyone who honestly studies these things. For example, almost the same identical language was used by prophets of old when they described the coming judgments of God upon certain areas of people. I have learned that in understanding many expressions in New Testament eschatology, it is absolutely necessary to go back to the Old Testament and see how the same expressions were used there. In that way, one lets the Bible interpret itself.

For an example of the way the writers of the Old Testament used highly imaginative language concerning the universe to describe events that happened, look especially at **Psalm 18**. The heading describes the Psalm as words from David concerning God's deliverance of "him from the hand of all his enemies and from the hand of Saul." It says:

"Then the earth shook and trembled; the foundations also of the hills moved and were shaken, because he was wroth.

"There went up a smoke out of his nostrils, and fire out of his mouth devoured: coals were kindled by it.

"He bowed the heavens also, and CAME DOWN" (one version says "he descended"): "and darkness was under his feet.

"And he rode upon a cherub, and did fly: yea, he did fly upon the wings of the wind.

"He made darkness his secret place; his pavilion round about him were dark waters and thick clouds of the skies.

"At the brightness that was before him his thick clouds passed, hail stones and coals of fire.

"The LORD also thundered in the heavens, and the Highest gave his voice; hail stones and coals of fire" **(Psalm 18:7-13)**. (See also **II Samuel 22:8-10**.)

In the midst of all these celestial and terrestrial scenes described by David, he said, "He . . . came down!" **(vs. 9)**. But students of the Bible should understand that this is the kind of language used by the writers when they are describing the wonderful works of God, usually in reference to His judgments, and in reference to His deliverances and great blessings to His people. We are not to take these verses literally in a naturalistic sense.

G. R. Beasley-Murray describes the "coming" of God to help David (in **Psalm 18**) thusly:

"The Lord of heaven and earth thus comes in all his glory, shaking the world to its foundations, causing the mountains to heave and the ocean floor to be exposed — all for the aid of one sick man! This is a clear expression of the association in a Hebrew's mind when he thought of the coming of God to aid his people: the stepping forth of the Creator evokes the trembling of the whole creation" (**G. R. Beasley-Murray, Jesus and the Kingdom of God**, p. 6).

When "the earth shook and trembled," when "the foundations also of the hills moved and were shaken," then it was that the LORD "CAME DOWN." So says **Psalm 18:7, 9**. This is beautiful apocalyptic language.

Concerning this same passage **(Psalm 18)**, **Milton Terry** said:

"The simplest reader of this psalm observes that, in answer to the prayer of the one in distress, Jehovah reveals himself in marvelous power and glory. He disturbs for his sake all the elements of the earth and the heavens. He descends from the lofty sky as if bending down the visible clouds and making a pathway of massive darkness under his feet. He seems to ride upon a chariot, borne along by cherubims, and moving swiftly as the winds . . . In the psalmist's thought winds, fire, hail, smoke, clouds, waters, lightnings, and earthquake are conceived as immediately subservient to Jehovah, who interposes for the rescue of his devout servant" **(Terry, Biblical Apocalyptics, p. 25).**

Terry gave a footnote on this by **Perowne** which said:

"David's deliverance was, of course, not really accompanied by such convulsions of nature, by earthquake, and fire, and tempest; but his deliverance, or rather his manifold deliverance, gathered into one, as he thinks of them, appear to him as marvelous a proof of the divine power, as verily effected by the immediate presence and finger of God, as if he had come down in visible form to accomplish them. — **The Book of Psalms**, new translation, with notes, etc., vol. i. p. 186. American ed., Andover, 1876" **(Terry, Biblical Apocalyptics, p. 25).**

Jesus used this same kind of language when He said, "they shall see the Son of man coming in the clouds of heaven with power and great glory" **(Matthew 24:30).**

God coming down! Jesus coming down! And "in the clouds of heaven with power and great glory!" What beautiful and powerful language describing the manifestation of Jesus as the Son of man in His kingdom!

And the language is not much different than we find used at times in modern life. General Wojcieck Jaruzelski of Poland "was 16 when Nazi Germany attacked Poland in 1939, and he recalls vividly how, on a clear September day 51 years ago, he and his family crossed into Lithuania as refugees. 'I thought then that the heavens had fallen on me', Jaruzelski recalls" **(Time**, Oct. 1, 1990).

But back to **Matthew 24:29:**

Dr. Warburton said:

" . . . this language was borrowed from the antient hieroglyphics: for as in hieroglyphic writing, the sun, moon, and stars were used to represent states and empires, kings, queens, and nobility; their eclipse and extinction, temporary disasters, or overthrow, &c. so in like manner, the holy prophets call kings and empires by the names of the heavenly luminaries; their misfortunes and overthrow are represented by eclipses and extinction; stars falling from the firmament are employed to denote the destruction of the nobility, &c."

(**Warburton's Divine Legation,** vol. 2, book 4, section 4, quoted by N. Nisbett, **Our Lord's Prophecies of the Destruction of Jerusalem,** pp. 22-23).

On this verse (**Matthew 24:29**), one writer of years ago said: "It requires but a slender acquaintance with the writings of the Old Testament prophets to enable us to observe the peculiarity. It is not only figurative, but the figures are of the boldest kind, involving analogies so remote, as in some instances to be scarcely discoverable. If revolutions in empires be the subject, the prophetic representation is filled with disturbance of the laws of the natural world, and the sun, moon, and stars, are exhibited in commotion. If a deliverer is promised to the Jews, the prophet expresses the promise by the rising of a star, and the like" (**Samuel Hinds,** pp. 209-210).

An example of the latter mentioned can be seen in **Numbers 24:17.** Illustrations will be given of the former as we move along in our study here.

Adam Clarke, in his commentary on this verse (**Matthew 24:29**) said:

"**Immediately after the tribulation,** &c. Commentators generally understand this, and what follows, of the end of the world and Christ's coming to judgment: but the word **immediately** shows that our Lord is not speaking of any **distant** event, but of something immediately consequent on calamities already predicted: and that must be the destruction of Jerusalem . . .

"In the prophetic language, great commotions upon the earth are often represented under the notion of commotions and changes in the heavens: —

"The fall of **Babylon** is represented by the stars and constellations of heaven withdrawing their light, and the sun and moon being darkened. See Isa. xiii. 9, 10.

"The destruction of **Egypt,** by the heaven being covered, the sun enveloped with a cloud, and the moon withholding her light. Ezek. xxxii. 7, 8.

"The destruction of the **Jews** by **Antiochus Epiphanes,** is represented by **casting down some of the host of heaven,** and the **stars** to the ground. See Dan. viii. 10.

"And this very destruction of **Jerusalem** is represented by the Prophet Joel, chap ii. 30, 31, by showing wonders in heaven and in earth — **darkening the sun, and turning the moon into blood.** This general mode of describing these judgments leaves no room to doubt the propriety of its application in the present case" (**Adam Clarke,** commentary on **Matthew 24:29**).

Take, for example, the case of the prophesied fall of **Babylon** to the Medes in 539 B.C., and how God used this celestial and universal language to describe the judgment that would come upon her:

"Behold, the day of the LORD cometh, cruel both with wrath and fierce anger, to lay the land desolate: and he shall destroy the sinners thereof out of it.

"For the stars of heaven and the constellations thereof shall not give their light: the sun shall be darkened in his going forth, and the moon shall not cause her light to shine.

"And I will punish the world for their evil . . ." **(Isaiah 13:9-11).**

This applied to **Babylon,** as mentioned in verse 1. Again, note the prophecy of Ezekiel against **Egypt:**

"And when I shall put thee out, I will cover the heaven, and make the stars thereof dark; I will cover the sun with a cloud, and the moon shall not give her light.

"All the bright lights of heaven will I make dark over thee, and set darkness upon thy land, saith the Lord GOD" **(Ezekiel 32:7,8).**

This applied to Egypt, as mentioned in **vss. 2, 12-16.**

And further, note in **Amos 8:9,** "And it shall come to pass in that day, saith the Lord GOD, that I will cause the sun to go down at noon, and I will darken the earth in the clear day." This had reference to the northern kingdom.

Or again, note the actions of the "little horn" mentioned by Daniel in **Daniel 8:9-10:**

"And out of one of them came forth a little horn, which waxed exceeding great, toward the south, and toward the east, and toward the pleasant land.

"And it waxed great, even to the host of heaven; and it cast down some of the host and of the stars to the ground, and stamped upon them."

Would you say this language was talking about something that was literally done in a materialistic way, or would you say that the language is symbolical and **represented** in celestial language something that would take place?

Isaiah 34 is a chapter of symbolical language depicting in principle the awful judgment of God, and illustrated by at least two places to be affected — **Idumea** and **Bozrah** (vss. 5-6). God's anger is against all nations, and His judgment is pictured in this chapter. That it is symbolical language is shown by "the mountains shall be melted with their blood" **(vs. 3).**

In **verse 4** God says:

"And all the host of heaven shall be dissolved, and the heavens shall be rolled together as a scroll: and all their host shall fall down, as the leaf falleth off from the vine, and as a falling fig from the fig tree" (vs. 4).

This is identical language as that given in **Revelation 6:13-14**: "And the stars of heaven fell unto the earth, even as a fig tree casteth her untimely figs, when she is shaken of a mighty wind.

"And the heaven departed as a scroll when it is rolled together; and every mountain and island were moved out of their places."

It has previously been thought that this passage in Revelation refers to a time in our future, but evidently it does not. It must apply to the judgment and destruction of Israel years ago in fulfillment of Jesus' prophecy. Notice the next two verses:

"And the kings of the earth, and the great men, and the rich men, and the chief captains, and the mighty men, and every bondman, and every free man, hid themselves in the dens and in the rocks of the mountains;

"And said to the mountains and rocks, Fall on us, and hide us from the face of him that sitteth on the throne, and from the wrath of the Lamb" **(Revelation 6:15-16)**.

How like that passage is what Jesus said in **Luke 23:28-30**:

"But Jesus turning unto them said, Daughters of Jerusalem, weep not for me, but weep for yourselves, and for your children.

"For, behold, the days are coming, in the which THEY shall say, Blessed are the barren, and the wombs that never bare, and the paps which never gave suck.

"THEN shall THEY begin to say to the mountains, Fall on us; and to the hills, Cover us."

This was language depicting the great tribulation in Israel in A.D. 67-70. This kind of language is used, picturing the response of sinful man to the awful judgment of God. Notice how God used the same language about Israel in **Hosea 10:8**:

"The high places also of Aven, the sin of Israel, shall be destroyed: the thorn and the thistle shall come up on their altars; and they shall say to the mountains, Cover us; and to the hills, Fall on us."

But back to **Isaiah 34** where God used such figurative language to describe His judgment against rebellious people. In **verse 8** He said, "For it is the day of the LORD's vengeance." This is not a future Armageddon, but was judgment of Idumea and Bozrah.

Then notice the highly symbolical language of **vss. 9-10**:

"And the streams thereof shall be turned into pitch, and the dust thereof into brimstone, and the land thereof shall become burning pitch.

"It shall not be quenched night nor day; the smoke thereof shall go up for ever: from generation to generation it shall lie waste; none shall pass through it for ever and ever."

Read this last verse over carefully. Is it symbolical and figurative language or not? Or does someone say it LITERALLY happened like that?

It is from passages in the Old Testament like this that writers in the New Testament (from Matthew right on to Revelation) draw from and use as a pattern for describing things they are talking about. So let us not take the words too NATURALLY! As you hear God speaking in **Isaiah 34** concerning the celestial happenings at those local judgment scenes, note that Jesus uses that same kind of language when talking about judgment upon Israel in His generation.

"Immediately after the tribulation of those days shall the sun be darkened, and the moon shall not give her light, and the stars shall fall from heaven, and the powers of the heavens shall be shaken" **(Matthew 24:29)**.

This is highly symbolical language, given in the style of the Old Testament prophets, to describe the shake-up of things at the judgment of Christ in the destruction of the land of Israel, Jerusalem and the Temple in A.D. 67-70. This imagery is taken from the Old Testament and pictures the final dissolution and destruction of the Jewish nation. It is a picturesque portrayal of the greatness and majesty of God in times of judgment. Even the earth and the heavens seem to dissolve in His presence, as in **Revelation 20:11** when earth and the heavens fled from the presence of Him Who sat on the great white throne.

Jesus said, "The powers of the heavens shall be shaken" **(Matthew 24:29)**. The writer of the book of Hebrews tells us about this in **Hebrews 12:26-28**:

"Yet once more I shake not the earth only, but also heaven. And this word, Yet once more, signifieth the removing of those things that are shaken, as of things that are made, that those things which cannot be shaken may remain. Wherefore we receiving a kingdom which cannot be moved . . ." Here is shown the removing of the old covenant and the reception of the new. The writer of Hebrews quotes from **Haggai 2:6-7** which says:

"Yet once, it is a little while, and I will shake the heavens, and the earth, the the sea, and the dry land; And I will shake all nations, and the desire of all nations shall come: and I will fill this house with glory, saith the LORD of hosts."

The writer of the book of Hebrews indicated that the fulfillment of that prophecy was in process at the time the book of Hebrews was written, shortly before Jerusalem was destroyed. Haggai may have had in mind something in connection with the rebuilding of the Temple many years ago (see **Haggai chapter 1**), which was in their immediate future, but the fulness of that promise was only reached with the beginning of New Testament times as the old covenant was done away with and the new brought in. What was promised in "a little while" did come to pass in the rebuilding of the Temple, but that Temple was only **typical** of what would take place years later. With this in mind, the writer of Hebrews said, ". . . but NOW he hath promised, saying, Yet once more I shake not the earth only, but also heaven" (**Hebrews 12:26**). God verily shook things up (heaven and earth) to bring about the elimination of an old system and to institute a new. Things that could be shaken were removed, and things which could not be shaken remained. A kingdom, which cannot be moved, was received. And the culmination of all this shaking took place at the ending of those days of tribulation — immediately afterwards. It was then that God brought about His new world order.

The Sun - Moon - Stars - Represented Mainly the Universe of Israel

The stars falling from heaven (**vs. 29**) represented the downfall of the entire Jewish commonwealth as represented by the leaders.

Princes and nobles of the Babylonian kingdom were called "stars" in **Daniel 8:10** and were said to be "cast down." Now the language can relate to Israel.

Jewish writers understood the light to mean the law; the moon, the Sanhedrin; and the stars, the Rabbis.

Joseph in a dream saw "the sun and the moon and the eleven stars" obeying him (**Genesis 37:9**), and there we see the same kind of typology used, as we know this referred to the brothers of Joseph finally having to yield to Joseph when he became a ruler in Egypt. The heavenly elements represent people in Old Testament language.

F. W. Farrar put it this way:

"The powers of heaven were being shaken. Suns and moons and stars — from Roman Emperors down to Jewish Priests — were one after another waxing dim, and shooting from their spheres. Clearly the day must be at hand of which the Lord had said that it would come **ere that generation passed away,** and that all the things of which He had spoken would be fulfilled" (**F. W. Farrar,** p. 414).

Jesus said that "the powers of the heavens shall be shaken" (**vs. 29**). What would Jewish people have understood these words to mean? Look at **Isaiah 51:16**:

"And I have put my words in thy mouth, and I have covered thee in the shadow of mine hand, that I may **PLANT THE HEAVENS, and LAY THE FOUNDATIONS OF THE EARTH**, and say unto **ZION**, Thou art my people."

Planting the heavens and laying the foundations of the earth was symbolical language for Zion's becoming God's people. God did not literally plant the heavens and lay the foundations of the earth at this late date of writing. It has to be symbolical. Therefore, it is only logical that the shaking of the powers of the heavens (and the passing away of the heavens and earth afterward) would mean the utter end of Israel, the ending of what God had planted and set.

You remember that Peter used similar language on the day of Pentecost when he quoted from **Joel 2**: "And I will shew wonders in heaven above, and signs in the earth beneath; blood, and fire, and vapour of smoke: The sun shall be turned into darkness, and the moon into blood, before that great and notable day of the Lord come" **(Acts 2:17, 19-20)**.

These events at Pentecost happened in "the last days" (of the Jewish age), and in connection with the anticipation of the "day of the Lord." This had nothing to do with any prediction of a futuristic (to us) day of the Lord (or Armageddon), but had everything in the world to do with that cataclysmic event of the coming of Christ in judgment upon Israel in those days. This "day of the Lord" occurred with the judgment of God upon Israel in A.D. 67-70. The "blood, and fire, and vapour of smoke" remained as proof that God had come on the scene, and that Jesus was at the right hand of God in Heaven.

If this be objected to on account of the use of the expression, "The day of the Lord," as though it could only apply to our own future, I remind you to look back at the prophecy against Babylon and note that the Lord said, "Behold, the day of the Lord cometh . . ." We need to disassociate from our minds any idea that "the day of the Lord" can only be one event in our own future. Any great judgment time of God upon a nation or group of people could rightly be called "the day of the Lord" (and **was** so called).

Take your exhaustive concordance and look up the numerous times this expression is used in the Old Testament. Notice here several in particular:

Isaiah 13:6 — Against Babylon.

Isaiah 34:8 — Against Idumea, Bozrah and all nations.

Ezekiel 30:2-3 — Against Egypt.

Joel 1:15, 3:14 — Against Israel. (The heavens would tremble, the

sun and moon be darkened, and the stars withdraw their shining).
Zephaniah 1:7, 14 — Against Judah.
Zechariah 14:1 — Against Jerusalem.

So we see in these passages that the wrath of God is displayed in judgment upon unbelieving and rebellious people. This is called "The day of the Lord" in Bible language. There were many such days of the Lord.

Referring to **Joel 2:28-32, C. D. Alexander** said:

"An adequate study of prophecy would soon teach that the figures used in this prophecy — signs in heaven and earth, the darkening of sun and moon, blood, fire and vapour of smoke, have nothing to do with the end of the world, but with the end of the Old Covenant and its earthly administration in the Jewish State. The same figures are frequently used in the Old Testament to denote the removal or overthrow of kingdoms, powers, and ordinances (see Isaiah 13 for example, where the same figures are used for the overthrow of Babylon). Peter's quotation was a warning to the Jewish people of his own day that the time of the removal of their order had come; their kingdom and state were about to go down in blood, and their sun was about to set—as took place in A.D. 70 when nation and Temple were destroyed by the Romans."

John Gill, Baptist theologian and pastor of years ago, said:

". . . **and the powers of the heavens shall be shaken;** meaning all the ordinances of the legal dispensation; which shaking, and even removing of them, were foretold by Haggai, chap. ii. 6, and explained by the author of the Epistle to the Hebrews, chap. xii. 26, 27, whereby room and way were made for Gospel ordinances to take place, and be established; which shall not be shaken, so as to be removed, but remain till the second coming of Christ" (**John Gill,** on Matt. 24:29).

When Jesus said that certain things would take place IMMEDIATELY after that tribulation OF THOSE DAYS, we have no right to interpret this as meaning that a couple of thousand years or so may come between the two. Let's give Jesus credit for knowing how to use language to make it mean what He said. "Immediately" means "immediately" — not later.

Jesus plainly said in **Luke 21:22** that "These be the days of vengeance, THAT ALL THINGS WHICH ARE WRITTEN MAY BE FULFILLED." The events described by Luke were those connected with the destruction of Jerusalem in A.D. 70, and notice that he said "THESE" were the days when all things which were written were to be fulfilled. Not some other days hundreds of years later. These tragic events WERE (not will be) the fulfillment of ALL the remaining prophecies concerning Israel. And if "ALL THINGS" were fulfilled then, how could any of these prophecies relate to Israel in OUR future?

Some Literal Signs Too

While I personally look on these things mentioned as apocalyptic language describing some great event as occurring, I do not mean to say that there were not actual and literal signs seen during those awful days. **Luke 21:25-26** says:

"And there shall be signs in the sun, and in the moon, and in the stars; and upon the earth distress of nations, with perplexity; the sea and the waves roaring;

"Men's hearts failing them for fear, and for looking after those things which are coming on the earth: for the powers of heaven shall be shaken."

There were to be celestial signs, Luke says.

F. W. Farrar, drawing from Josephus, Tacitus, and the Talmud, summed up a few of those things when he said:

"In Jerusalem men told how, at the Passover of A.D. 65, a mysterious light had gleamed for three hours at midnight in the Holiest Place; how the enormous gates of brass, which it required the exertions of twenty men to move, had opened of themselves, and could not be closed; how, at Pentecost, the priests had heard sounds as of departing deities, who said to each other, 'Let us depart thence . . .' " **(Farrar,** p. 416).

It might be well to look at some of the things **Josephus the historian** told us about. He gave us some of the details as he commented on "the destruction also of the entire city, with the signs and wonders that went before it" **(Josephus,** vol. 1, p. 8). In his book of the war of the Jews he said:

". . . while they did not attend, nor give credit, to the signs that were so evident and did so plainly foretell their future desolation; but, like men infatuated, without either eyes to see, or minds to consider, did not regard the denunciations that God made to them. Thus there was a star resembling a sword, which stood over the city, and a comet, that continued a whole year. Thus also, before the Jews' rebellion, and before those commotions which preceded the war, when the people were come in, great crowds to the feast of unleavened bread, on the eighth day of the month Xanthicus (Nisan), and at the ninth hour of the night, so great a light shone round the altar and the holy house, that it appeared to be bright day time; which light lasted for half an hour. This light seemed to be a good sign to the unskilful, but was so interpreted by the sacred scribes, as to portend those events that followed immediately upon it. At the same festival also, a heifer, as she was led by the high-priest to be sacrificed, brought forth a lamb in the midst of the temple. Moreover, the eastern gate of the inner (court of the) temple, which was of brass, and vastly heavy, and had been with difficulty shut by twenty men, and rested upon a basis armed with iron, and had bolts fastened very deep into the firm floor, which was there made of one entire stone, was seen to be opened of its own accord about the sixth hour of the night. Now, those that kept watch in the temple came hereupon running to the captain of the temple, and told him of it: who then came up thither, and not without great difficulty, was able to shut the gate again.''

And then **Josephus** in his account goes on to say:

"But the men of learning understood it, that the security of their holy house was dissolved of its own accord, and that the gate was opened for the advantage of their enemies. So these publicly declared, that this signal foreshowed the desolation that was coming upon them. Besides these, a few days after that feast, on the one-and-twentieth day of the month Artemisius (Jyar), a certain prodigious and incredible phenomenon appeared; I suppose the account of it would seem to be a fable, were it not related by those that saw it, and were not the events that followed it of so considerable a nature as to deserve such signals; for, before sun-setting, chariots and troops of soldiers in their armor were seen running about among the clouds, and surrounding of cities. Moreover at that feast which we call Pentecost, as the priests were going by night into the inner (court of the) temple, as their custom was, to perform their sacred ministrations, they said that, in the first place, they felt a quaking, and heard a great noise, and after that they heard a sound as of a great multitude, saying, 'Let us remove hence' " **(Works of Josephus,** vol. 1, book VI, Chapter V, pp. 453-454).

Luke's parallel account **(Luke 21:25-26)** says:

"And there shall be . . . upon the earth distress of nations, with perplexity; the sea and the waves roaring; Men's hearts failing them for fear, and for looking after those things which are coming on the earth."

"Nations" here could be those that made up the different countries which in their entirety were called Judaea, and included the Jews, the Galileans, the Samaritans, etc. Also, it could refer to the nations of the Roman Empire as well, with so many things taking place and changing about in those days. But more likely, Jesus had in mind those of Judaea, people whose lives were threatened with all the horrors and terrors of those days in the land.

"The 'roaring . . . of the sea' is reminiscent of **Isaiah 17:12**; in biblical prophecy the sea often symbolizes chaos or stands for a source of fear" (**Walter L. Liefeld, Expositor's Bible Commentary,** vol. 8, p. 1022).

Isaiah 17:12-13a says, "Woe to the multitude of many people, which make a noise like the noise of the seas; and to the rushing of nations, that make a rushing like the rushing of mighty waters! The nations shall rush like the rushing of many waters . . ."

The Jewish Talmud tells us that the Rabbis were expecting a coming destruction of Jerusalem. In the section called Toma, folio 39b, it says:

"Our Rabbis taught: During the last forty years before the destruction of the Temple . . . the doors of the **Hekal** would open by themselves, until R. Johanan b. Zakkai rebuked them, saying: **Hekal, Hekal,** why wilt thou be the alarmer thyself? (Note: Predict thy own destruction.) I know about thee that thou wilt be destroyed, for Zechariah ben Ido has already prophesied concerning thee: **Open thy doors, O Lebanon, that the fire may devour thy cedars**" (**The Soncino Talmud,** Seder Mo'ed, vol. III Toma, p. 186).

But all of these literal and natural, heavenly and earth-wise things which we read about occurring in those days, all happened **during** the days of that tribulation period. What verse 30 is telling us is that "the sign of the Son of man in heaven" comes at the **closing** of the tribulation period. "Immediately after the tribulation of those days . . ." (vs. 29). **Luke 21:25** ("there shall be signs") could have been referring to some of these kinds of things we have read about; but the "sign" (singular) of **Matthew 24:30** is something different entirely, which we shall discuss later. At the closing of the tribulation of those days, and following the sun and moon darkening, the stars falling, and the powers of the heavens being shaken, THEN it is that the sign of the Son of man in heaven appears. What this is we shall discuss later at **verse 30**. The Jewish universe collapses following the tribulation period, and then it is SEEN that the Son of man is in heaven at the right hand of power.

But it was after the tribulation of THOSE DAYS — not some future days. And the words of Mark confirm this — "But in those days, after THAT tribulation . . ." (**Mark 13:24**), showing that it cannot refer to any other time than immediately after that, the days of that same tribulation which had just been mentioned, and not some future time of tribulation. Language would not mean anything at all if Jesus had meant "Immediately after the tribulation of those days following at least another 1900 years or so, etc." Why not accept the statement of Jesus exactly as He gave it? If "immediately" does not mean "immediately," then words can be said to mean anything, and we have no way of knowing for sure what Jesus meant. Not only so, if by "immediately" we are told that it means hundreds or even thousands of years later, the wording would not even be grammatically correct, to say the least. **Mark 13:24,** "But in those days, after that tribulation," shows that immediately "after" means "in those days" that followed upon that tribulation. And Jesus said that ALL THINGS WOULD BE FULFILLLED IN THAT GENERATION **(Matthew 24:34).**

Some Bible teachers today imply that this does not mean what it says, but rather that things in the distant future are **looked on** as "imminent" and "soon," etc. For example, **Dr. John Newport** in his book, **The Lion and the Lamb** (Broadman Press, 1986, p. 127), in explaining John's use of the statement, "The time is at hand" in **Revelation 1:3,** says, "Notice that John states in verse 3: 'The time is near:' John, like the other prophets of the Bible, has little interest in exact dates. However, the future is always viewed as imminent." Then he said, "The distant future is always viewed as if it were immediate . . .. We call this the foreshortened future . . .. The foreshortened future concept was employed by John."

This I find difficult to believe. And where Dr. Newport gets his authority for saying that "the foreshortened future concept was employed by John," I do not know. What necessitates a person's accepting such a viewpoint (which is not even good Bible exegesis) is that a preconceived notion is already at hand in the belief that John (and Jesus) were talking NOT about something soon to happen, but about the end of OUR age and a future "second coming" of Christ. Because of this, such an explanation offers an "out" to the problem of John (and Jesus) saying what they did about the time element. I once had this problem too, and sought to find the solution in saying that God blended the "immediate" with the "future" (as two mountain ranges in the distance are seen as one). However, the more I have studied, the more I have come to the conclusion that this is not being honest with the language used by Jesus and John. The best solution to the problem is simply to accept what they said to mean exactly what they said, and what their hearers would have understood as meant by what they said. Of course, such an acknowledgement might change a little of our theology; but who is right — Jesus and John, or OUR theology?

The "Mountain Range" Interpretation

John Albert Bengel, orthodox theologian of the 18th century (1687-1752), was the originator of the "mountain range" interpretation of this discourse, an interpretation I also used a few years ago in my treatment of this passage, though I did not know the origin of it at that time. It was the only answer I could come up with.

In **Bengel's New Testament Commentary**, on Matthew 24:29, Bengel said:

"The English has **immediately**. You will say, it is a great leap from the destruction of Jerusalem to the end of the world, which is subjoined to it **immediately**. I reply, a prophecy resembles a landscape paint-ing, which represents distinctly the houses, paths, and bridges in the foreground, but brings together, into a narrow space, most widely severed valleys and mountains in the distance. Such a view should they who study prophecy have of the future to which the prophecy refers. And the eyes of the disciples, who in their question had connected the end of the temple with that of the world, are left somewhat in the dark (for it was not yet time to know; ver. 36). Hence they afterwards, with entire harmony, imitated the Lord's language, and declared that the end was at hand." (**J.A. Bengel**, vol. 1, p. 274).

But I ask, could Jesus be accused of being so reckless with His own use of language that He would equate the word "immediately" with a period of time extending hundreds (maybe thousands) of years into the distant future? I hardly think so. At least, I had to give up my own point of view on that when I began to see how wrong I was in attributing to Jesus what He did not actually say.

Milton Terry said:

"But we can find no word or sentence which appears designed to impress anyone with the idea that the destruction in question and the parousia would be far separate as to time. The one, it is said, will immediately follow the other, and all will take place before that generation shall pass away (**Milton S. Terry, Biblical Hermeneutics**, note on p. 439).

Then **Terry** asks (p. 443):

"On what valid hermeneutical principle, then, can it be fairly claimed that this discourse of Jesus comprehends all futurity? Why should we look for the revelations of far distant ages and millenniums of human history in a prophecy expressly limited to the generation in which it was uttered?"

Still later, **Terry** said:

"We are driven, then, by every sound principle of hermeneutics, to conclude that Matt. xxiv, 29-31, must be included within the time-limits of the discourse of which it forms an essential part, and cannot be legitimately applied to events far separate from the final catastrophe of the Jewish State." (same, p. 449).

John Broadus was a great scholar and teacher, but it seems to me that he certainly did not use sound Bible exegesis when he said (1886):

"So far as the passage relates to the destruction of Jerusalem, we may suppose that the events it indicates were to follow immediately after those predicted in 15-28. As regards the ulterior reference to the final *parousia* there may prove to be in like manner some close consecution, but only the fulfillment is likely to show" **(Broadus, p. 489).**

It is because of seeing "ulterior reference" to other things further out than what Jesus was talking about, that has created in the minds of many utter confusion as regards our Lord's interest in this passage of Scripture. No matter what we may think (or know) will happen in the future, it is not ours to insert them into these passages and thereby change the ONE meaning that Jesus was expressing to His disciples.

In studying apocalyptic language of the New Testament, I have gone back into the Old Testament — the source for much of the terminology used in the New Testament. As I checked out many of the various places where such language was used, especially in references to times of the Lord's visitation in judgment on nations and peoples, I saw that such language was **much stronger than the actual event itself.** This greatly interested me, for I realized that if it were this way in the Old Testament, the New Testament must be similar — for it was written with Hebrew terminology in mind. So I began to better understand some of the "celestial" and "heavenly" language used in conjunction with earthly events — the sun turning dark, the moon turning into blood, the heavens rolling back as a scroll, the Lord riding in a chariot, or on the wind, or on the clouds, the stars falling from heaven, etc., etc. I began to notice that when reference was made to judgment by the Lord on individuals, or nations, or the world, such language was used. Not that these things happened exactly this way, but it was a picturesque way of God's declaring HIS power, HIS majesty, HIS judgment, etc. But they are examples of GOD Himself being involved in such judgment. In our present study, Matthew 24:29-30 are classic examples of this. Understanding this has also helped me in better understanding the book of Revelation where John used the same kind of expressions.

So we see how Jesus used language that His people would understand — the same kind of language used in the Old Testament when great and mighty events occurred.

Mark and Luke both show that the question of the disciples (which some think referred to two or three different things) actually referred to only one event (or different events happening in the immediate proximity of each other). Notice: "when shall THESE THINGS be? and what shall be the SIGN of THY COMING, and of the end of the world?" and "what SIGN will there be when THESE THINGS shall come to pass?" (**Matthew 24:3** and **Luke 21:7**). Matthew puts the "sign" with His coming, and Luke puts the "sign" with "these things," together indicating they are one and the same in their minds. See also **Mark 13:4** where Mark says, "what shall be the SIGN when ALL these things shall be fulfilled?" If Matthew, Mark and Luke record the same conversation, then it has to be admitted that Jesus' answer referred to one and the same situation — and not two or three different events separated by many hundreds of years. It is unthinkable that the disciples had any other time factor in mind than when Jerusalem and the Temple would be destroyed, and they did connect these events together in His answer. It is only for later Bible students to try to make the chapter refer to different events separated by a period of hundreds or even thousands of years.

If Jesus had meant to include some far-off distant future event in this chapter, surely He would have told them He was talking about something different, but He didn't. He included it all together. So why don't we?

Jesus never said that after many years following the tribulation of THOSE DAYS (**Matthew 24:29**) which He was just describing, that they would see the sign of the Son of man coming, etc. Rather, He said, "IMMEDIATELY after the tribulation of THOSE DAYS . . . ."

This one word, "IMMEDIATELY," was the key word to finally bring me to understand that the coming (*Parousia*) Jesus spoke of came immediately after events leading up to the destruction of Jerusalem and the Temple in A.D. 70.

One may ask, "If these things have already happened, why is the future tense used in speaking of them (prophetically). These things **WERE** future to those in that generation that saw them come to pass; but if they occurred before that generation was over, then it stands to reason that they would not be future to us though they were to them. The same can be said for many of the things in the book of Revelation.

At this point, I am hopeful that it has been clearly shown that the judgment upon Israel, with all its horrible tribulation period, is closely connected with and involved with the coming of the Son of man and the manifestation of His kingdom. This is not to say that the destruction of Jerusalem **itself** was the *parousia*. This is only one of the things that happened in connection with that great event. There is a chronological order involved: (1) The great tribulation period, (2) The heavenly disturbances, with sun and moon darkened, and stars falling, and (3) The sign of the Son of man in heaven (and) the Son of man coming in the clouds of heaven. All of this is connected, but should be kept separate and in order in our minds. The time factor is the same — all happened in that generation. The Jewish age finally came to a close with the destruction of its city and its Temple; the entire Jewish government, economy, rulership, priesthood, rituals, sacrifices, all became dark and fell from heaven, so to speak, and the Son of man was seen sitting at the right hand of God, and coming in the clouds of glory.

Speaking of the parallel passage in **Mark 13:24-27, Ezra P. Gould** said:

"We come now to the coming of the Son of Man, with its accompanying portents, v. 24-27. It is placed after the destruction of Jerusalem, but in the same general period: **in those days, after that affliction.** The portents, the darkening of the sun and moon, and the falling of the stars belong to that event, and not to the destruction of Jerusalem. This separation of the two events which might seem to belong together, means that the fall of Jerusalem is a preparation for the Advent, which cannot take place without it. It is that end of the old order which must precede the beginning of the new" **(Gould, p. 249).**

The words of **Milton Terry** might be helpful here:

"Some expositors fall into the error of **identifying** the coming of the Son of man with the destruction of Jerusalem. These events are rather to be spoken of as coincident, in that the Messianic reign is conceived as following immediately after the tribulation of those days. The overthrow of Jerusalem was only one act of judgment of the King of glory, and should be so distinguished" **(Milton Terry, Biblical Apocalyptics, p. 242).**

In the teachings of Jesus in **Matthew 24,** His prophecy of the "coming of the Son of man" was given with the aspect of judgment upon His enemies (Israel) in mind. Redemption, or deliverance, for His own disciples in that day, was also spelled out. The reason for this is obvious. There were other events that would occur later, at another time; but in this discourse He is dealing with the question of the disciples as to when the Temple would be destroyed at the end of that age, and the coming of the Son of man. God "came" and "descended" many times in the Old Testament at times of judgment upon groups of people. Apocalyptic language was used to describe those events. Why should we not believe that Jesus would employ the same kind of language in His references to the coming wrath to be visited on Israel — language depicting His coming as the Son of man in this manifestation of His kingdom? At the same time, this did not preclude any other such visitation or coming in the future; indeed, we still have the **whole world** to think about, with the resurrection of ALL men from the graves, and a universal judgment that will be greater than just that for Israel. **For that reason, Jesus did not say that these other things would take place at His coming in His generation.**

And I assure you, that if Jesus did not "know the day nor the hour" of the impending destruction of Jerusalem (other than "this generation"), He certainly did not know the day nor the hour of other events that will take place some day later on, and He left those things out of His discourse because they were not involved; and certainly the revelation of any such future dates had not been given to Him by His Father. I venture to suggest that He believed much time would elapse after the destruction of Jerusalem, for He said in **Luke 21:24** that the Jews would "be led away captive into all nations: and Jerusalem shall be trodden down of the Gentiles, until the times of the Gentiles be fulfilled." All of this was to occur in history AFTER the burning and destruction and desolation of Jerusalem in A.D. 70. **Beyond that, His prophecy did not go.**

Section 5 •••••••••••••••••••••••••••

"THE SIGN OF THE SON OF MAN IN HEAVEN"

"And then shall appear the sign of the Son of man in heaven: and then shall all the tribes of the earth mourn, and they shall see the Son of man coming in the clouds of heaven with power and great glory" (Matthew 24:30).

Now we come to that passage in **Matthew 24** where the water really hits the wheel! There is so much to be said on just this one verse that it is necessary we take another complete section after this to deal further with the remaining part of the verse which says, "and they shall see the Son of man coming in the clouds of heaven with power and great glory," in addition to what is said in this section. This is the passage that has had so many varied interpretations. Interpreters (as with many other passages too, of course) just cannot seem to get together on a unified interpretation. But I believe that most expositors of this verse (**vs. 30**) in our times are in error in their interpretation. The main error is that this verse is put into the wrong time frame as to the usage of apocalyptic language here. And thusly, most interpreters fail to see the primary reference to Israel in the first century in relation to this passage.

Keeping in mind all that has already been said in this book on **Matthew 24**, it becomes almost impossible to give any other time factor for this passage than a past fulfilment. This is called the "preterite" or "preterist" interpretation ("preterite" being the adjective, and "preterist" the noun); and the word "preterite" simply means "past," and "preterist" one who holds to that interpretation. The past as we see it in this passage is that of A.D. 70.

Verse 30 with its reference to "the sign of the Son of man in heaven" and "the Son of man coming in the clouds of heaven" is inseparably connected with the same events considered in the previous verse, having to do (as we have tried to show) with the destruction of Jerusalem. And these were things to come to pass in that generation.

Remember, the disciples asked Jesus a three-fold question (**Matthew 24:3**). It involved (1) when the Temple would be destroyed, (2) what would be the sign of His coming, and (3) what would be the sign of the end of the world (age). The disciples did not indicate that they were talking about three different time periods, and the answer of Jesus indicated that all of these things would occur in that generation (see **verse 34**).

It is just not possible to separate these three things into separate time zones separated by hundreds of years. The disciples did not; they evidently thought they would all occur at the same time. And Jesus did not correct their understanding of this. Even dispensationalist and premillennialist **Thomas Ice** acknowledges that, "It is probably true that the disciples thought of the three events (the destruction of the temple, the coming of Christ, and the end of the age) as one event" **(Ice,** p. 271).

From some years back, in my studies of various commentaries, I kept seeing that some of them taught that the coming of the Son of man in **Matthew 24** referred to the coming of Christ in judgment on Jerusalem in A.D. 70 and not to His final coming at the end of the world. So I determined to search out what some of the older commentaries and writings had to say about this.

In September 1987 I was in meetings with several churches in Northern Ireland. On our way back from Ireland, at London my wife and I took a train to Cambridge, where we spent three days in order to do some research work at Cambridge University Library with this in mind. I had secured prior permission for this visit and also secured a letter of introduction from my own John B. Stetson University as per their request. I concentrated my search to the old rare books (1600-1850) on the subjects of the prophecy of **Matthew 24** relating to the coming of Christ in judgment on Jerusalem in A.D. 70, the dating of the book of Revelation, the identification of Babylon in Revelation 17 as old Jerusalem, etc. The library assistants were helpful in locating and bringing to my table a total of twenty-four such rare books containing sermons and commentaries by leading writers of many years ago from various countries, languages and denominations, none published later than 1856. For two and a half days I researched those books, made many pages of notes; and the assistants secured scores and scores of pages of photocopies of the many pages I needed for later reference and study. Evelyn was a terrific help as she searched the catalogue sections and secured information for use by the assistants in locating the books.

The walk each morning and return at night was just twenty-five minutes each way from our hotel, and afforded some of the most pleasant scenery for us to enjoy. We stayed through each day, and had a snack at the library restaurant for lunch.

Cambridge University is made up of many colleges, all in Cambridge, and the tremendous library serves them all. It is similar in some respects to Bodleian Library of Oxford University in Oxford, England, where I also did some research back in May of 1982, and then again for these present studies in April of 1989. (In April 1989

I also researched material at the British Museum Library in London during two of the days I was in meetings with a church in London.) There were a number of books I could not locate at Cambridge Library. In June of the next year, during a trip for meetings in Indiana, we stopped by Southern Baptist Theological Seminary in Louisville, Kentucky (where I had taken summer work in 1958); and we spent three days in the library there following up this matter. The library has the largest collection of religious books in America, I was told. We found many books by the old authors whose writings I wanted to see. I brought home with me about 1,000 pages of photostat copies of things I was looking for on this and other subjects which I needed.

But these were not all the sources for our research material. In addition to Cambridge University Library at Cambridge, England; and Bodleian Library at Oxford University at Oxford, England; and British Museum Library at London, England; and Southern Baptist Theological Seminary Library at Louisville, Kentucky; much less time has been spent at other libraries such as the Baptist College Library at Belfast, Northern Ireland; Southwestern Baptist Theological Seminary Library at Ft. Worth, Texas; Dallas Theological Seminary Library in Dallas, Texas; Trinity College Library in Dublin, Ireland; and Concordia Lutheran Seminary Library at Ft. Wayne, Indiana.

My findings from those books at those libraries, as well as from some other old books which I had in my own library, showed me that prior to the time when dispensationalism began to be promoted and became the major emphasis in eschatology, there were many who believed and taught that the prophecy of **Matthew 24** related to the coming of Christ in judgment on Jerusalem in the year A.D. 70, and that many of these believed that none of this prophecy applied to a final coming of Christ at the end of the world. (A number of them even believed that the **final** coming of Christ at judgment was fulfilled in Matthew 24.) This preterite view of **Matthew 24** (that is, that this prophecy was all fulfilled in A.D. 70) is also substantiated by later writers, though it seems to be true that this view has not been largely held in our own day and time. The emphasis of both the pre-tribulation and the post-tribulation rapturists has dominated the scene to the exclusion of this viewpoint in recent years. The reason for this is that the "great tribulation" of **Matthew 24:21, 29** has been relegated to a time in our future instead of leaving it where it belonged with the events surrounding the destruction of Jerusalem in A.D. 70 and God's wrath upon Israel. And in turn, the reason that this has been done, is because of the statement by Jesus that "IMMEDIATELY

AFTER the tribulation of those days . . . shall appear the sign of the Son of man in heaven: and . . . coming in the clouds of heaven with power and great glory" **(Matthew 24:29-30)**. If the second coming of Christ comes immediately after the tribulation, it has been reasoned, then it is only logical that this all has to be in the future (our future), because the second coming of Christ has not yet occurred. Of course, this creates some problems in trying to separate all this from A.D. 70 and putting it into our future when the rest of the chapter is talking about the events at A.D. 70; but some try to solve that problem by saying there is a "double reference" or else a "double fulfillment" in these prophecies! They say it referred to **both** the destruction of Jerusalem AND the future final coming of Christ, or else that it refers to two different things and different times; one, the destruction of Jerusalem, with the other passages referring to the final coming of Christ in our future. But all of this is pure speculation and not Bible exegesis! The problem is solved in understanding that the coming of the Son of man in **Matthew 24** is a coming of Christ in judgment on Jerusalem which all occurred when Jerusalem was destroyed in A.D. 70, and has nothing in the world to do with a second coming of Christ in our future. This does not preclude any teaching of a final resurrection and judgment elsewhere in the Bible, but this passage should not be manipulated and distorted in order to find the teaching in that chapter.

Another bit of confusion comes from the fact that numerous Bible students confuse "the great tribulation" of **Matthew 24:21, 29** with "the great tribulation" of **Revelation** 7:14. These are not the same, though they deal with approximately the same period of time. They are both represented by the time of 3½ years, but dealing with two different groups of people. The tribulation of **Matthew 24** deals with the trouble and tribulation which **Israel** went through during this awful time of judgment upon Jerusalem and all of Palestine; whereas, the tribulation of **Revelation 7** deals with the dreadful persecution the **Christians** underwent by Rome in those early days of Christianity, but including the persecution they had been enduring under the Jews as well. Concerning that tribulation, John said that he was their "brother, and companion in tribulation" **(Revelation 1:9)**. These two tribulations should not be confused; they relate to two different peoples altogether. It is only natural, then, that if someone believes they are the same tribulation, and they believe that **Revelation 7** refers to some **distant** tribulation just prior to the second coming of Christ, they will also believe that the tribulation of **Matthew 24** refers to the time in the future before the second coming of Christ (or between the rapture and the revelation if they are dispensationalists, which means they would have to put a rapture PRIOR to the tribulation mentioned in **Matthew 24**). But Jesus in **Matthew 24** spoke of "the tribulation OF THOSE DAYS," referring to the events of A.D. 67-70, and not to some later and much more future time. The sign of the Son of man in heaven was to be manifested immediately after the tribulation of THOSE DAYS, Jesus said, and was not something to occur **in the future** at some other time after that.

★★★★★★★★★★★★★★★

"And then shall appear the sign of the Son of man in heaven: and then shall all the tribes of the earth mourn, and they shall see the Son of man coming in the clouds of heaven with power and great glory" (Matthew 24:30).

What is the "sign of the Son of man in heaven"? Cyril, Hilary, Chrysostom, Augustine, Jerome, and Erasmus believed that the sign would be a cross appearing in the heavens. Another refers to the rending of the heaven or the appearing angels. Others felt it would be the star of the Messiah (**Numbers 24:17**). Older expositors thought Jesus meant that **Christ Himself** would be the sign.

"R. Hofman thinks that the reference is to that apparition in the form of a man which is alleged to have stood over the holy of holies for a whole night while the destruction of the capital was going on" (**Meyer's Commentary on the New Testament**, vol. 1, p. 423).

Hal Lindsey said, "Perhaps the 'sign of the Son of Man' will be a gigantic celestial image of Jesus flashed upon the heavens for all to see. This would explain how all men suddenly recognize who He is and see the scars from His piercing at the cross." (**Hal Lindsey, The Late Great Planet Earth**, p. 173).

But a lot of this kind of explanation seems a little ludicrous to me, and certainly speculative, to say the least.

That sign would not be a needed thing for a future generation of Jews 2,000 or more years away. That event was needed in **their** generation then, to vindicate the claims of Jesus in reference to His kingdom, to prove His Messiahship (as the Son of man), and to reveal His vengeance in the destruction of those who had killed Him and punished those early Christians. The expression could hardly be adaptable to some future generation of Jews. It was to the Jews of Jesus' day, who caused His death. Regardless of the unbelief of Jewish people today, present-day Jews are no more responsible for the death of Christ than are Gentile people everywhere. Unsaved Jews and Gentiles alike will face the judgment of God some day, but it was to the Jews of Jesus' generation that this prophecy was directed.

The Sign of the Son of Man in Heaven

"The sign of the Son of man IN HEAVEN" is the sign or proof that the Son of man is "in heaven" (as it says), in fulfillment of Daniel

7:13-14 which predicted that the Son of man would come "with the clouds of heaven" and "TO THE ANCIENT OF DAYS" (in Heaven), to receive His everlasting kingdom. His appearing in judgment was proof of that.

I am going to repeat this, with emphasis, as this is the crux of this whole section:

THE "SIGN OF THE SON OF MAN IN HEAVEN" IS THE SIGN OR PROOF THAT THE SON OF MAN IS "IN HEAVEN" (AS IT SAYS) IN FULFILLMENT OF **DANIEL 7:13-14** WHICH PROPHESIED THAT THE SON OF MAN WOULD COME "WITH THE CLOUDS OF HEAVEN" AND "TO THE ANCIENT OF DAYS" (IN HEAVEN), TO RECEIVE HIS EVERLASTING KINGDOM. HIS APPEARING IN JUDGMENT WAS THE PROOF OF THAT.

The very act of God's destruction of the Temple and Jerusalem itself through the instrumentality of the Roman armies was the manifestation of the power and glory of the Son of man, and it was proof to the Jewish people of the Messiahship of the Lord Jesus Christ. Apocalyptic language is used to describe the catastrophic events that took place at that time.

Remember, the disciples had asked, "WHAT shall be the sign of thy coming, and of the end of the world [age]?" **(Matthew 24:3)**. And now here Jesus is saying that after the abomination of desolation, after the great tribulation, after the powers that be fall from their lofty positions, then—THEN—it is that they will see the sign of the SON OF MAN IN HEAVEN! All that has happened ends up in climactic proof that Jesus Christ is in Heaven, reigning at the right hand of the Father, and judging His enemies on earth. Now is His *parousia*/coming! Now is His revelation of His power and glory! Now is the Son of Man seen coming in His kingdom!

J. Marcellus Kik said:

"The judgment upon Jerusalem was the sign of the fact that the Son of man was reigning in heaven. There has been misunderstanding due to the reading of this verse, as some have thought it to be 'a sign in heaven.' But this is not what the verse says; it says the sign of the **Son of man in heaven**. The phrase 'in heaven' defines the locality of the Son of man and not of the sign. A sign was not to appear in the heavens, but the destruction of Jerusalem was to indicate the rule of the Son of man in heaven" **(J. Marcellus Kik, An Eschatology of Victory**, p. 137).

David Chilton said:

"The destruction of Jerusalem was the sign that the Son of Man, the Second Adam, was in heaven, ruling over the world and disposing it for His own purposes. At His ascension, He had come on the cloud of heaven to receive the Kingdom from His Father; the destruction of Jerusalem was the revelation of this fact. In Matthew 24, therefore, Jesus was not prophesying that He would literally come on the clouds in A.D. 70 (although it was **figuratively** true). His literal "coming on the clouds," in fulfillment of Daniel 7, took place in A.D. 30, at the beginning of the 'terminal generation.' But in A.D. 70 the tribes of Israel would see the destruction of the nation as the result of His having ascended to the throne of heaven, to receive His kingdom." **(David Chilton, The Great Tribulation, p. 25)**.

In another book, **Paradise Restored, David Chilton** said:

" . . . the location spoken of is **heaven**, not just the **sky**; second, it is not the **sign** which is in heaven, but **the Son of Man** who is in heaven. The point is simply that this great judgment upon Israel, the destruction of Jerusalem and the Temple, will be the sign that **Jesus Christ is enthroned in heaven at the Father's right hand, ruling over the nations and bringing vengeance upon His enemies**. The divinely ordained cataclysm of A.D. 70 revealed that Christ had taken the Kingdom from Israel and given it to the Church; the desolation of the old Temple was the final sign that God had deserted it and was now dwelling in a new Temple, the Church" **(David Chilton, Paradise Restored, p. 100)**.

The wording of this passage refers us back to the expression, "The Son of man," as found in **Daniel 7:13**, which expression Jesus had used concerning Himself when referring to His coming (*parousia*) in the events associated with the destruction of Jerusalem and the Temple. In **Daniel 7:13-14** the Son of man was seen coming with the clouds of heaven to the Ancient of days and receiving His everlasting kingdom. This was a prophecy which was finally fulfilled in the ascension of Jesus to the Father (see **Acts 2:30-26**).

Even though the kingdom was given to Christ upon His ascension to the Father, it remained for the manifestation of this to be seen in some way by all of Israel. Jesus said that this took place in those final events leading up to the destruction of Jerusalem and the Temple in A.D. 70 Here was the "sign" that JESUS was the fulfillment of the Son of man who was seen in Daniel coming in the clouds of heaven **(Daniel 7:13)**. He WAS the Son of man "coming in the clouds of heaven" **(Matthew 24:30)**. This great calamitous ending of the city of Jerusalem and the Temple was this SIGN. It fulfilled what Jesus had said that Caiaphas the high priest would see. Caiaphas had asked Jesus if He were the Christ (Messiah), the Son of God. Jesus told him yes, and added, "Hereafter shall ye see the Son of man sitting on the right hand of power, and coming in the clouds of heaven" (**Matthew 26:64**). Caiaphas understood Jesus' prediction as a claim to Messiahship, as evidenced by his statement in the next verse, "He hath spoken blasphemy." The words of Jesus were symbolical and apocalyptic language, of course. Caiaphas would see BOTH Jesus "sitting on the right hand of power" (signifying authority) **and** "coming in the clouds of heaven" (signifying fulfillment in Jesus the "Son of man" [in **Daniel 7:13**] and Messiah). Not only he, if he were still living at the time, but all others of that generation too, saw this prediction fulfilled in those momentous days of A.D. 70 in the events of the complete destruction of all that he as high priest stood for.

No wonder Caiaphas "rent his clothes" when Jesus first told him this; but if Caiaphas was present at Jerusalem or nearby when these things happened, he would surely have been reminded of what Jesus had said.

They destroyed His Temple, and forty years later He destroyed theirs.

Milton Terry said:

"Matthew reads (xxvi, 64), 'From this time . . . ye shall see the Son of man sitting at the right hand of power, and coming on the clouds of heaven.' We maintain that this language cannot be naturally interpreted as a reference to an event belonging to a far distant period of time. It is something that is to take place **from this time onward**, and something which the high priest and his associates are to see. We quote with great satisfaction the comment of Gould in the **International Critical Commentary on Mark** (p. 252): 'This settles two things: first, that the coming is not a single event, any more than the sitting on the right hand of power; and second, that it was a thing which was to begin with the very time of our Lord's departure from the world. Moreover, the two things, the sitting on the right hand of power, and the coming are connected in such a way as to mean that he is to assume power in heaven and exercise it here in the world. The period beginning with the departure of Jesus from the world was to be marked by this assumption of heavenly power by the Christ, and by repeated interferences in crises of the world's history, of which the destruction of Jerusalem was the first' " (**Milton Terry, Biblical Apocalyptics,** pp. 222-223).

Of this verse, **John Lightfoot said:**

"**And then shall appear the sign of the Son of man.** Then shall **the Son of man** given a proof of himself, who they would not before acknowledge: a proof, indeed, not in any visible figure, but in vengeance and judgment so visible, that all the tribes of the earth shall be forced to acknowledge him the avenger. The Jews would not know him: now they shall know him, whether they will or no, Isa. xxvi. II. Many times they asked of him a **sign**: now a **sign** shall appear, that he is the true Messiah, whom they despised, derided, and crucified, namely, his signal vengeance and fury, such as never any nation felt from the first foundations of the world" (**John Lightfoot**, vol. 2, p. 320).

The destruction of Jerusalem was the outward and visible proof of the coming of the Son of man.

Tribes of the Earth Mourn

"... and then shall all the tribes of the earth mourn..." (**Matthew 24:30**).

The Jewish world came tumbling down in A.D. 70. The Jewish nation was decimated. The outward symbols of the old covenant, the ritualistic elements of the old religious system, the holy place (including the land, the city and the Temple) were completely destroyed. Nothing like this had ever happened to the Jewish people. For them, heaven and earth passed away. The world had ended. And it took all of this to show to them how wrong they had been in what they had done to Jesus Christ and then to His followers. But Jesus had promised that this would happen. And now "all the tribes of the earth [land] mourn." "All the tribes of the earth [land]" refers to the Jewish people who were divided into twelve tribes.

"And I will pour upon the house of David, and upon the inhabitants of Jerusalem, the spirit of grace and of supplications: and they shall look upon me whom they have pierced, and they shall mourn for him, as one mourneth for his only son, and shall be in bitterness for him, as one that is in bitterness for his firstborn.

"In that day shall there be a great mourning in Jerusalem, as the mourning of Hadadrimmon in the valley of Megiddon" (**Zechariah 12:10-11**).

We know that the above Scripture involved fulfillment at the death of Christ first of all, for that is where they actually and physically saw Him on the cross wounded for their transgressions (see **John 19:37**). It was in reference to the wounds inflicted upon Jesus at the time of His death that it could be asked, "What are these wounds in thine hands?" (**Zechariah 13:6**). And it was "in that day" (**Zechariah 13:1**) that "there shall be a fountain opened to the house of David and to the inhabitants of Jerusalem for sin and for uncleanness" (**Zechariah 13:1**).

But what happened at the cross (and prior) brought about the utter destruction and desolation of Jerusalem—that day of the Lord that had been promised upon Israel.

"Behold, the day of the LORD cometh, and thy spoil shall be divided in the midst of thee.

"For I will gather all nations against Jerusalem to battle; and the city shall be taken, and the houses rifled, and the women ravished; and half of the city shall go forth into captivity, and the residue of the people shall not be cut off from the city" **(Zechariah 14:1-2).**

This brought about the greatest time of mourning that Israel had ever seen. And it was in connection with this that the Bible says:

"And his feet shall stand in that day upon the mount of Olives, which is before Jerusalem . . . and the LORD my God shall come, and all the saints with thee" **(Zechariah 14:4,5).**

Be sure to notice the constant reference in Zechariah 13 and 14 of "in that day." It is all involved together.

And the "living waters" of **Zechariah 14:8** are the living waters of **Ezekiel 47:1-12** which pre-figured the "water of life" of **Revelation 22:1-2** which flows through the holy city, the New Jerusalem, the church, and which Jesus Himself promised in **John 7:37-39** as He referred to "as the scripture hath said," and which he identified as the Holy Spirit who would be given following His ascension and glorification.

The entire sermon of Peter in **Acts 2:14-36** was in connection with this coming "day of the Lord" (vs. 20) with the prior outpouring of the Holy Spirit upon the disciples (**vss. 17-18**). Three thousand of the Israelites mourned and repented at that time and were saved and received the promise that had been made to them. But to rebellious and sinful Israel as a whole, the final climax and culmination of the wrath of God upon the people came about with the "day of the Lord," involving the complete destruction of Jerusalem.

"And then shall appear the sign of the Son of man in heaven: and then shall all the tribes of the earth [land] mourn **(Matthew 24:30).**

This has reference to the tribes of Israel mourning. This is not talking about what happens to a Gentile world at some later time. There were "tribes" of Israel at that time, when Israel was destroyed in A.D. 70, but since then there have not been any such things as "tribes" of Israel, and no, never shall be. **Gentiles** are not referred to as "tribes" in the Bible.

"Behold, he cometh with clouds; and every eye shall see him, and they also which pierced him: and all kindreds of the earth [land] shall wail because of him" **(Revelation 1:7).**

You cannot literalize all of this into actual materialistic and physical events with reference to a coming of Christ to the Mount of Olives again at some time in our future. Much of this great affair is explained from the spiritual viewpoint by the Bible itself. We are trying to point out the clues and the explanations as we move along in this series.

Following the statement concerning the appearance of the sign of the Son of man in heaven, and that of all the tribes in the land mourning, it then says that "they shall see the Son of man coming in the clouds of heaven with power and great glory." We discussed this matter of the coming of the Son of man under **verse 27**, and more will be said later. It is necessary to see this not as a physical, bodily coming of Christ, but as an "apocalyptic" coming. Jesus did not have to be bodily present there in order for His presence to be perceived.

In **Exodus 19** it states that on Mount Sinai "the LORD descended upon it in fire" (**vs. 18**), "And the LORD came down upon mount Sinai, on the top of the mount (**vs. 20**)." But no one saw Him in bodily form or shape. Did Jesus have to appear in bodily and physical form in A.D. 70 in order to "come" at that time?

This is the heart of what is discussed in this series — that Jesus Christ did come in A.D. 70, but not in bodily and physical form.

The newly-published commentary of the Sunday School Board of the Southern Baptist Convention says:

"Jesus portrays his return with the typical apocalyptic imagery of cosmic upheaval. He does not intend his language to be taken as a literal scientific description of events but as a vivid metaphor, much as we speak of earth-shaking developments" **(Craig L. Blomberg, The New American Commentary**, vol. 22, p. 362). Dr. Blomberg was not a preterist, but his language is significant.

In my investigation and research into many, many books on this subject, I have yet to find a single author who satisfactorily and with proper Bible exegesis explained how this chapter could deal with both the destruction of Jerusalem and also a future (to us) second coming of Christ. Those who try to do so are up against a hard place, and they disagree among themselves as to which verses refer to which subject. This is dealt with more in detail in Section 9.

Present-day students of eschatology seem woefully ignorant of the writings of past theologians on these subjects. There was a time (prior to the mid-1800's) when the most prominent interpretation of **Matthew 24** was from the preterite standpoint, and the dating of the book of Revelation was believed to be at an earlier date than is now believed. In fact, it was believed by many that part of the prophecies of **Revelation** had to do with the destruction of Jerusalem ("that great city" which was responsible for "the blood of prophets and saints" **(Revelation 17:6, 18:8, 21, 24)**. As time went on, the emphasis changed and many reverted to the later date for **Revelation**; and as dispensationalism gained a foothold everywhere, the emphasis on **Matthew 24** having been completely fulfilled in A.D. 70 began to wane. In our own day and time, dispensationalism has been holding the frontlines in eschatology everywhere it seems, except that more scholars are now coming to the preterite position again. Many are now holding to an earlier date for Revelation, and many are accepting that there is no FUTURE tribulation and *"parousia"* taught in **Matthew 24** but that all was fulfilled in A.D. 67-70 as God's judgment on Israel. The preterite (past fulfillment) interpretation of both **Matthew 24** and the book of Revelation is gaining ground all over the country.

One dispensationalist author, editor and pastor, graduate of Dallas Theological Seminary (**Thomas Ice**), in a letter to me dated September 20, 1989, said:

"Many are moving toward a preterist interpretation of the Olivet Discourse and Revelation in our day. It is coming full cycle since the days of Darby. I have a very large collection of literature advocating that view, which was a very prominent view among both liberals and evangelicals 100-150 years ago."

And then he added in a letter of November 30, 1989, "I do think that dispensationalism will continue to grow increasingly unpopular as we head into the 1990's." (These statements do not mean that Dr. Ice himself is changing from a dispensationalist — far from it; but they simply indicate that he recognizes the reality of what is going on today among those who are studying eschatology.)

What the Older Authors Said About the Coming of the Son of Man in Matthew 24

It is purposeful on my part to review a number of authors of earlier years, giving sizeable quotations from a few of them, in order to give a larger perspective of the subject at hand than I could possibly do with simply my own words. Also, the weight of influence in this manner should be helpful in establishing the validity of the things I am trying to say. In other words, is it difficult to believe what I am saying if all these reputable authors of many years ago believed and taught the same thing? While it is true that some others of many years ago believed otherwise, yet the point is that my interpretation of these matters is not independent, but held by many scholars and commentaries of many years gone by. The books studied and referenced are only a drop in the bucket compared to all that is available, but my quotations may be fairly representative of the whole. We need to see what was taught before the days of dispensationalism began to take over. We shall take a look at a few dealing with just this passage in **Matthew 24:30** for example, and then come on up closer home.

Henry Hammond (1681)

One of the oldest of the writers was **Henry Hammond,** whose 949-page book, **Paraphrase and Annotations Upon All the Books of the New Testament** (5th edition corrected), was printed in London in 1681. On the question asked by the disciples in **Matthew 24:3** he said:

"**Coming** . . . the presence, or the coming of Christ is one of the phrases that is noted in this book to signifie the destruction of the Jews . . . A threefold **coming** of **Christ** there is, 1. in the flesh to be born among us, 2. at the day of doom to judge the **world, I. Corinthians 15:23.** and in many other places; and beside these, 3. a middle coming, partly in vengeance, and partly for the deliverance of his servants; in vengeance, visible, and observable on his enemies and crucifiers, (and first on the people of the Jews, those of them that remain impenitent unbelievers) and in mercy to the relief of the persecuted Christians. So 'tis four times in this chap. v. 27, 37, 39, and here.

" . . . That this is the meaning of his **coming in glory with his angels,** Matt. 16:27 hath been shewed already. So again Matt. 26:64, his coming **in the clouds of heaven,** though it may be thought to look toward his final third coming at the great day of doom, yet as the very Jews have observed, that that phrase signifies the infliction of judgment or punishment, so that it doth so there . . . " **(Henry Hammond, p. 119).**

Thomas Newton (1754)

In May of 1982 I came across an old rare book in the library of Cinderford Baptist Church in Cinderford, England, where I was preaching in eight days of meetings. The books in this library were going to be disposed of, and I was told that I could have this book entitled, **Dissertations on the Prophecies,** by **Thomas Newton,** written in 1754 and published in London in 1840. I note that some noted writers have quoted from this old book, so I feel fortunate to have it in my possession. (My copy evidently was not the first edition, for I find **N. Nisbett** quoting some of these same words in his own book which was printed in 1802.) Dr. Newton gathered much of his information from Eusebius, Josephus, the Jewish Talmud, etc., and his section on **Matthew 24** is a veritable storehouse of information because of this. Even though Thomas Newton was a premillennialist, his treatment of **Matthew 24** is as scholarly, historical and Scriptural as anything I have come across. He had no questions about the truthfulness of the Bible in these matters. Dr. Newton was Lord Bishop of Bristol and Dean of St. Paul's, London. He was born at Lichfield, England, on either December 21, 1703, or January 1, 1704 (I found two dates on his birth).

The book by Dr. Newton is 730 pages, and there are 69 pages given over to the prophecy of the destruction of Jerusalem in A.D. 70. On verses 29-30 (p. 374), Dr. **Newton** said the following:

" 'The coming of Christ' is also the same period with the destruction of Jerusalem, as may appear from several places in the Gospels, and particularly from these two passages; 'There are some standing here,' saith our blessed Lord, 'who shall not taste of death till they see the Son of Man coming in his kingdom,' Matt. xvi. 28, that is, evidently, there are some standing here who shall live, not till the end of the world, to the coming of Christ to judge mankind, but till the destruction of Jerusalem, to the coming of Christ in judgment upon the Jews. In another place, John xxi.22, speaking to Peter concerning John, he saith, 'If I will that he tarry till I come, what is that to thee?' what is it to thee, if I will that he live till the destruction of Jerusalem? as in truth he did, and long. 'The coming of Christ,' and 'the conclusion of the age,' being, therefore only different expressions to denote the same period with the destruction of Jerusalem, the purpose of the question plainly is, when shall the destruction on Jerusalem be, and what shall be the signs of it?' "

Then later, on pages 408-409, Dr. **Newton** said the following:

" 'Immediately after the tribulation of those days shall the sun be darkened, and the moon shall not give her light, and the stars shall fall from heaven, and the powers of the heavens shall be shaken.' Commentators generally understand this, and what follows, of the end of the world, and of Christ's coming to judgment; but the words 'immediately after the tribulation of those days,' show, evidently, that he is not speaking of any distant but of something immediately consequent upon the tribulation before mentioned, and that must be the destruction of Jerusalem . . . .

"Our Saviour proceedeth in the same figurative style, ver. 30 — 'And then shall appear the sign of the Son of Man in heaven; and then shall all the tribes of the earth mourn, and they shall see the Son of Man coming in the clouds of heaven, with power and great glory.' The plain meaning of it is, that the destruction of Jerusalem will be such a remarkable instance of divine vengeance, such a signal manifestation of Christ's power and glory, that all the Jewish tribes shall mourn, and many will be led from thence to acknowledge Christ and the Christian religion. In the ancient prophets, God is frequently described as coming in the 'clouds,' upon any remarkable interposition and manifestation of his power; and the same description is here applied to Christ. The destruction of Jerusalem will be as ample a manifestation of Christ's power and glory as if he was himself to come visibly in the clouds of heaven."

Then later, commenting on the verses of Matthew 24 down through verse 34, **Dr. Newton** said:

"It is to me a wonder how any man can refer part of the foregoing discourse to the destruction of Jerusalem, and part to the end of the world, or any other distant event, when it is said so positively here in the conclusion, 'All these things shall be fulfilled in this generation.' It seemeth as if our Saviour had been aware of some such misapplication of his words, by adding yet greater force and emphasis to his affirmation, ver. 35 — 'Heaven and earth shall pass away, but my words shall not pass away' " (p. 426).

N. Nisbett (1802)

At Cambridge University Library I found a book by **N. Nisbett**, printed in 1802, with this long title: **The Triumphs of Christianity Over Infidelity Displayed, or, the Coming of the Messiah, The True Key to the Right Understanding of the Most Difficult Passages in the New Testament.** In this book **Nisbett** said:

"To suppose, on the contrary, that these verses were intended to describe the final judgment of the world, is indeed violently to sever them from their manifest connection — not only with the preceding verses — but, as will presently appear, from the subsequent context; which, in the strongest terms which language can convey, asserts that all the things which he had before been describing, would be in that generation. It would be to violate all the rules of probability and just criticism and to charge the Evangelical Historians with such a confusion of ideas and such a perversion of language as would render them utterly unworthy of any regard; for, as the learned University Preacher has very justly observed — 'whenever the same word is used in the same sentence — or in different sentences, not far distant from each other; we ought to interpret it precisely, in the same sense, unless either that sense should involve a contradiction of ideas — or the Writer expressly informs us that he repeats the word in a fresh acceptation' " (p. 112).

Then on page 131 he said, " . . . the whole of the xxivth of Matthew, and particularly the 36th and following verses, relate solely to **the destruction of Jerusalem,** exclusively of **a second coming,** and of **the end of the world.**"(N. Nisbett, **The Triumphs of Christianity Over Infidelity Displayed,** Printed for the author by J. Atkinson, Deal, England, 1802, pp. 112, 131).

John Gill (1809)

Writing on this verse (**Matthew 24:30**) in his **Exposition of the New Testament** (1809) in vol. 2, p. 239, premillennialist **John Gill,** Baptist theologian and a predecessor of Charles H. Spurgeon, said:

" . . . he shall appear, not in person, but in the power of his wrath and vengeance, on the Jewish nation; which will be a full sign and proof of his being come: for the sense is, that when the above calamities shall be upon the civil state of that people, and there will be such changes in their ecclesiastical state; it will be as clear a point, that Christ is come in the flesh, and that he is also come in his vengeance on that nation, for their rejection and crucifixion of him, as if they had seen him appear in person in the heavens. They had been always seeking a sign, and were continually asking one of him; and now they will have a sign with a witness; as they had accordingly. **And then shall the tribes of the earth, or land, mourn,** that is, the land of Judea; for other lands and countries were not usually divided into tribes, as that was; neither were they affected with the calamities and desolations of it, and the vengeance of the Son of man upon it; at least not so as to mourn on that account, but rather were glad and rejoiced: and **they shall see the Son of man coming in the clouds of heaven with power and great glory.** The Arabic version reads it, **ye shall see,** as is expressed by Christ in ch. xxvi. 64, where the high-priest, chief priests, Scribes, and elders, and the whole sanhedrim of the Jews are spoken to: and as the same persons, namely, the Jews, are meant here as there; so the same coming of the Son of man is intended; not his coming at the last day of judgment; though that will be in the clouds of heaven, and with great power and glory; but his coming to bring on, and give the finishing stroke to the destruction of that people, which was a dark and cloudy dispensation to them: and when they felt the power of his arm might, if not blind and stupid to the last degree, see the glory of his person, that he was more than a mere man, and no other than the Son of God, whom they had despised, rejected, and crucified; and who came to set up his kingdom and glory in a more visible and peculiar manner, among the Gentiles."

Thomas Scott (1817)

Thomas Scott was rector of Aston Sanford, Bucks, and Chaplain to Lock Hospital in England. The sixth American edition of his commentary was published in 1817. On verses 29-31 Scott said:

"The language of these verses is suited, and probably was intended, to lead the mind of the reader to the consideration of the end of the world, and the coming of Christ to judgment: yet the expression, 'immediately after the tribulation of those days,' must restrict the primary sense to them, to the destruction of Jerusalem, and the events that were consequent to it. (**Notes, Is.** xiii, 10: xxxiv, 3-7. **Jer.** iv, 23-25. **Marg. Ref.**). The darkening of the sun and moon, the falling of the stars, and the shaking of the powers of the heavens, denote the utter extinction of the light of prosperity and privilege to the Jewish nation; the unhinging of their whole constitution in church and state; the violent subversion of the authority of their princes and priests; and the abject miseries to which the people in general, especially their chief persons, would be reduced, and the moral darkness to which they would be consigned. This would be an evident **sign** and demonstration of the Son of man's exaltation to his throne in heaven; whence he would come in his divine providence, as riding upon 'the clouds of heaven with power and great glory', to destroy his enemies, who would 'not have him to reign over them;' at which events all the tribes of the land would mourn and lament, whilst they saw the tokens and felt the weight of his terrible indignation." **(Thomas Scott,,** vol. 1).

It must be said that Thomas Scott added that "the whole passage will have a more literal and august accomplishment at the day of judgment." It is difficult for me to understand this statement, for after vss. 32-35 on the timing of these things, he said, "This absolutely restricts our primary interpretation of the prophecy to the destruction of Jerusalem, which took place within forty years." If the prophecy related to the destruction of Jerusalem, then we have no authority to give a double sense to it and say that it also applies to another event in our future.

This is the error of a number of expositors: while they very strongly believe that all of **Matthew 24** is a prediction of what would happen in A.D. 70, they turn right around and say that the passage will ALSO have a more literal fulfillment in our future. Honestly, this is doing injustice to the passage of Scripture with such interpretation, and adding to it what it does not say. At the same time, we do need to see what these older authors had to say about the passage as relating directly to the events of A.D. 70.

Adam Clarke (1837)

Adam Clarke, in his commentary on this verse, said:

"**Then shall appear the sign of the Son of man.** The plain meaning of this is, that the destruction of Jerusalem will be such a remarkable instance of Divine vengeance, such a signal manifestation of Christ's power and glory, that all the **Jewish tribes** shall mourn, and many will, in consequence of this manifestation of God, be led to acknowledge Christ and his religion. By . . . **of the land,** in the text, is evidently meant here, as in several other places, the **land of Judea** and its **tribes,** either its then **inhabitants,** or the Jewish people wherever found" **(Adam Clarke,** commentary on **Matthew 24:30).**

P. S. Desprez (1854)

P. S. Desprez was the evening lecturer of Collegiate Church, and

Senior Curate of St. George's, Wolverhampton, England. In his book, **The Apocalypse Fulfilled,** he made this simple strong statement:

"... Lord came, as he said, to destroy Jerusalem, and to close the dispensation" **(P. S. Desprez, The Apocalypse Fulfilled,** Preface, p. vi).

Carl August Auberlen (1856)

Dr. Carl August Auberlen was a Doctor of Philosophy, "Licentiage and Professor Extrordinarius of Theology" in Basil, Switzerland. His book, **The Prophecies of Daniel and The Revelation of St. John,** was translated by Rev. Adolph Saphir and published in 1856. Dr. Auberlen was a premillennialist. He made this statement:

"... Christ Himself represents the destruction of Jerusalem as His Messianic coming (Matt. xxiv. 28)." **(Carl August Auberlen, The Prophecies of Daniel and The Revelation of St. John,** p. 101).

David Brown (1858)

In my library is an old book written by **David Brown** in 1858, entitled **Christ's Second Coming: Will It Be Premillennial?** Dr. Brown was a postmillennialist. He was Professor of Divinity, Free Church College, Aberdeen, Scotland, and was one of the editors of the highly respected **Jamieson, Faucett and Brown Commentary** on the Bible. I have had this book on hand since at least 1957, since it was reproduced and distributed by The Old Paths Book Club in 1953. Here is what he says with reference to **Matthew 24:29-31:**

"... What is the direct and primary sense of the prophecy? Those who have not directed their attention to prophetic language will be startled if I answer, The coming of the Lord here announced is his **coming in judgment against Jerusalem** — to destroy itself and its temple, and with them the peculiar standing and privileges of the Jews as the visible Church of God, and set up 'the kingdom of heaven' (or gospel kingdom) in a manner more palpable and free than could be done while Jerusalem was yet standing. I say this application of the words, as their direct and primary sense, will probably startle those unacquainted with the prophetic style. But all hesitation on the subject will cease if we will but allow the Scripture to be its own interpreter" (p. 434).

Then in a footnote, Dr. Brown quotes **Dr. Urwick** from the book **Second Advent,** page 5, as saying:

" 'Many attempts,' says Dr. Urwick, 'have been made to anatomize this prophecy, and exhibit separately the parts which relate to the invasion of Jerusalem by Titus, and the parts which regard the judgment of the world at the last day. I have not met with any thing satisfactory in this way. If any man could have done it well, Bishop

Horsley was the man: he had learning, ingenuity, power, and determination enough for it. Yet one cannot read the sermon in which he attempts to separate the prophecy of the 'coming' from the prophecy of the destruction of Jerusalem, without feeling that a giant is grappling with a difficulty he cannot master. The statement of our Lord, 'Verily I say unto you, This generation shall not pass, till these things be fulfilled,' puts it, I think, beyond question, that the whole range of the prediction was to have an accomplishment before the then race of human beings should all have died from the face of the earth "(**David Brown,** p. 441).

Henry Cowles (1881)

"This passage is too closely connected with what immediately precedes and immediately follows, to be wrenched out of these connections and applied definitely to the final judgment" (**Henry Cowles, Matthew and Mark,** p. 27).

Incidentally, someone may wonder why these writers of some years back usually spoke in terms of the events of 70 A.D. applying only to that time and not to "the final judgment" instead of saying that they did not apply to the Rapture, future Great Tribulation period, etc. The reason is simply that back then, the dispensational ideas of a pre-tribulation rapture, etc., were not even being taught (had not really had time to be promoted much since its invention a few years prior). What Christians in those days believed was simply that Christ will come some day and raise the dead and judge the world.

The Baptist Faith and Message statement adopted by the Southern Baptist Convention in 1963 says:

"God, in His own time and in His own way, will bring the world to its appropriate end. According to His promise, Jesus Christ will return personally and visibly in glory to the earth; the dead will be raised; and Christ will judge all men in righteousness."

Nothing is said about a tribulation period, nor a millennial period here, either. I know that 1963 is not too far back, but this statement was in harmony with other preceding statements of faith. This belief as stated has characterized most of the church creeds through the years. The older writers, writing before the days when dispensational teachings were in full swing, simply spoke of the "final judgment," and wanted to distinguish the events of **Matthew 24** from that coming day. These writers did not believe that **Matthew 24** was teaching primarily about events to take place **in our future.**

F. W. Farrar (1882)

F. W. Farrar, Fellow of Trinity College, Cambridge, Canon of Westminster, and Chaplain in Ordinary to the Queen, said:

"... the contemplated coming was first fulfilled in the catastrophe which closed the Jewish dispensation, and the inauguration of the last age of the world" **(Farrar,** p. 429).

John A. Broadus (1886)

Dr. John A. Broadus (1827-1895, Baptist author, preacher, and president of Southern Baptist Theological Seminary from 1889 until 1895) also said that this last public discourse of Jesus was an unfolding of what He had previously said to His disciples in **Matthew 16:27-28** where He had said:

"For the Son of man shall come in the glory of his Father, with his angels; and then he shall reward every man according to his works. Verily I say unto you, There be some standing here, which shall not taste of death, till they see the Son of man coming in his kingdom."

Dr. Broadus said, "Six months earlier (in 16:27 f.) he had declared that he would come again in the glory of his Father, as the sovereign Judge of mankind; and that some of them then present would live to see him 'coming in his kingdom.' We there found it necessary to understand that the particular coming to which this last phrase especially refers took place at the destruction of Jerusalem, which made Christianity completely and manifestly distinct from Judaism, and established the Messianic kingdom in its permanent present state. The prediction then briefly made by our Lord is now more fully unfolded" **(John A. Broadus,,** vol. 1, Matthew, p. 479).

Then later, Dr. Broadus has another interesting statement. While he believed that the final coming of Christ is referred to in **Matthew 25:31-46**, he believed that **much more** of both **Matthew 24** and **25** (down to Matthew 25:31) referred to the destruction of Jerusalem and NOT a future (to us) second coming of Christ than most commentators today would acknowledge. He said:

"It is practically impossible to suppose that v. 30 f. relates **simply** to the destruction of Jerusalem. As the latter part of the discourse (25:31-46) clearly refers to the second coming of our Lord, it seems unavoidable to suppose a similar reference here; see also the corresponding passage, 13:41. But v. 34 will presently declare that 'all' the foregoing matter will occur during the existing generation. Then we cannot believe (with Meyer and others) that the Saviour mistakenly expected his *parousia* to be within that generation, it follows that v. 29-31 must refer to the destruction of Jerusalem" **(John A. Broadus,** vol. 1, p. 491).

Ezra P. Gould (1896)

Rev. Ezra P. Gould, Professor of New Testament Literature and Language, Divinity School of the Protestant Episcopal Church, Philadelphia, in his commentary on **Mark,** speaks of the interpretation which he held concerning the coming of the Son of man as recorded in both **Matthew** and **Mark**. He said:

"A third interpretation, the one adopted here, holds that the event predicted in the second part did take place in that generation, and in connection with the destruction of Jerusalem. The event itself, and the signs of it, interprets according to the analogy of prophecy, figuratively. It finds numerous instances of such use in O.T. prophecy. God coming in the clouds of heaven with his angels, and preceded or announced by disturbances in the heavenly bodies, is the ordinary prophetic manner of describing any special Divine interference in the affairs of nations. See especially Dan. 7:13, 14, 27, where this language is used of the coming of the Son of Man, i.e. of the kingdom of the saints, to take the place of the world-kingdoms. The prophecy becomes thus a prediction of the setting up of the kingdom, and especially of its definite inauguration as a universal kingdom, with the removal of the chief obstacle to that in the destruction of Jerusalem" (**Ezra P. Gould,** p. 241).

Milton S. Terry (1898)

Milton S. Terry, 19th century Methodist Episcopalian, graduate of Yale Divinity School, pastor of churches, and professor of Hebrew and Old Testament exegesis and theology at Garrett Biblical Institute, said in reference to **Matthew 24:**

". . . all these sayings of Jesus are capable of a self-consistent and satisfactory explanation of a prophecy of what was in the near future when he uttered them. The overthrow of the Jewish temple and the subsequent going forth of the new kingdom of Christ in the world are the main subject. We adopt this hypothesis as the only tenable explanation of the language which all three synoptists ascribe to Jesus on this occasion of his concluding his teaching in the temple" (**Milton S. Terry, Biblical Apocalyptics,** p. 218).

I highly recommend this 512-page book by Dr. Milton S. Terry as one of the most scholarly and comprehensive books dealing with the prophetic utterances of Jesus interpreted from the preterist standpoint. The last half of this book is a commentary on the book of Revelation.

Dr. Milton S. Terry wrote another book entitled, **Biblical Hermeneutics. Dr. Wilbur M. Smith,** well-known Bible scholar and former professor at Moody Bible Institute, said that this book is "the most exhaustive single work in our language on the history and interpretation of the Scriptures." In this book Dr. Terry said concerning **Matthew 24:30:**

"The language of Matt. xxiv, 30, concerning 'the Son of man coming in the clouds of the heaven with power and much glory,' is taken from Daniel's night vision (Daniel vii, 13) in which he saw the Son of man coming to the Ancient of days and receiving from him dominion, and glory, and a kingdom. That vision was a part of the composite of world-empire, and signified that 'the kingdom and dominion, and the greatness of the kingdom under the whole heaven, shall be given to the people of the saints of the Most High, whose kingdom is an everlasting kingdom, and all dominions shall serve and obey him' (Dan vii, 27). The kingdom received from the Ancient of days is no other than the kingdom symbolized by the stone cut out of the mountain, in chap. ii, 34, 35, which 'became a great mountain and filled all the land.' This is the kingdom of Messiah, which the Chiliasts believe to be yet future, but which is more generally believed to be the Gospel dispensation, a kingdom not of this world, and not inaugurated with phenomenal splendour visible to mortal eyes. Like the stone cut out of the mountain, and the mustard seed, it is small and comparatively unimportant at its beginning, but it grows so as to fill the earth. This kingdom, according to Jesus' own testimony (Luke xvii, 20), 'comes not with observation;' that is, says Meyer, 'the coming of the Messiah's kingdom is not so conditioned that this coming could be **observed** as a visible development, or that it could be said, in consequence of such observation, that here or there is the kingdom.' It may safely be affirmed, therefore, that this language concerning the coming of the Son of man in the clouds means no more on the lips of Jesus than in the writings of Daniel. It denotes in both places a sublime and glorious reality, the grandest event in human history, but not a visible display in the heavens of such a nature as to be a matter of scenic observation. The Son of man came in heavenly power to supplant Judaism by a better covenant, and to make the kingdoms of the world his own, and that parousia dates from the fall of Judaism and its temple. The mourning of 'all tribes of the land' (not all the nations of the globe) was coincident with the desolation of Zion, and our Lord appropriately foretold it in language taken from Zech. xii, 11, 12" (**Milton S. Terry, Biblical Hermeneutics**, p. 446-447).

Concerning the "sign of the Son of man," **Dr.** Terry said further:

" 'The sign of the Son of man' may mean the ruin of the Jewish temple, considered as a sign or token that the old aeon thereby is ended, and the new Messianic aeon is begun. 'The sign of the prophet Jonah' (Matt. xii, 39; xvi, 4) was no miraculous phenomenon in the heavens. The analogy between Christ and Jonah for three days and three nights (Matt. xii, 40) may be compared with John ii, 19-21 as suggesting that 'the temple of his body,' which was raised up in three days, was a prophetic sign that upon the ruin of Judaism and its temple there would rise that nobler 'spiritual house' (I Peter ii,

5), 'which is his body, the fulness of him who filleth all in all' (Eph. i, 23)" **(Milton S. Terry, Biblical Hermeneutics, p. 452).**

Now the fact that preachers and writers of the early nineteenth century and before believed and taught that ALL of **Matthew 24** referred to the events at the destruction of Jerusalem and the Temple in A.D. 70 does not necessarily make this true. But it is a weighty consideration when one realizes that their teachings began to fade out as modern-day dispensationalism began to make its inroads and became so widely accepted everywhere. And even though in our immediate area of time, the teachings of dispensationalism are undergoing a more thorough scrutiny by serious Bible scholars, it still remains for some of these prior teachings to be restored to their rightful place in the emphasis on eschatology today. I predict: the tide will turn, and truth will win out!

Please understand that I am not saying that ALL of these writers I quote believed that the entire chapter of **Matthew 24** referred **only** to the events surrounding the destruction of Jerusalem in A.D. 70; but I am wanting to show that these men ALL went further than most modern-day writers do in their assigning the major part, if not all of the chapter, to that period of time in the past, and agreeing that the coming of the Son of man in **Matthew 24** referred to what happened in A.D. 70 and not to be something out in our future. It is interesting to me that for many years some of us have not seen the alternative to previously held views on this subject. It is always difficult for us to enter into a new area of understanding about something when all we have heard or been taught in our past has been something else. Then when we do begin to find the answer to the problem, we also begin to learn that others have seen the answer long before, but we didn't know about it. I think the Holy Spirit uses our aggressive research to help us to discover these things.

Dr. George L. Murray

I have a book in my library which more than thirty years ago impressed my mind concerning this particular verse. **Dr. George L. Murray,** in his book, **Millennial Studies,** said the following concerning this passage:

" 'They shall see the Son of man coming in the clouds of heaven with power and great glory.' It is not surprising that this clause is so generally accepted as referring to the Lord's return, for that seems to be its obvious meaning. It is, however, very easy for us to forget that some words are not used today with the meaning they had two thousand years ago. Our Lord Jesus Christ was familiar with the language of the Old Testament and frequently used its figures of speech. In the Old Testament a Divine visitation of a providential nature was frequently referred to as a coming of the Lord. In Genesis 11:5 we read, 'the Lord came down to see the city.' In Exodus 3:8, God says, 'I am come down to deliver them.' In Psalm 72:6 the Psalmist says, 'He shall come down like rain upon the mown grass.' Isaiah, showing the folly of looking to Egypt for help, says, 'So shall the Lord of hosts come down to fight for Mount Zion, and for the hill thereof' (Isaiah 31:4). None of these passages suggests that God came in visible and personal form to dwell upon the earth at that time; neither is that suggested by Matthew 24:30. We take second place to no one in our conviction that the Lord will return personally and visibly, but we cannot blind ourselves to the fact that on this occasion He was using Old Testament figures of speech, which frequently described God as coming with clouds. The Lord said to Moses, 'Lo, I come unto thee in a thick cloud' (Exodus 34:5). 'Who maketh the clouds His chariot: who walketh upon the wings of the wind' (Psalm 104:3). Many other passages could be cited to show that Divine visitations were spoken of as the coming of the Lord in the clouds. 'Clouds and darkness are round about Him' (Psalm 97:2). The words, 'They shall see the Son of man coming in the clouds of heaven,' do not present too much difficulty, for even to this day men speak of seeing God in some manifestation of His power. Those whose minds were spiritually enlightened could certainly see the Son of man in the clouds of heaven which came down so darkly upon Jerusalem at this time" **(George L. Murray, pp. 122-124).**

R. V. G. Tasker (1961)

Coming closer to our times now, let us take a look at what **R. V. G. Tasker** in the **Tyndale New Testament Commentaries** (1961) had to say about this prophecy of Jesus:

"But, we may well ask, are these the only possible alternatives? Is it not also possible to regard these verses as a cryptic description in the symbolism of poetry of the Roman conquest of Jerusalem and of the spread of the Christian Church which followed it? The sack of 'the holy city' in which over a million people were slain would inevitably appear to those who witnessed it a world-catastrophe of the greatest magnitude; and only language symbolic of cosmic disturbance, such as the darkening of the sun, the failure of the moon to give light, and stars falling from the sky, was adequate to describe it. In using such language Jesus was following the example of the ancient prophets. As Levertoff remarks (p. 80), 'These are figures, or symbols of divine acts effecting great changes in the world, and are not to be taken literally. The Old Testament prophets employed such imagery in their announcements of God's interventions in the history of nations; cf. Is. xiii.10, xxxiv. 4; Am. viii. 9; Ezk. xxxii. 7, 8; Joel ii. 28-32.' Indeed, poets all down the ages have used such language to describe the upheaval caused by cataclysmic historical events. Thus in our own day A. E. Housman in his poem, **Epitaph on an Army of Mercenaries,** refers to the first world war as 'the day when Heaven was falling, the hour when Earth's foundation fled'. It may well be, then, that R. A. Knox is right when he says, 'You must understand the portents of verse 29 as an allegorical way of referring to dynastic changes (A.D. 69-70 was 'the year of the four emperors'); and you must identify 'the coming of the Son of man' in verse 30 with some verified experience, e.g. the voice which was heard, according to Tacitus, crying out 'The gods are departing'. The type of language used by the Roman historian in the passage from which this quotation is taken is certainly instructive. Contending hosts were seen meeting in the skies, arms flashed, and suddenly the Temple was illumined with fire from the clouds. Of a sudden the doors of the shrine opened and a superhuman voice cried: 'The gods are departing': at the same moment the mighty stir of their going was heard.' The destruction of the Jerusalem Temple was indeed a divine visitation, which one familiar with the language of Jewish prophecy could describe as a coming of the Son of man on **the clouds of heaven with power and great glory.** It was in fact only after the old order ended with the destruction of the Temple that world evangelism by the Christian Church, now entirely separate from Judaism, could be conducted in earnest. Not till then could the **trumpet** of the gospel be sounded throughout the world. Not till then could the Son of man, having 'visited' the old Israel in judgment, **send his angels (i.e. His messengers) to gather together his elect from the four winds, from one end of heaven to the other,** a result which could be obtained only when the gospel had been preached to the whole world (29-31)." (R. V. G. Tasker, pp. 226-227).

Loraine Boettner

More recently, under the heading, **The Coming of God or of Christ in Judgment,** Dr. **Loraine Boettner** (a Presbyterian, postmillennialist, and author of a number of books), wrote:

"In the Olivet discourse recorded in Matthew 24 we have in figurative language a prediction of Christ's coming in Judgment on the apostate nation of Israel, which coming occurred in the year 70 A.D. Said He: 'But immediately after the tribulation of those days (we have already seen that the 'tribulation' referred to the horrors connected with the siege and fall of Jerusalem), the sun shall be darkened, and the moon shall not give her light, and the stars shall fall from heaven, and the powers of the heaven shall be shaken: and then shall appear the sign of the Son of man in heaven: and then shall all the tribes of the earth mourn, and they shall see the Son of man coming in the clouds of heaven with power and great glory' (vss. 29, 30). And in verse 34 we have the time of this coming fixed very definitely: 'Verily I say unto you, This generation shall not pass away, till all these things be accomplished'" **(Loraine Boettner, p. 254).**

On page 252 of this same book, Dr. Boettner had written under the heading, "Various Ways in Which Christ Comes," these words:

"In reply to the objection that we cannot watch for the coming of Christ unless we think of His Second Coming as imminent, it is important to keep in mind that the word 'come' or 'coming' is used in different senses. There are various ways in which Christ comes. Unless we recognize this we only involve ourselves in error. Premillennialism fails to do justice to the **manifold** comings of Christ. It is so absorbed with the final and so-called Second Coming that it stubbornly refuses even to acknowledge that there are others. The present writer has read numerous premillennial books which treat at length the final Coming but which either ignore or scoff at the idea that there are other ways in which Christ comes. We agree that there will be one great, final, visible, glorious, personal Coming. But we find that Scripture teaches there are also other ways in which He comes."

Incidentally, it was **Dr. Boettner's** book, **The Millennium,** which a pastor friend in Kentucky gave to me in 1979 that had a real impact on my mind as I was studying things related to the Second Coming of Christ. I recommend that you get a copy of this book and read it if you are seriously interested in eschatology. The quotations above were taken from the revised edition of 1984, a copy of which the author personally gave to me later. He wrote to me on November 1, 1984, after he had read my book, **The Millennium — The Big Question,** and said, "I received real help from the one on the Millennium. It is, in my opinion, the best of its kind I have seen anywhere." Now that meant a lot to me, coming from Dr. Boettner. He did not know at that time that it was **his** book in 1979 which had helped me. We had further correspondence on different matters up until his death on January 3, 1990.

Cornelius Vanderwaal

". . . the judgment Jesus sent on Jerusalem is to be regarded as a 'coming' on his part (to deliver His people and to strike His enemies with covenant wrath)" **(Cornelius Vanderwaal, p. 77).**

Foy E. Wallace, Jr.

Another writer, **Foy E. Wallace, Jr.** (Church of Christ), says:

"The mention in Luke's narrative of the distress upon the land of Judea, the mass massacre of the inhabitants by the sword, the carrying away of the captives into all the surrounding nations, the encompassing of the city by foreign armies, and the trodding down of Jerusalem by the Gentiles permanently — all of these things can be descriptive of only one event of history: that final crisis of the ages concerning Jerusalem, in which transition from the dispensation of Judaism, and the consequent expansion of the New Kingdom of Christ, are seen in these evidences to be the main subject of Matthew 24 — the conquest and establishment of Christianity in all the world" (p. 345).

"The teaching of both the Old and New Testaments concerning the kingdom of Christ is: that it contemplates the full length of time from his ascension to heaven after his resurrection to his descension from heaven at the end. 'For he must reign, till he hath put all enemies under his feet' — I Corinthians 15:25. The overthrow of Jerusalem and the temple was the final sign to the world that he was seated 'on the right hand of power,' as he had declared in Matthew 26:64 to the high priest of the Jews: and as further announced to this Jewish official that he and his fellow officials of the Sanhedrin should thereafter see it. Methinks they did — at the destruction of their capital city and their national temple" (**Foy E. Wallace, Jr.**, pp. 346-347).

On another page, **Dr. Wallace** said:

"As it is biblically certain that the God of heaven in times of old descended, in the Old Testament metaphor, on the clouds of heaven to execute judgment on ancient wicked nations and cities (Isaiah 13 and 19), so certainly did the Son of man come in the clouds with his angels of power to execute judgment on the once great city of Jerusalem, guilty of his blood and the blood of his saints and martyrs" (**Foy E. Wallace, Jr.**, p. 461).

J. Barton Payne

J. Barton Payne expressed himself thusly:

"The Jerusalem Bible here proposes that the 'coming' be understood as a figure for divine judgment, in light of the immediately preceding stress . . . on the criminal treatment to be suffered by the apostles: 'The coming which is here foretold is not concerned with the world at large but with Israel: it took place at the moment when God 'visited' his now faithless people and brought the OT era to an end by the destruction of Jerusalem and its temple" (**J. Barton Payne**).

David Chilton

A more recent writer, **David Chilton**, pastor of The Church of the Redeemer, a Presbyterian Church in California, said, "The Olivet Discourse (Matthew 24, Mark 13, and Luke 21) is not about the Second Coming of Christ. It is a prophecy of the destruction of

Jerusalem in A.D. 70" (**David Chilton, Paradise Restored**, p. 224).

George M. Bowman

George M. Bowman of Canada had this to say about verse 30:

". . . Jesus said, 'And then shall appear the sign of the Son of man in heaven: and then shall all the tribes of the earth mourn, and they shall see the Son of man coming in the clouds of heaven with power and great glory' (**Matt. 24:30**). Whatever this passage means, one thing is certain: it had to take place within the generation in which it was spoken by Christ because he said (**verse 34**) that the then current generation would not pass until all these things were fulfilled.

"The phrase, 'they shall see the Son of man coming in the clouds of heaven with power and great glory', refers to a language familiar to the Jews. It does not say that Christ was coming to earth. Prophetic language of the Old Testament clearly shows that the Lord coming on a cloud speaks of his coming in judgment. And that is exactly what Christ did when Jerusalem and the temple were destroyed. People saw him come in judgment, but it was not a visible appearance of Christ in person" (**George M. Bowman**, p. 34).

Most students of the Bible, when studying various passages, will go to the various commentaries to see what those authors have to say on particular verses. While many commentaries are available and easily accessible, many of them are not, especially the older ones. In this book, by references here and there, we have documented quotations from many of these men, not only from commentaries but from other writings. Our research can be helpful to those who would be needing additional information but who would not have access to these books. And even if all these books were available and accessible, we have brought together these passages, giving page numbers and volume numbers and other information for some who are interested in studying these things. But there is still so much more than what I list in this book!

The use of quotations from other authors in this book does not mean that all these men held to the same identical view I have expressed in this book. They are quoted where what they said is needed at that point in our writing, to further confirm or to illustrate what I am saying at that point.

So what is the purpose of all this documentation of what these writers and preachers had to say about **Matthew 24**? Simply this: It cannot be denied that the view that the COMING OF CHRIST in judgment on Jerusalem as mentioned in Matthew 24 was taught by these men. While it is true that many of our commentaries teach that **Matthew 24:29-30** refer to the actual bodily and future (to us) return of Christ, it is obvious that this viewpoint was not held by these men quoted. This is evidenced by the large number of writers and preachers and Bible scholars who insisted that proper exegesis of that passage required that it stay in context with the events Jesus had mentioned relative to the destruction of Jerusalem. These writers were of different denominations, from different countries, lived over a period of many years, and were different in their views on the millennium as well, but were convinced in agreement that **Matthew 24:29-30** was fulfilled in Christ's coming in judgment on Jerusalem in the year A.D. 70. And there are many others besides them, too, who gave this same interpretation, which at one time was said to be the consensus of the Bible scholars on the matter. This view is now gaining ground again, in spite of increased vigor on the part of many to maintain the teachings of dispensationalism relative to eschatology.

Others in the past, with critical bias, suggested that even Jesus **expected** that He would bodily, physically and visibly return to earth in connection with the events of A.D. 70, and that He was mistaken because He did not do so! Others said that Jesus knew better but misled His disciples in that matter with a good purpose and reason for doing so. Believing the nature of Christ to be what it was, we can dismiss the latter idea most vehemently. And as to the other, no, He was not mistaken. But our understanding of this passage has been clouded because we have tried to force a literal, physical, bodily return of Christ into what He promised in **Matthew 24**. He DID come, but in spiritual power and judgment. This passage does not invalidate a final day of reckoning. Jesus predicted both the destruction of Jerusalem and His *parousia*/coming in the same context. If the first did come to pass, why would He have been mistaken about the other? He wasn't! His *"parousia"* was fulfilled then too, as He promised.

An alternative to the modernists' view was to insist that Jesus did not err about His second coming, but that the passage in question **(Matthew 24:29-30)** actually refers to **our** future. But this takes that passage out of context, as I have shown in this book. Futurism and dispensationalism became so influential and accepted by so many that the teaching of these men I have quoted became relegated to the background, and are just now beginning to be seen again as the proper alternative to the modernists' position, and one which is based on precise and literal exegesis of the passages involved.

Some others who did not feel the passage refers to our future only, said it had a double fulfillment — referring to the events of A.D. 70 **and** our future. Still others used a double reference interpretation — that is, they believed some parts of the passage referred to A.D. 70, and other parts referred to our future. Those who believe the latter usually find a transition verse somewhere in the chapter. (I deal with this in detail in Section 9.) All these different viewpoints show us how far Bible teachers are willing to go in order to avoid the plain common-sense literal interpretation of this passage of Scripture. To change the meaning of the passage does not solve the problems that they find therein.

It is obvious that the dispensationalists went even further than simple futurism, when they claimed that not only did **Matthew 24:30** refer to the second coming of Christ in our future, but they taught also that a prior rapture of Christians would take place seven years (or some, 3½ years; and some, 45 days) before that second coming, and that the tribulation mentioned in **Matthew 24:29** was to be such a stated period of time between the rapture and the revelation of Christ from Heaven in our future. I have already shown in other writings of mine how this pre-tribulation rapture teaching got started back in the late 1700's and the early 1800's. Dispensationalists and others make the "tribulation" of **Matthew 24:29** refer to some future time just before the second coming of Christ to earth (whether pre- or post-tribulation rapturists), when it is so evident and obvious that Jesus was referring to the great tribulation which came to the Jews during the siege of Jerusalem and its destruction ending in A.D. 70

The dispensationalists and others do wrong to make this tribulation be a stated period of time in our future in connection with a future second coming of Christ. And I repeat here what I have claimed before, that the **ONLY PLACE** in the Bible where a passage of Scripture is used to promote such a **SEVEN YEARS** tribulation period between the Rapture and the Second Coming of Christ, is in **Daniel 9:24-27**. This is where J. N. Darby got it from, and Dr. Harry Ironside said that Darby was the first to do this in **connection with a pre-tribulation rapture**. But **Daniel 9:24-27** has **NOTHING** to do or say about any future (to us) tribulation period, and certainly nothing to do with a future (to us) second coming of Christ. It is a prophecy already fulfilled during the 3½ years of the ministry of Christ and 3½ years later, in the midst of which (the 70th week) He was "cut off" (crucified).

Section 6 ••••••••••••••••••••••••••

"COMING IN THE CLOUDS OF HEAVEN"

" . . . and they shall see the Son of man coming in the clouds of heaven with power and great glory" (Matthew 24:30b).

Does God come down to planet earth? Yes, He does, if we are to believe what the writers of the Bible tell us.

It might be well here to consider that all through the Bible God is depicted as coming down, descending, coming in the clouds, and coming in various ways both at times of salvation and at times of judgment. Various figures of speech are used to depict God's making His judgments known to man. It is not unlikely that the writers of the New Testament used the same kind of language in depicting the same things.

In the passage under consideration at the moment, Jesus is pictured as "coming in the clouds of heaven." We have seen in the previous section of this book that the coming of Christ in **Matthew 24:30** was His coming in revelation of His power and majesty and kingdom at the time Jerusalem was destroyed in A.D. 70. He is depicted here as "coming in the clouds of heaven." The Jewish mind understood this kind of language in the sense it was written. We need to do so also. The language does not mean those things happened in a literal and naturalistic way. We want to discuss this terminology in order to better understand how language like this was used in the Bible, and what it means here.

Genesis 37:5-11 (especially **verse 9**) explains the language concerning the sun, the moon, the stars, etc., as we discussed previously. In this case in **Matthew 24** the reference is to Israel. We find help in interpreting such New Testament passages by going back to the Old Testament where these things are first mentioned.

Here in **Matthew 24** Jesus adopted the same kind of language as used in **Daniel 7:13**, and by this He indicated that the manifestation of the kingdom which had been given to Him was fulfilled at the time of the destruction of Jerusalem.

The first part of **Matthew 24:30** was dealt with in our previous section entitled, **The Sign of the Son of Man in Heaven.** This section will now deal with the last part of that verse — "and they shall see the Son of man coming in the clouds of heaven with power and great glory."

To "see" the Son of man coming in His kingdom does not mean that they would literally see Jesus physically coming from Heaven.

The word is used more like as found in **Matthew 5:8**, "Blessed are the pure in heart: for they shall see God." Seeing God would not be literally seeing someone with the physical eye, for God cannot be seen in that way. God is "the invisible God" **(Colossians 1:15)**. (See also **I Timothy 1:17**). Moses forsook Egypt and "endured, as seeing him who is invisible" **(Hebrews 11:27)**.

Can one see someone who is not visible? Yes, if the definition of "see" does not restrict the meaning to physical eyesight, which it does not. By being born again, we "see the kingdom of God" **(John 3:3)**. By being pure in heart, we "see God" **(Matthew 5:8)**. Those at Jerusalem would "see the Son of man coming in the clouds of heaven." This is apocalyptic language in the same sense as the sun being darkened, the moon not giving her light, and the stars falling from heaven **(vs. 29)**. The "powers of the heavens" being shaken no doubt refers to the spiritual institutions of Judaism being shaken loose.

The Son of man being seen as coming in the clouds of heaven was a fulfillment of Jesus' prediction to Caiaphas the high priest, "Hereafter shall ye see the Son of man sitting on the right hand of power, and coming in the clouds of heaven" **(Matthew 26:64)**.

To "see" meant "to recognize, to be aware, to perceive." The events occurring at Jerusalem in A.D. 70 would cause the tribes of Israel to recognize that Jesus' pronouncements concerning Himself were now validated; He was indeed the Son of man and the Messiah!

"Seeing" Jesus is not always done in a physical way. Take, for example, when Jesus talked to His disciples about His departure from this life and the coming of the Holy Spirit. He said, "Yet a little while, and the world seeth me no more; BUT YE SEE ME" **(John 14:19)**. He reinforced this statement in **John 16:16** when He said, "A little while, and ye shall not see me: and again, a little while, and YE SHALL SEE ME." His disciples did not understand this **(vs. 17)**, but that is because He was talking to them in spiritual language. He was referring to His later presence with them in the person of the Holy Spirit. His being in them would be the same as their seeing Jesus. He did come, and His presence was literally with them; but it was not a physical person they saw, nor did they see Him with physical eyes.

Likewise, when the Son of man came in His kingdom, the tribes of the land did "see the Son of man coming in the clouds of heaven with power and great glory" **(Matthew 24:30)**, but it was not a physical person they saw nor did they see Him with physical eyes. But they did know that He had come!

"The Greek word for 'see' *(eido)* is used by both Luke and John.

According to James Strong, *eido* can be used in a very broad sense. It can mean **to know, be aware, have knowledge, perceive, be sure, understand,** etc. It is very obvious that the Greek word *eido* does not always mean to 'see literally' or to perceive with the senses" **(Clyde F. Whitehead, Israel versus Israel, p. 244).** This is the way they saw Jesus coming in the clouds of heaven in A.D. 70.

In **Matthew 21:40** in the parable where the lord "cometh" and destroys the wicked men, Jesus indicated that this represented the time when the kingdom of God would be taken from the Jews and given to those who would bring forth the fruits thereof — clearly referring to the time when Jerusalem would be destroyed, as is evident in the following chapters. This was when the "lord cometh." And our Lord did "come" in judgment on Israel less than 40 years later.

In the July-August 1991 edition of **Restoration of Our Theological Structure,** revised and reprinted February 1992, editor **Raymond P. Joseph** illustrated the sovereignty of God over nations, even in their destruction, and illustrated by what happened in A.D. 67-70:

"The Jewish Josephus, the official historian appointed by the Roman government, is recording the events which occurred in Palestine in A.D. 68-70, events which we know today as 'The Destruction of Jerusalem.' The Christians of Jesus' day knew that He had foretold His return in judgment on Jerusalem, in Matthew Chapter 24. Jesus warned the Christians to flee, and they did. So, true to His Word, Jesus came back to Palestine, this time as the Rider on the White Horse of Revelation Chapter nineteen. The Roman armies under General Titus wreaked destruction on the city of Jerusalem, completely destroying the Temple, until not one stone was left upon another" **(Raymond P. Joseph, p. 4).**

As to the coming of Christ at the judgment of Jerusalem in A.D. 67-70, with this thought at least agreed **David S. Clark** in his book, **The Message from Patmos:**

". . . It is certain that the destruction of Jerusalem bulks more largely in the prophecies of the New Testament than our premillennial friends are wont to admit. The bulk of Matt. 24, Mark 13, and Luke 21, concerns the destruction of Jerusalem. Moreover Christ said: 'There are some standing here who shall not taste of death till they see the Son of Man coming in his kingdom,' and 'This generation (Christ's generation not some future one) shall not pass till all these things be fulfilled.' All this shows that Christ used this language to describe some near event which he called a 'coming of the Son of Man.' It may be so in this verse seven, 'And they also which pierced him;' very probably many of his crucifiers lived to see the judgment executed upon Jerusalem." **(David S. Clark, p. 25)**.

Dr. John Gill said (on the parallel **Mark 13:26**):

"Ver. **26, And then shall they see the Son of man,** etc. Not in person, but in the power of his wrath and vengeance; of which the Jews then had a convincing evidence, and full proof; and even of his being come in the flesh, as if they had seen him in person: this shows, that the sign of the Son of man, in Matt. xxiv. 30, is the same with the Son of man: **coming in the clouds with great power and glory**; not to judgment, but having taken vengeance on the Jewish nation, to set up his kingdom and glory in the Gentile world" **(Dr. John Gill,** Commentary on Mark 13:26).

Some people have an idea of a God way up in the Heaven somewhere, Who sent angels down to help His people occasionally, and Who sometimes spoke to His servants in some way, and Who at one time came down to earth in the person of Jesus, and who will again come to this earth at some time in our future. And this is about as far as it goes. But a careful survey of the Bible indicates that God has always been close to this earth, and that He appeared and came down to judge, or to save, or to communicate with His people, many, many times. God really "came down" from Heaven to planet earth again and again. And in the New Testament likewise, it is recorded that God chose to "come down" to this earth. He came in the person of Jesus to put away sin. He came in the person of the Holy Spirit to indwell believers. He came in the judgment upon Israel in A.D. 70 and revealed His tribulation and wrath upon a sinful nation. The whole Bible, from the picture of God walking with Adam in the cool of the day, to the passage in Revelation where it says God will dwell among His people, is a long story filled with the comings of God to earth on behalf of those He created and loved and saved. And His presence will forevermore be with those of us who belong to Him.

Various "Comings" of Christ

The word "coming" as found in **Matthew 24:3, 27, 37** and **39** is from the Greek noun *"parousia"* which means "arrival, or presence." It does not have the meaning of the word "return" though in some cases it could involve that meaning also. The word involves an "event" as well as the idea of "duration"; in other words, it is not only something that happens, but it can mean that whoever has come is now here; that is, the person arrives, and also is here now. It can mean either or both.

Of interest concerning the use of the word *"parousia"* is something a friend, Robert Whitelaw, told me. Some years ago he was in Athens,

Greece, visiting a power plant. He told me that he found that *"parousia"* is the very word used today in Greek on an electric control panel to signify **"ON,"** i.e., **presence** of electric power. As I have mentioned before, the word does not only mean "coming" in the sense of **arrival**, but it can signify **presence** also in the sense of being present.

The word "coming" as found in **Matthew 24:30** (**"they shall see the Son of man coming"**) and **Matthew 24:48** ("My lord delayeth his coming") is from the Greek word *"erchomai"* and is a verb. It has the same basic meaning, except that it denotes the action of His coming.

There are various "comings" of Christ mentioned in the New Testament, though not all from the same Greek word. The "coming" of Christ is not one single solitary event.

Jesus told His disciples, "Ye shall not have gone over the cities of Israel, till the Son of man be COME" **(Matthew 10:23)**. Whatever He was talking about here, He was referring to a "coming" in a very short while.

His *parousia* "coming" was manifested on the Mount of Transfiguration, and Peter said of that event, "We made known unto you the power and COMING (*parousia*) . . . when we were with him in the holy mount" (II Peter 1:16, 18). Even though lasting only briefly, the transfiguration of Jesus was a literal manifestation or revelation of His glorious coming and presence.

As Jesus gave the Great Commission to the disciples, He told them, ". . . and, lo, I am with you alway, even unto the end of the world" **(Matthew 28:20)**. This verse indicates His continuous presence in the world in relationship to His disciples, but without physical presence. No less is it true that His coming/presence in A.D. 70 would be true without a **physical** presence.

Following His ascension, He came to His disciples in the person of the Holy Spirit as He had promised. He had told them, "I will not leave you comfortless: I will COME to you. . . . But the Comforter, which is the Holy Ghost, whom the Father will send in my name . . ." **(John 14:18, 26)**.

Paul indicated that Christ has come to abide in the heart of each believer, and he said, "Now if any man have not the Spirit of Christ, he is none of his. And if Christ be in you . . ." **(Romans 8:9, 10)**.

The Holy Spirit lives in the life of each individual believer (see **Romans 8:11, I Corinthians 3:16** and **6:19**), and Paul equates this with Christ being in us.

Jesus told the church at Pergamos, "Repent; or else I will COME unto thee quickly, and will fight against them with the sword of my mouth" **(Revelation 2:16)**. This was a conditional coming.

Likewise, Jesus told the church at Ephesus, "Remember therefore from whence thou art fallen, and repent, and do the first works; or else I will COME unto thee quickly, and will remove thy candlestick out of his place, except thou repent" **(Revelation 2:5)**.

And He told the church at Sardis, "If therefore thou shalt not watch, I will COME on thee as a thief, and thou shalt not know what hour I will come upon thee" **(Revelation 3:3)**.

Jesus said, "For where two or three are gathered together in my name, there am I in the midst of them" **(Matthew 18:20)**. When believers meet together in the name of Jesus, He is present there also.

Jesus appeared to Saul on the road to Damascus, and the men who journeyed with Saul heard His voice though they saw no man. "I have APPEARED unto thee" **(Acts 26:16)**. "And the men which journeyed with him stood speechless, hearing a voice, but seeing no man" **(Acts 9:7)**. Ananias told Saul that God had chosen him to know his will and to "see that Just One, and shouldest hear the voice of his mouth" **(Acts 22:14)**. Saul saw Jesus, but not physically.

Ananias told Saul that "the Lord, even Jesus, that APPEARED unto thee in the way" had sent Ananias so that Saul could receive his sight **(Acts 9:17)**.

Telling of this Damascus-road experience later, Paul said that Jesus told him, "I have APPEARED unto thee" and "I will APPEAR unto thee" **(Acts 26:16)**.

Of this experience Paul wrote later, ". . . have I not seen Jesus Christ our Lord?" **(I Corinthians 9:1)**.

But Saul (Paul) never saw Jesus with his physical eyes, nor did Jesus appear in bodily form.

And more in reference to our present studies, the Son of man came in A.D. 70 at the time of the destruction of Jerusalem and the Temple when the Jewish age ended. " . . . when shall these things be? and what shall be the sign of thy COMING, and of the end of the world [age]?" **(Matthew 24:3)**. "Verily I say unto you, This generation shall not pass, till all these things be fulfilled" **(Matthew 24:34)**.

The "Coming" of Christ at the Great White Throne Judgment

Revelation 20:11-15 gives us the picture of a time when ALL are seen as resurrected and standing before the "great white throne." Jesus Christ Himself is seated upon that throne **(Acts 17:31; John 5:22, 27)**. Where that throne is supposed to be located we are not told, but we are told that heaven and earth flee away from the awful sight.

The old heaven and earth were Judaism, which now has fled away. (We shall deal with this in detail in Section 8.) John's prophecy now advances to the time when the final destinies of all who have ever lived are pronounced by the One on that throne.

James Stuart Russell, in his book, **The Parousia** (1887), gives allowance for the millennial period not being in the scope of John's statement that these things would all happen "shortly." He said, ". . . we are disposed to regard the whole parenthesis as relating to matters still future and unfilfilled" (p. 523). This is obvious, as the thousand years period evidently extends for a long indefinite period of time, only the beginning of which could be said to "shortly come to pass" (Revelation 1:1).

But Russell takes the resurrection and great white throne judgment scene and brings it back to fit into the "things which must shortly come to pass" (Revelation 1:1). I prefer to leave this scene at the **end** of the millennial period. The reason I do this is because **Revelation 20:5** says that "the rest of the dead lived not again until the thousand years were finished." This puts the resurrection and great white throne judgment scene at the **conclusion** of the thousand years period. (This thousand years period represents the time the martyred saints are reigning with Christ in Heaven — actually, Christ's reign during this gospel age.)

It is not said that Jesus actually and physically steps His feet onto this earth for that judgment. But He is **present** for that judgment. The throne no doubt symbolizes the authority and rule of Jesus Christ. All of mankind, of the whole world, could not literally stand in front of a literal chair-like throne all at one time. This mystery is not explained to us in this passage. John uses this beautiful symbolic language to picture these things for us. But we do know that when Jesus Christ judges the whole world, He will be **present,** and He will be the judge.

One of the earlier preterist writers (**Henry Hammond, 1681**) who held to the preterite interpretation of Matthew 24, and taught that the second coming of Christ took place in fulfillment thereof in A.D. 70, termed the final day of judgment a **third coming** of Christ. He wrote that the "coming of Christ . . . at the day of doom to judge the world" was "his final third coming at the great day of doom" (p. 119).

But even so, if Jesus Christ's being **PRESENT** on the great white throne be called a "coming of Christ," yet the Bible still does not say that this judgment will take place on this earth. **He comes to judge, but not in a materialistic, physical, fleshly manner.** At least, we do not read this in this passage of Scripture in **Revelation 20:11-15.**

Many teach that Christ will some day in our future come to this earth, and then reign on this earth for a thousand years. **The Bible does not teach this.** Neither does it teach that Christ will come to this earth and reign on this earth, **at all;** not at anytime in our future does it say that He will do this. The "comings" of Christ in the New Testament do not refer to any such event.

As mystical and even contradictory as it may seem, Jesus Christ is here right now in the lives and hearts of His believers, in the person of the Holy Spirit; and He is also in Heaven, seated at the right hand of God the Father, ruling over the affairs of this world.

When Jesus Christ "comes" and sits upon the great white throne of judgment, this will not be a "coming" to this earth, nor in any naturalistic, materialistic and physical manner. This judgment will be accomplished in the spiritual world, in another dimension than this materialistic natural world of ours made up of earthly thrones and judicial councils. His reign and His rule and His judgment are spiritual matters. The great summation of the final judgment of all mankind is pictured in symbolic language in **Revelation 20:11-15.** Those who are lost are "cast into the lake of fire." Death and Hell, both intangible and abstract subjects, are pictured as also being cast into the lake of fire. In these words we are being told that Death and Hell will be no more. Death will ultimately be banished. And Hell which has captured the souls of men after bodies have died, will be no more. This "second death" will have no power over God's people forever; and God will be all in all!

But it is important that we recognize the fact that most all of the passages in the New Testament which are generally used to picture a coming of Christ in our future to judge the world, are actually passages referring to the coming of Christ which the disciples expected in their generation (Matthew 24:34) and which Jesus had promised would take place before all of them were dead (Matthew 16:28).

The comings of Christ are not one single solitary event. But His first coming in human form as a sin-offering, and His apocalyptic coming in judgment on Israel in that generation (apart from a sin-offering), were spoken of in the New Testament as His first and His second appearances. " . . . now once in the end of the world [age] hath he appeared to put away sin by the sacrifice of himself. . . . and unto them that look for him shall he APPEAR the second time without sin unto salvation" **(Hebrews 9:26-28).** The "day approaching" of Hebrews 10:25, which they saw, was the soon-coming judgment on Israel and the release of His people from the bondage of the Jewish age: " . . . and so much the more, as ye see the day approaching" **(Hebrews 10:25).**

The view of various comings of Christ has been held by different theologians, as for example, Dr. John Owen who preached and wrote in the 17th century. (See **John Owen, The Works of John Owen,** vol.

9, pp. 138-139). Another later theologian was Dr. E. Y. Mullins, former president and professor of theology at Southern Baptist Theological Seminary in Louisville, Kentucky. (See **E. Y. Mullins, The Christian Religion in its Doctrinal Expression,** p. 459). One more recent one was well-known writer and theologian Loraine Boettner. (See **Loraine Boettner, The Millennium,** pp. 252-262). There are others, of course, which we could mention if we took the time to look them up and list them.

Old Testament Passages Where God Came Down

In the Old Testament there are many passages where we find the same kind of language used to describe God's coming to bring judgment into the world and to manifest His power, as we find also in **Matthew 24.**

In **Genesis 18:21** the Lord said concerning Sodom and Gomorrah, "I will GO DOWN now, and see whether they have done altogether according to the cry of it." That visit and investigation resulted in the Lord's raining "upon Sodom and upon Gomorrah brimstone and fire from the LORD out of heaven" **(Genesis 19:24).**

Deuteronomy 33:2: "The LORD CAME from Sinai, and rose up from Seir unto them; he shined forth from mount Paran, and he CAME with ten thousands of saints."

Isaiah 31:4: ". . . so shall the LORD of hosts COME DOWN to fight for mount Zion, and for the hill thereof."

Isaiah 64:3: ". . . thou CAMEST DOWN, the mountains flowed down at thy presence." When was this done? "When thou didst terrible things which we looked not for, . . ."

Isaiah 66:15: "For, behold, the LORD will COME with fire, and with his chariots like a whirlwind, to render his anger with fury, and his rebuke with flames of fire."

Psalm 18:9: "He bowed the heavens also, and CAME DOWN."

Psalm 47:5: "The hills melted like wax at the PRESENCE of the Lord."

Psalm 50:3: "Our God SHALL COME, and shall not keep silence: a fire shall devour before him, and it shall be very tempestuous round about him."

Psalm 96:13: ". . . for he COMETH, for he COMETH to judge the earth."

Psalm 97:5: "The hills melted like wax at the PRESENCE of the LORD, at the PRESENCE of the Lord of the whole earth."

Psalm 144:5: "Bow thy heavens, O LORD, and COME DOWN: touch the mountains, and they shall smoke."

Hosea 8:1: "Set the trumpet to thy mouth. He shall COME as an eagle against the house of the LORD, because they have transgressed my covenant, and trespassed against my law."

Micah 1:3-4: "For, behold, the LORD COMETH forth out of his place, and will COME DOWN, and tread upon the high places of the earth.

"And the mountains shall be molten under him, and the valleys shall be cleft, as wax before the fire, and as the waters that are poured down a steep place."

If the writers of the Old Testament used such highly symbolic language to picture the actions of God, is it not likely that the writers of the New Testament, and Jesus in particular, would use the same kind of imagery to describe events of historic proportions? Why should Jesus not have used symbolical language like this from the Old Testament to describe events at the destruction of Jerusalem, etc.?

In **Genesis 11:5** where it says, "the LORD CAME DOWN to see the city and the tower, which the children of men builded," and then said, " . . . let us GO DOWN, and there confound their language" (vs. 7), how did He come down? It was by judgment on the people, by scattering them abroad upon the face of all the earth **(Genesis 11:8)**.

When the Lord God saw the afflictions of His people in Egypt and said, "I am COME DOWN to deliver them out of the hand of the Egyptians," etc. **(Exodus 3:8)**, how did He come down? It was by judgments upon the land of Egypt until Pharaoh finally let the people go.

So, in the Old Testament this expression of God coming down is used to express some great act of God, either in judgment or of blessing, as the case might be.

At Babel, when God scattered the people, He was not physically seen.

In Egypt, when He delivered His people, He was not physically seen.

At Jerusalem, when Christ came and Jerusalem was destroyed, He was not physically seen.

But — HE CAME DOWN! And His coming was in judgment on Israel and blessing for the true people of God. And His coming was just as real as God coming down in the Old Testament to manifest His power and judgments.

It is not necessary for us to agree with the assumption that there is no such thing as any other "coming" of Christ except a future final return of Christ to judge the world. His presence (*parousia*) in the events of history indicate that even though He sits on the right hand of God the Father (indicative of His present reign), He has revealed His presence and power over and over again in various events.

He told Caiaphas the high priest that, "Henceforth ye shall see the Son of man sitting at the right hand of power, and coming on the clouds of heaven" **(Matthew 26:64)**. Here Jesus appropriates to Himself the title "Son of man" as found in **Daniel 7:13** where it says, ". . . behold, one like the Son of man came with the clouds of heaven, and came to the Ancient of days." Here He is both coming with the clouds of heaven and also coming to the Ancient of days. Caiaphas and others (note the "ye" — plural, not "thou" — singular) would see Jesus manifested as the Son of man; they would see Him "sitting at the right hand of power." And notice it is to be "henceforth" (from that time on), and not simply in some single event in particular in the future. Jesus revealed His presence in power and glory through a number of events after that.

Dr. E. Y. Mullins, former President and Professor of Theology in Southern Baptist Theological Seminary, Louisville, Kentucky, said:

"Jesus, in Matthew 26:64, says in reply to the high priest's question, 'Henceforth ye shall see the Son of man sitting at the right hand of power, and coming on the clouds of heaven.' The phrase translated 'henceforth' (*ap'arti*) does not mean 'hereafter,' as if some future time were in view. It means from the time when Jesus spoke the words — 'from now on.' He means that the era of God's power, as exerted in and through His Son, has begun. The Son of man is 'henceforth' the ruler of history.

"Events which followed upon these words of Jesus confirmed them. His death was a departure from the earth, and certainly his resurrection from the dead was a return in power. Of course it did not take the place of the great event of the future, the *Parousia,* when he shall return to judge the world. (See Acts 1:11). The gift of the Holy Spirit on the day of Pentecost was another great event belonging to the series in the near future. The destruction of Jerusalem was clearly included in the near events portrayed in his great prophecy. These events were comings of Christ. They were witnessed by men who heard his words and who remained alive, according to his prediction, until the fulfilment." **(Edgar Young Mullins, The Christian Religion in its Doctrinal Expression, pp. 456-459).**

J. Marcellus Kik said:

"The third and final clause of the verse 30 reads: 'And they shall see the Son of man coming in the clouds of heaven with power and great glory.' This clause has been thought to relate definitely to the second, visible, and personal coming of the Lord. But in the light of well-defined Biblical language, the reference is rather to a coming in the events of His providence in judgment against His enemies and in deliverance of His people" **(J. Marcellus Kik, pp. 73-74).**

And they saw it — yes, they did! Not with the naked human eye, but with the eyes of understanding and perception. This was proof that Jesus was on the right hand of God and that He had allowed this terrible destruction. They did indeed understand this. They saw it!

Commenting on the coming of the Lord in I Thessalonians 4:15, **Butler's Bible Readers Commentary** had this to say:

"The coming again of the Lord is not one single act, as his resurrection, or the descent of the Spirit, or the final coming in judgment, but the great complex of all these the result of which shall be his taking his people to himself, to be where he is. This receiving is begun in his resurrection, carried on in the spiritual life, further advanced when each by death is fetched away to be with him, fully completed at his coming in glory, when they shall for ever be with him in the perfected resurrection state" **(Butler's Bible Reader Commentary).**

While the above writer did not mention the "coming of the Son of man" at the judgment of Israel in A.D. 70, yet he does show us the necessity of not limiting the "coming" of Christ to just one single solitary event in our future. We must give way in our interpretation for these other events which were definitely classified as "comings" and "appearances" of the Lord.

Appearances of Christ After His Ascension

There are a number of places in the New Testament where we read that Jesus Christ appeared to people here on earth after His ascension to glory.

Jesus appeared to Stephen:

"But he, being full of the Holy Ghost, looked up stedfastly into heaven, and saw the glory of God, and Jesus standing on the right hand of God,

"And said, Behold, I see the heavens opened, and the Son of man standing on the right hand of God" **(Acts 7:55-56).**

The persecutors of Stephen considered his remarks as total blasphemy and stoned him to death. They displayed the same venom in their spiritual system as was shown back with Caiaphas the high priest when he "rent his clothes" after hearing Jesus say, "Hereafter shall ye see the Son of man sitting on the right hand of power, and coming in the clouds of heaven" **(Matthew 26:64-65).**

Jesus appeared to Saul of Tarsus:

"And as he journeyed, he came near Damascus: and suddenly there shined round about him a light from heaven:

"And he fell to the earth, and heard a voice saying unto him, Saul, Saul, why persecutest thou me?"

"And the men which journeyed with him stood speechless, hearing a voice, but seeing no man" **(Acts 9:3-4, 7).**

Jesus appeared to Peter when he fell into a trance:
"Peter went up upon the housetop to pray about the sixth hour . . . And saw heaven opened, and a certain vessel descending unto him. . . . And there came a voice to him, Rise, Peter; kill, and eat. But Peter said, No so, Lord . . ." **(Acts 10:9, 11, 13-14)**.

Jesus appeared to Paul warning him away from Jerusalem:
"And it came to pass, that, when I was come again to Jerusalem, even while I prayed in the temple, I was in a trance;

"And saw him saying unto me, Make haste, and get thee quickly out of Jerusalem" **(Acts 22:17-18)**. Paul said here that he "saw" the Lord!

And later on it was said, "The Lord stood by him, and said, Be of good cheer, Paul: for as thou hast testified of me in Jerusalem, so must thou bear witness also at Rome" **(Acts 23:11)**.

And on the island of Patmos, John saw the "Son of man" (Revelation 1:13), and "out of his mouth went a sharp twoedged sword" **(Revelation 1:16)**. John said, "And when I saw him, I fell at his feet as dead. And he laid his right hand upon me, saying unto me, Fear not; I am the first and the last" **(Revelation 1:17)**.

Let's get Jesus out of a box! We have kept him boxed in to a "first coming" and a "second coming" and not allowed Him the freedom to come and go as He pleases. But He breaks out of our doctrinal boxes and does what He wants to do. He even came and stood with the three Hebrew children in the midst of the burning fiery furnace ("the form of the fourth is like the Son of God") **(Daniel 3:25)**, and that was even before his "first" coming!

It is certainly true that in the New Testament we see Jesus coming (appearing) again and again as it pleased Him. So why should anyone think it strange that He said He would come before that generation was over, before some standing around Him then would be dead? As to how and when He comes, He picks His own places and manner in which to come. In the first century, A.D. 70, He came once again and was present in the events of those fateful days. His coming then was in both salvation and judgment — salvation to His people who were now delivered from the bondage of the Jewish system and their oppressors, and judgment upon the entire nation of Israel. He promised His disciples that He would BE WITH THEM until the end of the age **(Matthew 28:20)**; and He was, over and over, again and again, "the Lord working with them, and confirming the word with signs following" **(Mark 16:20)**.

Old Testament Passages Where God Came "In the Clouds"
Even though I have previously given a number of passages from the Old Testament, illustrating how symbolic and apocalyptic language is used of God's judgments and power when they speak

of His coming down from heaven to earth, it will also be appropriate here to mention a number of places in the Old Testament describing God not only as coming, but as COMING IN THE CLOUDS. Understanding this kind of language will help us to understand some of the New Testament expressions with the same wording.

God's coming down to earth on the clouds is mentioned a number of times in the Old Testament, and the expression "on the clouds" signified His great judgment, His redemption, His glory, etc. These celestial things mentioned in **Matthew 24:27-31**, including His coming in, or on, or with, the clouds, as the case might be in various passages, are no different in essence than prophecies or statements we find in the Old Testament about God Himself. Look at some of these places:

Exodus 16:10: ". . . the glory of the LORD appeared in the CLOUD."

Exodus 19:9: "I come unto thee in a thick CLOUD."

Exodus 34:5: "And the LORD DESCENDED IN THE CLOUD, and stood with him there. . . ."

Leviticus 16:2: " . . . for I will appear in the CLOUD upon the mercy seat."

Numbers 11:25: "And the LORD came down in a CLOUD."

Psalm 18:9-12: "He bowed the heavens also, and came down. . . . Yea, he did fly upon the wings of the wind. . . . His pavilion round about him were dark waters and thick CLOUDS of the skies. At the brightness that was before him his thick CLOUDS passed. . . ."

Psalm 97:2-5: "CLOUDS and darkness are round about him." Read the rest of this passage and note the symbolical language used.

Psalm 104:3: "Who maketh the CLOUDS his chariot: who walketh upon the wings of the wind."

Isaiah 19:1: "Behold, the LORD rideth upon a swift CLOUD, and shall come into Egypt."

Daniel 7:13: ". . . one like the Son of man came with the CLOUDS of heaven, and came to the Ancient of days." (Here is prophecy of the ascension of Jesus to the Father, using that same language the Hebrew mind so well understood). Can this be literal? How then did the Son of man **come with the clouds** while at the same time He **came to God in Heaven?** From this it is very evident that the expression "came with the clouds" is symbolical language depicting some event of deity.

Joel 2:1-2: " . . . for the day of the LORD cometh, for it is nigh at hand; A day of darkness and of gloominess, a day of CLOUDS and of thick darkness. . . ."

Nahum 1:3: "The LORD hath his way in the whirlwind and in

the storm, and the CLOUDS are the dust of his feet."
Zephaniah 1:14-15: "The great day of the LORD is near. ... That day is a day of wrath, ... a day of CLOUDS and thick darkness. ..."

Is it not realistic to assume that Jesus adopted this same type of apocalyptic language in speaking of God's destruction of Jerusalem by the Roman soldiers? It does not mean that Jesus physically and bodily came riding down on a cloud out of Heaven any more than these other passages meant that God did likewise. Many expressions in the New Testament can best be explained by referring to their meanings in the Old Testament, especially those that relate to prophecy.

New Testament Passages Where Jesus Comes in the Clouds

Now to follow through after reading these Old Testament passages we have just cited, let us look at a few in the New Testament and see how the same imagery carries forward into the language of Jesus and the apostles:

Matthew 24:30: "... they shall see the Son of man COMING IN THE CLOUDS of heaven with power and great glory."

Matthew 26:64: "Hereafter shall ye see the Son of man sitting on the right hand of power, and COMING IN THE CLOUDS of heaven."

Mark 13:26: "And then shall they see the Son of man COMING IN THE CLOUDS with great power and glory."

Mark 14:62: "Ye shall see the Son of man sitting on the right hand of power, and COMING IN THE CLOUDS OF HEAVEN." (Here it says that they will see Him "coming in the clouds of heaven" while He is "sitting on the right hand of power.") Surely anyone can see that this is highly apocalyptic language. If literal and bodily, how could He do both at the same time? His sitting on the right hand of the Father and His coming in the clouds of heaven are expressions of great magnitude, expressing the realization of the people as to the claims of Jesus Christ as the Son of man in His glory.

And in the book of **Revelation (1:7)** is found the same kind of language expressing the same thing: "Behold, he COMETH WITH CLOUDS; and every eye shall see him, and they also which pierced him: and all kindreds of the earth shall wail because of him." This is not some futuristic prophecy for our time or later; this prophecy is right in line with the others which tell us that Jesus was coming in the clouds to bring judgment upon Israel for their sins. The ones who pierced Him would see this. The peoples of the land would mourn when this happened.

Dr. John Owen said, "So upon or in the destruction of Jerusalem (the same work), Luke xxi. 27, the Son of man is said to 'come in a cloud, with power and great glory' — and they that escape in that desolation are said to 'stand before the Son of man', verse 36" **(John Owen, The Works of John Owen, vol. 9, p. 139).**

Revelation 14:14: "Behold a white CLOUD, and UPON THE CLOUD one sat like unto the Son of man." This "Armageddon" vision depicted here involves the land of Israel, which was destroyed by the Roman soldiers. "And the winepress was trodden without the city . . ." etc. **(vs. 20).** Josephus the historian describes in vivid words the historical incidents of such horrible bloodshed in those days that caused John to make a prediction like this.

But we are getting into the book of Revelation here, and much more on this should await some other time and some other book on that subject alone. But let me give here a quotation from **Kenneth Gentry** in his recent book, **The Beast of Revelation:**

"The references in Revelation to His coming have to do with His coming in judgment, **particularly upon Israel.** This is evident in the theme verse of Revelation found in Revelation 1:7: 'Behold, He is coming with the clouds, and every eye will see Him, even those who pierced Him; and all the tribes of the earth will mourn over Him. Even so, Amen.' This cloud-coming of Christ in judgment is reminiscent of Old Testament cloud-comings of God in judgment upon ancient historical people and nations (Pss. 18:7-15; 104:3; Isa. 19:1; Joel 2:1, 2; Hab. 1:2ff.; Zeph. 1:4, 15)" **(Kenneth Gentry, The Beast of Revelation, p. 26).**

Can anyone tell me why we should consider all these passages in the Old Testament to be figurative language, but that in the New Testament they would have to be literal (that is, natural and physical)? Isn't it more logical to think that the writers of the New Testament (and Jesus) would naturally do the same as the Old Testament writers did, and use this kind of language metaphorically? Didn't the same God inspire the prophecies in both testaments? Why should He then deal with them differently?

Can one see Christ in any other way than physical? Jesus said to His disciples, "Yet a little while, and the world seeth me no more; but ye see me: because I live, ye shall live also" **(John 14:19).** Jesus was saying here that after He was gone, while the world would no longer be able to see Him, the disciples would certainly see Him; but surely we understand He did not mean that He would be physically seen.

The *parousia*/coming of the Son of man in that generation was the commencement of His coming in judgment, which took place first in the destruction of His enemies (i.e., Jerusalem). This judgment will continue on into the future until that judgment is completed as represented by the picture of the great white throne judgment of **Revelation 20:11-15.** (See also **Acts 17:31**). Jesus had said,

"For the Father judgeth no man, but hath committed all judgment unto the Son. . . . And hath given him authority to execute judgment also, because he is the Son of man" **(John 5:22, 27)**. He began exercising that judgment in the events of A.D. 67-70.

According to **Luke 21:27-28**, it was right after Jesus said, "And then shall they see the Son of man coming in a cloud with power and great glory," that He said, "And when these things begin to come to pass, then look up, and lift up your heads; for your redemption draweth nigh."

This, of course, did not refer to the redemption of their souls, which had already taken place; nor did it refer to the redemption of their bodies, which takes place at the resurrection. But it referred to their personal redemption from all they had been undergoing at the hands of the Jewish people. They would now be delivered from all of that. In view of this prospect, they were to lift up their heads and be glad.

And concerning their deliverance from the awful tribulation that did come upon that nation, Jesus had said, "Watch ye therefore, and pray always, that ye may be accounted worthy to escape all these things that shall come to pass, and to stand before the Son of man" **(Luke 21:36)**. This is in line with John's vision in the book of Revelation concerning those awful things that were predicted to happen, and he said, "For the great day of his wrath is come; and who shall be able to stand?" **(Revelation 6:17)**. As to who would be able to stand, only those servants of God who were redeemed, who were figuratively sealed in their foreheads **(Revelation 7:3)** so that they would not be harmed during that dreadful time. They would be the ones who would be able to stand before the Son of man.

A Premillennial Coming of Christ

We have been talking about the coming of Christ (the *parousia*) at the time of the fall of Jerusalem in 70 A.D. Following this time was and is the church age, believed by many of us to be that same interval of time spoken of by John the Revelator as "the thousand years," and by modern Bible scholars as "the millennium." So, in this respect, this *parousia*/coming of Christ in A.D. 70 was a **premillennial** coming of Christ! (I just had to throw this in for the fun of it, though the thought is not original with me!)

★★★★★★★★★★★★★★

"... and then shall all the tribes of the earth mourn ..." **(Matthew 24:30)**.

The above portion of **verse 30** follows that which spoke of "the sign of the Son of man in heaven"; and before that part which says "they shall see the Son of man coming in the clouds of heaven," etc. But I wanted to cover the matter of the Son of man coming in the clouds first, and so now this.

This part of verse 30 is reminiscent of **Zechariah 12:11-12** where it says, "In that day shall there be a great mourning in Jerusalem, as the mourning of Hadadrimmon in the valley of Megiddon. And the land shall mourn, every family apart. . . ." The tribes' mourning in A.D. 67-70 was in fulfillment of this Old Testament prophecy. It was to the tribes of the land of Israel to which this passage had reference.

Allan A. MacRae said:

"Thus the English word 'earth' could mean the entire globe or it could be used to indicate a small amount of soil. The Hebrew word *eres* which is translated 'earth' hundreds of times, is often used in the sense of country or land, as 'the land of Israel.' The English and Hebrew usages are far from identical and a translator often has difficulty in selecting the word that will fit the particular context" **(Allan A. MacRae, The Prophecies of Daniel, p. 22).**

The same thing holds true in the New Testament. The Greek word *ge* translated "earth" also means "land." In this particular case it is talking about the tribes of the **land** of Israel.

Jesus said, ". . . they [all the tribes of the earth/land — the Jews] shall see the Son of man coming in the clouds of heaven with power and great glory" **(vs. 30).** Here **(vs. 30)** the Christians will have already fled from Jerusalem as Jesus instructed them in **verse 16**, and it is the Jewish tribes in the land which see the manifestation of Christ's power and glory.

On **verse 30**, **Henry Hammond** said, "30. And this shall appear to be a signal punishment upon the Jews, and they shall with sorrow (though too late) take notice of it as a notable act of revenge of the crucified Christ upon those that were thus guilty of his death . . ." **(Henry Hammond,** v. 1, p. 116, new ed.).

★ ★ ★ ★ ★ ★ ★ ★ ★ ★ ★ ★ ★ ★

"And he shall send his angels with a great sound of a trumpet, and they shall gather together his elect from the four winds, from one end of heaven to the other" (Matthew 24:31).

This is not speaking of a Rapture of the saints into Heaven at some future (to us) coming of Christ! (Just three verses later He will say this was to happen in that generation). Please note that the older commentaries do **not** apply this to a Rapture!

After the coming of the Son of man, he would then gather His elect ones. He would do then with His elect ones what He could not do with rebellious Jerusalem prior to His death. He had lamented, "O Jerusalem, Jerusalem, thou that killest the prophets, and stonest them which are sent unto thee, how often would I have GATHERED thy children together, even as a hen GATHERETH her chickens under her wings, and ye would not!" **(Matthew 23:37).**

It is not a physical gathering He is talking about, but a spiritual one. After lamenting that the people of Jerusalem would not allow Him to gather them together, He uttered these words of "desolation," "Behold, your house is left unto you desolate" (**vs. 38**). And then He made the statement, "For I say unto you, Ye shall not see me henceforth, till ye shall say, Blessed is he that cometh in the name of the Lord" (**vs. 39**). (This was a quotation from **Psalm 118:26**).

When would this happen? It certainly did not happen any time prior to the destruction and desolation of Jerusalem. They never acknowledged Him as coming in the name of the Lord; and not until the *"parousia"* coming of Christ in A.D. 70 did they "see" Him as such. Jesus had said to the high priest, "And ye shall SEE the Son of man sitting on the right hand of power, and coming in the clouds of heaven" (**Mark 14:62**).

And this is what Jesus had predicted to His disciples in the last verse studied, " . . . and they shall SEE the Son of man coming in the clouds of heaven with power and great glory" (**Matthew 24:30**). They **did** SEE Him then and had to acknowledge that He was the Blessed One, the Messiah, Who came in the name of the Lord.

But by then it was too late! They acknowledged Him only in the same way as Jesus said some would in **Matthew 7:22-23**, "Lord, Lord, have we not prophesied in thy name? and in thy name have cast out devils? and in thy name done many wonderful works? And then will I profess unto them, I never knew you: depart from me, ye that work iniquity."

This was not a promise of salvation for Israel in general by any means, other than for the elect who were among those who witnessed the awful holocaust of God's fierce anger against Israel. They had rejected Him, and He had not been able to **gather** them together, and so God brought desolation upon the place. Now with Jerusalem and the Temple completely demolished, it is next in order to GATHER the true people of God together, even as He had previously desired to do with the people of Jerusalem.

"Angels" means "messengers" according to the definition of the Greek word *aggelos*. This word is translated "messengers" in **Matthew 11:10, Mark 1:2, Luke 7:24, 27; 9:52, II Corinthians 12:7, James 2:25**, etc. It can refer either to spiritual beings who carry God's message, or it can refer to earthly men who preach the gospel.

"Not the angels, **i.e.**, ministering spirits, so called, not from their nature, but their office, as being sent forth by God and Christ; but men-angels, or messengers, the ministers and preachers of the Gospel, whom Christ would call, qualify, and send forth into all the world of the Gentiles, to preach his Gospel, and plant churches there still more, when that at Jerusalem was broken up and dissolved. These are called **angels,** because of their mission and commission from Christ, to preach the Gospel" **(John Gill, An Exposition of the New Testament, p. 239, on St. Matthew 24:31).**

In general, the trumpet being blown signified anticipated victory **(Joshua 6:4-5, Judges 7:19-22),** a new time period **(Psalm 81:30),** preparation for battle **(Ezekiel 7:14),** and a warning and alarm **(Ezekiel 33:3, Joel 2:1).** More specifically, it spoke of gathering the people together for some purpose; and a trumpet was in connection with God's revealing Himself in some way (see **Exodus 19:16).**

A trumpet sound was for calling the people together. "And when they shall blow with them, all the assembly shall assemble themselves to thee at the door of the tabernacle of the congregation" **(Numbers 10:3).**

The trumpet here in **Matthew 24:31** is the GOSPEL MESSAGE by which men are brought into this oneness of the children of God.

The elect of God will be gathered from the north, south, east and west as by "a great sound of a trumpet," reminiscent of "the great trumpet" of **Isaiah 27:12-13** where it says:

"And it shall come to pass in that day, that the LORD shall beat off from the channel of the river unto the stream of Egypt, and ye shall be gathered one by one, O ye children of Israel. And it shall come to pass in that day, that THE GREAT TRUMPET SHALL BE BLOWN, and they shall come which were ready to perish in the land of Assyria, and the outcasts in the land of Egypt, and shall worship the LORD in the holy mount at Jerusalem."

"The Jews say, that 'in the after-redemption (**i.e.,** by the Messiah) all Israel shall be gathered together by the sound of a trumpet, from the four parts of the world. Zohar in Lev. fol. 47:1'" **(John Gill).**

In **John 11:51-52** the high priest had "prophesied that Jesus should die for that nation; And not for that nation only, but that also he should GATHER TOGETHER in one the children of God that were scattered abroad."

This gathering was not physical, but spiritual, and did not occur immediately upon the death of Jesus. It took the culmination of all events through the destruction of the Jewish system before Christianity could be seen for what it really was, and all could enter into that new phase of spiritual development then established.

Here we have the answer to the kind of thing that the Psalmist was talking about in **Psalm 50:3-5:**

"Our God shall come, and shall not keep silence: a fire shall devour before him, and it shall be very tempestuous round about him.

"He shall call to the heavens from above, and to the earth, that he may judge his people.

"Gather my saints together unto me; those that have made a covenant with me by sacrifice."

"This . . . trumpet announces the inauguration of the New Covenant, and is to be compared with the trumpet which announced the inauguration of the Old Covenant (Exodus 19:16, 20:18)" **(Roderick Campbell, p. 73).**

Henry Hammond, one of the older of the commentators, expressed it thusly:

"31. And he shall, as with an herald and a loud sounding trumpet, gather together all the persevering believers, that remnant whom he purposed to preserve from this destruction, wheresoever they are in any part of Judaea, (see Rev. vii. 12) and rescue them from this common calamity: see ver. 40, 41, and Rev. vii. 3, 4, etc." **(Henry Hammond, v. 1, p. 116 new ed.).**

But His deliverance of the early Christians was only the beginning of any gathering that would be taking place as time went on.

Nisbett's definition of "from one end of heaven to the other," was, "From the four quarters of the land; from one end of the Jewish dominion to the other" **(Nisbett, p. 28).** We know, of course, that the statement had more of a universal meaning than that limited definition, though the idea no doubt was included.

Milton S. Terry said:

"This verse has been understood, figuratively, of the sending forth of the messengers of the Gospel to gather unto Christ an elect Church in place of the outcast Israel. In that sense it was a procedure which followed the *parousia* and still continues" **(Milton S. Terry, Biblical Hermeneutics,** footnote, p. 447).

This gathering of God's people would continue right on through the conversion of Gentiles who would "sit down" with those of the Old Testament saints. "And I say unto you, That many shall come from the east and west, and shall sit down with Abraham, and Isaac, and Jacob, in the kingdom of heaven" **(Matthew 8:11).**

This process actually began during that transition period from Christ to the destruction of Jerusalem. In Acts we are shown how God began to bring in the Gentiles (Cornelius, **Acts 10-11**). And when they had their conference at Jerusalem about this, James declared that what had happened was in fulfillment of the words of the prophets" **(Acts 15:15).** He said,

"Simeon hath declared how God at the first did visit the Gentiles, to TAKE OUT OF THEM a people for his name.

"And to this agree the words of the prophets; as it is written,

"After this I will return, and will build again the tabernacle of David, which is fallen down; and I will build again the ruins thereof, and I will set it up:

"That the residue of men might seek after the Lord, and all the Gentiles, upon whom my name is called . . ." **(Acts 15:14-17)**.

The dispensational premillennialists want to stretch the time of fulfillment of that period out into a future millennium, but James declared its past fulfillment in the days of early Christianity. And it might have been only a small start at that time, but was destined to become an ever-increasing process especially after the demise of the Jewish system. God's people would be gathered from everywhere!

The process continues until all of God's people have been gathered together. "That in the dispensation of the fulness of times he might GATHER TOGETHER in one all things in Christ, both which are in heaven, and which are on earth; even in him" **(Ephesians 1:10)**. This passage does not refer just to the "fulness of time" which led up to the actual fulfillment itself, but it refers to the fulness of the times in the sense of all that went along with the time being reached — that is, of all the blessings that followed that point of time.

Here is seen the oneness in Christianity, consisting of both saved Jews and saved Gentiles. And it could possibly refer to the final control of all things which have been put under the feet of Jesus **(Acts 2:34-35, I Corinthians 15:25)**. This passage **(Ephesians 1:10)** would not refer, however, to any universal reconciliation or restoration as envisioned by some.

Writing of the parallel passage to **Matthew 24:31** in **Mark 13:27**, **Ezra P. Gould** (1896) wrote:

"All the processes by which men are brought to the acknowledgement of Christ and the obedience of the kingdom belong to the gathering of the elect. The angels represent the invisible heavenly agencies in an earthly event. The introduction of them means that there is that invisible, Divine side to a human transaction. Back of all that men are doing for the conversion of the world, is the Lord Christ with the hosts of heaven. . . . As for the time, it begins then, at the time of the consummation of the Jewish age, because Judaism was the great obstacle at that time to the universal spread of the kingdom. Under its influence, Christianity threatened to become a mere appendage of Judaism, to have the particularism, formalism, and legalism of that religion grated upon it in such a way that it could never become a universal religion. With the removal of this obstacle, could begin, not the gathering of the elect, but the gathering of them from the four quarters of the world, the universal gathering" **(A Critical and Exegetical Commentary on the Gospel According to St. Mark, p. 252)**.

John Ellicott's comments on John 11:52 are worth noting here:

"**And not for that nation only** — Caiaphas had said 'die for the people,' using the word which meant the people of the Jews. St. John said, 'die for that nation,' using the wider words which meant the nation as one of the nations of the earth. He now passes to a wider meaning still. He had lived to see a partial fulfilment of the ingathering of the 'other sheep' of chap. x. 16, and he thinks of that death as for God's children in all nations, who shall be one flock under one shepherd" (**John Ellicott, Ellicott's Commentary on the Whole Bible,** vol. 5, p. 486).

". . . unto him shall the gathering of the people be" (**Genesis 49:10**).

Commenting on **Matthew 24:31, Dr. George L. Murray** in his book, **Millennial Studies,** said:

" 'And he shall send his angels with a great sound of a trumpet, and they shall gather together his elect from the four winds, from one end of heaven to the other.' We know that no Bible scholar will deny that the word, translated **angels** in this passage, is also translated **messengers** at least seven times in the New Testament, and in neither case does it apply to a celestial being. Three times the word is used of John the Baptist. In Luke 9:52 the term is applied to the disciples of Christ. In II Corinthians 12:7 the same word is used in describing the messenger of Satan that came to buffet the apostle Paul, while in James 2:25 it is used to designate the spies hidden by Rahab. In the book of Revelation, Jesus Christ commanded John to write to the angel of each of the seven churches in Asia, but our Lord was not dictating letters to the angels who do His will and behold His face, but to the ministers of the seven churches in Asia Minor. Christ's ministers and messengers were therefore the *angelous* or **angels** commissioned to gather His elect from the four winds of heavens by the preaching of the gospel. This world-wide mission, which really began with the destruction of Jerusalem, removed the shackles of Judaism and formally brought to an end the old dispensation. The blowing of the great trumpet is also a figurative expression. The metaphor abounds in Scripture in connection with such important pronouncements as the day of Jubilee and other similar occasions. The messengers of Christ were now to go forth in His name, heralding the day of Jubilee for as many as should believe the Gospel" (**Murray,** pp. 124-125).

When prophecy speaks of gathering people from "one end of heaven to the other" (**Matthew 24:31**) it is not talking about a gathering of people from heaven. As for example, see **Deuteronomy 30:4-5** where God said to Israel:

"If any of thine be driven out unto the OUTMOST PARTS OF HEAVEN, from thence will the LORD thy God gather thee, and from thence will he fetch thee: And the LORD thy God will bring thee into the land which thy fathers possessed, and thou shalt possess it. . . ." This is simply a "heavenly" expression signifying to the uttermost limits of where people are.

"From one end of heaven to the other" (vs. 31). This is the same kind of expression as in **Deuteronomy 4:32,** " . . . ask from the one side of heaven unto the other." God is not suggesting here that Israel go up into Heaven to inquire of Him, but rather, the expression is one of universality — encompassing all areas. As one can look out and see where "heaven" touches the earth in one direction, then the same in the opposite direction, so in that sense God is saying "from one end of heaven to the other."

Of this verse **John Lightfoot** said:

"**And he shall send his angels,** &c. When Jerusalem shall be reduced to ashes, and that wicked nation cut off and rejected, then shall the Son of man send his ministers with the trumpet of the gospel, and they shall gather together his elect of the several nations from the four corners of heaven: so that God shall not want a church, although that ancient people of his be rejected and cast off: but, that Jewish church being destroyed, a new church shall be called out of the Gentiles" (**John Lightfoot,** vol. 2, p. 320). (**Jamieson, Faucett and Brown Commentary** also quotes this passage from Lightfoot in its commentary, as well as **Milton Terry** in **Biblical Hermeneutics,** p. 447).

Adam Clarke, in his commentary on this verse, said:

"**Shall gather together his elect.** The **Gentiles,** who were now **chosen** or **elected,** in place of the rebellious, obstinate **Jews,** according to our Lord's prediction, Matt. viii. 11, 12, and Luke xiii. 28, 29. For **the children of the kingdom,** (the **Jews** who were **born** with a **legal right** to it, but had now finally **forfeited** that right by their iniquities) **should be thrust out.** It is worth serious observation, that the Christian religion spread and prevailed mightily **after** this period: and nothing contributed more to the success of the Gospel than the **destruction of Jerusalem** happening in the very **time** and **manner,** and with the very **circumstances,** so particularly foretold by our Lord. It was **after this period** that the kingdom of Christ began, and his reign was established in almost every part of the world" (**Adam Clarke,** commentary on **Matthew 24:31**).

The gathering together of God's people is not done instantaneously. This "gathering" takes place during the entire gospel age in which we now live.

John Tindall Harris said:

"Pentecost was the coming of the Kingdom in its initial form; but the Advent of the King in the glory of His *Parousia* did not take place until the destruction of Jerusalem. They came in the dispensation of the Lord's *Parousia* — the day of Christ — in which we are now living. In this dispensation of the *Parousia* the Church is now being gathered" **(John Tindall Harris, The Writings of the Apostle John, p. 171).**

George R. Beasley-Murray said:

"The unity of Gentiles and Jews in one people in the kingdom of God, while 'sons of the kingdom' would be excluded, is evident from Matt. 8:11-12/Luke 13:28-29. The universal implication of Mark 13:27 could well envisage the gathering of the elect of all nations along with the penitents of Israel into a single community under the lordship and in the fellowship of the Son of man" **(George R. Beasley-Murray, Jesus and the Last Days, c. 1993, p. 434).**

In **Zechariah 2:10-11** is a prophecy of the Christian age which followed the Jewish age:

"Sing and rejoice, O daughter of Zion: for, lo, I COME, and I will dwell in the midst of thee, saith the LORD.

"And MANY NATIONS SHALL BE JOINED TO THE LORD in that day, and shall be my people: and I will dwell in the midst of thee. . . ."

This is not a so-called future "millennial" promise for a period of time after a future "second coming" of Christ, but a gospel promise for this age — fulfilled in the gathering of people to Christ, in this age in which Judaism has now been supplanted by true spiritual Israel — God's redeemed people. God **did** come (as He said); Jesus came in judgment on the old system, and now the way into the holiest **(Hebrews 9:8)** is manifested, and God is dwelling in the midst of His redeemed people who have been "gathered" to Him. No temple is needed now **(Revelation 21:22)** as God dwells directly in the midst of His people **(Revelation 21:3).** This reminds us of what Jesus told the woman at the well:

" . . . the hour cometh, when ye shall neither in this mountain, nor yet at Jerusalem, worship the Father. . . . But the hour cometh, AND NOW IS, when the true worshippers shall worship the Father in spirit and in truth. . . . God is a Spirit: and they that worship him must worship him in spirit and in truth" **(John 4:21-24).**

Jesus foresaw the dissolution of the entire ritualistic worship system of the Jewish (and Samaritan) people, and the ensuing age when God's elect would be gathered out of all nations to worship Him in spirit and in truth as He personally dwelt in their midst. God does right now dwell in the hearts of His people everywhere. The old temple is gone, and God Himself (and Jesus) are the temple of the new city **(Revelation 21:22),** the holy Jerusalem which is the city of God, made up of all God's redeemed people.

This was also true before Jerusalem was destroyed (since Pentecost), but it took the utter destruction of the Jewish system to make it clear that God does not dwell in temples made with hands **(Acts 7:48)**, but that His presence would be found in His gathered people.

Dispensationalists believe that the Church is in a "parenthetic" period of time, and that God's prophetic clock stopped in the time of Christ and will not start again until Jesus comes again in our future. They believe that the Jews looked on their age as **their** present age, and that the age to come was believed by them to be after Messiah comes and reigns with His people. As dispensationalists believe that the rejection of Christ led to the postponement of the kingdom until Christ comes again, they believe that the age to come refers to a millennium (in the future, following a future second coming of Christ).

J.N. Darby, the founder of what is known as modern-day dispensationalism, said:

"Really, this is not a dispensation. The Jews had a 'this world' and 'a world to come,' 'this age' and an 'age to come.' Messiah was to bring in the 'age to come.' The age of the law went on and Messiah did come, but they would not have Him, and the whole thing stopped: then comes the church between that and His second coming; and this is why I said this is not strictly a dispensation, but when Messiah comes again, it will close this time, and then will be the last day of this age" **(The Collected Writings of J.N. Darby, vol. 25, pp. 243-244).**

But the Bible does not teach that the kingdom was postponed. True, the kind of kingdom the Jews were looking for did not come, but Christ's kingdom did; and He is now in glory, reigning from the right hand of His Father **(Acts 2:30-36).** The end of the Jewish age did come, and the new age (or dispensation) is here. Paul speaks of it thusly in **Ephesians 1:10,** "That in the dispensation of the fulness of times he might gather together in one all things in Christ, both which are in heaven, and which are on earth; even in him." That process of gathering is now in effect, in fulfillment of what Jesus said in **Matthew 24:31.** And this "fulness of times" mentioned in **Ephesians 1:10** began at the time as referred to in **Galatians 4:4,** "But when the fulness of the time was come, God sent forth his Son. . . ."

The Galatians passage referred "to a point of time, marking the completion of the preparation for our Lord's coming; here, apparently, to a series of 'seasons,' 'which the Father hath put in His own power' (Acts 1:7) for the completion of the acts of the Mediatorial kingdom described in the words following" **(Ellicott's Commentary, vol. 4, p. 13).**

"The whole Gospel **times** (plural) are meant, with the benefits to the church **dispensed** in them severally" **(Jamieson, Faussett and Brown Commentary**, vol. 3, p. 399).

Someone said that it took forty years for Israel to get to the promised land, and that it took spiritual Israel forty years to get to the New Jerusalem.

The Kingdom of God

True, the word "kingdom" is not found in **Matthew 24**. But it is found elsewhere in connection with the coming of the Son of man, such as in **Matthew 16:28**, "Verily I say unto you, There be some standing here, which shall not taste of death, till they see the Son of man coming in his kingdom." In the events of **Matthew 24** we find that kingdom manifested.

When in **Mark 1:15** Jesus said, "The time is fulfilled, and the kingdom of God is at hand," He was saying that the time arranged by God for the fulfillment of the promises of the kingdom of God had now come. Jesus really did initiate the work of God **in the world**, which was to culminate in the completed process at the end of history in the resurrection of all the dead and the judgment of all mankind. The development of this work carries us from His birth through His miracles, His death, His resurrection, His ascension, Pentecost, and finally the manifestation of His kingdom to all of Israel through the events of A.D. 66-70. These events are called the "coming of the Son of man in his kingdom."

In other words, there is:

1. An **arrival** of the kingdom of God (**Mark 1:15** and **Matthew 12:28**) at the ministry of Christ. To the Jews, this was evidenced in His miracles. To the disciples, this was also evidenced at Pentecost. But Jesus technically "received" the kingdom upon His ascension (**Daniel 7:13-14, Acts 2:30-36**). That was His crowning day!
2. **A manifestation** of the kingdom at Pentecost at the fall of Jerusalem and the Temple, and in all the signs and wonders in between.
3. A **consummation** of the kingdom (**I Corinthians 15:24**) at the "end" when He delivers the kingdom over to God the Father. All will be resurrected, either to life or damnation, and Death and Hell will be destroyed forever.

It is not the initiation, or the beginning, of the kingdom of God which we see in the events of A.D. 67-70. This was the manifestation of that kingdom, in which Christ's power and glory were revealed. The kingdom had its beginning years earlier, as **Mark 1:15** and **Matthew 12:28** said, beginning with the ministry of Christ. It was an inward thing — in the hearts of men. When Jesus said, "The kingdom of God is **within** you" **(Luke 17:21)**, He used the word *"entos"* for "within" — not simply "in the midst of you," but actually "within you." It is the same word as found in "within the cup" **(Matthew 23:26)**, which, of course, means **inside** the cup — not "in the midst of the cup." We need to understand the varying degrees of progress in the growth of the kingdom, and the events involved in that growth, right on up to the final consummation of that kingdom when it is turned over to God the Father at the end of history **(I Corinthians 15:24)**. During **this** age, after Christ had sat down on the right hand of the Father **(Acts 2:33)**, He remains in authority until all enemies are subdued **(Acts 2:33-35)**. The last enemy to be conquered is death itself **(I Corinthians 15:25-26)**, which will occur when the final resurrection takes place **(Revelation 20:14)**.

The kingdom of Heaven is the same as the kingdom of God. Even the Jews of Jesus' day understood that.

Dr. Robert L. Lindsey, Southern Baptist missionary to Israel, who studied Hebrew and lived and worked among Hebrew-speaking people, said:

" . . . the rabbis often talked about 'the Kingdom of Heaven,' by which they meant 'the Kingdom of God.' They were afraid of transgressing the command not to 'take the name of the Lord in vain' so, as was their habit, they said that if the actual name of the Lord is not said you cannot transgress this commandment at all: use some evasive synonym and you will not break this law. The expression in Hebrew is *malchut shammayim,* Kingdom of Heaven, Heaven being an evasive synonym for God" **(Robert L. Lindsey,** pp. 23-24).

Our emphasis in this series on **Matthew 24** is that of the **manifestation** of that kingdom. Christ had come, inaugurating the kingdom of God. He proved its existence by His mighty miracles. After His resurrection and before His ascension, He told the disciples that ALL power (authority) in Heaven and earth had been given to Him **(Matthew 28:18)**. (See also **Ephesians 1:20-21**). **There is no greater authority in all the universe than this!** He then took up that reign at the right hand of the Father. He had come to the "Ancient of days," "and there was given him dominion, and glory, and a kingdom, that all people, nations, and languages, should serve him: his dominion is an everlasting dominion, which shall not pass away, and his kingdom that which shall not be destroyed" **(Daniel 7:13-14)**. And from that elevated position in glory, His kingdom was **manifested** to Israel in power at Pentecost **(Acts 2)**, and in the events of A.D. 67-70, and His glory and power revealed to all in His coming (arrival, *parousia*) in judgment on all those who had violently opposed that kingdom.

"The sign of the Son of man in heaven" (**Matthew 24:30**) appeared in those events, demonstrating that He was truly seated in glory as the Son of man and Messiah; and in apocalyptic language it states that they would see "the Son of man coming in the clouds of heaven with power and great glory" (which they did in **Matthew 24:30**).

This event is what **Matthew 24** is all about. To go from the **inauguration** of the kingdom to the **manifestation** of that kingdom is quite a jump. And to go from the manifestation of the kingdom to the **consummation** of the kingdom is also a big jump. To really understand the **progress** and **growth** of the kingdom would require a study of all the references to the kingdom in especially the New Testament. Other books can better deal with that than we can here.

Summary

Let us summarize some of the things we have said in this section:

1. The "sign" of the Son of man in Heaven was the destruction of Jerusalem.
2. Jesus was present at the destruction of Jerusalem, but He was not physically seen.
3. Various "comings" of Christ are mentioned in the New Testament.
4. Old Testament passages mentioned God coming down.
5. Jesus appeared on numerous occasions after He left the earth.
6. Old Testament passages spoke of God coming in the clouds.
7. The tribes of Israel in the land would mourn when their city was destroyed.
8. Jesus would send his angels/messengers out with the trumpet of the gospel to gather the people of God.
9. Jesus came in His kingdom, which was part of the kingdom of God.

Section 7 ●●●●●●●●●●●●●●●●●●●●●●●●

"THIS GENERATION SHALL NOT PASS . . ."

"Now learn a parable of the fig tree; When his branch is yet tender, and putteth forth leaves, ye know that summer is nigh:

"So likewise ye, when ye shall see all these things, know that it is near, even at the doors.

"Verily I say unto you, This generation shall not pass, till all these things be fulfilled" (Matthew 24:32-34).

★ ★ ★ ★ ★ ★ ★ ★ ★ ★ ★ ★ ★ ★

With this passage Jesus begins to summarize what He had been teaching in the previous verses. In answer to their question, "When shall these things be? and what shall be the sign of thy coming, and of the end of the world [age]?" He enumerated a number of things that would happen before the end came. Deceivers and false Christs would come. Wars and rumours of wars would be prevalent. There would be famines, pestilences, and earthquakes. They would be delivered up to be afflicted and would even be put to death. The gospel would be preached in all the world, and then the end would come. The abomination of desolation, the pagan Roman armies, would surround the holy city. There would be a time of great tribulation. Then the Son of man would come in the clouds of heaven.

So He says, "When you see all these things, you will know that the time has now come for the Son of man to come."

He uses a parable of the fig tree to illustrate this. He says:

"Now learn a parable of the fig tree; When his branch is yet tender, and putteth forth leaves, ye know that summer is nigh:

"So likewise ye, when ye shall see all these things, know that it is near, even at the doors" **(Matthew 24:32-33)**.

This is a universal illustration. Many trees lose their leaves during winter. After winter is over, when the new green leaves begin to show up on the trees, we know that spring is right around the corner. Jesus said that just like you know summer is coming when you see the new leaves on the tree, so when all these things have come about which I have mentioned, you know that the end is near — that the Son of man is about ready to appear, just like someone standing at the door waiting to come in.

This is a simple illustration, and we should not attach other meanings to it than Jesus intended to convey. I shall say more about this later, especially about the "fig tree."

The parallel passage in **Luke 21:28** says, "And when these things begin to come to pass, then look up, and lift up your heads; for YOUR REDEMPTION DRAWETH NIGH."

As **John Gill** said:

". . . not the redemption of their souls from sin, Satan, the law, the world, death, and hell; for that was to be obtained, and was obtained, before any of these signs took place; nor the redemption of their bodies at the last day, in the resurrection, called the day of redemption; for this respects something that was to be, in the present age and generation . . . , but the deliverance of the apostles and other Christians, from the persecution of the Jews, which were very violent and held till these times, and then they were freed from them: or by **redemption** is meant, the Redeemer, the Son of man, who shall now come in power and glory, to destroy the Jews, and deliver his people; and so the Ethiopic version renders it, **for he draws nigh who shall save you**" (John Gill, on Luke 21:28, vol. 5, **John Gill's Commentary,** 1851).

We know that it was the contemporary people of Jesus' day who would see these things happen. Jesus said, "So likewise YE, when YE shall see all these things, know that it is near, even at the doors" (vs. 33). He said, "YE." THEY would see these things. Therefore, this could not be something to happen 2,000 years, more or less, in the future. It **had** to be during the time when the disciples could see these things coming on them, which would indicate that it (He) was "near, even at the doors."

"When ye shall see all THESE things, know that it (He) is near, even at the doors." Even the Scofield Reference Bible marginal note says that "it" means "he." So, when all THESE things (all the things already mentioned which are commonly understood by commentators to apply to the events leading up to the destruction of Jerusalem) begin to come to pass, then He (Christ) will be "near, even at the door."

★★★★★★★★★★★★★★

"Verily I say unto you, This generation shall not pass, till all these things be fulfilled" (Matthew 24:34).

★★★★★★★★★★★★★★

Jesus very plainly said here that ALL of the things He had mentioned would come to pass in that generation. This would include the persecution of the disciples, the gospel being preached in all the world, the abomination of desolation, the great tribulation, and the coming of the Son of man.

One commentary frankly acknowledges, "This is a troublesome

verse" (**The New Jerome Commentary,** p. 667). And why is it troublesome to the writer of this Catholic commentary? It is because he believes, "The greatest event, the coming of the Son of Man with the kingdom, is still to come" (p. 688). Rather than simply acknowledging, as Christ said, that "**ALL**" those things would be fulfilled in that generation, he wants to tear part of the prophecy out and make it fit into a future scheme of things. And this is why the verse is troublesome to many other people as well. They want to make the verse read, "some of these things," instead of, "all these things," as Jesus said.

We should accept these words of Jesus exactly as He gave them. The reason this is not done in most cases is because modern interpreters try to separate the coming of the Son of man from the rest of the things mentioned, thinking that Jesus was talking about something a couple thousands of years or so down the road somewhere, instead of about His coming in judgment on Israel in A.D. 70. As discussed before, one cannot split the chapter up like that. The word "generation" applied to that generation of people living at the time He spoke, not to a generation of people thousands of years later.

Verse 34 stands out clear and plain in defining and limiting the time involved in the matter of when all the things He had been talking about would take place. All of those things right on up through the preaching of the gospel to all nations would happen, and then the end would come (**vs. 14**). It was then they would see the abomination of desolation, indicating they should flee to the mountains, for it was then that great tribulation would occur. And it was to be "immediately" after that tribulation that they would see the Son of man coming in the clouds. They **did** see all those things take place, and they did flee before the tribulation took place which ended in A.D. 70. Therefore, when Jesus said that all those things would take place in that generation, and they did, the coming of the Son of man was to be understood to occur immediately thereafter.

Thomas Newton (1754) said:

"He proceeds to declare that the time of his coming was at no very great distance, and to show that he hath been speaking all this while of the destruction of Jerusalem, he affirms with his usual affirmation, ver. 34, 'Verily I say unto you, This generation shall not pass, till all these things be fulfilled!' It is to me a wonder how any man can refer part of the foregoing discourse to the destruction of Jerusalem, and part to the end of the world, or any other distant event, when it is said so positively here in the conclusion, 'All these things shall be fulfilled in this generation.' It seemeth as if our Saviour had been aware of some such misapplication of his words, by adding yet greater force and emphasis to this affirmation, ver. 35 — 'Heaven and earth shall pass away, but my words shall not pass away' " (**Thomas Newton, p. 426**).

Meaning of the Word "Generation" in This Verse

The word "generation" as used in Matthew 24:34 is from the Greek word *"genea"* which means, "by implication an **age** (the period or the persons)."

This word has the same meaning as the word "generation" found in **Luke 11:50-51**:

"That the blood of all the prophets, which was shed from the foundation of the world, may be required of THIS GENERATION;

"... verily I say unto you, It shall be required of THIS GENERATION."

Judgment upon Israel, and all the things mentioned in Matthew 24, would come upon THAT generation. It did, during the lifetime of many of those who lived at that time.

Several other passages in the New Testament where this identical word (same in the Greek — *genea*) is used, would be:

Luke 1:50: "And his mercy is on them that fear him from generation to generation."

Acts 13:36: "For David, after he had served his own generation by the will of God, fell on sleep, and was laid unto his fathers, and saw corruption."

Hebrews 3:10: "Wherefore I was grieved with that generation, and said, They do alway err in their heart; and they have not known my ways."

About the best verse I can think of which clearly shows the meaning of this word ("generation/*genea*") as used in **Matthew 24:34**, is **Matthew 1:17**:

Matthew 1:17: "So all the generations from Abraham to David are fourteen generations; and from David until the carrying away into Babylon are fourteen generations; and from the carrying away into Babylon unto Christ are fourteen generations."

Here are 42 generations. If "race" (for example) were meant by this word, does this passage mean there were **42** races of Israel, all of whom came from Abraham's blood? This passage ought to really settle the matter as to the meaning of the word.

Many irrelevant meanings have been given to this word "generation" by many different expositors. (See a listing of them in **Meyer's Commentary** on this verse, volume 1, page 420. I shall not take the space to quote them all here.) None of them seem reasonable when the proper definition is considered. Some authors have produced questionable writings based on one or more of these irrelevant meanings — which are not meanings at all! By the word "generation" in **Matthew 24:34** Jesus meant the same period of time as referred to in **Matthew 16:28:**

"Verily I say unto you, There be some standing here, which shall not taste of death, till they see the Son of man coming in his kingdom."

Thomas Scott said in his commentary on **vss. 32-35:**

"Our Lord here answers the former part of the apostle's questions, concerning the time when these events would take place. In general he assured them, that their approach would be as certainly determined by the signs that he had mentioned, as the approach of summer was by the budding and the tender branch of the fig-tree, and that they would all be accomplished before the generation was passed away. This absolutely restricts our primary interpretation of the prophecy to the destruction of Jerusalem, which took place within forty years" **(Thomas Scott, vol. 1).**

"This Generation" Not in Our Times Nor Our Generation

In **Acts 2:40** Peter urged his hearers to save themselves "from this untoward generation." What did he have in mind? He had in mind the coming fate upon that generation of Israel from which converts would save themselves. This is the same as when Jesus said, "Verily I say unto you, All these things shall come upon this generation" **(Matthew 23:36)**, as He told the Jews of the impending judgment about to fall on them.

In **Matthew 24:34** He simply reiterated what He had already said in the previous chapter as to how all those things would happen in that generation.

Ezra P. Gould (1896) said, " . . . there is general consent now that the prophecy is restricted in time to that generation, v. 30. In general, the historical interpretation of prophecy is fairly settled" **(Gould, p. 249).**

"We must not miss the clear references to the **contemporary expectation.** Enclosing the relevant portion of the discourse, we have Christ's own time-element designation. In 23:36, he dogmatically asserts '**all** these things shall come upon **this** generation.' He closes the relevant portion of the prophecy by repetition of the time frame: Matthew 24:34 says, 'Verily I say unto you, **this** generation shall not pass, till all these things be fulfilled.' And just forty years later Jerusalem was destroyed! Contextually the 'this generation' of Matthew 24:34 **must** speak of the same idea as that of Matthew 23:36." **(Kenneth L. Gentry, Jr., He Shall Have Dominion, p. 162).**

Of this verse, **John Lightfoot** said:

"**This generation shall not pass, &c.** Hence it appears plain enough, that the foregoing verses are not to be understood of the last judgment, but, as we said, of the destruction of Jerusalem. There were some among the disciples (particularly John), who lived to see these things come to pass. With Matt. xvi. 28, compare John xxi. 22. And there were some Rabbins alive at the time when Christ spoke these things, that lived till the city was destroyed, viz. Rabban Simeon, who perished with the city, R. Jochanan Ben Zaccai, who outlived it, R. Zadoch, R. Ismael, and others" (**John Lightfoot,** vol. 2, p. 320).

John Gill, predecessor of Charles Spurgeon, said:
"**Verily I say unto you, this generation shall not pass,** etc. Not the generation of men in general; as if the sense was, that mankind should not cease, until the accomplishment of these things; nor the generation, or people of the Jews, who should continue to be a people, until all were fulfilled; nor the generation of Christians; as if the meaning was, that there should be always a set of Christians, or believers in Christ in the world, till all these events came to pass; but it respects that present age, or generation of men then living in it; and the sense is, that all the men of that age should not die, but some should live **till all things were fulfilled;** see Matt. xvi. 28, as many did, and as there is reason to believe they might, and must, since all these things had their accomplishment, in and about forty years after this: and certain it is that John, one of the disciples of Christ outlived the time by many years; and, as Dr. Lightfoot observes, many of the Jewish doctors now living, when Christ spoke these words, lived until the city was destroyed; as Rabban Simeon, who perished with it, R. Jochanan ben Zaccai, who outlived it, R. Zadoch, R. Ismael, and others: this is a full and clear proof, that not any thing that is said before, relates to the second coming of Christ, the day of judgment, and the end of the world; but that all belong to the coming of the Son of man, in the destruction of Jerusalem, and to the end of the Jewish state" (**John Gill,** on **Matthew 24:34, An Exposition of the New Testament,** vol. 2, 1809, p. 240).

Some say (a modern innovation) that the "generation" Jesus mentioned would be the generation following the proclamation of Israel as a nation in 1948. Then, taking 40 years as a generation, they even timed the second coming of Christ for the year 1988 — 40 years later (and I am writing this paragraph in August of 1988 when a number of these modern gurus have proclaimed September 12, 1988, as the anticipated date of the Rapture!). And this in spite of the fact that some of their counterparts were previously saying the Rapture would take place in 1981 and were sadly embarrassed by its lack of occurrence. They too taught that Christ would come in 1988, a generation from the time Israel became a nation, but believing there would be a tribulation for seven years before that coming and a Rapture seven years prior to that coming at the beginning of that seven years of tribulation, surely then the Rapture would be in 1981!

Such thinking on the part of these folks was occasioned by their belief that when Jesus told them the fig tree putting forth new leaves was a sign that summer was near, and that likewise when they saw all those things they would know that it was near, even at the door **(Matthew 24:32-34)**, and that the generation would not pass till all those things were fulfilled. That much is absolutely true, and Jesus said it; but the mistake on the part of these modern-day prophets is in believing that the "fig tree" Jesus mentioned referred to Israel, and that the "generation" Jesus mentioned referred to the 40 years following the beginning of the state of Israel in May of 1948. And their mistake also is in believing that Jesus said just "fig tree" alone. Read **Luke 21:29**, and you will see that He said, "Behold the fig tree, AND ALL THE TREES." So He could not be using just a fig tree to illustrate Israel; and not only so, He never mentioned anything in the world about the beginning of a nation or state of Israel. He said, "THESE THINGS," and He was referring to those things which He had predicted would come prior to the destruction of Jerusalem, etc. When they saw those things begin to come to pass, they would know that "the kingdom of God is nigh at hand" **(Luke 21:31)**.

Hal Lindsey, in his book, **The Late Great Planet Earth,** put it this way:

"When the Jewish people, after nearly 2,000 years of exile, under relentless persecution, became a nation again on 14 May 1948 the "fig tree" put forth its first leaves.

"Jesus said that this would indicate that He was 'at the door' ready to return. Then He said, 'Truly I say to you, **this generation** will not pass away until all these things take place' **(Matthew 24:34 NASB).**

"What generation? Obviously, in context, the generation that would see the signs — chief among them the rebirth of Israel. A generation in the Bible is something like forty years. If this is a correct deduction, then within forty years or so of 1948, all these things could take place. Many scholars who studied Bible prophecy all their lives believe that this is so" **(Hal Lindsey,** pp. 53-54).

It is interesting that chapter 2 of Lindsey's book is headed, **When is a Prophet a Prophet?** And his second chapter heading is, **Do We Really Live and Learn?** with the first sentence in the chapter reading, "It's ironic that man never seems to learn from past mistakes, especially when they relate to major catastrophes." We know, of course, that Lindsey's (and others') predictions of the Lord's return in 1988 or so did not take place, and so that theory they used about the meaning of "generation" has been thrown out the window.

Why do not Bible teachers simply accept the meaning of the word to be what Jesus meant it to be?

"Dispensationalism tried to make 'this generation' refer to the 'terminal generation,' as Hal Lindsey calls it, but Jesus always meant the generation that witnesses the preaching and death of Jesus, as any concordance will reveal" (**Dale Moody, p. 556**).

It might be helpful to notice what a number of translations say about this verse in connection with the meaning of "this generation":

New English Bible: "I tell you this: the present generation will live to see it all."

Today's English Version: "Remember this! All these things will happen before the people now living have all died."

Moffatt's Translation: "I tell you truly, the present generation will not pass away, till all this happens."

Weymouth's Translation: "I tell you in solemn truth that the present generation will certainly not pass away until all this has taken place."

These translations hit the nail on the head. The meaning of the word was that of the "present" generation in the time of Christ; not some future generation thousands of years away.

When Jesus said, "This generation shall not pass, till all these things be fulfilled" (**vs. 34**), these things (just mentioned) included "the Son of man coming in the clouds of heaven with power and great glory" (**vs. 30**), because He was to come immediately after the tribulation at the end (**vss. 29-30**).

This passage (**vs. 34**) was responsible for showing me that the coming of Christ "in the clouds of heaven with power and great glory" WHATEVER IT MEANS — happened in that same generation to which Jesus spoke. His coming was part of the "ALL THINGS" which He said would occur in THAT generation.

The Word "Generation" Here
Does Not Mean "A Race" of People

It is unfortunate that some have defined this word "generation" so as to mean "race," and try to make Jesus say that all these things would happen before the "race" of Jews had passed away. But Jesus was not talking about any "race" of Jews.

God told Israel that they were to keep the Passover as "a feast to the LORD throughout your generations" (**Exodus 12:14**). What did He mean here? Different "races" of people, or rather different periods of time?

The word "generation" as used in this verse does **not** mean "kind, nation, offspring, stock." On this **C.I. Scofield** says (p. 1034, old edition, **Scofield Reference Bible**):

"Gr. *genea*, the primary definition of which is, 'race, kind, family, stock, breed.' (So all lexicons.) That the word is used in this sense here is sure because none of 'these things,' the world-wide preaching of the kingdom, the great tribulation, the return of the Lord in visible glory, and the regathering of the elect, occurred at the destruction of Jerusalem by Titus, A.D. 70. The promise is, therefore, that the generation — nation, or family of Israel — will be preserved unto 'these things'; a promise wonderfully fulfilled to this day."

Mr. Scofield is wrong here. He used the wrong Greek word with his definition, for the definition he gives is for the Greek word, *"genos."* But this is not the word used in **Matthew 24:34**. The word used in **Matthew 24:34** is certainly *"genea,"* but this has a different definition which is, "by implication an **age**."

If the verse meant "kind, nation, offspring, stock," then it would have had the Greek word *"genos,"* but it did not; the word is *"genea,"* and Scofield's definition of that word is not correct.

The word *"genea"* is used in **Luke 1:50**, "from generation to generation." It is used in **Acts 13:36**, "he had served his own generation." It is used in **Hebrews 3:10**, "I was grieved with that generation." As can easily be seen, this word means an age or period of time, not a race of people.

An example of the use of the word *"genos"* (which is **NOT** used in **Matthew 24:34**) would be **I Peter 2:9**, "But ye are a chosen generation, a royal priesthood, an holy nation. . . ." Here it is evident that this is the word that means "kind, nation, offspring, stock." But this is not the word used in **Matthew 24:34**.

Another Greek word for "generation" is *"gennema"* and means "offspring — fruit." This particular word is found in **Matthew 23:33** where Jesus said, "Ye serpents, ye generation of vipers, how can ye escape the damnation of hell?" But this word is also not the one that is used in **Matthew 24:34**.

It is bad that Mr. Scofield made this error as he supposedly checked out the Greek lexicons, for it has certainly played havoc with the theology of some later Bible teachers.

What Jesus meant by all those things happening in that generation, including the *parousia*/coming of Christ, was that they would all happen while some of those folks to whom He preached were still alive, as we pointed out from **Matthew 16:28**.

A study of the passages where Jesus used this word (*genea*/generation) shows that Jesus generally used the word in connection with the people who were right then and there in His own time. The places in Matthew where this exact word is used are: **Matthew 11:16; 12:39, 41, 42, 45; 16:4; 17:17; 23:33, 36; 24:34.** Look them up and see for yourself. Also, there are twenty-one other times in the New Testament where this exact word is used; a concordance will show you where they are.

Once again, the meaning of the word "generation" (*genea*) in Matthew 24:34 is, "by implication, an **age** (the period or the persons): — age, generation, nation, time." (See **Strong's Concordance**).

David Chilton, in his book **The Great Tribulation,** has covered this point very well. He said:

"Some have sought to get around the force of this text by saying that the word **generation** here really means **race,** and that Jesus was simply saying that the Jewish race would not die out until all these things took place. Is that true? I challenge you: Get out your concordance and look up every New Testament occurrence of the word **generation** (in Greek, *genea*) and see if it **ever** means 'race' in any other context. Here are all the references for the Gospels: Matthew 1:17; 11:16; 12:39, 41, 42, 45; 16:4; 17:17; 23:36; 24:34; Mark 8:12, 38; 9:19; 13:30; Luke 1:48, 50; 7:31; 9:41; 11:29, 30, 31, 32, 50, 51; 16:8; 17:25; 21:32. **Not one** of these references is speaking of the entire Jewish race over thousands of years; **all** use the word in its normal sense of **the sum total of those living at the same time.** It always refers to **contemporaries.** (In fact, those who say it means "race" tend to acknowledge this fact, but explain that the word suddenly **changes** its meaning when Jesus uses it in Matthew 24! We can smile at such a transparent error, but we should also remember that this is very serious. We are dealing with the Word of the living God.)" **(David Chilton, The Great Tribulation,** p.3).

"Although attempts have been made to interpret **this generation** as the Jews, or as the human race in general, it is more likely that originally it meant the generation living at the time of Jesus." (**J.C. Fenton,** p. 391).

"Israel" is Not a "Race," Anyway

By any stretch of the imagination, could the word "generation" as used by Christ here, mean "the race" of Israel — that this race would still be in existence at a future second coming of Christ in our future? This would be like saying, "Things are going to happen to you in the future, and you will still be there when it happens to you." Now would that kind of language mean anything? Of course, it is obvious that if something is to happen to anyone, they will still be around — in anything, everything, anytime, anywhere. That is certainly no argument.

But on the matter of whether the "race" of Israel would be intact in our future; that is another thing. It is felt that something should be said here concerning that matter.

In my book, **Israel in Bible Prophecy**, I made the statement, "There is no Jewish Race." I quoted from **Encyclopaedia Brittanica** when I said this. Here is what I said:

"The **Encyclopaedia Brittanica** (1973), vol. 12, page 1054, actually states: 'The Jews As A Race: The findings of physical anthropology show that, contrary to the popular view, there is no Jewish race. Anthropometric measurements of Jewish groups in many parts of the world indicate that they differ greatly from one another with respect to all the important physical characteristics.'

The reason behind this, of course, is mixed bloodlines through the mixed marriages bringing about the most mixed racial origins of these people today. On top of that, the majority of so-called Jews in the world today are not Jews at all (even with the mixed blood), because their ancestry is that of the Khazars whose ancestors go far back to the Turks and Huns, and who as a nation in A.D. 740 adopted the Jewish religion and became known as Jews. (See my book, **Israel in Bible Prophecy**, for further historical documentation on this).

Encyclopaedia Judaica Jerusalem itself also says this, under the heading **Anthropology, Physical:**

"It is a common assumption, and one that sometimes seems ineradicable even in the face of evidence to the contrary, that the Jews of today constitute a race, a homogeneous entity easily recognizable. From the preceding discussion of the origin and early history of the Jews, it should be clear that in the course of their formation as a people and a nation they had already assimilated a variety of racial strains from people moving into the general area they occupied. This had taken place by interbreeding and then by conversion to Judaism of a considerable number of communities. . . .

"Thus, the diversity of the racial and genetic attributes of various Jewish colonies of today renders any unified racial classification of them a contradiction in terms. Despite this, many people readily accept the notion that they are a distinct race. This is probably reinforced by the fact that some Jews are recognizably different in appearance from the surrounding population. That many cannot be easily identified is overlooked and the stereotype for some is extended to all — a not uncommon phenomenon" (**Encyclopaedia Judaica Jerusalem**, 1971, vol. 3, p. 50).

Also, **Encyclopedia Americana** says:
"**Racial and Ethnic Considerations.** Some theorists have considered the Jews a distinct race, although this has no factual basis. In every country in which the Jews lived for a considerable time, their physical traits came to approximate those of the indigenous people. Hence the Jews belong to several distinct racial types, ranging, for example, from fair to dark. Among the reasons for this phenomenon are voluntary or involuntary miscegenation and the conversion of Gentiles to Judaism" (**Encyclopedia Americana,** 1986, vol. 16, p. 71).

Also, **Collier's Encyclopedia** says:
"A common error and persistent modern myth is the designation of the Jews as a 'race.' This is scientifically fallacious, from the standpoint of both physical and historical tradition. Investigations by anthropologists have shown that Jews are by no means uniform in physical character and that they nearly always reflect the physical and mental characteristics of the people among whom they live" (**Collier's Encyclopedia,** 1977, vol. 13, p. 573).

Being a Jew means that one is of the Judaistic religion or a convert to it, or else in the "brotherhood" of those who are. Many of the "Jews" are Communists and atheists, in fact.

Being a Jew has nothing to do with race as such. Sammy Davis, Jr. became a Jew. Elizabeth Taylor became a Jew when she married Eddie Fisher. In June of 1991 Tom Arnold and Roseanne Barr, the T.V. entertainer, renewed publicly their wedding vows, and he was celebrating his conversion to Judaism.

Jews can be of different races. It is like someone who is a Catholic or a Protestant; they can be of any race or color. In Israel they have a peculiar law which says what their government says is a Jew. I quote this from **Funk and Wagnall's New Encyclopedia,** vol. 14, p. 214: "In 1970 the Israeli Knesset adopted legislation defining a Jew as one born of a Jewish mother or a convert." It matters not who the father is, nor to what race he belongs. And a convert can be from any race. So you see, we are not talking about a "race" of people when we talk about the Jewish people.

In May of 1991 the government of Israel air-lifted 14,087 "Jews" from Ethiopia. Months earlier 15,000 others of them had been brought to Israel. These were the black-skinned people who called themselves **Beta Israel** (House of Israel) "whose ancestors had intermarried with the natives, as the black skin of the modern Falashes indicates." These are black people, very unlike most of the other people in Israel today. They are like the Jews of North Africa, the Jews of Yemen, the Jews of Persia, the Jews in India, the Jews of China, the Jews in the Pacific Lands, Japan, Philippines, Dutch

East Indies, New Zealand and Latin America, in that they are different nationalities and from different races, and yet are known as "Jews." The so-called Jews of today are NOT a race of people, but people of mixed races and ancestry whose common tie is the Judaistic religion.

H.G. Wells, in **The Outline of History,** said:

"There can be little doubt that the scattered Phoenicians in Spain and Africa and throughout the Mediterranean, speaking as they did a language closely akin to Hebrew and being deprived of their authentic political rights, became proselytes to Judaism. For phases of vigorous proselytism alternated with phases of exclusive jealousy in Jewish history. On one occasion the Idumeans, being conquered, were all forcibly made Jews. There were Arab tribes who were Jews in the time of Muhammad, and a Turkish people who were mainly Jews in South Russia in the ninth century. Judaism is indeed the reconstructed political ideal of many shattered peoples — mainly Semitic. . . . The main part of Jewry never was in Judea and had never come out of Judea" (**H.G. Wells,** p. 505).

Many Christians do not know that the vast majority of so-called Jews in the world today are the Ashkenazim Jews, while the remainder of them are the Sephardim Jews. The Ashkenazim Jews have as their background not the nation of Israel but a country called Khazaria, which country at one time was the largest country in Europe. The

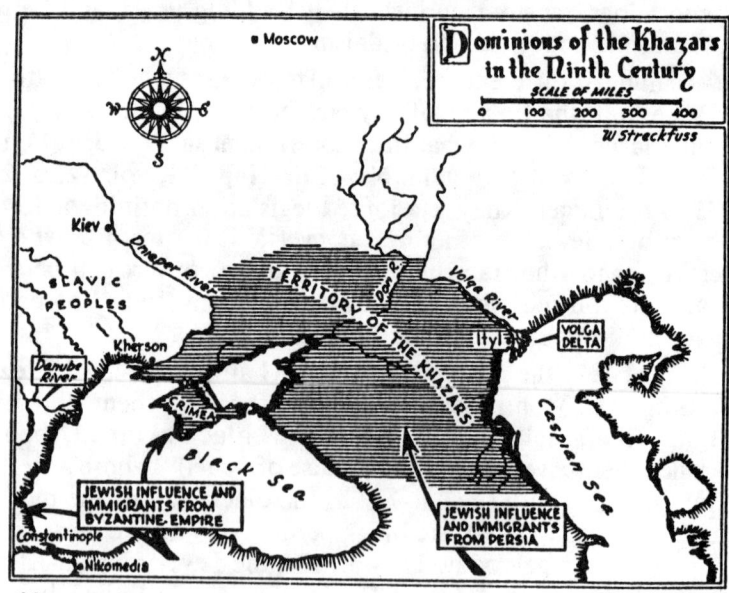

(Map copyrighted by and used through the courtesy of The Jewish Publication Society of America, Philadelphia, Pa.)

settlers of Khazaria were Turks and Huns. In A.D. 740 King Bulan of Khazaria decided to adopt the Judaistic religion for his country. A number of Jews were already living there. So he converted to Judaism, along with all his officials, and his whole nation ended up being known as a nation of Jews. In 970 Russia came in and dominated the situation, and the Khazars were scattered, many of them going down into Poland and Lithuania, where at the dawn of our modern civilization the largest concentration of Jews were found. Today, the largest percentage of so-called Jews in the world have as their background this group of people. This is fully documented in detail in my book, **Israel in Bible Prophecy**. Naturally, these people are not a "race" of Jews, and yet it is thought by some that they constitute the major portion of the 14,000,000 so-called Jews in the world today. Their features are different than the Sephardim Jews; their language backgrounds are different (the Ashkenazim speaking Yiddish, and the Sephardim with their Hebrew and many of them who speak Spanish on account of their own mixed-up background in Spain). In Israel they have their separate organizations, and the nation there is divided between these two mixed-up bloodlines of people. In the 12th century the Ashkenazim Jews made up only 6.7% of the Jews, but around 1965 they numbered 11,000,000 or about 86% of all the Jews in the world. Think of the implications of this!

Thomas Ice, strong dispensationalist and executive director of the Pre-Trib Research Center in Washington, D.C., said recently, ". . . and the fact that ethnic Israel has been reestablished as a nation and now controls Jerusalem is a strong indicator that we are near the end of the church age" (**Thomas Ice, Pre-Trib Perspectives**, p. 3). If by "ethnic" he means "racial," in no way can it be said that "ethnic" Israel has been reestablished. This is a hoax that is being perpetrated in the name of good Christian theology and eschatology! There is no Jewish race today, let alone this being a sign that we are near the end of the church age. This is like pulling a rabbit out of a hat to prove a point!

Just as a sidelight here, let me say that those premillennialists today who hold to the viewpoint that so-called Israel's being set up as a nation in Palestine is Biblical fulfillment, and/or that the Jews will all be restored some day to Palestine before a millennial reign of Christ, along with a rebuilt Temple and re-instituted sacrifices, may not be aware "that those who held the premillennial theory in the second and third centuries, seem not to have believed in any literal, territorial restoration of the Jews at all, — much less in their millennial supremacy over all nations, and the re-establishment of their religious peculiarities" (**David Brown**, p. 339).

So Scofield must have been wrong when he tried to attach this meaning of race to the word "generation" in **Matthew 24:34,** as though Jesus meant the race of Israel would be preserved intact until all these things that He mentioned would take place. And sad it is that so many have followed Scofield's interpretation. What Jesus meant is exactly the same as what He meant in the other passages in Matthew where He used the same word in referring to the people of HIS day and time. THAT generation would not pass away until ALL those things were fulfilled which He had predicted.

But even if Jesus had meant "this race" when He said "this generation," what would that have proved? For certainly that nation of people which was in existence at the time He spoke these words, was still around when all those things He mentioned happened in A.D. 67-70. It is only a strained interpretation that tries to put this group of people with their destruction out into our future, when their nation and their Temple were actually destroyed completely in A.D. 70.

In a recent book, **Palestine is Coming,** by **Kermit Zarley,** it was stated that "British Minister of State Lord Moyne supported his government's White Paper of 1939 by publicly opposing further Jewish immigration. He argued that Jews were not demonstrably the true descendents of the ancient Hebrews and therefore without legitimate claim to the Holy Land. He meant that Jews were hardly a pure race, being a much more heterogeneous group than popularly conceived. For this, he was assassinated by the Stern Group on November 6, 1994" **(Kermit Zarley, p. 131).**

His assassination goes to show how truth suffers at the hands of those whose personal interests are felt to be greater. Many are unwilling to acknowledge the genetic composition of those who go by the name "Jews" today, and Bible expositors will glibly (and ignorantly) declare that the generation of which Jesus spoke was the "Jewish race"! There is no Jewish race today, if we are to believe what authoritative sources say about the matter. This, therefore, could not have been what Jesus meant by "generation," C.I. Scofield and others to the contrary.

The prediction of judgment upon Israel was for THAT generation. That generation of opposers of Christ had said, "His blood be on us, and on our children" **(Matthew 27:25).** And it was. That judgment came about in A.D. 67-70, and the nation was decimated. Some say that the Jews today are guilty of the crucifixion of Jesus Christ. This is not true any more than are Gentiles who reject Him now. The nation that was officially guilty of the death of Christ received its judgment. God's judgment is not upon Jews today because of what others did many years ago. We need to understand this. In the same vein, we could say that the Germans of today are not guilty of what Adolph Hitler and Nazi Germany did to the Jews back in the 40's. It works both ways. So why continue to hold Germans as such to be guilty of what others did? We need to be fair and logical in all our thinking about these matters. It is just like the white people of America still being condemned by some for what their ancestors did to the Negroes years ago in bringing them to America and keeping them as slaves. White Americans of today should not be held to blame for what others did many years ago. We could go on with other examples. But God is the judge. He judged Israel. We are not to blame Jews of today. We all ought to be very careful not to ever be guilty of any kind of **racism**, regardless of who is under consideration.

The "All Things" of That "Generation" Included the "*Parousia*/Coming" of Christ

When Jesus said that "all these things" would occur before that generation was over, He included ALL those things which He had been discussing in answer to the disciples' questions. "All these things" are spelled out for us from **verse 4** right on down through **verse 33** which precedes **verse 34**. "ALL" of these things, nothing excepted. They would all occur in that generation. These are not ambiguous words. The meaning is plain and obvious.

And if all these things were to occur in that generation, it necessarily follows that "the Son of man coming in the clouds of heaven with power and great glory" was one of those things that would occur in that generation (**vs. 30**), for He was answering the disciples' question as to "when shall these things be? and what shall be the sign of thy coming, and of the end of the world [age]?" All these things, He said, would happen in that generation.

Just because most of us have been taught through the years that what Jesus was talking about was some event to occur in our future some day, does not change the fact that **HE** said those things would occur in that generation. If His teaching on this does not agree with our concept, what are we to do? We must make our concepts agree with His teaching, that is what. It is difficult for people to let go of preconceived ideas about things. But truth is truth, and Jesus said all these things would happen in that generation. We have previously pointed out other passages that plainly stated that He would come before all of them died (**Matthew 16:28**, etc.).

"But we can find no word or sentence which appears designed to impress any one with the idea that the destruction in question and the parousia would be far separate as to time. The one, it is said, will immediately follow the other, and all will take place before that generation shall pass away" **(Milton Terry, Biblical Hermeneutics, p. 439).**

Writing on **Mark 13:30** (the parallel passage of Matthew 24:34), **G.R. Beasley-Murray** said:

"The meaning of 'this generation' is now generally acknowledged. While in earlier Greek *genea* meant 'birth,' 'progeny' and so 'race,' in the sense of those descended from a common ancestor, in the LXX it commonly translates the term *dor,* meaning 'age,' 'age of man,' or 'generation' in the sense of contemporaries. On the lips of Jesus 'this generation' always signifies the contemporaries of Jesus, but at the same time always carries an implicit criticism. For Mark the eschatological discourse expounds the implications of the prophecy of judgment in verse 2, and so implies the perversity of 'this generation,' which must suffer the doom predicted.

"This generation is not to pass away until '**all these things** happen' (*tauta panta genetai*). The first term, *tauta,* appeared previously in verse 29: 'When you see **these things** happening. . . .' A clearer precedent for *tauta panta,* however, appears in the question of the disciples in verse 4: 'When will all these things be, and what is the sign when all these things will be completed?' The response to the request for a sign has been given, above all in verses 14-15; the question concerning the 'when' is answered in verse 30. In view of Mark's setting of the statement, however, it is difficult to exclude from '**all these things**' the description of the parousia in verses 24-27" **(G.R. Beasley-Murray, Jesus and the Kingdom of God, pp. 333-334).**

Meyer's Commentary on **verse 34** says, "That the second advent itself is intended to be included, is likewise evident from ver. 36, in which the subject of the day and hour of the advent is introduced." And then he added, on verse 36:

"The affirmation of ver. 34, however, does not exclude the fact that no one knows the **day and hour** when the second advent, with its accompanying phenomena, is to take place. It is to occur during the **life-time of the generation then existing,** but no one knows on what **day** or at what **hour** within the period thus indicated."

"The plain teaching of the passage is that before some of those who heard him speak should die the Son of man would come in glory, and his kingdom would be established in power" **(Terry, Biblical Apocalyptics, p. 220).**

The Word "Quickly" in the Book of Revelation

It is absolutely certain that the early disciples following the ascension of Jesus, did indeed expect a soon-coming of Jesus Christ from Heaven, and that even in their lifetime. From where did they get this anticipation, if not from Jesus Himself?

Modern interpreters of the New Testament say that the word "quickly" in Revelation (pertaining to Christ's coming) means "suddenly" and not "soon." But the Greek word for "quickly" as used in reference to Christ's coming **(Revelation 2:5, 16; 3:11; 22:7, 12, 20)** is not the same word as used **elsewhere** when "in haste" is meant. (See **Luke 14:21; 16:6; John 13:27; Acts 12:7; 22:18**.) The word is *"tachu,"* and does not necessarily nor generally mean "suddenly," but has the meaning of **"shortly, i.e., without delay, soon."** The use of this word in Revelation is in accord with the time statements of **Revelation 1:1**, "things which must shortly come to pass," and **Revelation 1:3**, "for the time is at hand." It seems clear to me that the writer of the book of Revelation would have understood by his own use of these various words that the "coming" of Christ was to be expected soon (to that generation to whom he wrote).

If an "imminent" coming of Christ is taught at all in the New Testament (and it was), then it becomes necessary for the student of that New Testament to discover exactly to which area of time that imminence applies. Men have taught such an imminent return of Christ for nearly 2,000 years, and **NONE** of them have been correct except those who taught it prior to A.D. 70. Only during that generation from Christ until that date (from A.D. 30 to 70) could it be said that Christ's coming was imminent and would occur in that generation **(Matthew 24:34)**. And it was during that period of time that the writers of the New Testament constantly wrote of a soon-coming Christ.

Verse 33 defines the time when the coming of the Son of man would be there by saying, ". . . when ye shall see all these things, know that it is near, even at the doors." Then **verse 34** defines when they could expect to see all these things fulfilled, by saying, "This generation shall not pass, till all these things be fulfilled." In other words, they would see them in that generation. So those things would point toward His soon-coming, and in their generation would be the time they would see those things come to pass. So both **verse 33** and **verse 34** act in a confirmatory way to each other.

H. Wayne House and **Thomas Ice** believed that this means **not** the generation in which Christ was speaking, but the generation to which the signs will be given, that is, the future generation at the time of a future second coming of Christ. They said:

"Since the phrase 'all these things' governs the timing of 'this generation' (regardless of how it has been used in other contexts), one has to determine what 'all these things' are and when they will be fulfilled. Then we will know whether 'this generation' referred to those in Christ's day or to a future generation" **(H. Wayne House and Thomas D. Ice, p. 286).**

This argument should be dismissed. If the word "generation" does indeed refer to people in a particular period of time, then when Jesus said "THIS" generation, He had to mean those of His generation for **they were the ones who saw these things come to pass.** And Jesus plainly said that after these things were seen, right on through the preaching of the gospel to all nations, the end would come. He said "THIS generation" — not some generation thousands of years later.

And in a real sense, **verse 34** itself governs when it was to be understood that "all these things" would occur, rather than the other way around as House and Ice have it. Once understanding the true meaning of the word "generation," and knowing the historical facts of those events actually happening during the 40 years after Christ, it can be seen that what Jesus meant was that all of those things would happen in that particular period of time in which He was talking to those disciples. By saying this, He was emphasizing that those things **would** all occur in **THAT** generation, and that some of them would live to see it. **THAT** time was "this" generation! (I mean, "this" generation to them.)

It is beyond doubt that the people in Jesus' day saw all of those things come to pass in **their** generation, including the preaching of the gospel to all the nations (as we showed in an earlier section of this book), and Jesus said, ". . . and then shall the end come." It seems to me that only someone with a dispensational futuristic point of view would try to change the meaning of this to something else. Jehovah's Witnesses and dispensationalists evade this argument by denying that "these things" ever happened in that first century! But denying the obvious does not eliminate the facts.

And one cannot summarily dismiss the meaning of what Jesus said simply by suggesting that **WE** can determine when "these things" will be "regardless of how it has been used in other contexts." We **must** pay attention to how the word "generation" is used in other contexts, and how Jesus used the word elsewhere is evidently the meaning here in verse 34 as well.

Greg L. Bahnsen and **Kenneth L. Gentry, Jr.** show how the context (the previous **chapter 23**) proves that Jesus was talking about the generation of His own day and time. They said:

"In Matthew 23 Jesus sorely rebukes the 'scribes and Pharisees' **of His own day** (Matt. 23:2ff.), urging **them** finally to 'fill up then the measure of your fathers' who killed the prophets (23:31-32). He says that they are a 'generation' of vipers (23:33), that will persecute and slay His disciples (23:34). He notes that upon **them** will come all the righteous blood shed on the earth (23:35). He then dogmatically asserts: 'Verily I say unto you, all these things shall come upon this generation' (23:36)" **(Greg L. Bahnsen** and **Kenneth L. Gentry, Jr.,** p. 266).

Speaking on **Matthew 24** at First Baptist Church of Lakeland, Florida, where we are members, on Sunday morning March 27, 1991, **Dr. Ed Hindson,** vice president of Missouri Baptist College in St. Louis, Missouri, and now secretary of the Pre-Trib Research Center in Washington, D.C., said, "There **will come** a generation in which these things take place."

But that is not what Jesus said. Jesus said, "THIS generation shall not pass, till all these things be fulfilled" **(Matthew 24:34)**. The expression "this generation" does not mean the same to us today as it did when used in speaking to the disciples, for many generations have gone by since then. We can look back now and say that it all happened in THAT generation in which Jesus spoke, even as He said it would.

David Brown (1858) said:

"Does not this tell us plainly as words could do it, that the whole prophecy was meant to apply to the destruction of Jerusalem? There is but one way of setting this aside, but how forced it is, must, I think, appear to every unbiased mind. It is by translating, not 'this **generation,**' . . . but 'this **nation** shall not pass away:' in other words, the Jewish nation shall survive all the things here predicted! Nothing but some fancied necessity, arising out of their view of the prophecy, could have led so many sensible men to put this gloss upon our Lord's words. Only try the effect of it upon the perfectly parallel announcement in the previous chapter: 'Fill ye up then the measure of your fathers. . . . Wherefore, behold, I send you prophets, and wise men, and scribes: and some of them ye shall kill and crucify; and some of them shall ye scourge in your synagogues, and persecute from city to city . . . **that upon you** may come all the righteous blood shed upon the earth, from the blood of righteous Abel unto the blood of Zacharias, whom ye slew between the temple and the altar. **Verily I say unto you, All these things shall come upon this generation'** . . . Matt. xxiii. 32, 34-36). Does not the Lord here mean **the then existing generation of the Israelites?** Beyond all question he does; and if so, what can be plainer than that this is his meaning in the passage before us? In this case, the coming of the Lord here announced is just a figurative coming to 'judge' and destroy Jerusalem, with all the judicial consequences of that coming" **(David Brown,** p. 435).

John Broadus said:

"The emphasis is on 'all.' All the things predicted in v. 4-31 would occur before or in immediate connection with the destruction of Jerusalem. But like events might again occur in connection with another and greater coming of the Lord, and such seems evidently to be his meaning" (**Broadus, p. 492**).

I emphasize the first part, especially, that ALL the things mentioned in vss. 4-31 would occur in connection with the destruction of Jerusalem. His second thought is a "might" (Broadus' own word) — not Bible exegesis at all, even though it was Dr. Broadus who said this, and especially when he adds, "and such seems evidently to be his meaning." If the "all" takes in everything mentioned in connection with the destruction of Jerusalem, then how could it be "evidently . . . his meaning" that "like events might again occur in connection with another and greater coming of the Lord?"

Even my post-tribulational, premillennial friend, **Henry Hudson**, editor of **Echoes of the Ministries**, in his Vol. 11, No. 2 issue of his publication, acknowledges the very obvious meaning of this word "generation" in **verse 34**. He says:

"Many commentators play around with the word 'generation' (*genea*), and thinking to avoid embarrassment, project its application to the generation which will be alive during the last days immediately preceding the Second Coming of the Messiah. Others, expand its meaning to include the whole nation of Israel, which, in spite of the intensity of the great tribulation, will nevertheless be preserved as a nation right up till the end of this present age. However, if Scripture be compared with Scripture, such verbal games are soon exposed as being nothing but armchair gymnastics (cf. Matthew 11:16; 12:41-45; 23:36; Luke 11:50, 51; Hebrews 3:10). The word is generally used to signify a people belonging to a particular period of time, or more loosely, to a period defined by what might be considered as an average life span of a man" (**Henry Hudson, p. 32**).

But even after hitting the nail on the head with that paragraph, Dr. Hudson messes up his whole argument by saying on the next page, "In order to accept what I have just said, there needs to be some appreciation for the possible twofold application of biblical prophecy, that is, the prophetic message had direct practical association with the original hearers, but it also anticipated a final fulfillment at the end of the age." You see, this is where Biblical exegesis breaks down, and speculation enters into the picture. There is absolutely nothing to indicate that Matthew chapter 24 "anticipated a final fulfillment at the end of the age." What was predicted for that generation, happened in that generation; and nothing was said about its happening AGAIN at some later time.

"It was to this event, the most awful in history — 'one of the most awful eras in God's economy of grace, and the most awful revolution in all God's economy of grace, and the most awful revolution in all God's religious dispensations' — that we must apply those prophecies of Christ's coming in which every one of the Apostles and Evangelists fixed these three most definite limitations — the one, that before that generation passed away all these things would be fulfilled; another, that some standing there should not taste death till they saw the Son of Man coming in His kingdom; and third, that the Apostles should not have gone over the cities of Israel till the Son of Man be come. It is strange that these distinct limitations should not be regarded as a decisive proof that the Fall of Jerusalem was, in the fullest sense, the Second Advent of the Son of Man which was primarily contemplated by the earliest voices of prophecy" (**Farrar**, p. 489).

The importance and significance of what happened in A.D. 70 is not fully appreciated by Bible students today. This is partly because the historical setting and the prophetic fulfillment have been overlooked, and this in turn is because most Bible students are "futuristic" inclined in their thinking when they read ANY prophecies. We need to see and understand that Matthew 24 was a prophecy that has already been fulfilled, and therefore has no future fulfillment at all today. On this premise, then, we can better try to understand the meaning and significance of what has already happened.

We need to read these New Testament prophecies with first century glasses on, not 20th century glasses! We need to understand that these future prophecies were given to the disciples with reference to THEIR future — not OUR future. It is so easy to read the New Testament and just simply take for granted that EVERYTHING applies to us and to OUR future. But this is not true. Jesus spoke to the generation in which He lived.

To sum up the comments on this verse, it might be well to quote from an old commentary of 1843, **The Four Gospels: With a Commentary**, by **Abiel Abbot Livermore:**

"34. This generation shall not pass, etc., i.e., those then living would witness the fulfillment of Jesus' predictions; which was the case, for the destruction of Jerusalem took place about forty years after, and many then living were involved in the great catastrophe. John long survived the event, and Lightfoot speaks of some Rabbins who also outlived it. It is apparent from this verse, that Jesus has been previously speaking of the downfall of the Jews, not of future judgment. At the time Jesus uttered these words there was peace with the Romans, and no prospect of the Jews venturing to contend with them; or, if they did, of the temple, city, and nation being wholly destroyed. Yet forty years accomplished it all. What boundless confidence ought we ever to repose in the promises and warnings of Jesus, since he has so clearly established his claim of an unerring prophet!" **(Abiel Abbot Livermore, p. 288)**.

Who Are the "Chosen People" of God?

Right here would be a good place to discuss this matter of the "race" or "bloodline" of Israel as being the criteria for being God's "chosen people." A simple fact, unthought of evidently by most of the T.V. evangelists and publications which dwell on these things, is that God's CHOICE of a group of people for his particular favor and blessings, was NEVER made on the basis of race or blood! NOT ONE TIME in the Bible is any such reference made.

The selection, or choice, was made on the basis of COVENANT. And the covenant was made to a group of people of MIXED racial background. And the truth of the matter is, that Gentiles could enter into this covenant relationship also by circumcision. During most of the history of this covenant people in the Old Testament, there was a tremendous amount of blood-mixing in the group. The nation of Israel was not a nation based on race, but on covenant. The covenant was the focal point of the relationship to God.

Within this covenant people were the true believers, those who kept faith with God. Being part of the covenant people alone, through the rite of circumcision, etc., did not make one **truly** a Jew. As Paul said in **Romans 2:28-29**:

"For he is not a Jew, which is one outwardly; neither is that circumcision, which is outward in the flesh: But he is a Jew, which is one inwardly; and circumcision is that of the heart, in the spirit, and not in the letter; whose praise is not of men, but of God."

There was always this true Jew among the nation of Israel, and the combined number of them could properly be called "the remnant." They were truly "spiritual Israel." Of Nathaniel, Jesus said, "Behold an Israelite indeed, in whom is no guile!" **(John 1:47)**. But to the unbelieving Jews, Jesus said, "If ye were Abraham's children, ye would do the works of Abraham . . .. Ye are of your father the devil, and the lusts of your father ye will do" **(John 8:39, 44)**. These unbelieving Jews were not children of Abraham nor of God. "If God were your Father, ye would love me" **(John 8:42)**.

The true believers among the Jews in Jesus' day were the true Jews; they were the faithful; they were the remnant. They were spiritual Israel. They were the ones who had no trouble in accepting Jesus as the Messiah He claimed to be. They accepted Him and were born again, becoming sons of God **(John 1:11-12)**. His "own" rejected Him, but as many of those who accepted Him, they became the sons of God.

It was this remnant of people, the spiritual Israel, the believing Jews, to whom applied the NEW COVENANT — a covenant not made in stone, but written in their hearts **(Jeremiah 31:33)**. Spiritual Israel which had existed before Christ, and during the time of Christ, continued right on this side of Christ as more and more Jews accepted the gospel, as shown by the book of Acts. Those being saved in the early days of Christianity were known as "the firstfruits unto God and to the Lamb" **(Revelation 14:4)**. They were the firstfruits, the first ones, who were converted to Christianity. They are spoken of in **Revelation 7:3-8** as 144,000 who were sealed, to be protected against the coming wrath of God upon the land of Israel. They all did escape to Pella when the land of Israel was devastated and Jerusalem was destroyed.

Gentiles who by faith came into this believing body of people became part of the same body. They were like branches grafted into the main tree. (See **Romans 11:17, 19.**) Unbelieving Jews who were not spiritual Israel could also be grafted into the same spiritual tree **(Romans 11:23)**. In this one body there is "neither Jew nor Greek" **(Galatians 3:28)**, but all of them, both Jew and Gentile, are "Abraham's seed, and heirs according to the promise" **(Galatians 3:29)**.

And in all of this there is not, and never was, any acceptance by God on the basis of race of any of these people — either under the old covenant or the new, either before Christ or afterwards. All were saved by faith, all were God's people (true Israel) by faith in God. The NATION was only a nation because to that group of people was given the covenant, though only those in that nation who were obedient to the covenant were God's true people (spiritual Israel).

When the old covenant ceased to be **(Hebrews 10:9** — "He taketh away the first, that he may establish the second"), then the nation of Israel ceased to be, for it was based on that covenant which God had given to them. The new covenant was one which had the laws written in their hearts, not just on stone **(Hebrews 10:16)**. The way into the holiest, into the realm of the new covenant, was not MANIFESTED until the Temple was destroyed ("the way into the holiest of all was not yet made manifest, while as the first tabernacle was yet standing," **Hebrews 9:8)**. And when God spoke of a new covenant, He thereby declared that the first one would become old, as the writer of Hebrews said, ". . . that which decayeth and waxeth old is ready to vanish away" **(Hebrews 8:13)**. By the time the Temple at Jerusalem was destroyed, all the Jewish religious rituals, ceremonies, and everything were gone. God's people had entered into the new covenant through Jesus. The old covenant was gone. And there was no more a nation of Israel which has been based on that old covenant.

Any people other than Christians, calling themselves "ISRAEL" today, are not based on the NEW COVENANT; and the old covenant has vanished away. Those of the present-day nation of Israel, created by man and not by God, reject the new covenant of God which came through Jesus, and thereby they forfeit all claims to any promises of God and any inheritance under His covenant.

So, remember, even the old nation of Israel (before A.D. 70) was not based on race, but on covenant. When that covenant ceased to be, Israel as a nation ceased to be. All true Israelites, who were under that covenant, entered right on into the new covenant, and they continued to be God's chosen people, inheriting the promises of God, along with any and all Gentiles who did and would enter that same body of people. That same body of people exists today. They are the "chosen generation, a royal priesthood, AN HOLY NATION," etc. **(I Peter 2:9)**. In times past the Gentile members of this nation "were not a people, but are now the people of God" **(I Peter 2:10)**.

So the line of God's people always existed, and continued right on through the New Testament and into our age. These are the true people of God whom God had in mind from the very beginning. "For the promise, that he should be the heir of the world, was not to Abraham, or to his seed, through the law, but through the righteousness of faith" **(Romans 4:13)**. God promised Abraham that through his seed all nations on earth would be blessed. He did not have a "race" of Jews in mind, though His plan was to use the NATION of Israel (made up of mixed peoples) to bring about His purposes.

And as to any blood-race of Jews today, it is incredible to think that God would let His promises apply to any so-called land of Israel whose present-day population is made up of such an admixture of peoples that encyclopedia after encyclopedia bears witness to the fact that there is no such thing as a "Jewish race" of people today, which witness involves not only those in the nation of Israel today, but all the other so-called Jewish people in the world.

Conclusion

So we come back to our proposition, which is that our understanding of the word "generation" in Matthew 24:34 has to be that of a time period which would include some of those living in Jesus' day. This is the only sensible interpretation of this passage when all factors involved are considered — which is what we have tried to do. Therefore, it is our belief that **ALL** the things Jesus mentioned prior to **verse 34** actually took place in the first century, and more precisely, during the time ending with A.D. 70

Section 8 ●●●●●●●●●●●●●●●●●●●●●●●●●●

"HEAVEN AND EARTH SHALL PASS AWAY"

"Heaven and earth shall pass away, but my words shall not pass away" (Matthew 24:35).

★★★★★★★★★★★★★★★

It has been generally believed that Jesus here meant that even though these physical heavens and earth will pass away some day, that is not true about His word which will never pass away. Whether this physical earth and solar system ever pass away is not the point in this chapter. There is more to this statement of Jesus than meets the eye. Jesus has been talking in apocalyptic language, and heaven and earth passing away could mean here just what He has been talking about — that the heaven and earth of the old Jewish order will pass away, and that His word concerning all this is sure to come to pass.

At first glance, it looks as though Jesus was simply saying in this verse, "My words will be here when the world has passed away." But is the physical world or universe what Jesus had in mind? Were a literal heaven and earth in His thoughts? Remember now, what Jesus had been talking about — what He had already said in this chapter would pass away. We have been discussing the passing away of the Jewish nation and the old religious order of things.

Go back to Matthew 5:18 and see where Jesus said, "Till heaven and earth pass, one jot or one tittle shall in no wise pass from the law, till all be fulfilled." Here He said that the law would not pass away until what? Until two other things passed away. What were they? First, "Till heaven and earth pass," and secondly, "till all (the law) be fulfilled." We know the law **was** fulfilled in Christ, and all prophecies relating to Israel were fulfilled by A.D. 70. We all realize that because of this the old covenant system was becoming a thing of the past (**Hebrews 8:13**). But how could this be, when "heaven and earth" had not passed away, for Jesus said, "Till heaven and earth pass, one jot or one tittle shall in no wise pass from the law"? Maybe we can understand this better if we realize He was not talking about the literal heaven and earth, but something else. Something else would have to pass away before it could be said that the law was not still in effect.

In the New Testament especially, the destruction of heaven and earth refers not to the physical universe, but rather, it relates to the final passing of the disobedient nation of Israel. All would be fulfilled, every jot and tittle, when heaven and earth passed away (**Matthew 5:18**).

We have to go to the Old Testament to see what "heaven and earth" means in prophetic language.

In **Deuteronomy 32:1**, in the song of Moses, God is talking to Israel when He says: "Give ear, O ye heavens, and I will speak; and hear, O earth, the words of my mouth."

In the song of Moses, God is depicting the fate of Israel when He says: "For a fire is kindled in mine anger, and shall burn unto the lowest hell, and shall consume the earth with her increase, and set on fire the foundations of the mountains" (**vs. 22**).

Is God talking here about burning up the earth? No, He is talking about bringing judgment upon Israel. He had already told them of the type of judgment they could expect. "The LORD shall bring a nation against thee from far, from the end of the earth, as swift as the eagle flieth; a nation whose tongue thou shalt not understand" (**Deuteronomy 28:49**).

In the song of Moses, God is telling His people that He had delivered them from the oppressor, but that if they would become disobedient He would bring all sorts of trouble upon them. It was a song of deliverance, but also a song of warning. In **Revelation 15:2-4** we see the saints singing the song of Moses, and also the song of the Lamb, after they had gotten their victory over the Beast.

But apocalyptic and symbolical language is used in the song of Moses in describing the judgment of God. When Israel is finally destroyed, it is as though heaven and earth are burned up.

In **Isaiah 51:13** God said that He had "stretched forth the heavens, and laid the foundations of the earth." Once again, is God speaking here of the literal heavens and earth?

Read on in this **same passage** to verse 16: "And I have put my words in thy mouth, and I have covered thee in the shadow of mine hand, that I may **plant the heavens, and lay the foundations of the earth, and say unto Zion, Thou art my people."**

Read that verse again. It could not be talking of the formation of the literal heavens and earth, for that had taken place more than 3,000 years before! So, then, what is He talking about? The verse explains itself. He is talking about "Zion." He is talking about "my people." In other words, He is talking about **Israel**. He is talking in this verse about the formation of Israel.

So in **Matthew 24:35** Jesus must be talking about the passing away of **Israel** when He speaks of heaven and earth passing away. This is what the entire 24th chapter of Matthew is about — the passing away of old Israel.

Now there will be a **new** Israel — a **new** heavens and earth; but more about that later.

In Bible figurative language, "heavens" refers to governments and rulers, and "earth" refers to the nation or people.

With this in mind, we can look at the very first chapter of Isaiah, in which God begins to give predictions of coming invasions and captivities of His people; and in **Isaiah 1:2** He said:

"Hear, O heavens, and give ear, O earth: for the LORD hath spoken, I have nourished and brought up children, and they have rebelled against me."

To whom is He speaking when He addresses, "O heavens" and "O earth"? He is talking to Israel. This shows very clearly that "heavens and earth" are symbolical language for Israel. In this passage He went on to say:

"Hear the word of the LORD, ye rulers of Sodom; give ear unto the law of our God, ye people of Gomorrah" (**vs. 10**). Now God was not speaking to Sodom and Gomorrah, for they had been destroyed many years previously. But the rulers and people of Israel were likened to the people of Sodom and Gomorrah, and it was to the "heavens and earth" also that He was speaking. The "heavens and earth" and also "the rulers of Sodom and Gomorrah" referred to Israel as a nation.

In **Isaiah 24** we have a picture of God's promise of judgment on Israel through the Assyrians. But Israel is spoken of as the "earth." Read in particular verses 1 and 19-20:

"Behold, the LORD maketh the earth empty, and maketh it waste, and turneth it upside down, and scattereth abroad the inhabitants thereof."

"The earth is utterly broken down, the earth is clean dissolved, the earth is moved exceedingly."

"The earth shall reel to and fro like a drunkard, and shall be removed like a cottage; and the transgression thereof shall be heavy upon it; and it shall fall, and not rise again."

And in **Isaiah 34:4-5** God said:

"And all the host of heaven shall be dissolved, and the heavens shall be rolled together as a scroll: and all their host shall fall down, as the leaf falleth off from the vine, and as a falling fig from the fig tree.

"For my sword shall be bathed in heaven: behold, it shall come down upon Idumea, and upon the people of my curse, to judgment."

We know this is not to be taken literally — that the literal heavens would be dissolved and rolled together as a scroll — for He said that His "sword shall be bathed in **heaven**" and then followed that by explaining what He meant — that the sword would "come down upon **Idumea.**"

The rulers and their people would face judgment from the Lord. God said, "my sword," and He used the armies of heathen people to accomplish His purpose.

In **Jeremiah 22:29** God says, "O earth, earth, earth, hear the word of the Lord." And in verse 1 (along with verses 11, 18 and 24) we read that the words were for the people of Judah, concerning the time when they would be taken "into the hand of Nebuchadrezzar king of Babylon, and into the hand of the Chaldeans" (**vs. 25**). It was not the whole physical earth God was talking to, but the **people**.

If the dissolving of heaven and earth were to be taken literally in all the passages of the Old Testament where such language is used, it would necessarily mean that the heavens and earth were to be destroyed **numerous times**! The language has to be figurative.

This brings us back to our comments on the cosmic disturbances mentioned in **Matthew 24:29**, when "shall the sun be darkened, and the moon shall not give her light, and the stars shall fall from heaven, and the powers of the heavens shall be shaken." There Jesus was not talking about the literal heavens coming apart. He was talking about the rulers and the dignitaries of the nation of Israel falling. This happened in **A.D. 70** and there was no more a nation of Israel.

Isaiah 13:13 said, "Therefore I will shake the heavens, and the earth shall remove out of her place, in the wrath of the LORD of hosts, and in the day of his fierce anger." Some, who take the literalistic interpretation approach to all prophecy, might apply this to the end of the world's history. But prophecies like this actually applied to spiritual things — the passing away of the old, and the transformation of things into newness of life.

Haggai 2:6-7 (a Messianic prophecy) said, "Yet once, it is a little while, and I will shake the heavens, and the earth, and the sea, and the dry land; And I will shake all nations. . . ." This passage applies to the change of things which were brought about by the passing away of the old and the introduction of the new. The coming of Christ made possible this great change. This change would involve the passing away of the old Judaistic system with all its ceremonies, rites, rituals, sacrifices, etc. As the writer of Hebrews said, as he "borrowed" words from Haggai 2:6:

"Whose voice then shook the earth: but now he hath promised, saying, Yet once more I shake not the earth only, but also heaven.

"And this word, Yet once more, signifieth the removing of those things that are shaken, as of things that are made, that those things which cannot be shaken may remain.

"Wherefore we receiving a kingdom which cannot be moved . . ." **(Hebrews 12:26-28)**.

In **Haggai 2:21-22** God said, "I will shake the heavens and the earth; And I will overthrow the throne of kingdoms, and I will destroy the strength of the kingdoms of the heathen." Here we see the connection between shaking the heavens and the earth, and the overthrow of kingdoms and powers.

While the coming of Jesus Christ made possible the passing away of the old and the introduction of the new through the institution of the new covenant (so vividly discussed by the writer of Hebrews), yet much of all this was not eliminated completely until A.D. 70 when Jerusalem and the Temple were completely destroyed and the old **actually** ceased to be. As the writer said in **Hebrews 8:13**, "In that he saith, A new covenant, he hath made the first old. Now that which decayeth and waxeth old is READY to vanish away."

While the coming of Christ, and especially His death, made possible this new area of things, yet the manifestation of all this was not possible until the Temple itself and all its rituals were completely abolished. As the writer of Hebrews said, "The Holy Ghost this signifying, that the way into the holiest of all was not yet made manifest, while as the first tabernacle was yet standing" **(Hebrews 9:8)**. In the destruction of the Temple in A.D. 70, after it was no longer standing, it was manifested that the old covenant had vanished away, and the new heaven and new earth of this gospel dispensation were now in effect.

In all of this we see that from Christ until A.D. 70 there was a gradual transition from the old age to the new. He came in the end of the age **(Hebrews 9:26)**. The old was **ready** to vanish away **(Hebrews 8:13)**. The new was manifested after the Temple was destroyed **(Hebrews 9:8)**.

Concerning the expression, "ready to vanish away," found in Hebrews 8:13, **George Eldon Ladd** said, "Whether or not these words refer to the historical destruction of Jerusalem by the Romans in 70 A.D., they at least affirm the dissolution of the old Mosaic order, because the new order of redemption reality has come" **(George Eldon Ladd, The Last Things, p. 27)**.

Milton Terry interprets **II Peter 3** as referring to a change to the gospel age rather than to a literal destruction of the earth. Referring to the interpretation given them by the literalists to such passages as **Isaiah 51:16; 65:17; 66:22; II Peter 3:10-13; Revelation 20:11; 21:1** as relating to "a literal prophecy of the destruction of the world by fire, and the creation of a new world in its place," Dr. Terry said:

"That these texts may intimate or dimly foreshadow some such ultimate reconstruction of the physical creation, need not be denied, for we know not the possibilities of the future, nor the purposes of God respecting all things which he has created. But the contexts of these several passages do not authorize such a doctrine. Isaiah li. 16, refers to the resuscitation of Zion and Jerusalem, and is clearly metaphorical. The same is true of Isa. lxv. 17, and lxvi. 22, for the context in all these places confines the reference to Jerusalem and the people of God, and sets forth the same great prophetic conception of the Messianic future as the closing chapters of Ezekiel. The language of 2 Pet. iii, 10, 12, is taken mainly from Isa. xxxiv. 4, and is limited to the parousia, like the language of Matt. xxiv, 29. Then the Lord made 'not only the land but also the heaven' to tremble (Heb. xii, 26), and removed the things that were shaken in order to establish a kingdom which cannot be moved (Heb. xii, 27, 28)." **(Milton S. Terry,** footnote in **Biblical Hermeneutics,** p. 489).

In **Isaiah 65:1** God is quoted as saying, "I am sought of them that asked not for me; I am found of them that sought me not: I said, Behold me, behold me, unto a nation that was not called by my name." Reference is made here to the Gentiles who would behold the Lord — those who had not been called by His name. Paul brings this out in Romans 10:20 as he refers to this prophecy.

The passage goes on to say in **Isaiah 65:9,** "And I will bring forth a seed out of Jacob, and out of Judah an inheritor of my mountains: and mine elect shall inherit it, and my servants shall dwell there." Here is mentioned a "seed" coming out of Judah who will be his elect.

In verses **13-14** fleshly Israel is contrasted to this spiritual Israel — the elect.

Then in verse **15** He said concerning fleshly Israel, "And ye shall leave your name for a curse unto my chosen: for the Lord GOD shall slay thee, and call his servants by another name." These servants would bless the Lord "because the former troubles are forgotten, and because they are hid from mine eyes" (**vs. 16**). And it was in **this** context that God said, "For, behold, I create new heavens and a new earth: and the former shall not be remembered, nor come into mind . . . for behold, I create Jerusalem a rejoicing, and her people a joy" (**vss. 17-18**). This is the New Jerusalem of Revelation 21:10 — that holy city, the bride, the Lamb's wife, the church, God's people in this new dispensation.

And it was in this same context that God said, "For, behold, the LORD will come with fire, and with his chariots like a whirlwind, to render his anger with fury, and his rebuke with flames of fire"

(Isaiah 66:15). The Lord comes! And He did come, with the fires of His fury upon the land of Israel. And as a result, it could be said, "For as the new heavens and the new earth, which I will make, shall remain before me, saith the LORD, so shall YOUR SEED and YOUR NAME remain" **(Isaiah 66:22)**. Out of the ruins of the old heavens and the old earth, and the old Jerusalem, there comes a new earth and a new Jerusalem. This was the "seed out of Jacob" **(Isaiah 65:9)** and the "nation that was not called by my name" **(Isaiah 65:1)**. The whole situation has changed, and all things are new **(Revelation 21:5)**.

Jesus said, "**TILL** heaven and earth pass, one jot or one tittle shall in no wise pass from the law, till all be fulfilled" **(Matthew 5:17)**.

I used to see just "till all be fulfilled." The law would remain until it was all fulfilled, and then it would pass away.

But I had not noticed the other "till" — "TILL heaven and earth pass. . . ." Not one jot or tittle of the law would pass until heaven and earth passed.

Now is He talking about the literal heaven and earth? If so, then the law has not yet passed, and is not yet fulfilled — for certainly the literal heaven and earth have not passed away.

But this language speaks of Israel (the heavens and earth of **Isaiah 51:16**) passing away. With the passing away of Israel, all the old covenant became a thing of the past. All was fulfilled. See **Luke 21:22** where it says of Israel's destruction, "For these be the days of vengeance, that all things which are written may be fulfilled." And Jesus said, "This generation [the generation during which He lived] shall not pass, till all these things be fulfilled" **(Matthew 24:34)**.

Some of the old Reformation preachers understood the meaning of those words, "heaven and earth," as meaning the political or governmental areas of life. For example, the most respected **John Owen**, writing of the demise of the Roman Empire, said that it "was shivered to pieces by many barbarous nations; who, settling themselves in the fruitful soils of Europe, began to plant their heavens, and lay the foundations of the earth, growing up into civil state," etc. **(John Owen**, vol. 8, p. 265). Here John Owen had reference to the shaking of the Roman Empire, but later in this book I give a lengthy quotation of his where he had the reference to the Jewish religious structure which was removed before the full realization of the new covenant in the kingdom of Christ.

Speaking of the "restoration of God's people into a glorious condition after all their sufferings," **John Owen** said that this was "held out under the same term, and you have a plentiful demonstration of this point." He then quoted from **Isaiah 65:17, 18, II Peter 3:13**, and **Revelation 21:1** (vol. 8, p. 255). These passages, of course, refer to the new heavens and new earth. Once again, however, John Owen had in mind the condition of God's people following the passing away of the old heavens and old earth of the Papacy government and rule, whereas it seems the writers from which he quoted were referring to the church following the destruction of Babylon, which was old Jerusalem, and represented all the Jewish religious structure. Nevertheless, later in this book I give you a lengthy summary of Dr. Owen's interpretation of **II Peter 3**, where he applies the destruction of the old heavens and earth to the destruction of the Jewish system, and the new heavens and new earth to the new order under Christ.

But his understanding of the meaning of the heavens and the earth is well taken, and it would profit us to understand this also in our studies on **Matthew 24** and related passages. **John Owen** said:

"Not to hold you too long upon what is so plain and evident, you may take it for a rule, that, in the denunciations of the judgments of God, through all the prophets, heaven, sun, moon, stars, and the like appearing beauties and glories of the aspectable heavens, are taken for governments, governors, dominions in political states, as Isa. xiv 12-15; Jer. xv. 9, li. 25." His footnote then gives Isa. 13:13; Ps. 68:8; Joel 2:10; Rev. 8:12; Matt. 24:29; Luke 21:25; Isa. 60:20; Obad. 4; Rev. 8:13; 11:12; 20:11 (**John Owen**, vol. 8, p. 255, in a sermon entitled **Shaking and Translating of Heaven and Earth**, preached on April 19, 1649).

The "Heavens and the Earth" Represent Israel

In **Isaiah 51:15-16** God said:

"But I am the LORD thy God, that divided the sea, whose waves roared: The LORD of hosts is his name.

"And I have put my words in thy mouth, and I have covered thee in the shadow of mine hand, that I may plant the heavens, and lay the foundations of the earth, and say unto Zion, Thou art my people."

God is not talking here about something that happened at creation's date **3,000 years before!** He is talking about His people Israel. "The heavens and the earth" represent Israel in this language.

And the downfall of governments is represented by heavenly disturbances. For example, **Isaiah 34:4** (nations); **Jeremiah 4:23-25** (Jews by Babylon); **Ezekiel 32:7** (destruction of Egypt).

The shaking of heaven and earth, and planting the heavens and foundation of the earth, are Bible language referring to change, transformation, and making into a new thing, of God's people.

Some of us may have to re-orient our thinking to understand the meaning of these passages. The Hebrew people understood this kind of language. It was their style. We need to see things in context, and the context of these New Testament passages had reference to the first century — not the end of the Roman Empire, not the Reformation period, and not a future state of the world at the end of time — but of what was to take place in the generation of those living in the time of Christ.

This same kind of language was used over and over again in the Old Testament as has been previously pointed out when we dealt with **Matthew 24:29** in this book.

Jesus used this kind of language in the above-mentioned verse **(Matthew 24:29)**, and He used this same kind of language in verse 35 when He said, "Heaven and earth shall pass away." Why should Jesus use a different kind of prophetic language than was used in the Old Testament and that was understood by the Hebrew mind?

One thing I have learned about literalism and symbolism in the Bible, is this: **History** and **events** are generally given in **literal** language, and **prophecies** are generally given in **symbolical** language. When God created the heavens and the earth, that was a historical event; the language describing that event is literal. When God is describing the downfall of Israel in prophetic terms, He uses symbolical language, like the destruction of the heavens and the earth. He does not mean that He will actually destroy the heavens and the earth; that is prophetic and symbolical language.

In **Hebrews 1:10-12** we have the same kind of language:

"Thou, Lord, in the beginning hast laid the foundation of the earth; and the heavens are the works of thine hands:

"They shall perish; but thou remainest; and they all shall wax old as doth a garment;

"And as a vesture shalt thou fold them up, and they shall be changed."

Matthew 24:35 could be the same as a condensed paraphrase of these verses in Hebrews, for they are talking about the same thing. In fact, just about all the book of Hebrews is about the passing away of the old heavens and earth of the old covenant and nation of Israel, as is so plainly brought out in **Hebrews 12:26-28**, where it speaks of the shaking of heaven and earth, and the removing of those things that can be shaken, and our receiving a kingdom which cannot be shaken or moved. Read it!

J. Stuart Russell said:

"What, then, is the great catastrophe symbolically represented as the shaking of the earth and heavens? No doubt it is the overthrow and abolition of the Mosaic dispensation, or old covenant; the destruction of the Jewish church and state, together with all the institutions and ordinances connected therewith. There were 'heavenly things' belonging to the dispensation: the laws, and statutes, and ordinances, which were divine in their origin, and might be properly called the **'spiritualia'** of Judaism — these were the heavens, which were to be shaken and removed. There were also 'earthly things:' the literal Jerusalem, the material temple, the land of Canaan — these were the **earth**, which was in like manner to be shaken and removed. The symbols are, in fact, equivalent to those employed by our Lord when predicting the doom of Israel. 'Immediately after the tribulation of those days (the horrors of the seige of Jerusalem) shall the sun be darkened, and the moon shall not give her light, and the powers of the **heavens shall be shaken**' (Matt. xxiv. 29). Both passages refer to the same catastrophe and employ very similar figures; besides which we have the authority of our Lord for fixing the event and the period of which He speaks within the limits of the generation then in existence: that is to say, the reference can only be to the judgment of the Jewish nation and the abrogation of the Mosaic economy at the Parousia'' (**J. Stuart Russell**, pp. 289-290).

The literal earth is not predicted to pass away. In fact, in **Psalm 104:5** David said that God "laid the foundations of the earth, that it should not be removed for ever."

And in **Ecclesiastes 1:4** Solomon said, "One generation passeth away, and another generation cometh: but the earth abideth for ever."

In **Matthew 24:35** Jesus is not speaking of the passing away of the literal heavens and earth, but of the coming destruction of Israel and Jerusalem and the Temple and all the rituals and ceremonies involved in their existence and practices. There was to be a new heavens and a new earth as a result, of which we speak shortly.

We must point out that the phrase, "heaven and earth," in the Bible is certainly not **limited** to Israel; but such usage is so prominent that we need to be made aware of this, else we shall miss the real message when we come across the expression in numerous passages where it is so used. Many are unaware of this expression having this meaning. But the references we have given show this to be the obvious meaning.

II Peter 3:1-13

The question then arises, "What about II Peter 3 where it tells of "the day of the Lord," and the heavens passing away, and the earth being burned up (**vs. 10**)?

This chapter has to be understood in the context of all these other passages which have been given. In writing prophetically, it is natural that Peter would also use the same kind of language and expressions as used in prophecy in the Old Testament. Why not? The people to whom he wrote would understand him on that basis.

Let us analyze what Peter said in **II Peter 3:1-13**:

★★★★★★★★★★★★★★

"This second epistle, beloved, I now write unto you; in both which I stir up your pure minds by way of remembrance:

"That ye may be mindful of the words which were spoken before by the holy prophets, and of the commandment of us the apostles of the Lord and Saviour:

"Knowing this first, that there shall come in the last days scoffers, walking after their own lusts,

"And saying, Where is the promise of his coming? for since the fathers fell asleep, all things continue as they were from the beginning of the creation.

"For this they willingly are ignorant of, that by the word of God the heavens were of old, and the earth standing out of the water and in the water:

"Whereby the world that then was, being overflowed with water, perished:

"But the heavens and the earth, which are now, by the same word are kept in store, reserved unto fire against the day of judgment and perdition of ungodly men.

"But, beloved, be not ignorant of this one thing, that one day is with the Lord as a thousand years, and a thousand years as one day.

"The Lord is not slack concerning his promise, as some men count slackness; but is longsuffering to us-ward, not willing that any should perish, but that all should come to repentance.

"But the day of the Lord will come as a thief in the night; in the which the heavens shall pass away with a great noise, and the elements shall melt with fervent heat, the earth also and the works that are therein shall be burned up.

"Seeing then that all these things shall be dissolved, what manner of persons ought ye to be in all holy conversation and godliness,

"Looking for and hasting unto the coming of the day of God, wherein the heavens being on fire shall be dissolved, and the elements shall melt with fervent heat?

"Nevertheless we, according to his promise, look for new heavens and a new earth, wherein dwelleth righteousness."

★★★★★★★★★★★★★

Let me suggest to start with that this passage is not to be taken literally (naturally) any more than **Luke 3:5** was taken literally: "Every valley shall be filled, and every mountain and hill shall be brought low; and the crooked shall be made straight, and the rough ways shall be made smooth."

Peter tells his readers that he wants them to remember and be mindful of the words of the prophets. Do you know of any words of the prophets in the Old Testament regarding the passing away of heavens and earth **IN A LITERAL SENSE?** We have noted some instances in the Old Testament about the **dissolving** of the heavens (same word as used here in **verse 13**), and as we discuss this passage we shall notice some other places as well. But none of the places refer to a literal passing away of heaven and earth. And yet Peter is wanting to remind his readers of the words of the holy prophets. Keep this in mind.

Keep in mind also that Peter had previously written **(I Peter 4:7)**, "**But the end of all things is at hand.**" Naturally, he was not talking about the end of our present heavens and earth, for if he were, he was mistaken, for that has not happened, and nineteen hundred years have gone by. He meant an end was at hand to the old heavens and earth of Judaism under the judgment of God — the end of the world (Jewish age) which Jesus has predicted would happen in that generation **(Matthew 24:34)**. This occurred later, just a few years after Peter had written it. So here he now reminds his readers not only of the words of the holy prophets, but also of "the commandment of us the apostles of the Lord and Saviour" **(II Peter 3:2)**. The apostles had referred to the same things as spoken by the holy prophets in the Old Testament.

The Last Days

Then in **II Peter 3:3** Peter said that scoffers would come in "the last days," saying, "Where is the promise of his coming?" **(vss. 3-4)**. We have gone to great length in this book to show how "the last days" were those of **their** age, the Jewish age, and not our age. Nearly forty years went by after Jesus said He was going to come in judgment on Israel, and people would be asking in those last days, "When is He coming? He said He was going to come in 'this generation' and these things would all take place which He promised, but He has not come yet. When will the promise be fulfilled?" This is what Peter said they would be asking in the closing days of that age — in "the last days." Not **our** last days, but **their** last days.

The *"Parousia"* Like in Noah's Day

The coming of Christ which is in question here is that of His *parousia*/coming in A.D. 70, the same as we have been discussing throughout this book.

Peter said, "for since the fathers fell asleep," etc. **(vs. 4)**. This had to be Jews asking the question, "Where is the promise of his coming?" and not Gentile unbelievers of today. It was **their** fathers who had fallen asleep.

The same could be said of the expression, "from the beginning of the creation" (same verse). Modern Gentile unbelievers do not refer to the "creation." They believe the earth is either of everlasting origin or else came into being through some other means than by God's divine creation. They would not be speaking in terms of a beginning of creation. These were the Jews in Peter's time who would be making this statement.

Peter says next (**vss. 5-7**) that those who would ask that question were ignorant of a former example of a prophesied judgment which came to pass — the flood. He said that "the world that then was, being overflowed with water, perished" (**vs. 6**). The word "world" is from the Greek word *"kosmos"* which means the world in its orderly arrangement, including the inhabitants. Scofield's note on this word in **Matthew 4:8** also says, "When used in the N.T. of humanity, the 'world' of men, it is **organized** humanity — humanity in families, tribes, nations — which is meant." It was this "world" which perished — not the earth itself. In **Matthew 24:37** Jesus likewise compares His coming in judgment on Israel "as the days of Noe were."

In **II Peter 2:5** it says that God "spared not the old world, . . . bringing in the flood upon the world of the ungodly." In **II Peter 3:6** it says, "Whereby the world that then was, being overflowed with water, perished." But afterwards, the **earth** was still here; it was not destroyed. The end of the world was not the destruction of the earth, but the destruction of ungodly sinners. This is what Peter meant in **II Peter 3:7** when he says, "the heavens and the earth, which are now, by the same word are kept in store, reserved unto fire against the day of judgment and perdition of ungodly men." It was to be the world of ungodly men which was to perish — not the literal earth itself.

As **Don Preston** put it, "We understand from Peter that in Noah's day the world, the moral world, or society, perished. We understand that Peter foresaw the coming dissolution of another society, the Jewish world. This is exactly what happened in 70 A.D." (**Don K. Preston, II Peter 3 — The Late Great Kingdom**, p. 38).

In Noah's day, the **literal** heavens were not destroyed by the flood. The **literal** earth was not destroyed by the flood. It was the **PEOPLE** who were destroyed.

"But," Peter said, "**the heavens and the earth**, which are now, by the same word are kept in store, reserved unto fire against the day of judgment and perdition of ungodly men" (**vs. 7**).

Why would Peter not be talking about the same heavens and earth which were talked about in the Old Testament in prophetic passages? Indeed, as the "world" of mankind with its system and arrangement passed away (not the earth), so Peter was predicting a coming judgment and destruction of Israel — the heavens and earth of prophecy. The "perdition of ungodly men" (vs. 7) is not talking about the literal heavens and earth vanishing, but of that nation of ungodly men passing away. This would happen shortly.

In a rather new book on prophecy, a recent writer, **David P. Crews,** said as regards to **verse 7:**

"The 'heavens and earth' are simply the Jewish religious/political authorities and the land of Palestine and the people who lived there. They were the 'ungodly men' — ungodly because they had rejected and killed the Christ, and still rejected him — who were being 'kept' (by the gracious mercy of God who wanted all to repent and come to him) unto the **day of judgment and destruction.** This phrasing tells us that this is another 'day of the Lord' just like the ones we see exampled in the Old Testament" **(David P. Crews,** p. 96).

God Gave Them 40 Years to Repent

Peter indicates that God is concerned that men not perish, but that they should come to repentence; and the reason God had waited this long was His unwillingness to see people perish. He gave them forty years to repent, and they did not. God cannot wait forever. The forty years were extra — thrown in for good measure to faithless Israel whose end should have come when they nailed Jesus to the cross!

But the promise of God is certain, and He will keep His word. "Heaven and earth shall pass away, but my words shall not pass away" **(Matthew 24:35).** The end of the Jewish age would come in that generation. "Verily I say unto you, This generation shall not pass, till all these things be fulfilled" **(Matthew 24:34).** The fact that God was waiting this long meant nothing to the mind of God, for with Him "one day is with the Lord as a thousand years, and a thousand years as one day" **(II Peter 3:8).** He never gave a precise number of days, for that would be man's numbering system for man's mind. In God's mind it is different, and in His mind it could not matter how short or how long because He is timeless.

The Day of the Lord

Then Peter connects "his coming" (vs. 4) with "the day of the Lord" (vs. 10), and it would come as "a thief in the night," He said. The idea of a thief coming was also used in **Matthew 24 (verses 43-44)** in connection with the Son of man coming, as well as in **I Thessalonians 5:2** where it stated "that the day of the Lord so cometh as a thief in the night."

Someone may say this expression, "day of the Lord," certainly puts this into our future, at a future coming of Christ, rather than in A.D. 70 when Christ came at the time of judgment on Israel. Those who are more futuristic in their interpretation of prophecy might say that. But the fact is that "the day of the Lord" is an expression also taken from the Old Testament and was used many times as regards to the judgments and destruction of various nations. That is the way it is used here. It does not have to have a meaning with reference to some future time to us of drastic judgments of God upon our world. But **it usually meant a time when God Himself would punish or judge people by the means of armies of other people.** The invading armies of other nations brought judgment and destruction upon various nations, and these times were each called "the day of the Lord" when they were proclaimed of the Lord. (In the New Testament such a day would be called "the day of Christ" as well if it had to do with the Messianic kingdom.)

"It is commonplace in prophecies of judgment for the destruction to be at the immediate hand of an invading nation and the destruction nonetheless to be declared a direct act of God" **(Randall Otto, p. 92).**

In **Ezekiel 30:3** a prophecy is given concerning a coming "day of the LORD." But in **verse 10** it is clearly pointed out that what is involved would be the destruction wrought by "Nebuchadrezzar king of Babylon." This is the way "the day of the Lord" was to come at so many times in the Bible, including that one predicted in **II Peter 3.**

Whenever the expression, "day of the Lord," was used in the Bible with reference to the people under discussion, it seems that the term referred to the next great epochal judgment of God. When one considers the passages in **I Peter** regarding the soon-approaching event which was to take place, it lends support to the idea that this passage in **II Peter 3** goes right along with these other passages in depicting a "near" event. In **II Peter 3:1** Peter wrote to stir up their memory of what he had written before, as well as what had been spoken by the holy prophets.

In his previous epistle, Peter had written that God was "ready to judge the quick and the dead" **(I Peter 4:5).** He wrote them that "the end of all things is at hand" **(I Peter 4:7).** He wrote them that "the time is come that judgment must begin at the house of God" **(II Peter 4:7).** Other references in **I Peter** give the same emphasis. In this epistle Peter was talking about the "day of the Lord" that was to occur in their generation. It was a "near" event.

Let us see how this expression was used in the Old Testament. How it was used there would certainly be the way any writers of the New Testament would use it — else there would be a **change** of definition necessary for New Testament Hebrews to understand what was meant. The expression was **primarily** used in connection with judgment against Israel, both in the Old Testament and the New Testament.

In **Isaiah 13:6** the Bible said that "the day of the LORD is at hand [near]," and we know from verse 1 that this was speaking of Babylon when God would "lay the land desolate: and he shall destroy the sinners thereof out of it" **(vs. 9)**.

Notice, too, in this same passage **(vs. 10)** that it mentions the stars not giving their light, the sun being darkened, and the moon not causing her light to shine — in that day of the Lord when He punishes Babylon ("the world") "for their evil, and the wicked for their iniquity" **(vs. 11)**. Here again we see **cosmic disturbances** representing the cessation of rulers in high places — in this case in Babylon itself.

In **Ezekiel 13:5** is mentioned "the day of the LORD" as being the time when four years later Jerusalem was destroyed and the people carried away into captivity to Babylon.

In **Ezekiel 30:3** it was prophesied, "the day of the LORD is near," and this was in reference to Egypt's destruction by "Nebuchadrezzar the king of Babylon" **(vs. 10)**.

In **Joel 1:15** it was prophesied, "the day of the LORD is at hand," and in **2:1**, "the day of the LORD cometh, for it is nigh at hand." Notice, in **2:10** the cosmic disturbances are mentioned — the earth quaking, the heavens trembling, the sun and moon darkening, the stars withdrawing their shining — all pointing to the downfall of rulers at the time of invading armies used by God in His day to bring judgment upon His people. In verse 11 God even calls the invading army, "his army."

And when in **Joel 2:28-31** God said the Spirit would be poured out before "the great and the terrible day of the LORD come," we are aware that Peter quoted from this passage on the day of Pentecost, saying it was fulfilled in their day **(Acts 2:16-20)**. We know the day of the Lord was to follow this, as the passage says, which it did just 37-40 years later in the siege and final destruction of Israel and Jerusalem. Note how the cosmic disturbances are mentioned in **Joel 2:30-31** and quoted in **Acts 2:19-20** in connection with "that day of the Lord," the same as Jesus did in **Matthew 24:29**.

Still other Old Testament references to "the day of the Lord" can be located by the use of a concordance, but we shall not go further here.

While the various references to "the day of the Lord" in the Old

Testament referred to various nations, etc., the reference in ALL such expressions in the **New Testament** are to that "day of the Lord" in A.D. 67-70 when the nation of Israel was involved — the only nation in the New Testament concerning which prophecy was made with reference to "the day of the Lord." Israel was to be destroyed at the *parousia*/coming of Christ in A.D. 70.

So, as we come to **II Peter 3:10**, is there any reason why we should think otherwise of "the day of the Lord" mentioned here? I think not. Peter is speaking here prophetically about the coming destruction of Israel through the armies of Rome and its subsidiaries in A.D. 67-70. And he uses the cosmic disturbance symbols exactly like they were used in the Old Testament when the different days of the Lord occurred — "in the which the heavens shall pass away with a great noise, and the elements shall melt with fervent heat, the earth also and the works that are therein shall be burned up." Both the heavens and the earth (symbolically) were to be destroyed. Both the rulers and the people were to be destroyed in this day of the Lord as prophesied to take place at "his coming."

To throw light on **II Peter 3:10**, recent author **Randall Otto**, speaking of the cosmic disturbances as mentioned in **Matthew 24:29; Mark 13:24-25;** and **Luke 21:25-26** said:

"The prophet's use of the language of cosmic catastrophe is not intended to be taken literally, for it is clear that it generally has to do with instances of judgment either upon apostate Israel or upon its pagan neighbors that issue from God by means of a national army!" **(Randall Otto, p. 103).**

On another page, Otto said:

"Once again, it is common for Bible readers unfamiliar with the apocalyptic imagery of the Old Testament to take these words as literal events associated with a final cosmic conflagration. Indeed, there are even some who are considered biblical scholars who willfully ignore this Old Testament imagery in their insistence on a literal destruction of the universe" **(Randall E. Otto, p. 226).**

Otto then goes on to say that the text of **II Peter 3:10** is the same kind of apocalyptic text as found in the symbolic imagery of **Isaiah 13:9-10; 24:23; Ezekiel 32:7-8ff; Joel 2:30 ff, Amos 8:9;** and **Zephaniah 1:14-18.**

In like manner, **David P. Crews** said:

"Here again, we are tempted to think that the physical universe is the subject of this prophecy. It is from this verse and others like it that so many have obtained the idea that the universal creation, including this planet Earth, will be consumed and destroyed in some 'end time' event. Once again, however, we are hearing a prophecy, and again we are seeing the apostle use symbols" **(David P. Crews, p. 98).**

It is true that many of the commentaries generally have agreed and taught that this passage in **II Peter 3** refers to the **literal** destruction of the world by fire at the final coming of Christ. Some of those who hold to this view include John Calvin, John Trapp, B.H. Carroll, Matthew Henry, Matthew Poole, Heinrich Meyer, Albert Barnes, Charles Ellicott, A.R. Fausset, Broadman Commentary, John A. Bengel, to name a few I have at hand at the moment in my library. John Bengel even goes so far as to say that even the stars would be dissolved.

". . . and the stars . . . also shall be dissolved with the earth. They are mistaken, who restrict the history of the creation and the description of this destruction only to the earth and to the quarter of the heaven which is nearer to the earth, but feign that the stars are older than the earth, and will survive it. It is not to the heaven only which surrounds the earth, but **to the heavens**, that both dissolution and restoration are ascribed, ver. 10 and 13" **(John A. Bengel,** 1687-1752, vol. 2, p. 779).

But even so, in spite of numerous commentaries which give the literal interpretation to this passage in **II Peter 3**, let us keep in mind that Peter had the **SAME MEANING** in this passage as was expressed in all the Old Testament passages mentioning "the new heavens and the new earth." And the apocalyptic and symbolic kind of language used would have been the same as well. Why should it be any different in **II Peter 3** than in all those Old Testament passages? I have found that the Bible itself interprets passages of Scripture better than many commentaries do. But, of course, it took me a long time to discover some of this myself.

It hardly seems possible to me that "the heavens being on fire shall be dissolved" of **II Peter 3:12** would have any different meaning than the "all the host of heaven shall be dissolved" of **Isaiah 34:4**. The latter refers to Bozrah and Idumea and their judgment **(vs. 6)** at the day of the Lord's vengeance **(vs. 8)**. Both are symbolic expressions, neither of which refer to the actual heavens being burned up.

And as we have seen earlier (in **Psalm 104:5** and **Ecclesiastes 1:4**), this earth will stand forever. See also the following passages:

"And he built his sanctuary like high palaces, like the earth which he hath established for ever" **(Psalm 78:69)**.

"Praise him, ye heavens of heavens, and ye waters that be above the heavens. . . .

"He hath also stablished them for ever and ever: he hath made a decree which shall not pass" **(Psalm 148:4,6)**.

"... the world also is stablished, that it cannot be moved" **(Psalm 93:1)**.

"... the world also shall be established that it shall not be moved ..." **(Psalm 96:10)**.

And God promised after the flood that He would nevermore destroy **all** of mankind again. "I will not again curse the ground any more for man's sake; for the imagination of man's heart is evil from his youth; **neither will I again smite any more every thing living, as I have done**" (Genesis 8:21).

Some may say that God made a covenant with Noah, and that the rainbow would be a reminder of that covenant between Noah and the world, that "the waters shall no more become a flood to destroy all flesh" **(Genesis 9:15)**. And this, some say, does not rule out God's destruction of the entire world by **fire** some day — that He will not do it with a flood, but He will do it with fire. They feel that **II Peter 3** teaches this. But no, **Genesis 8:21** plainly declared that God would never "again smite any more every thing living, as I have done."

God did destroy nations, but never again the whole world. And we do not know of any prediction anywhere in the Bible that says He will destroy this entire universe.

The word "earth" **(II Peter 3:7)** here means "land" and refers prophetically to the land of Israel. "Burned up" refers to the utter destruction that took place in those days throughout the entire land of Palestine. As the "world" of sinners was destroyed in the flood, so here the "earth/land" of Israel was completely destroyed.

The "heavens" would pass away in this day of the Lord, Peter said **(vs. 10)**. Yes, they would pass away just like the heavens were predicted to be removed in the Old Testament when "the day of the Lord" came, at various times. This is prophetic language. When the rulers of the nation which God destroyed passed away, it was said the heavens passed away. The invading armies did this. But in the New Testament we are thinking of the nation of Israel — the only nation under consideration in the whole New Testament. When the heavens passed away, it was Israel which passed away.

It is interesting that the word "coming" here in **verse 12** ("unto the coming of the day of God") is the same identical word in the Greek (*"parousia"*) as used of the "coming" of Christ Himself in numerous places in the New Testament.

The Elements Shall Melt

In **II Peter 3:10**, Peter said that when the day of the Lord came and the heavens passed away, "the elements shall melt with fervent heat." We need to examine the meaning of this word "elements," which is the same word as is used several other times in the New Testament. The Greek word for "elements" is *"stoicheion"* and means "something orderly in arrangement — element, principle, rudiment." The word itself can refer to the parts of which our universe is made, and it can also refer to the rudimentary things of religion (as well as other things too, of course). At this point in our interpretation, given the symbolic fulfillment of the passing away of the heavens and the earth, we would connect this word to Israel. The elements that would be done away with would be those things related to Israel which would be abolished.

We find this word first in **Galatians 4:3** where Paul said, "Even so we, when we were children, were in bondage under the **elements** of the world."

Here Paul was saying that the Jewish people before Christ and salvation were living under the worldly ceremonies and ordinances of the old covenant, though now they no longer needed the law as a schoolmaster as they had graduated to Christ by faith. The "elements" were no longer needed. Actually, it took the events of A.D. 67-70 for the complete elimination of these "elements" from the lives of the people. All was destroyed in the holocaust of those eventful days — the day of the Lord.

Then in **Galatians 4:9** the word is used again. "But now, after that ye have known God, or rather are known of God, how turn ye again to the weak and beggarly **elements**, whereunto ye desire again to be in bondage?" Paul follows this by saying that because "Ye observe days, and months, and times, and years," that he was afraid he had bestowed his labor upon them in vain (**vss. 10-11**). Turning again to the legality of the old law and its system was the same as going back to an "elementary" religious system. The whole system would be "burned up" shortly.

In **Colossians 2:8** Paul encourages the Colossian Christians not to go back into these elementary things of the old law. He uses the same word for "elements" (*"stoicheion"*), though here translated "rudiments." "Beware lest any man spoil you through philosophy and vain deceit, after the tradition of men, after the **rudiments** of the world, and not after Christ." The spiritual lives of these Christians could be spoiled if they listened to those Judaizers who tried to get them to return to the old way. These things would soon go up in smoke. They were only elementary and not needed in mature Christian living.

Then in the same chapter, **Colossians 2:20**, Paul said, "Wherefore if ye be dead with Christ from the **rudiments** of the world, why, as though living in the world, are ye subject to ordinances . . .?" These ordinances would soon "perish" (be destroyed), he said (vs. **22**).

These "elements" of religion were destined to be "burned up," because in a real sense the death of Christ had already brought them to naught. In **Colossians 2:14-17** Paul said:

"Blotting out the handwriting of ordinances that was against us, which was contrary to us, and took it out of the way, nailing it to his cross;

"And having spoiled principalities and powers, he made a shew of them openly, triumphing over them in it.

"Let no man therefore judge you in meat, or in drink, or in respect of an holyday, or of the new moon, or of the sabbath days:

"Which are a shadow of things to come; but the body is of Christ."

And in **Ephesians 2:14-15** Paul said:

"For he is our peace, who hath made both one, and hath broken down the middle wall of partition between us;

"Having abolished in his flesh the enmity, even the law of commandments contained in ordinances; for to make in himself of twain one new man, so making peace."

If these other four places in the New Testament are the only places anywhere in the New Testament that the word for "elements" can be found, except in **II Peter 3:10**, would you not think that the meaning in **II Peter 3:10** would be the same as in these other places? Other than those four other places, this is the only place the word is used.

Jesus had said, "I am come to send FIRE on the earth; and what will I, if it be already kindled?" (**Luke 12:49**). This was not to be literal fire, but the fire of His wrath and justice, and a change of religious systems.

In **Lamentations 2:3** it says, ". . . he burned against Jacob like a flaming fire, which devoureth round about." This did not mean that everything was burned up, but rather that judgment came upon all.

After the "heavens" of the rulership of the Jewish people had passed away, the "elements" themselves of the old ordinances, etc., would also pass away ("be burned up"). All of this came to pass by A.D. 70 when Jerusalem and the Temple were completely destroyed. This was all at "his coming" at that "day of the Lord" when the Roman armies fulfilled the plan of God so that a new "heavens and earth" could be brought into existence.

When Peter said "the elements shall melt with fervent heat" in **II Peter 3:12**, the Greek word for "melt" there is *"teko* which means "to liquefy." But interestingly, in verse 10 where those same identical words (in English in the King James version) are used: "the elements shall melt with fervent heat," the Greek word for "melt" is different. It is *"luo,"* which means "break up, destroy, dissolve, loose, melt, put off." In actuality, this is what happened to those "elements" of the old Jewish religion — they were broken up, destroyed, dissolved, loosened and put off. This is how the elements melted in that day of the Lord when the heavens and the earth felt the judgment of God.

The New Heavens and the New Earth

Peter said, "Nevertheless we, according to his promise, look for new heavens and a new earth wherein dwelleth righteousness" (**vs. 13**).

The thing that struck me about this particular verse is that the looking forward to a new heavens and a new earth was based upon **"HIS PROMISE."** It is according to His promise, Peter said, that we look forward to a new heavens and a new earth. Where in the Bible can we find this **promise** of a new heavens and a new earth? If we locate it, it should reveal to us whether Peter is speaking of a literal heavens and earth passing away, or if he is using this terminology in a symbolic way.

The only prophecies ("promise" referred to in **vs. 13**) in the Old Testament specifically mentioning the new heavens and new earth are found in **Isaiah 65:17** and **Isaiah 66:22**. These are the only two places in the Old Testament where this promise of new heavens and a new earth can be found, and neither of these speak of a literal heavens and earth passing away. Nor do they speak of a literal new heavens and new earth.

Commentaries generally apply the fulfillment of these prophecies to the gospel age (as opposed to dispensationalists and some premillennialists who apply them to a future millennium after a future second coming of Christ). The new heavens and new earth referred to the spiritual world order which was brought into being through Christ. But the old had to pass away before the new could come into being.

We shall discuss these two passages in Isaiah which speak of the new heavens and new earth.

Isaiah 65-17

Isaiah 65:17: "For, behold, I create new heavens and a new earth: and the former shall not be remembered, nor come into mind." The results of the creation of new heavens and a new earth are seen in the rest of the chapter — the creation of another Jerusalem (a new Jerusalem) — and the blessings which **premillennialists** say will take place **literally** during a millennium here on earth after Jesus comes in our future (see specifically verses **20 and 25**). But this passage is a grand depiction of the gospel age after Christ came in judgment in A.D. 70 and took away the old heavens and the old earth. Now we have the new heavens and the new earth of the gospel age.

The famed **Charles Spurgeon** of the Metropolitan Tabernacle in London said (in a sermon on **Isaiah 65:17-19**):

"Did you ever regret the absence of the burnt-offering, or the red heifer, or any one of the sacrifices and rites of the Jews? Did you ever pine for the feast of tabernacle, or the dedication? No, because, though these were like the old heavens and earth to the Jewish believers, they have passed away, and we now live under new heavens and a new earth, so far as the dispensation of divine teaching is concerned. The substance is come, and the shadow has gone: and we do not remember it" (**Charles Spurgeon**, Metropolitan Tabernacle Pulpit, vol. xxxvii, p. 354).

In this gospel age we now have the new Jerusalem supplanting the old Jerusalem which was destroyed in A.D. 70. This new Jerusalem is more fittingly described in **Revelation 21 and 22**. John said:

"And I saw a new heaven and a new earth: for the first heaven and the first earth were passed away; and there was no more sea.

"And I John saw the holy city, new Jerusalem, coming down from God out of heaven, prepared as a bride adorned for her husband" (**Revelation 21:1-2**).

This new Jerusalem in the new heavens and new earth is **not** a materialistic city. **IT IS THE BRIDE, THE LAMB'S WIFE**, as it says. The angel told John, "Come hither, I will shew thee the bride, the Lamb's wife" (**Revelation 21:9**). And what is it that symbolizes the bride of Christ? It says, "And he carried me away in the spirit to a great and high mountain, and shewed me that great city, the holy Jerusalem, descending out of heaven from God" (**Revelation 21:10**). This is the bride of Christ, the new Jerusalem, which is the new people of God since Christ came in the day of the Lord in A.D. 70 and destroyed the old Jerusalem — the faithless wife of Jehovah. The description of this new city, which city we are, is shown in **Revelation 21 and 22** and is our heritage for **this life and the life to come, both for time and eternity.**

Max King said:

"Peter said, in anticipating the **imminent** end of all things (the coming of Christ and the end of the then existing heaven and earth) (I Pet. 4:7), 'nevertheless we, according to his promise, look for new heavens and a new earth.' This promise of a new heaven and earth is taken from Isa. 65:17-19 and 66:22-24, and had a limited fulfillment in Israel's return from Babylonian captivity. But beyond the limited restoration, this prophecy (as many other prophecies) was understood as having an ultimate, final meaning and fulfillment through Christ in 'the age to come'. The city of Jerusalem was the focus of this new heaven and earth, not only in its limited fulfillment in Israel's return from Babylon (Isa. 65:18, 19), but also in its ultimate fulfillment in Christ in the New Covenant aeon, as seen in chapters 21 and 22 of Revelation" **(Max King, p. 256).**

Isaiah 66:22

Isaiah 66:22: "For as the new heavens and the new earth, which I will make, shall remain before me, saith the LORD, so shall your seed and your name remain."

We are the seed of Christ and Abraham. "And if ye be Christ's, then are ye Abraham's seed, and heirs according to the promise" **(Galatians 3:29).**

The Old Testament had said, ". . . the Lord GOD shall slay thee, and call his servants by another name" **(Isaiah 65:15).** It was just two verses later that God said, "For, behold, I create new heavens and a new earth" **(vs. 17).**

"But ye are a chosen generation, a royal priesthood, AN HOLY NATION, a peculiar people; . . . Which in time past were not a people, but are now the people of God" **(I Peter 2:9-10).**

All this had been prophesied in the Old Testament. "And they shall call them, The holy people, The redeemed of the LORD: and thou shalt be called, Sought out, A city not forsaken" **(Isaiah 62:12).**

This was the city for which Abraham looked: "For he looked for a city which hath foundations, whose builder and maker is God" **(Hebrews 11:10).**

These were the **PROMISES** of God concerning a new heavens and a new earth and a new city (the new Jerusalem). There was no **literalistic** interpretation to be given those passages in Isaiah. No literal heaven and earth would be destroyed, and no literal heavens and earth would be created. And Peter said, "Nevertheless we, **ACCORDING TO HIS PROMISE,** look for new heavens and a new earth, wherein dwelleth righteousness" **(II Peter 3:13).** This was the kind of new heavens and new earth Peter was looking for.

Interestingly, just seven verses before the promise of the new heavens and new earth in **Isaiah 66:22,** the Lord said:

"For, behold, the LORD will come with fire, and with his chariots like a whirlwind, to render his anger with fury, and his rebuke with flames of fire.

"For by fire and by his sword will the LORD plead with all flesh:

and the slain of the LORD shall be many" **(Isaiah 66:15-16)**.

Those two verses indicate in figurative language God's part in causing the old heavens and earth to disappear. The fire and sword represented invading armies.

Commenting on **Isaiah 66:22, Edward J. Young** said: "With this verse the prophet makes known the foundation for the entire preceding line of thought. By **your** seed and **your** name he has in mind the spiritual Israel of which he has been speaking. **Seed** refers to the descendants of the people of God, who form the subject of this address. Their perpetuity is to be assured. **Name** indicates reputation; forever the Church will be recognized by the people whom God has chosen to be His own. To assure God's people of this perpetuity and constant recognition God institutes a comparison with the new heavens and the new earth. As God originally created the heavens and the earth, so now He is going to make (the participle suggests near futurity) **new heavens** and a **new earth**, which will stand before Him (i.e. under His constant care and protection; cf. 48:19; 53:2). The old Israel will pass away; but from it there will spring the remnant that has survived the judgment, and together with it will be a great influx of Gentiles, all of which will form the true Israel of God under the new dispensation. In the old dispensation this Israel of God (the Church) had been practically identical with the literal nation, but in the new the Gentiles should be fellow heirs, and of the same body, and partakers of his promise in Christ by the gospel, '. . . to the intent that now unto the principalities and powers in heavenly places might be known by the church the manifold wisdom of God . . .' (Eph. 3:6, 10). The promise is strengthened by **saith the Lord**" **(Edward J. Young, Commentary on the Book of Isaiah, vol. 3, pp. 535-536)**.

David Chilton said, "Because of the 'collapsing-universe' technology used in this passage, many have mistakenly assumed that St. Peter is speaking of the physical heaven and earth, rather than the dissolution of the Old Covenant world order" **(David Chilton, The Days of Vengeance, p. 540)**.

The new heavens and new earth of **II Peter 3:13** are not a picture of that which is to be in the eternal state following the great white throne judgment. The promise is taken from those two passages we have previously mentioned in Isaiah. They refer to this present dispensation, the gospel age. Spiritual blessings are pictured by earthly blessings. Many passages in the Old Testament, thought to refer to the eternal blessings Christians will have in glory or at least out in eternity, actually refer to this present age. **Kenneth Gentry** spoke well on this when he said:

"First, numerous prophetic references speak of *factors inappropriate to the eternal state*, such as the overcoming of active opposition to the kingdom (e.g., Psa. 72:4,9; Isa. 11:4, 13-15; Mic. 4:3), birth and aging (e.g., Psa. 22:30-31; Isa. 65:20; Zech. 8:3-5), the conversion of people (Psa. 72:11), death (e.g., Psa. 22:29; 72:14; Isa. 65:20), sin (e.g., Isa. 65:20, Zech. 14:14-17), suffering (e.g., Psa. 22:29; 72:2, 13, 17), and national distinctions and interaction (e.g., Psa. 72:10-11, 17; Isa. 2:2-4; Zech. 14:16-17)" **(Kenneth Gentry, He Shall Have Dominon, p. 208).**

Douglas Wilson said:

"Some of the terms of the promise in Isaiah are these: we know that death will remain in the new heaven and new earth (65:20), home construction will continue (65:21), agriculture will continue (65:21), as will worship (66:23). The **new heavens and new earth** is therefore not a phrase which describes the eternal resurrection state." **(Douglas Wilson, p. 30).**

Neither is **Isaiah 65:17-25** a picture of a 1,000-years millennium after a future second coming of Christ, as believed by premillennialists. But it is a picture of God's new spiritual world order to the extent that the gospel permeates the lives and hearts of men and women in this present age. It is a picture of Christ's present kingdom on earth. It is a picture of the new covenant operating in the lives of God's people. So much a transformation is this from the old order, that it is said, "the former shall not be remembered, nor come into mind." **(Isaiah 65:17).**

John Calvin said:

"**For, lo, I will create new heavens and a new earth.** By these metaphors he promises a remarkable change of affairs; as if God had said that he has both the inclination and the power not only to restore his Church, but to restore it in such a manner that it shall appear to gain new life and to dwell in a new world. These are exaggerated modes of expression; but the greatness of such a blessing, which was to be manifested at the coming of Christ, could not be described in any other way. Nor does he mean only the first coming, but the whole reign, which must be extended as far as to the last coming, as we have already said in expounding other passages" **(John Calvin, John Calvin's Commentaries, vol. 8, pp. 397-398).**

Writing on **Matthew 24:27** but conveying the same thoughts we are trying to suggest here, **Dr. John Lightfoot** said this:

"That the destruction of Jerusalem is very frequently expressed in Scripture as if it were the destruction of the whole world, Deut. xxxii. 22; 'A fire is kindled in mine anger, and shall burn unto the lowest hell' (the discourse there is about the wrath of God consuming that people; see ver. 20, 21), 'and shall consume the earth with her increase, and set on fire the foundations of the mountains.' Jer. iv. 23; 'I beheld the earth, and lo, it was without form, and void; and the heavens, and they had no light,' &c. The discourse there also is concerning the destruction of that nation, Isa. lxv. 17; 'Behold, I create new heavens and a new earth: and the former shall not be remembered,' &c. And more passages of this sort among the prophets. According to this sense, Christ speaks in this place; and Peter speaks in his Second Epistle, third chapter; and John, in the sixth of the Revelation; and Paul, 2 Cor. v. 17, &c." (**John Lightfoot**, vol. 2, pp. 18-319).

In his volume 3, **Dr. Lightfoot** spoke further on his views on this subject. He said:

"With the same reference it is, that the times and state of things immediately following the destruction of Jerusalem are called 'a new creation,' 'new heavens,' and 'a new earth,' Isa. lxv. 17; 'Behold, I create a new heaven and a new earth.' When should that be? Read the whole chapter; and you will find the Jews rejected and cut off; and from that time is that new creation of the evangelical world among the Gentiles.

"Compare 2 Cor. v. 17 and Rev. xxi. 1, 2; where, the old Jerusalem being cut off and destroyed, a new one succeeds; and new heavens and a new earth are created.

"2 Pet. iii. 13: 'We, according to his promise, look for new heavens and a new earth.' The heavens and the earth of the Jewish church and commonwealth must be all on fire, and the Mosaic elements burnt up; but we, according to the promise made to us by Isaiah the prophet, when all these are consumed, look for the new creation of the evangelical state" (vol. 3, p. 453).

Dr. Lightfoot had previously said:

"That the destruction of Jerusalem and the whole Jewish state is described as if the whole frame of this world were to be dissolved. Nor is it strange, when God destroyed his habitation and city, places once so dear to him, with so direful and sad an overthrow; his own people, whom he accounted of as much or more than the whole world beside, by so dreadful and amazing plagues. Matt. xxiv. 29, 30, 'The sun shall be darkened, &c. Then shall appear the 'sign of the Son of man,' &c; which yet are said to fall out within that generation, ver. 34. 2 Pet. iii. 10, 'The heavens shall pass away with a great noise, and the elements shall melt with fervent heat,' &c. Compare with this Deut. xxxii. 22, Heb. xii. 26: and observe that by **elements** are understood the Mosaic elements, Gal. iv. 9, Coloss. ii. 20: and you will not doubt that St. Peter speaks only of the conflagration of

Jerusalem, the destruction of the nation, and the abolishing the dispensation of Moses" **(John Lightfoot,** vol. 3, p. 452).

John Brown, in his commentary on **Matthew 5:18** says:
" 'Heaven and earth passing', understood literally, is the dissolution of the present system of the universe, and the period when that is to take place, is called the 'end of the world'. But a person at all familiar with the phraseology of the Old Testament Scriptures, knows that the dissolution of the Mosaic economy, and the establishment of the Christian, is often spoken of as the removing of the old earth and heavens, and the creation of a new earth and new heavens" **(John Brown,** vol. 1, p. 170. Quoted by **Gary DeMar** in **Biblical Worldview**).

Dr. John Owen

We were driving back from a Bible conference on Long Island, New York, and we stopped by the **Great Christian Books** store at Elkton, Maryland. We spent the night in the Walt Hibbards' home. He was showing us around the store, and I saw a brand new set of Dr. John Owen's books on a shelf (reprinted in 1990). I commented, "I need something from volume 9 in that set of books." Mr. Hibbard instantly said, "It's on page 131." Sure enough, there it was. He knew exactly what I was looking for. I bought the new volume and brought it home with me.

Dr. John Owen was a Puritan preacher in the 17th century. I had heard that Dr. J. I. Packer said that John Owen was the greatest theologian of all time. My interest in his works was because I had read somewhere that John Owen had dealt with **II Peter 3** from a preterist standpoint. I want to quote a section from his book. It is a little lengthy, but because of who this man was please read it carefully and consider all that he says in relation to the things I have been writing in this book.

****

"It is evident, from sundry places in the New Testament, what extreme oppositions the believing Jews met withal, all the world over, from their own countrymen, with and among whom they lived. They in the meantime, no doubt, warned them of the wrath of Christ against them for their cursed unbelief and persecutions; particularly letting them know, that Christ would come in vengeance ere long, according as he had threatened, to the ruin of his enemies. And because the persecuting Jews, all the world over, upbraided the believers with the temple and the holy city, Jerusalem, their worship and service instituted of God, which they had defiled; they were given to know, that even all these things also should be destroyed, for their rejection of the Son of God. After some continuance of time, the threatening denounced being not yet accomplished, — as is the manner of profane persons and hardened sinners, Eccles. viii. 11, — they began to mock and scoff, as if they were all but the vain pretences, or loose, causeless fears

of the Christians. That this was the state with them, or shortly would be, the apostle declares in this chapter, verses 3, 4. Because things continued in the old state, without alteration, and judgment was not speedily executed, they scoffed at all the threats about the coming of the Lord that had been denounced against them."

****

"I shall only observe, by the way, not to look into the difficulties of these verses, that I not be too long detained from my principal intendment, — that the apostle makes a distribution of the world into heaven and earth, and saith, they 'were destroyed with water, and perished.' We know that neither the fabric or substance of the one or other was destroyed, but only men that lived on the earth; and the apostle tells us, verse 5, of the heavens and earth that were then, and were destroyed by water, distinct from the heavens and the earth that were now, and were to be consumed by fire; and yet, as to the visible fabric of heaven and earth, they were the same both before the flood and in the apostle's time, and continue so to this day; when yet it is certain that the heavens and earth whereof he speaks were to be destroyed and consumed by fire in that generation. We must, then, for the clearing our foundation, a little consider what the apostle intends by 'the heavens and the earth' in these two places: —

"1. It is certain, that what the apostle intends by the 'world,' with its heavens and earth, verses 5, 6, which was destroyed by water; the same or somewhat of that kind, he intends by 'the heavens and the earth' that were to be consumed and destroyed by fire, verse 7. Otherwise there would be no coherence in the apostle's discourse, nor any kind of argument, but a mere fallacy of words.

"2. It is certain, that by the flood, the world, or the fabric of heaven and earth, was not destroyed, but only the inhabitants of the world; and therefore the destruction intimated to succeed by fire, is not of the substance of the heavens and the earth, which shall not be consumed until the last day, but of persons or men living in the world.

"3. Then we must consider in what sense men living in the world are said to be the 'world,' and the 'heavens and earth' of it. I shall only insist on one instance to this purpose, among the many that may be produced, Isa. li. 15, 16. The time when the work here mentioned, of planting the heavens, and laying the foundation of the earth, was performed by God, was when he 'divided the sea,' verse 15, and gave the law, verse 16, and said to Zion, 'Thou art my people;' — that is, when he took the children of Israel out of Egypt, and formed them in the wilderness into a church and state. Then he planted the heavens, and laid the foundation of the earth, — made the new world; that is, brought forth order, and government, and beauty, from the confusion wherein before they were. This is the planting of the heavens, and laying the foundation of the earth in the world. And hence it is, that when mention is made of the destruction of a state and government, it is in that language that seems to set forth the end of the world. So Isa. xxxiv. 4; which is yet but the destruction of the state of Edom. The like also is affirmed of the Roman empire, Rev. vi. 14; which the Jews constantly affirm to be intended by Edom in the prophets. And in our Saviour Christ's prediction of the destruction of Jerusalem, Matt. xxiv., he sets it out by expressions of the same importance. It is evident, then, that in the prophetical idiom and manner of speech, by 'heavens' and 'earth,' the civil and religious state and combination of men in the world, and the men of them, are often understood. So were the heavens and earth that world which was then destroyed by the flood.

"4. On this foundation I affirm, that the heavens and earth here intended in this prophecy of Peter, the coming of the Lord, the day of judgment and perdition of ungodly men, mentioned in the destruction of that heaven and earth, do all of them relate, not to the last and final judgment of the world, but to that utter desolation and destruction that was to be made of the Judaical church and state; for which I shall offer these two reasons, of many that might be insisted on from the text: —

"(1.) Because whatever is here mentioned was to have its peculiar influence on the men of that generation. He speaks of that wherein both the profane scoffer and the those scoffed at were concerned, and that as Jews; — some of them believing, others opposing the faith. Now, there was no particular concernment of that generation in that sin, nor in that scoffing, as to the day of judgment in general; but there was a peculiar relief for the one and a peculiar dread for the other at hand, in the destruction of the Jewish nation; and besides, an ample testimony, both to the one and the other, of the power and dominion of the Lord Jesus Christ — which was the thing in question between them.

"(2.) Peter tells them, that, after the destruction and judgment that he speaks of, verse 13, 'We, according to his promise, look for new heavens and a new earth,' etc. They had this expectation. But what is that promise? where may we find it? Why, we have it in the very words and letter, Isa. lxv. 17. Now, when shall this be that God will create these 'new heavens and new earth, wherein dwelleth righteousness?' Saith Peter, 'It shall be after the coming of the Lord, after that judgment and destruction of ungodly men, who obey not the gospel, that I foretell.' But now it is evident, from this place of Isaiah, with chap. lxvi., 21, 22, that this is a prophecy of gospel times only; and that the planting of these new heavens is nothing but the creation of gospel ordinances, to endure for ever. The same thing is so expressed, Heb. xii. 26-28.

"First, There is the foundation of the apostle's inference and exhortation... — 'Seeing that I have evinced that all these things, however precious they seem, or what value soever any put upon them, shall be dissolved, — that is, destroyed; and that in that dreadful and fearful manner before mentioned, — in a way of judgment, wrath, and vengeance, by fire and sword; — let others mock at the threats of Christ's coming. — he will come, he will not tarry; and then the heavens and earth that God himself planted, — the sun, moon, and stars of the Judaical polity and church, — the whole old world of worship and worshippers, that stand out in their obstinacy against the Lord Christ, — shall be sensibly dissolved and destroyed. This, we know, shall be the end of these things, and that shortly.' "

****

"1. Because in every such providential alteration or dissolution of things on the account of Christ and his church, there is a peculiar coming of Christ himself. He cometh into the world for the work he hath to do; he cometh among his own to fulfil his pleasure among them. Hence such works are called 'his coming;' and 'the coming of his day.' Thus James exhorts these very Jews to whom Peter here writes, with reference to the same things, James v. 7-9, 'Be patient unto the coming of the Lord.' But how could that generation extend their patience to the day of judgment? 'Nay,' saith he, 'that is not the work I design, but his coming to take vengeance on his stubborn adversaries;' which he saith, verse 8, 'draweth nigh,' is even at hand; yea, Christ, 'the judge, standeth before the door,' verse 9, 'ready to enter;' — which also he did within a few years. So upon or in the destruction of Jerusalem (the same work), Luke xxi. 27, the Son of man is said to 'come in a cloud, with power and great glory;' — and they that escape in that desolation are said to 'stand before the Son of man,' verse 36. So, in the ruin and destruction of the Roman empire, on the account of their persecution, it is said that 'the day of the wrath of the Lamb was come,' Rev. vi. 16, 17" (John Owen, vol. 9, pp. 132, 133-135, 138-139).

★★★★★★★★★★★★★★

More on Symbolic Language of Prophecy

The type of language used in **II Peter 3** can be observed in numerous places in the Old Testament. Take, for example, the **fourth chapter of Jeremiah**. Here God is talking to and concerning Judah and Jerusalem (**vs. 5**), and He is speaking of sending destruction upon them from the north (**vs. 6**). The language used to describe the results of this visitation is found in **verses 23-28**:

"I beheld the earth, and, lo, it was without form, and void; and the heavens, and they had no light.

"I beheld the mountains, and, lo, they trembled, and all the hills moved lightly.

"I beheld, and, lo, there was no man, and all the birds of the heavens were fled.

"I beheld, and, lo, the fruitful place was a wilderness, and all the cities thereof were broken down at the PRESENCE of the LORD, and by his fierce anger.

"For thus hath the LORD said, The whole land shall be desolate; yet will I not make a full end."

This is apocalyptic figurative language describing the desolation of Judah by invading forces. The cosmic language simply means that the presence of Jehovah was revealed in judgment upon the people. The "presence" of the Lord (**vs. 26**) has the meaning of being in a fearful way, against someone or something. It would be like the word for "coming" in the New Testament (*"parousia"*), when it referred to judgment passages.

Similarly, in Micah is found this same kind of language, when God is talking about the destruction of Samaria and Jerusalem:

"For, behold, the LORD COMETH forth out of his place, and WILL COME DOWN, and tread upon the high places of the earth.

"And the mountains shall be molten under him, and the valleys shall be cleft, as wax before the fire, and as the waters that are poured down a steep place" **(Micah 1:3-4)**.

Then after mentioning that all of this is because of the sins of Jacob, and Israel, and Samaria, and Jerusalem **(vs. 5)**, He further declared,

"Therefore I will make Samaria as an heap of the field, and as plantings of a vineyard: and I will pour down the stones thereof into the valley, and I will discover the foundations thereof" **(Micah 1:6)**.

This destruction of these places were spoken of as the Lord coming forth and coming down **(vs. 3)**, though we know the results were accomplished through human instrumentality. Likewise, in **II Peter 3**, the fall and destruction of the nation of Israel and the city of Jerusalem and the Temple in New Testament times were said to occur at the coming of Christ, and the event is couched in apocalyptic language of the heavens and the earth. We can understand New Testament prophecy a lot better if we understand how terminology was used in the Old Testament.

When the expression is used concerning the heavens and the earth waxing old like a garment, and being changed (see **Psalm 102:26**), it is like Isaiah said in **Isaiah 50:9**, "they all shall wax old as a garment," as he spoke of PEOPLE who would be destroyed.

In the very next chapter God spoke of the heavens and earth vanishing:

"Lift up your eyes to the heavens, and look upon the earth beneath: for the heavens shall vanish away like smoke, and the earth shall wax old like a garment, and they that dwell therein shall die in like manner . . ." **(Isaiah 51:6)**.

Then in that same chapter God tells of forming Israel, describing this as planting the heavens and the foundations of the earth:

". . . that I may plant the heavens, and lay the foundations of the earth, and say unto Zion, Thou art my people" **(Isaiah 51:16)**.

ISRAEL was the heavens and the earth that God had formed, and someday that same heavens and earth would pass away as described in **II Peter 3**.

In **Deuteronomy 32:1**, after the formation of Israel, God said,

"Give ear, O ye heavens, and I will speak; and hear, O earth, the words of my mouth." To whom was God talking — the literal heavens and earth? No, He was talking to Israel.

And when He said in that same chapter (vs. 22) "For a fire is kindled in mine anger, and shall burn unto the lowest hell, and shall consume the earth with her increase, and set on fire the foundations of the mountains," He was not talking about the destruction of the earth. The verse before this tells what He was talking about, how that Israel had provoked Him to anger, and He would consume them with those who were not His people (vs. 21).

This is the way language is used in the Old Testament. It was adopted for like use in the New Testament.

This kind of language in relation to Israel began in the Bible in **Genesis 37:9** when Joseph told his brothers his dream. He said, "Behold, I have dreamed a dream more; and, behold, the sun and the moon and the eleven stars made obeisance to me." His father understood the meaning of that dream and asked, "What is this dream that thou hast dreamed? Shall I and thy mother and thy brethren indeed come to bown down ourselves to thee to the earth?" **(vs. 10)**.

Later, it was to be said that the nation of Israel which had been formed was the heavens and the earth **(Isaiah 51:16)**.

So, this passage in **II Peter 3** is not speaking of a transformation and renewal of the physical components of the material earth some day. As in the case of Noah's day, a new earth came about through a change in the people themselves — not the physical components of the earth as a result of the flood. People were destroyed, and a new era began. For all concerned, it was a new heavens and a new earth. So likewise, the new heavens and new earth of **II Peter 3** (based on the promises of Isaiah) consist of a renewed people of God following the disintegration of the old system of Judaism and all that went along with it. A shaking of "heavens and earth" took place, **(Hebrews 12:26-29)** which resulted in only the spiritual things that could not be removed being left.

Roderick Campbell, with reference to II Peter 3, says:

"Peter is preparing his hearers for the "fiery trial" which he sees looming in the days ahead — a trial which is certain to test their faith. His hearers have not yet fully grasped the significance of the great change introduced by the advent of Christ. The external fabric of the Old Covenant still stands, in outward appearance seemingly as secure and glorious as it was before (except for the rending of the temple veil). Some of the Christians are still clinging tenaciously to the ancient symbolic rites and ceremonies. From our vantage point it is easy to accuse them of lack of vision. But we should bear in mind that Peter and his audience were living in the midst of a persecuting world. Moreover, the destruction of their sacred city and temple was then imminent. Peter had heard the doom of their magnificent temple pronounced by the lips of Jesus — a doom which, Jesus said, some of the generation then living would witness with their natural eyes. In the midst of that crumbling world, Peter calls to mind Isaiah's promise of "new heavens and a new earth." By the eye of faith, he sees this new creation emerging from the dust and debris of that once glorious order of things which was so dear to every loyal Hebrew heart (cf. 2 Cor. 3:7). He and his hearers are standing within the threshold of the new age, an age which, although potentially and actually present, has not yet been made fully manifest to his hearers, who are no doubt still, for the most part, babes in Christ." (**Roderick Campbell, Israel and the New Covenant, p. 115**).

"But the day of the Lord will come as a thief in the night; in the which the heavens shall pass away with a great noise, and the elements shall melt with fervent heat . . ." **(II Peter 3:10)**.

Some say that this will occur someday in our future through a nuclear explosion. This would have to be some mighty nuclear explosion to affect the heavenly bodies! We recall that elsewhere we have discussed the heavenly bodies (sun, moon, stars, etc.) as representing the leaders of Israel, and the earth as representing the nation or people. Here both are seen as being obliterated. This would include their entire system of the old Mosaic rituals, ceremonies and regulations under which they labored and carried on their religious practices.

John Allfree, in England, says:

" . . . we may say that Peter, James, Paul and John, when speaking to or writing to Jewish brethren, speak of their days as the last days and warn of a terrible judgment that was about to happen, a judgment that would result in the heavens and the earth, or the world, passing away" **(John Allfree, p. 7)**.

In **Hebrews 1:10-12**, the writer said,

"And, Thou, Lord, in the beginning hast laid the foundation of the earth; and the heavens are the works of thine hands:

"They shall perish; but thou remainest; and they all shall wax old as doth a garment;

"And as a vesture shalt thou fold them up, and they shall be changed . . ."

Here God is not talking about a physical universe burning up some day, but of the heavens and earth of Israel which would soon pass away. There would be a folding up and a change made, even as an old garment is laid aside and a new one put on.

This thought is further carried out in **Hebrews 8:13**, "In that he saith, A new covenant, he hath made the first old. Now that which decayeth and waxeth old is ready to vanish away."

Here the old is not only decayed and waxed old and laid aside, but is ready to vanish away.

It was already in process, but by A.D. 70 it was a fully accomplished fact. The old was gone and the new had taken its place. There was now new heavens and a new earth, according to the promises found in Isaiah, which we have discussed in these pages — the only pages I know of where those promises are found; and Peter mentioned this in **II Peter 3:13**. That promise of new heavens and a new earth was now fulfilled. There were now new heavens and a new earth, a new temple, a new priesthood, a new people of God, a new Jerusalem, a new city. In **Revelation 21:5** God said, "Behold, I make all things new." This promise was fulfilled in the first century and is a reality for God's people today.

"Heaven and earth shall pass away" (**Matthew 24:35**). **Herman Ridderbos** of Holland said, " 'Pass away' here means become part of the past so that its significance is gone and no longer need be taken into account" (**Herman Ridderbos**, p. 502).

The heavens and earth of old Israel passed away in this sense, and their importance in the economy of God's redemption for man is no longer of any present significance. There is now a new heavens and a new earth.

"Heaven and earth shall pass away." They did, by A.D. 70.

Section 9 ••••••••••••••••••••••••••

NO MAN KNOWS THE DAY NOR THE HOUR

The twenty-fourth chapter of Matthew is the heart of New Testament prophecy. Someone has said that it is **The Little Apocalypse**. In this one chapter Jesus summed up for His disciples the things leading up to and ending with the *parousia*/coming of the Son of man. He told them that the end of the age would come within that generation, that the gospel would be preached in all the world, that the abomination of desolation would be present in the holy place, that a great tribulation would be upon the people, but that His disciples would be spared, and that the end would come with the destruction of the Temple and the coming of the Son of man in the clouds of Heaven.

In eight sections preceding this one, we have tried to cover these things in detail, considering every verse in Matthew 24 up to this point. We now come to the ninth and last section of the commentary itself upon this chapter. We arrive now at verse 36, which some say is a transition verse where Jesus leaves off speaking about the destruction of Jerusalem and begins talking about a future (to us) second coming of Christ.

★★★★★★★★★★★★★★

"But of that day and hour knoweth no man, no, not the angels of heaven, but my Father only" (Matthew 24:36).

★★★★★★★★★★★★★★

But is this such a "transition" verse, as some would describe it? Is this a point in the chapter where Jesus no longer is talking about the subject which has been being discussed, but now He is dealing with an entirely new subject — that of another coming of the Son of man than the one He has already told them about? In other words, is He now telling them of something additional that will happen (which would be in our future), and He concludes saying anything else about what would happen during that generation?

The answer to this question determines what kind of eschatology we are going to have. The answer determines much of what we would believe about the second coming of Christ. So what is the answer to this question? Is verse 36 a "transition" verse or not?

The answer is a strong, emphatic **NO**! This is not a transition verse! Jesus does not conclude talking about anything here. He is still talking about the same event which He has been talking about all along. Most of this section is written to prove just that, and to show that it could not be otherwise.

"All These Things"/"Thy Coming"

In **Mark 13:32** is a parallel passage to this verse, and the words are almost identical: "But of that day and that hour knoweth no man, no, not the angels which are in heaven, neither the Son, but the Father." This passage said that even Jesus Himself did not know the exact day nor the hour of that event.

What was Jesus talking about in this verse? Mark records the question of the disciples this way:

"Tell us, when shall these things be? and what shall be the SIGN when ALL THESE THINGS shall be fulfilled?" **(Mark 13:4)**.

Whereas **Matthew 24:3** asked about the "sign of thy coming," **Mark 13:4** asked about the "sign when all these things shall be fulfilled." SAME THING! Those things asked about included the coming of Christ in judgment on Jerusalem. And the disciples in their question in Mark 13:4 never mentioned the coming of Christ, but yet Jesus said in verse 32 that no man knew the day nor the hour when those events would take place. These verses are parallel **(Matthew 24:36** and **Mark 13:32)** and refer to the same identical thing — the events of the destruction of Jerusalem as took place in A.D. 70 when Christ came in judgment there.

Disciples to Flee "In that Day"

Not only so, but notice that **Luke 17:31** refers to "that day." But read the rest of the verse to see what Jesus was referring to. He said, "In THAT DAY, he which shall be upon the housetop, and his stuff in the house, let him not come down to take it away" — clearly referring to the haste the disciples would be in to leave Jerusalem in A.D. 67. The time is the same as in **Matthew 24:17**, much prior to the verse we are discussing at verse 36.

"That day" of Matthew 24:36 is the same "that day" as in Luke 17:31

Jesus was not introducing a new subject in **Matthew 24:36** when He said, "But of THAT DAY." The word "that" has to refer to something which precedes it, and in this instance it would have to refer to the time mentioned in the previous verses.

One cannot make "that day" of **Luke 17:31** refer to a past event (to us), and "that day" of **Matthew 24:36** refer to a future event (to us).

No Transition Verse

This is not a transition verse, suddenly shifting without any introduction to some other event which would not take place until 2,000 years or so later! Jesus was telling His disciples that no one knew when Jerusalem would be destroyed — that the matter was in God's knowledge only. They could only know that, "This generation shall not pass, till all these things be fulfilled" (vs. 34).

Read all of the parallel passages in **Matthew 24:1-42, Mark 13:1-33, Luke 17:20-37,** and **Luke 21:5-36,** and see if by any stretch of the imagination one can see Jesus talking about two different events in His teachings in these passages.

Now some might teach that when the writings of Matthew, Mark and Luke were all put together, it was not understood nor remembered exactly which things Jesus mentioned first, and that maybe the passage got mixed up and we don't actually know what Jesus meant from what we read here, and that it just appears that He was talking about the destruction of Jerusalem when He had actually talked also about a future second coming hundreds and hundreds of years later. Well, if you want to believe that is the way of it, go right ahead; but I personally prefer to just simply accept these passages as we have them in our Bible. I may be ignorant of some things, but I don't want to become more ignorant than I already am (which I would if I were to try messing around with changing these verses so they will say what I THINK Jesus MEANT to say!). Let the textual critics decide how they think it all ought to read, but I am not that smart so will stick with it as it reads in our Bible.

We have been accustomed to thinking that this verse relates to our not having knowledge of the time of a future (to us) second coming of Christ. But this relates to the time of the events surrounding the destruction of Jerusalem and the Temple, plus the coming of Christ, for this is what Jesus had been talking about. The parallel passage in **Mark 13:32** adds the words, "neither the Son," indicating that even He Himself, while He was on earth in human form, did not have certain knowledge about some things; and in this case He said that He did not know the exact time of the fulfillment of this matter, except that it would all occur within that generation, during the lifetime of some of those who were still living at that time.

Jesus, as a man, did not possess all the attributes of omniscience. **Luke 2:52** says that "Jesus increased in wisdom and stature, and in favour with God and man." If Jesus had to develop like any other man, then it is understandable that He did not know the day nor the hour when these events would take place. We assume that at age thirty he was still growing, and was therefore limited as to any omniscient knowledge at that time. But He was aware, with things shaping up like they were, that it would all be in that generation.

The reason that some expositors (as, for example, **Marcellus Kik** in **An Eschatology of Victory,** p. 67) say that here the subject changes to that of a second coming of Christ in our future, is because of their interpretation that the second coming of Christ (in our future) is found in this chapter, and they have to find a transition verse somewhere. To them, this is the most logical verse. (As will be pointed out later, still others have used other verses as a transition point, and there has been much disagreement on this.)

It has been said that by the use of that word "But" in verse 36, Jesus changed the subject to something else. But the word "but" is a connecting word, and is just like the word "but" found in verses 43 and 48. The subject is not changed in verses 43 and 48, so why should it be changed in verse 36?

When Jesus said, "But of THAT DAY," to what day did He refer as not being known? To what had He just referred? He had just said, "So likewise YE, when YE shall see all these things, know that **IT** is near, even at the doors" (**Matthew 24:33**). And to what does "IT" of verse 33 refer? He had just told them in the previous verse that when the branch puts forth the new leaves, SUMMER is nigh. And to what does "summer" refer? What was He illustrating here by the approach of summer? He had just concluded His statements regarding the events to IMMEDIATELY follow the tribulation; and so when "ALL these things" (**vs. 33**) are accomplished, then "summer is nigh." This was the "end of the age" and the dawning of a new age (the kingdom of God) for Christians. And that generation would not pass until ALL those things were fulfilled (**vs. 34**).

All of this subject matter is connected and cannot be separated into two events a couple of thousand or more years apart, as many people do.

"Those Days" and "That Day"

It has been proposed that prior to verse 36 the plural word "days" is used (**vss. 22, 29**), which refers to the events surrounding the destruction of Jerusalem, and that in **verse 36** Jesus shifts gears and starts talking about "that day" (singular) which (they say) refers only to a future second coming of Christ. But does that argument hold up when compared to other passages Jesus gave? No, it does not! Look at **Luke 17:31**, for example, where Jesus said, "IN THAT DAY, he which shall be upon the housetop, and his stuff in the house, let him not come down to take it away. . . ." Here we find Jesus using the singular expression ("that day") which, as anyone can plainly see, is referring to the same situation as in **Matthew 24:17** ("Let him which is on the housetop not come down to take any thing out of his house"), which indicates to us very clearly that the singular expression "that day" refers to events surrounding the destruction of Jerusalem and not to some future event thousands of years later. So when Jesus uses the expression, "But of that day," in **verse 36,** He is still referring to the same subject He has been talking about all along. It is only logical that the word "that" refers to the "it" or "he" of **verse 33,** which in turn could apply only to the event of **verse 30.** It is not logical that the word "that" would refer to something entirely new and different than He had been talking about, as He had not introduced any new subject matter at all. There is no "transition" verse here. Of course, Scofield's notes (see heading over **Luke 17:22**) say that Jesus was foretelling His future second coming in the balance of that chapter, but this cannot be for the simple reason just given.

"That day" is the culmination of "those days."

"This Generation," but Not the Day Nor the Hour

Then some say with reference to the destruction of Jerusalem that Jesus said, "This generation shall not pass, till all these things be fulfilled" **(Matthew 24:34),** but that concerning a future second coming of Christ He said, "But of that day and hour knoweth no man, no, not the angels of heaven, but my Father only" **(Matthew 24:36).** The time of one event could be known ("this generation") but the day or hour of the other event could not be known ("knoweth no man, etc."), they say. But this is a flimsy argument in attempting to separate one situation into two separate events. A thing can be understood to occur within a generation (forty years or so) but still not be understood to occur at some **known** "day and hour." The disciples could know the generation, but not the day and the hour.

An illustration of this might be the gestation period and birth of a baby. Everybody knows the baby will be born in approximately nine months or so, but nobody knows the day nor the hour. That is exactly the way it was with what Jesus was talking about. In fact, He somewhat used that illustration himself when He said, in **verse 8,** "All these are the beginning of sorrows (birth pangs)."

On **Mark 13:32 John Lightfoot** (1859) said:

"Of what **day** and **hour?** That the discourse is of the day of the destruction of Jerusalem is so evident, both by the disciples' question, and by the whole thread of Christ's discourse, that it is a wonder any should understand these words of the **day and hour** of the last judgment" **(John Lightfoot,** vol. 2, p. 442).

Dr. John Gill said:

"Ver. 36. **But of that day and hour knoweth no man, etc.** Which is to be understood, not of the second coming of Christ, the end of the world, and the last judgment; but of the coming of the Son of man, to take vengeance on the Jews, and of their destruction; for the words manifestly regard the date of the several things going before, which can only be applied to that catastrophe and dreadful desolation: now, though the destruction itself was spoken of by Moses and the prophets, was foretold by Christ, and the believing Jews had some discerning of its near approach; see Heb. x.25, yet the exact and precise time was not known . . ." **(John Gill,** on **Matthew 24:36,** 1809 ed., vol. 2, p. 241).

N. **Nisbett** said:

"But though the time was hastening on for the completion of our Lord's prophecy of the ruin of the Jews; yet the exact time of this judgment, laid hid in the bosom of the Father. Verse 36. 'Of that day and hour knoweth no man, no, not the angels of heaven, but my Father only.' St. Mark has it: 'Neither the Son, but the Father;' but the sense is the same. Some men of great learning and eminence have thought that our Lord is here speaking, not of the destruction of Jerusalem, but of that more solemn and awful one of the day of judgment. But I can by no means think that the Evangelists are such loose, inaccurate writers, as to make so sudden and abrupt a transition, as they are here supposed to do; much less to break through the fundamental rules of good writing, by apparently referring to something which they had said before; when in reality they were beginning a new subject, and the absurdity of the supposition will appear more strongly, if it is recollected that the question of the disciples was, 'When shall these things be?' 'Why,' says our Saviour, 'of that day and hour knoweth no man, no, not the angels of heaven, but my Father only' " (**N. Nisbett,** pp. 38-39).

His mind and spirit, so acutely sensitive to spiritual things and the way of God's dealings with man, Jesus could sense, He could feel, He could understand, that the things He was talking about would surely come to pass as an inevitable consequence of Israel's unbelief and rejection of spiritual values. He read the signs of the time accurately and perfectly. But He had no way of knowing the exact time of many things, such as the resurrection of the dead (both saved and lost), the final judgment of the world, the ultimate destruction of Satan, etc. Those things are left for the future to unfold in God's own due time. And in like manner, He did not know the exact timing of the destruction of Jerusalem, though He could and did predict all the things which He mentioned in Matthew 24 as to occur within that generation.

He emphasized this again in **verse 44,** and then again in **verse 13** of the next chapter.

But of great importance in proving that there is no "transition" verse at **verse 36,** simply notice that the expression "the coming of the Son of man" in **verses 37 and 39** (AFTER the so-called "transition" verse) is the same as the expression "the coming of the Son of man" in **verse 27** and in **verse 30** (BEFORE the "transition" verse). So there can be no transition at **verse 36**. The same subject is discussed on both sides of that verse.

More on "That Day"

Let me go over this matter again, as a clear understanding of this is absolutely necessary if Matthew 24 is to be fully understood. Some put the stress on the words, "that day," as though "that day" is something different than what has gone before. More precisely, they believe that "that day" refers to a future final return of Christ (future to us) rather than to the time of and the events of the destruction of Jerusalem and the Temple in A.D. 70. But let us look further to see if this is so.

In **Luke 17, verses 26-29,** Jesus mentioned the days of Noah and the days of Lot, and likened the coming of Christ to the destruction that took place in those days. He said, "Even thus shall it be in the day when the Son of man is revealed" (**vs. 30**). Now the same reference to Noah is found in **Matthew 24:37-39,** which (note carefully) is AFTER the supposed transition **verse 36**, and so, according to that view, would apply to a future final return of Christ. But go back to **Luke 17** now, and see that AFTER mention of Noah and Lot, it says "IN THAT DAY, he which shall be upon the housetop, and his stuff in the house, let him not come down to take it away" (**vs. 31**). These are the SAME instructions given by Jesus in Matthew 24:17-21 **BEFORE THE SUPPOSED TRANSITION VERSE** which related to the disciples fleeing from Judaea in A.D. 67 — not at a coming of Christ in our future.

Those who believe in a transition verse at **verse 36** are up against a hard place on this, because the references to Noah and Lot are incorporated into the teachings of Jesus both before and after the supposed transition verse. The plain matter of fact is that if this teaching of Jesus regarding Noah and Lot referred to what happened at Jerusalem in the first century in what He had to say in the book of Luke, then it is only evident that it would refer to the same thing in **verse 36** of **Matthew 24,** and this follows the supposed "transition" verse. So there is no transition verse. Only by manipulating Scriptures, or else by giving two utterly different meanings to the same illustrations of Jesus, can the "transition" verse theory hold up.

So we cannot have it both ways. The reference to "the days of Noe" in **Matthew 24:37** has to refer to the events of A.D. 67-70 and not to any future final coming of Christ, because in Luke the same reference and illustration is given in connection with **verse 31** about the disciples not coming down from the housetop (which in Matthew 24 certainly is up in the first section BEFORE the supposed transition verse).

The verdict? There is no transition verse. The whole passage relates to the same thing — not to two different comings of Christ. Read it carefully and make sure! Compare the two passages very closely. Why have interpreters not seen this? Or is there some explanation for this of which I am not aware?

Please note how certain verses compare with other verses in these two gospel accounts — verses from Matthew 24 which are both BEFORE **and** AFTER the so-called transition point. Rather than quoting, let me just give the references, and please do look them up!

Compare **Matthew 24:17-18** with **Luke 17:31**.
Compare **Matthew 24:26-27** with **Luke 17:23-24**.
Compare **Matthew 24:28** with **Luke 17:37**.
Compare **Matthew 24:37-39** with **Luke 17:26-27**.
Compare **Matthew 24:40-41** with **Luke 17:35-36**.

Luke put all these five events into one time frame, and it is generally acknowledged that this is true. But if Luke did not separate this section in his gospel into two sections, then neither was it to be done with Matthew 24. Please spend a few moments studying these passages together and see if your honest mind will not cause you to agree that Matthew 24 also is all in one time frame as well.

This means, of course, that the "that day" of **verse 36** is of the same time frame as "in those days" of **verses 22 and 29**.

As for those who break Matthew 24 into two sections of different time frames, let them try dividing up **Luke 17** and **Luke 24** the same way! It just doesn't work! We cannot wiggle out of the obvious truth of this matter simply because we might want to find a future (to us) second coming of Christ in this passage.

The "THAT DAY" of **Matthew 24:36** is the same time frame as the "THAT DAY" of **Luke 17:31**.

There is no transition verse in Matthew 24. The whole passage refers to the same events in the same time frame — "This generation shall not pass, till all these things be fulfilled" (**vs. 34**).

And anyway, why would Jesus be telling His disciples about **TWO** comings of Christ in the same discourse, when they had only asked him about **ONE**? That would have been rather confusing to them, to say the least! (Just as a number of interpreters are confused about it all when they try to insert two comings of Christ into the passage instead of just the one which Jesus is describing.)

So, then, this expression about no man knowing the day nor the hour is not an expression that was meant for us to use today to signify that nobody can know when Jesus is going to return in our future. This expression definitely was in connection with no one knowing the day nor the hour when the Son of man would come and judgment would fall upon Israel back in the first century. It sounds good for people to use it, for that signifies that no one can accurately be a date setter for some future coming of Christ. But this is not what was meant. It meant that the time of the destruction of Jerusalem was not known — the time of the *parousia*/coming of Jesus.

Rather than face this obvious fact, so many Bible teachers attempt to divide Matthew 24 into two different sections — the first dealing with the destruction of Jerusalem, and the second dealing with a final coming of Christ in our future. They indicate that there is a transition point in the chapter where it no longer discusses the destruction of Jerusalem, but rather it begins discussing a future (to us) second coming of Christ. They have to find a "stopping point" for the first section in order to do this, and a point where the discussion changes from one subject to another. While we have discussed mainly **verse 36** being this focal point used by so many, this is not the only point that is used by some.

As **Dr. Milton Terry** said:

"When, however, the one school of interpreters attempt to point out the dividing line, there are as many differences of opinion as there are interpreters. In Matt. xxiv and xxv, for example, the transition from the one subject to the other is placed by Bengel and others at xxiv, 29; by E. J. Meyer at verse 35; by Doddridge at verse 36; by Kuinoel at verse 33; by Eichorn at xxv, 14, and by Wetstein at xxv, 31 **(Terry, Biblical Apocalyptics,** p. 217).

Dr. B. H. Carroll used verse 29 as the starting point of a new subject. He said, " . . . for everything in the prophecy from the previous line drawn just under Matthew 24:28 relates to the final event. The destruction stops squarely with Matthew 24:28 and Luke 21:24" **(B. H. Carroll,** vol. 2, p. 262).

And there were those a hundred years ago who made the transition verse much earlier in the chapter than these others to whom we have referred. **Ezra Gould** said, "Those who divide the prophecy into two parts, one referring to the destruction of Jerusalem, and the other to the end of the world, make the division at v. 20" **(Gould,** p. 249).

The necessity for these men to find a transition verse in this chapter, of course, is because each one of them is **assuming** that a future (to us) second coming of Christ is also taught in that chapter, rather than the entire chapter's dealing with only the time frame of the events surrounding the destruction of Jerusalem.

To illustrate, here is an example of **J. Marcellus Kik**, who along with Doddridge, as mentioned above, chose verse 36 as the transition verse. He said:

"Now with verse 36 Christ commences a new subject, namely, his second coming and the events preceding it. This verse may be termed the 'transition' text of the chapter" **(Kik, p. 67)**.

And on page 69 of the same book **Kik** said:

"It is thus obvious that in Matthew 24:36 Christ passes from the subject of the destruction of Jerusalem to the subject of His Second Coming. It is a transition verse. It is a transition from the judgment against the Jewish nation to the subject of His coming to judge the world. He could give a definite indication of the time of the destruction of Jerusalem, 'but of **that day and hour** knoweth no one, not even the angels of heaven, neither the Son, but the Father only.' As Spurgeon states in his commentary on this verse: 'There is a manifest change in our Lord's words here, which clearly indicates that they refer to His last great coming to judgment' " **(Kik, p. 69)**.

R. T. France, whom I quoted under **verse 29,** also says that at **verse 36** the emphasis changes.

If these passages (from **verse 36** on) had been given on some other occasion, or even if Jesus had indicated that He was NOW referring to a different event, we could feel that He was talking about two different things. But He did not do this. And the way Matthew places the verses does not indicate two different things, which indicates that Matthew himself understood Jesus to be referring to the same time frame.

There being no consensus of opinion on this, it might be proper to analyze why it is thought so necessary to have a transition verse anywhere at all. It is only because it is felt that the last of the chapter simply cannot refer to the same event as the events in the first part of the chapter. There would not be all this difference of opinion if all would agree that Jesus was speaking of the same event in both parts of the chapter. And why would He not be, except for our own preconceived notions about the matter?

But how can what these authors say be true, when the same expressions are found in both sections of Matthew 24? If the same expressions are found in both sections of the chapter, so close together like this, they evidently speak of the same thing. For example, **verse 27** mentions "the coming of the Son of man." **Verse 30** mentions "the Son of man coming in the clouds of heaven." Then in **verse 37**, after the so-called transition point, it mentions "the coming of the Son of man." Likewise, in **verse 39** it mentions "the coming of the Son of man." Then in **verse 44**, "the Son of man cometh."

Are there two *"parousia"* comings — one **before verse 36**, and another **after verse 36** (or whatever transition verse is used)?

Doesn't it stand to reason that if these same phrases, mentioning the same identical thing, are found in both sections, where it is said that the destruction of Jerusalem is referred to in one, and the coming of Christ in the other, then they are all referring to the same identical time frame? Would Jesus have used the same identical expression IN SO MANY PLACES in this same chapter to refer to two different things? Don't we suppose that He would have known this would have gotten us all confused if He had done that?

With so many variations as to the interpretation of where one subject ends and the other begins, it is no wonder that **Dr. John A. Broadus** said, "Every attempt to assign a definite point between the two topics has proved a failure" **(Broadus,** p. 480).

No Bible scholar has yet been able to reconcile the passages which they felt told of two different events, at least not to any satisfactory degree.

The statement of **J. Stuart Russell** is worthy of note when he said, "There is not a scintilla of evidence that the apostles and primitive Christians had any suspicion of a twofold reference in the predictions of Jesus concerning the end" **(J. Stuart Russell,** p. 545).

William Barclay also believed that verses 36-41 referred to a future (to us) second coming of Christ, but he had other thoughts about **verses 30-35.** After discussing the other possibilities as to an understanding of **Matthew 24:32-35,** he said:

"But there is a third possibility. What if their reference is, in fact, to the prophecy with which the chapter began, the siege and fall of Jerusalem? If we accept that, there is no difficulty. What Jesus is saying is that these grim warnings of his regarding the doom of Jerusalem will be fulfilled within that very generation — and they were, in fact, fulfilled forty years later. It seems by the best course to take 32-35 as referring, not to the Second Coming, but to the doom of Jerusalem, for then all the difficulties in them are removed" **(William Barclay,** p. 315).

So what William Barclay is saying is that if these verses are accepted as applying to past events — that is, to the fall of Jerusalem in A.D. 70, the difficulties of interpretation vanish. This is true. But then, why did Barclay not just go on and include **verses 36-41** in that same kind of interpretation, and help to eliminate the difficulty folks have with the rest of that passage? You **cannot** separate these passages from each other. If one event happened in that generation, so did any others. Jesus said "all these things" would happen in that generation, and I believe He meant exactly that.

Some say that "signs" were given which point to the destruction of Jerusalem and the Temple, but that no sign was given concerning the coming of Christ. That is simply not true, for everything and every sign pointing forward to the destruction of Jerusalem and the Temple **ALSO** pointed forward to the coming of the Son of man. It was all to be in that generation, though no one could know the day nor the hour. He did not give a day nor an hour concerning the destruction of Jerusalem and the Temple either.

I strongly insist that if you really want to see the truth of the matter, that you read the several parallel passages relating to this — in **Matthew 24, Mark 13, Luke 17** and **Luke 21** — all at the same reading. You cannot escape seeing that the events relating to the destruction of Jerusalem and the coming (*parousia*) of Christ, were all involved in the same time frame. Language does not allow for the separation of these events into two periods separated by a couple of thousands off years or so. What applies to one, applies to the other, as is seen when analyzing all four of these passages.

It seems to me that those of us who believe the Bible had better get back to accepting what it says, instead of rationalizing about the matter and trying to make it mean what it does not say. Only with **previously held concepts** on this matter could it ever be thought that Jesus was talking about two different things at least 2,000 years apart! The passage itself would not lead anyone to believe that two comings of Christ are taught in this chapter.

Perhaps it is because of this obvious problem of trying to divide this chapter up into two time frames, that the dispensationalist futurists have simply said the **WHOLE** of this chapter 24 of Matthew deals with our **future** and not to anything in the first century. Therefore, they say, there will have to be a future preaching of the gospel to all the world, a future abomination of desolation, a future Temple, a future great tribulation period, etc., so that there can be a future *parousia* / coming of the Son of man. And all because they do not want to acknowledge that there was a *parousia* / coming of Christ in A.D. 70.

I know that for many years I did not see this. Back as far as forty years ago I saw that Matthew 24 told about an awful time that would come to Israel in that first century generation. I had the commentaries of **Albert Barnes** in my library which helped me to see that. But I made the "great tribulation" of verse 21 extend through many centuries so that **AFTER** the great tribulation Christ could come.

Honest study finally caused me to understand that verse 29 would not allow that, for it said, **"IMMEDIATELY"** after that tribulation Christ would come. The writer was talking about something that would happen immediately after the siege and destruction of Jerusalem and the Temple in A.D. 67-70. This convinced me that Jesus was saying that His *"parousia"*/coming would be in connection with the events of those days in the first century. From there, it did not take much more study of this chapter for me to finally realize that the entire chapter **(24)** of **Matthew** dealt with the great tribulation and coming of Christ, which all took place in the first century. So the point we are brought to is a firm belief that the commentaries and authors are wrong if they try to split this chapter up and make one part tell about the events of the destruction of Jerusalem and the Temple, and the other part to tell about a second coming of Christ in **our** future. And some of them, to get around this problem (as they see it), simply say that Jesus was talking about two different "comings" in that chapter. This is rationalization as well as bad hermeneutics and bad exegesis of the Bible. The *parousia*/coming of Christ as mentioned in **verses 3, 27, 30, 37, 39,** etc., is the **ONLY** coming of Christ in that entire chapter.

★★★★★★★★★★★★★★

"But as the days of Noe were, so shall also the coming of the Son of man be.

"For as in the days that were before the flood they were eating and drinking, marrying and giving in marriage, until the day that Noe entered into the ark,

"And knew not until the flood came, and took them all away; so shall also the coming of the Son of man be.

"Then shall two be in the field; the one shall be taken, and the other left.

"Two women shall be grinding at the mill; the one shall be taken, and the other left.

"Watch therefore: for ye know not what hour your Lord doth come" (Matthew 24:37-42).

In these six verses Jesus is still talking about the destruction of Jerusalem and the Temple and his *parousia*/coming as the Son of man. Twice here He uses the expression "the coming of the Son of man," and then the expression, "your Lord doth come."

In these verses Jesus is saying that the coming events in Israel, including His coming as the Son of man, would be like the time when the flood came and TOOK THEM ALL AWAY. As the flood came and took them all away, so the judgments on Israel will take them all away. The unbelieving and Christ-rejecting Jews in the land of Israel would be taken away in judgment.

Jesus emphasized that just like in the days of Noah when they were eating and drinking, and marrying and giving in marriage, with no sense of apprehension of the coming flood, so also would it be in those days prior to the destruction of Jerusalem.

Paul reminded his readers in **I Corinthians 7:29**:

"But this I say, brethren, the time is short: it remaineth, that both they that have wives be as though they had none."

Paul knew that in the face of approaching disaster and all the things related to it, marriage should be a matter of secondary importance. Paul spoke of "the present distress" **(vs. 26)**. But Jesus said that even with the approaching events of His generation, people would still be marrying and carrying on as though nothing would ever happen.

Some think that they can find a future (to us) **Rapture** in this passage of Scripture, where two shall be in the field and one shall be taken and the other left; and two shall be grinding at the mill, and one shall be taken and the other left. They think that being "taken" means that they will be "caught up" in a Rapture at a future second coming of Christ. But this is not talking about that. It is talking about people being "taken" in judgment — not to Heaven.

Jesus' words in **Luke 17** likewise liken the destruction of Jerusalem and Judaea in A.D. 67-70 to Lot and the destruction of Sodom and Gomorrah. Jesus said:

"Likewise also as it was in the days of Lot; they did eat, they drank, they bought, they sold, they planted, they builded;

"But the same day that Lot went out of Sodom it rained fire and brimstone from heaven, and destroyed them all.

"Even thus shall it be in the day when the Son of man is revealed" **(Luke 17:28-30)**.

Just like Sodom and Gomorrah were destroyed by fire and brimstone from heaven, so Jerusalem would be destroyed by the fires of God's vengeance acting through the Roman armies which would come into that land.

And just like Lot was saved from the fires of Sodom and Gomorrah by escaping outside the cities, so the early Christians escaped the tribulation that fell upon Jerusalem and Judaea by escaping outside the city and land over to Pella, where they were preserved from the wrath of God that soon fell upon the land.

In this passage, it mentions the Son of man being "revealed." In **Matthew 24** it mentions "the coming of the Son of man." Both of these expressions refer to the same thing. His *parousia* / coming was

His *apokalupto* / revelation.

In **Luke 17:32** we also find the expression, "Remember Lot's wife." I daresay you do not hear many sermons on this verse as a text, because most preachers do not get the picture that Jesus is presenting here. Jesus is reminding his hearers of how Lot's wife was turned into a pillar of salt when she hesitated and looked back upon the city. He was suggesting to them that this could be the fate of any who did not hurry and get out of Judaea and Jerusalem when the Roman armies showed up — how theirs could be a similar fate by being caught in the situation at Jerusalem, etc., if they did not heed His words and get out of the city immediately when they saw the Roman armies surrounding the city. While not experiencing fire and brimstone, they could be slaughtered during those horrible days of tribulation there.

We need to be reminded again here, that in **Luke 17:31** Jesus said, "In **THAT DAY**, he which shall be upon the housetop, and his stuff in the house, let him not come down to take it away: and he that is in the field, let him likewise not return back." Those who seek to find a transition verse in **Matthew 24:36** because Jesus used the expression "that day" rather than "those days" (to signify a change in what was being discussed), need to be reminded that here Jesus is using that same expression **"THAT DAY"** which relates to the time of danger from which the disciples were to flee, and which time in **Matthew 24** is described in **verses 17-18** in a passage far before a so-called transition **"THAT DAY"** is found in **verse 36**.

Then Jesus tells them to watch for they do not know the hour their Lord will come. They cannot know the day nor the hour, but they knew it would be in that generation.

Would it have made sense for Jesus to urge His disciples to "watch" for something that was not to take place for another 2,000 years or so?

★★★★★★★★★★★★★★

"But know this, that if the good man of the house had known in what watch the thief would come, he would have watched, and would not have suffered his house to be broken up.

"Therefore be ye also ready: for in such as an hour as ye think not the Son of man cometh" (Matthew 24:43-44).

Here Jesus repeats His same admonition for His disciples to be on the watch and be ready for His coming in judgment upon that wicked city of Jerusalem. Israel's house was ready to be broken up. Christians who escaped from the city and land would not be affected by the awful things that would happen there.

Paul taught in **I Thessalonians 5:2-3**, "For yourselves know perfectly that the day of the Lord so cometh as a thief in the night.

"For when they shall say, Peace and safety; then sudden destruction cometh upon them, as travail upon a woman with child; and they shall not escape."

But Christians were to be watching and ready. They were not to be caught up in that judgment that was to come. Paul said further in the passage just mentioned:

"And ye, brethren, are not in darkness, that that day should overtake you as a thief.

"Ye are all the children of light, and the children of the day: we are not of the night, nor of darkness" **(I Thessalonians 5:4-5)**.

★ ★ ★ ★ ★ ★ ★ ★ ★ ★ ★ ★ ★ ★

Then in the next few and last verses of **Matthew chapter 24**, Jesus describes the contrast between His waiting people who would be ready for Him, and the wicked ones who would not be prepared for that day. He said:

"**Who then is a faithful and wise servant, whom his lord hath made ruler over his household, to give them meat in due season?**

"**Blessed is that servant, whom his lord when he cometh shall find so doing.**

"**Verily I say unto you, That he shall make him ruler over all his goods.**

"**But and if that evil servant shall say in his heart, My lord delayeth his coming;**

"**And shall begin to smite his fellowservants, and to eat and drink with the drunken;**

"**The lord of that servant shall come in a day when he looketh not for him, and in an hour that he is not aware of,**

"**And shall cut him asunder, and appoint him his portion with the hypocrites: there shall be weeping and gnashing of teeth**" **(Matthew 24:45-51)**.

The lord would come in a day and an hour of which the evil servant would not be aware. The wicked servant would not be prepared nor watching for that time. Jesus said, "But of that day and hour knoweth no man, no, not the angels of heaven, but my Father only" **(Matthew 24:36)**.

No one would know the day nor the hour, but they could be ready and watching. These words were given by Jesus to His disciples to encourage them to do just that. These last few verses especially stress the kind of lifestyle that could develop on the part of those who were not looking for the lord to come. The statement of the wicked servant that "My lord delayeth his coming" **(vs. 48)** reminds us of what Peter said would be said in those last days by the scoffers: "Where is the promise of his coming?" **(II Peter 3:4)**. But the promise was sure, and that day would come. It did come, in awful judgment upon a wicked and perverse generation.

Commenting on **I Thessalonians 5:9**, Adam Clarke (1831) in his commentary, said:

"For God hath not appointed us to wrath. So then it appears that some were **appointed to wrath**, . . . **to punishment**; on this subject there can be no dispute. But **who** are they? **When** did this appointment take place? And for what **cause?** . . . If we look carefully at the apostles' words, we shall find all these difficulties vanish. It is very obvious that, in the preceding verses, the apostle refers simply to the destruction of the Jewish polity, and to the terrible judgments which were about to fall on the Jews as a **nation**; therefore, they are the **people** who were appointed **to wrath**; and they were thus appointed, not from **eternity**, nor from any indefinite or remote time, but from that time in which they utterly rejected the offers of salvation made to them by Jesus Christ and his apostles . . ." **(Adam Clarke's Commentary)**.

Many have left dispensationalism and have accepted the fact that Jesus was talking about the destruction of Jerusalem and the Temple in A.D. 70 in **Matthew 24**. But some of those who have progressed that far in their understanding of that passage, have not yet seen that **ALL** of **Matthew 24**, and not just part of it, was fulfilled in the generation of Christ and His hearers. I can easily understand how this is with them, having gone through this same process of thinking. And I know why there is a reluctance to see the whole picture as being in the past. So, of course, this is what we have tried to do in this book — to make clearer and plainer the whole picture by throwing as much light on it as we can. That "light" consists of the product of our own research and study and thinking, triggered by the things said in many books we have read, both old and contemporary. I think the arguments being presented in this series are irrefutable and unanswerable as to the validity of these views. Many are seeing the picture better, for which we are grateful.

Section 10 ●●●●●●●●●●●●●●●●●●●●●●●●●

CONCLUSION

We have tried in the preceding sections of this book to give a comprehensive and detailed commentary on the 24th chapter of Matthew. We know of no other commentary with as much material on this one chapter such as is contained in this book. Material has been presented from many other authors, of different denominations and persuasions and of different time periods. We have not been alone in our views.

This book in its entirety has attempted to interpret the 24th chapter of Matthew from the standpoint of what the discourse meant to the disciples themselves — the ones to whom the message was first given. The message was future for them, but is past for us. The time factor was summed up in the **34th verse:**

"**Verily I say unto you, This generation shall not pass, till all these things be fulfilled**" **(Matthew 24:34).**

It has been pointed out that **"all these things"** included the things the disciples asked Jesus about: (1) The destruction of the Temple, (2) the coming of the Son of man, and (3) the end of the age. It has been shown that other passages in the New Testament testified to this same nearness of time for which those things were predicted to occur.

The **parousia**/coming of Christ coincided with the end of that age and the destruction of Jerusalem and the Temple in A.D. 67-70. It was all in **that** generation.

Our personal interpretation of New Testament prophecy is that the entire 24th chapter of Matthew, most of the book of Revelation (all except part of chapter 20), plus most Scripture passages which we have previously assigned to a **future** second coming of Christ, were all fulfilled in the first century during that generation in the time of the apostles. This has been termed the "preterist" interpretation of these prophetic messages.

But God's past dealings with His people do not mean that **all** prophecy has been fulfilled. A world cannot be visualized which is to have no future resurrection and final judgment for all of mankind **(Revelation 20:11-15)**. This world still has to meet God. All lost people must give account to God for their rejection of Christ. And Christians in this present age, which began with Christ and the end of the Jewish age, have a glorious future not only in this life but also in the life which is to come. Jesus will continue to reign during this gospel age — the dispensation of the fulness of times (**Ephesians 1:10**) — until all enemies are put under His feet (**Acts 2:34-35; I Corinthians 15:25-26**. There will be a resurrection, and there will be a final judgment for all men, with Jesus Christ as the judge. He will then deliver the kingdom up to the Father, "that God may be all in all" (**I Corinthians 15:28**).

This book does not cover many other things I would like to get into. We have concentrated on **Matthew 24**. It is hoped that we can continue from this point, and with related subjects, in another book that will cover more than just **Matthew 24**. We are continuing to publish smaller books on further related subjects, which in due time may also be put into a larger book — life and health and finances permitting. Our smaller books are mailed out **free** to those on our mailing list as each one is published.

This book, no doubt, will generate many questions, but it offers an alternative to the view of the so-called "delay of the *parousia*" as expressed by the liberals who say that Jesus was mistaken when He promised His disciples a soon return.

We need to reexamine all those passages regarding the *parousia/* coming of Christ and see how they fit into the context of fulfillment in the first century. As I see it, this does not preclude a resurrection in the future for all men, nor a final judgment for the entire world. But our mistake in the past has been that of assigning all of the second coming of Christ passages to that final eventful time in our future. It is very evident that the teachings of Jesus and the writers of the New Testament spoke of a **soon-coming** *parousia*, and not something to occur hundreds or thousands of years later. We might have to deprogram our minds in order to accept this; but facts are facts.

As this series of studies on **Matthew 24** are brought to a close, I think I can do no better to convey my feelings about the teachings of the entire series, than to quote what **Dr. Milton S. Terry** (1898) said in his book, **Biblical Apocalyptics:**

"Finally, it is important to observe that the preterist and historical method of interpretation followed in this volume conserves the substance of every fundamental doctrine of the Gospel of Christ. It may helpfully modify some current conceptions of 'the great and notable day of the Lord;' for it treats the imagery of collapsing skies, and falling stars, and sounding trumpets, and dissolving mountains, and great white throne, and scores of similar figures of thought as expressing great realities, but not spectacular physical phenomena. Our interpretation no more denies or sets aside the doctrines of eternal judgment, of heaven and hell, of resurrection of the dead, and the coming and kingdom of Christ than does the refusal to affirm the literal 'fire and brimstone' of future retribution deny or invalidate

the doctrine of eternal reward and punishment beyond this mortal life.

"Nearly nineteen centuries of the manifested power and glory of Christianity in the world ought to have thrown some light on the nature of the coming and the kingdom of Christ. It can scarcely be a question among intelligent believers in Christ that the beginning of the era of our Lord and Saviour was the most signal and significant epoch in the history of mankind. It marked a 'fulness of times,' a crisis of ages. The exact point of transition from the old to the new may be with many an open question. But whether we place it at the birth of Jesus or at the time of his crucifixion, when he cried, 'It is finished,' or at his resurrection, or at his ascension, or at Pentecost, or at the fall of Jerusalem, the great commanding fact is still before us that the manifestation of the Christ, with which all these events must ever appear in vital relation, opened a new era in human civilization.

"We now submit the thought that these nineteen centuries of Christian light and progress are relatively but the misty morning twilight of the great day of Christ. It may be that he must reign a thousand times a thousand years before he shall have put all his enemies under his feet (I Cor. xv, 25). The coming of Christ in his kingdom and power and glory is not one instantaneous act or event. It is a long-continuing process comprehensive of his entire work both of redemption and of judgment. He comes in the power of his Spirit to convict the world respecting sin and righteousness and judgment (John xvi, 8); he comes in like manner to forgive the sins of the penitent and to lead the disciple into all the truth; he comes and is present wherever two or three are gathered together in his name. He has been coming through all the Christian centuries to receive unto himself the faithful souls who have looked for his heavenly appearing and glory (John xiv, 3; xvii, 22-24). As truly as Jehovah came of old in the clouds of heaven to execute judgment on the Egyptians (Isa. xix, 1), so did the Son of man come in the clouds and with the angels of his power to execute judgment on the great city that was guilty of his blood and drunken with the blood of his saints and martyrs. He sitteth at the right hand of Power and sendeth forth continually his innumerable company of angels to minister for them that shall inherit salvation. Such triumphal administration of judgment, mercy, and truth has been, is now, and shall for ages be the work of his Messianic reign. And in full accord with these revelations of his power and glory we cry out with the Hebrew psalmist:

> The Lord cometh, he cometh to judge the earth:
> He shall judge the world with righteousness,
> And peoples with his truth.

And we also respond with the Christian apocalyptist:

> Amen: come, Lord Jesus." (**Milton S. Terry, Biblical Apocalyptics**, pp. 480-481).

Section 11 ••••••••••••••••••••••••••

PERSONAL TESTIMONY BY THE AUTHOR

My journey in eschatology has been a long one. My conversion took place in 1936, at the age of fifteen. Though raised in a Baptist church (Southside Baptist Church at Jacksonville, Florida, then known as First Baptist Church of South Jacksonville), I became associated with a large interdenominational church in Jacksonville. This was Faith Temple, whose pastor was Robert Witty, who later became a Baptist and pastor of the Central Baptist Church as well as president of the Luther Rice Seminary. My conversion experience took place while I was attending this church, though not at the church but out by the river while my folks were fishing and I was reading the New Testament.

After being graduated from Landon High School, I operated a Christian book store and edited a religious publication for Faith Temple. At the age of 18, in September 1940, I was ordained as pastor of a small Baptist Church at Jacksonville and continued to run the book store at the other church. I became acquainted with the books written by such men as W. E. Blackstone, Arno Gabelein, William Pettingill, Harry Rimmer, William Evans, Louis Talbot, Harry A. Ironside, J. E. Strombeck, Clarence Larkin, etc., and of course the Scofield Reference Bible (several of which I still use, for the format and print style to which I got accustomed and liked). I was an avid reader. I listened to the radio broadcasts of Charles E. Fuller of the Old Fashioned Revival Hour. I listened to the messages and read the little books by Dr. M. R. DeHaan of the Radio Bible Class in Grand Rapids, Michigan. Dr. DeHaan's printer in Grand Rapids, Michigan (Northwestern Printing Co.), printed the first of my own little books starting in 1944. These men were all pre-tribulation rapturists and premillennial in their views on the second coming of Christ.

From the time right after I was first saved, I started reading Evangelist John R. Rice's **Sword of the Lord** publication, in 1937, when he first published it in Texas. This paper was influential in my life and ministry, and I preached many of the sermons I read in this paper. John R. Rice also taught the pre-tribulation rapture and a premillennial second coming of Christ. In the latter part of 1942, John R. Rice wrote and asked me to move to Wheaton, Illinois (where he was then located) and to become "assistant to the editor," which I did. This relationship lasted for only a few months, as I wanted to go into full-time evangelism on my own.

John L. Bray and John R. Rice, Wheaton, Illinois, January 10, 1943.

But I thought a lot of John R. Rice. I stayed in his home, knew his family, went with him to meetings in Wisconsin, shared the same hotel and guest rooms with him. We always remained friends, and I was saddened by his death December 29, 1980. He was a tremendous influence for evangelism and soul-winning in America. Many of his books were in my library, though most of them have been given away by now. Interestingly, in all the years I knew him, he never fussed at me for being a Southern Baptist, though he was an independent Baptist. We corresponded on numerous occasions about Bible questions, including a problem or two which I had in my mind on prophecy matters.

During the few months I lived in Wheaton, Illinois, working with Evangelist John R. Rice, I attended some of the night classes at Moody Bible Institute in Chicago, just 30 miles away — a school standing strongly for the Bible as the word of God and the fundamentals of the faith, though strongly entrenched in the pre-tribulation rapture and premillennial teachings.

My membership was with Southside Baptist Church in Jacksonville, Florida, when I went into full-time evangelism on my own in 1943. Dr. W. Herschel Ford was my pastor. He was a dear friend to both me and our family. He took me visiting with him. We ate out together. I loved his books, the "Simple Sermon" series, and I preached them! One of his books, in particular, in which I took the most interest was, **Seven Simple Sermons on the Second Coming**. They were well outlined and easy to follow, so I preached them! One of my own early little books, **The Great Tribulation**, was patterned after one of the sermons in his book. Dr. Ford wrote the introduction in one of the first little books I ever published (**Heaven, Hell and Salvation**), and when he died some years ago, I felt I had lost a good friend.

Many of my evangelistic meetings in 1943-1945 were conducted in the North with churches of **Independent Fundamental Churches of America**. Many of these pastors were graduates of Moody Bible Institute in Chicago and Dallas Theological Seminary in Dallas, Texas. Incidentally, when Dallas Theological Seminary was born in 1924, it was the only seminary in the world that held to premillennialism. There were no others.

In April of 1946 I was in meetings in Cairo, Illinois, and while there I read a book by Dr. Harry A. Ironside, **The Great Parenthesis**, a book which is now out of print though I still have my copy in my library. Dr. Ironside taught that the church age is a parenthesis in God's plan, and that God takes up again at the Rapture where He left off at the beginning of this age; therefore, the prophecies looking toward a second coming of Christ do not apply to this age, but only to a Tribulation period following the Rapture and looking toward the later return of Christ to the earth. When I read this and got it "straight" in my mind (!), I preached with vim, vigor and authority on all the details of the end-time, especially in relation to the second coming of Christ. But somehow I never got the prophecy on Daniel's 70th week straight in my mind. Dr. Ironside's view seemed logical, so I adopted it without much study in Daniel itself which was the basis for such a belief.

The title of Dr. Ironside's book was based on his teaching that there is a **"Great Parenthesis"** between the 69th and the 70th week of Daniel's prophecy found in **Daniel 9:24-27**, which he said had already lasted over 1900 years. Later in my life, looking back at this, it seemed to me that anyone would have known that nothing comes between a 69th and a 70th week, in anything; that where one ends, the other begins; and it has seemed this way to me for many years now.

The three years (1946-1949) of study at John B. Stetson University, DeLand, Florida, did nothing to change my futuristic views. While in college I was pastor of the Raiford Baptist Church at Raiford, Florida, 115 miles away; and after that I did some more evangelistic work.

In 1951 I married, and Evelyn and I moved to the pastorate of First Baptist Church in Clewiston, Florida. While there I published the little book, **The Great Tribulation** — one of the sermons I had preached, based on Dr. W. Herschel Ford's book.

Time went on. In 1953 I was in Miami, Florida, pastor of Orchard Villa Baptist Church (now Palm Springs Baptist Church after relocating to Hialeah). Suddenly one day I realized what I was doing. As I really began to study and think about some of these things about prophecy, I saw I was just "dishing out" what others had taught, as many others were doing, without a complete and solid analysis of those things for myself. I began to see that certain things in the Bible did not square up with some of the points I had been making. I had difficulty reconciling my teachings with what it seemed the Bible really taught. I do not mean that I had not studied. I had read and studied the Bible through, over and over again; my well-worn Bibles would testify to that.

But I learned to read the books of others in a very critical way, examining every statement they made for actual proof if they said something which seemed "fuzzy" or not correctly related to Scriptures I knew; and I refused to believe anything just because it "fit" into a system I had previously learned. (It is amazing how much material written in books one has to overlook when he does this).

I came to the place where I was willing to preach what I saw the Bible taught, whether I understood all of it or not. And if I later saw someting different than I was teaching then, I would change and go on teaching whatever it was I saw in its new light, as I understood it, regardless of any and all of my friends who might not see things just the same way.

As I said, I began to feel that it was a question as to whether the Bible actually taught some of the things I had been teaching. It was my intense love and devotion for the Bible as the word of God, as well as my independent research into its teachings, that finally separated me from some of the dogmatic and theoretical assertions I had been making. This has been my position ever since.

It was along then, in the early 50's, that I read **Albert Barnes'** Commentary and saw how he placed the Great Tribulation of **Matthew 24** back into the first century when Jerusalem was destroyed. I began to try to understand that passage more clearly — first believing that the tribulation period of **Matthew 24:21** would have to be extended for many years into the future for it to say that the Son of man would come **immediately** after that tribulation (**vs. 29**). This, I later felt, would cause one to be a post-tribulation rapturist, though not involving a futuristic seven years of tribulation as taught by so many. Later on still, I saw that I had no right to stretch that tribulation like a rubber band, way out into our future. In fact, it was some years later before I realized that the coming of Christ was indeed seen immediately after the tribulation of **Matthew 24:21**, and that both the great tribulation and the *parousia*-coming of Christ took place in the first century (as well as the end of that age). When I finally came to see this, a number of questions arose. I did not let the questions stop me from going on in my studies. I did learn that the more one understands, the more he will see there is yet to learn.

I have continued studying and digging, wading into everything by everybody, and really studying the Bible for myself on these things — comparing what others taught with what the Bible actually seems to say. My library began to fill up with many volumes dealing with various aspects of the second coming of Christ and related events, with more books on these subjects than anything else in my library. The difference was, I now read and studied with a supremely critical view of everything. Only God knows the many hours I spent studying these things. I don't want ever to believe, teach and preach things because I have been "brainwashed" into anything. Paul said, "Prove all things; hold fast that which is good" **(I Thessalonians 5:21)**. Consequently, I was not too dogmatic on many of those things for a number of years, because I was unwilling to say things of which I was not sure. Only the Holy Spirit can lead, step by step, into a knowledge of His word. The greatest interpreter of the Bible is the Holy Spirit — not college, seminary, Bible institutes, professors, Bible teachers, radio and television preachers, new books being published, and all the rest. And we need to spend more time with the Bible itself than with books **about** the Bible! So, for a long time I just preached what the Bible said without trying to compartmentalize various aspects of the Second Coming of Christ. What I didn't know and understand, I just didn't preach. That is being honest with God, myself, and my hearers (and readers).

I never fell out with others because we did not see eye to eye on details of prophecy — not even those preachers who shared my pulpit when I was a pastor. I have always felt it strange that some people separate themselves from other good Christians simply over the matters of details of prophecy. There are bigger things over which we could differ.

In May of 1980 a situation occurred which proved very embarrassing to me, but which turned out to be the beginning of a transformation in my ministry, as far as my views on eschatology were concerned. I had been invited to be with two churches in Germany — one on Sunday morning, and the other for meetings Sunday night through Wednesday; then I was to go on to meetings in Egypt. The previous year I had preached at both churches, with meetings of several nights at Rheinland Baptist Church in Einsiedlerhof. During those meetings the church reached its highest attendance since starting a year before, and we saw 26 conversions take place. Now I looked forward to those meetings.

On Saturday, the day before I was to preach, both pastors met with me, and they seemed disturbed. The pastor of the church where I was to conduct meetings asked me, "Are you a 'pre-trib'?" I asked him to define his terms so that I would know exactly what he was asking. The other pastor immediately responded by asking me, "Do you believe the rapture takes place before the 70th week of Daniel?" At that time I still had not done much studying in the prophecies of Daniel, and as mentioned before, had not given any special study to that particular prophecy of Daniel 9:24-27. Certainly I had never preached on it nor did I have any plans to do so. I answered simply,

"I don't know." As a result, and because I did not declare myself a "pre-tribulation rapture" preacher and would not agree that the rapture would occur prior to a tribulation period which according to one of them was presumably taught in Daniel 9, I was handed $200 and taken to the train station for Frankfurt. The pastor said, "No pre-tribulation rapture, no meetings!" Just like that! The pastor showed me that in this church's by-laws was a stipulation that one must believe in the pre-tribulation rapture to even belong to the church!

But I said that if you get a lemon, make a lemonade out of it; so I rode on a cruise boat up the River Rhine and did some sightseeing, as I did not have to be in Cairo, Egypt, until that Saturday. That experience revolutionized my life and ministry!

If it had not been for that incident in 1980, it is most likely my views of eschatology would not be the same as they are today. As a result, I began to dig in and study harder than ever before, and to piece together a lot of things that had been on my mind for a long time. As the pieces came together, so did the formation of various new books. But progress in understanding kept growing, taking me step by step to the point where I now stand as expressed in this series of studies in this present book. But it was nearly ten years later that I came to the understanding that not only **Matthew 24** but most all the book of Revelation had already been fulfilled in the first century.

My quest for knowledge on the New Testament prophecies led me to the libraries of some of the world's leading universities and seminaries. At these places I was able to track down many of the authors of years ago and learn what they taught. Our experience of several days at Cambridge University in Cambridge, England, in September 1987, for example, was recorded in Section 5 of this book.

I had just preached a sermon on **Has Jesus Already Returned to Planet Earth?** at Orangefield Baptist Church in Belfast, Northern Ireland. I was told that the message helped them to understand some of the passages in the New Testament relating to Christ's coming in that generation. That message was later printed in a little book, now out of print. But I still did not see that so many other New Testament passages relating to the coming of Christ, also related to those same events mentioned in **Matthew 24**; that is, they had been fulfilled in the past also.

At Cambridge University Library I found sufficient old books to have an influence on me toward feeling that not only **Matthew 24** but the book of Revelation too was fulfilled in the first century. I brought much material home with me in photocopies.

Later I did research for several days at Oxford University (Bodleian

Library).

I kept on studying. It might be appropriate to mention that other books which I later read also had an influence on my thinking. I did much of my reading while in campaigns overseas.

In January 1988 I was in meetings on Providence Island, Colombia. While there I read the entire 784 page book by **Max King** entitled **The Cross and the Parousia of Christ**. I wrote him later that it was an exhaustive book — that it had exhausted me in reading it! The book greatly intrigued me and raised many questions in my mind, though I never agreed with Max King's ideas of resurrection (and we corresponded later about this). I noted that in my own library at that time I had 29 of the books listed in the bibliography in the back of his book.

In June 1988, I got around to reading a book entitled **What Happened in A.D. 70?** written by **Ed Stevens**, editor of **Kingdom Counsel** in Bradford, Pennsylvania, which he had sent to me some time previously. This was a powerful little book on preterism. Ed and I have engaged in a number of conversations and communications.

In November 1988, I preached in meetings at Providence Baptist Church in Monrovia, Liberia. During that week of meetings, I read both of **Milton Terry**'s books — **Biblical Hermeneutics** and **Biblical Apocalyptics**. Dr. Terry was a 19th century Methodist Episcopalian and graduate of Yale Divinity School. He held several pastorates and became professor of Hebrew and Old Testament exegesis and theology at Garrett Biblical Institute. The scholarship of these books impressed me deeply, and the latter further clinched in my mind the matters that were developing there.

In October of 1990, while in meetings in Bucharest, Romania, I read **J. Stuart Russell**'s *The Parousia*. This book, written in England in 1878 by a Congregational minister, is perhaps the most important book on the preterist interpretation of the second coming of Christ of any book ever written.

From 1985 to 1992 there came forth from the various publishers up-to-date books on prophecy with the preterist interpretation, all of which I read. Some of these were: David Chilton's **Paradise Restored**, and **Days of Vengeance** (large commentary on the book of Revelation); Kenneth R. Gentry's **Before Jerusalem Fell**, and **The Beast of Revelation**; Gary DeMar's **Last Days Madness**; Arthur M. Ogden's **The Avenging of the Apostles and Prophets**; Joseph Balyeat's **Babylon, the Great City of Revelation**; etc. And there were others. Most of these are still available (see Bibliography in back for addresses).

Many other books have been studied and referred to, as indicated by the bibliography in the back of this book. Those I have mentioned were some of the most significant to me, not only in helping me to formulate these teachings in my mind, but to confirm the impressions I had as to what the Bible really taught on these matters. I do not agree with all of these in all the things they say, any more than they would agree with all I have written in this book, but they were particularly instrumental in helping me to come to the position I personally hold today. When I retired from the pastorate in 1976 in order to do overseas evangelism for the next nineteen years, I sold and gave away many of the books in my library. But when I began to study eschatology in earnest, I began to accumulate many more books on this subject. I have many, many commentaries and books on the book of Revelation itself. I have a number of full sets of commentaries. But books alone were not enough. I had to see these things for myself. And I am a slow learner.

One of the reasons I am laboring on this personal aspect of my ministry so much, is that I feel I must show cause for this present emphasis on prophecy from the standpoint in which I present it. Otherwise some who read what I am now writing and who know me from years back, or even read other books of mine not too many years back, will feel that I contradict myself and they would not understand. More than 2,000,000 of our smaller books have gone out all over the world, starting in 1944. I do not want to be misunderstood. We do not reprint any of those little books which do not at present represent our views.

Then too, by giving testimony to my own experience, I might encourage many others to do likewise. I know how easy it is for Christians to get "polarized" into the same mold of thinking about things; independent thought, creative study, and reliance on the Holy Spirit for illumination are not nearly so common as is supposed. From experience, I know it is difficult to break away from tradition! But inner peace, freedom, and liberty of conscience only come as the fetters of prejudice, misguided opinions, and inherited beliefs are all put on the table to be analyzed by the truth of the word of God itself.

It becomes easier, when one has spent many years in reading and studying the Bible, and researching many books and analyzing all kinds of interpretations, to finally reach some valid conclusions for oneself. But it is also true that with such background and experience, one learns that there is so much more yet to be learned. I pity the young student, not long started out, who reads a few modern books on prophecy, and suddenly he knows it all and is a world expert on prophetic matters! We see too much of this.

To be sure, there will be those who keep right on preaching and teaching those things that are not found in the Bible, simply because they have their minds already geared to it, and it would be extremely embarrassing for them to really study the Bible's teachings **in depth** and come to conclusions that would cause them to "change horses in the middle of the stream." I can understand this! And I can be far more tolerant with them about this than they possibly would be with me (some of them, anyway), but I am just as doggedly determined to preach the truth of the infallible word of God as they are — and even more so perhaps. At the same time, I do not disassociate myself from anyone simply because he does not agree with me on these matters. Would to God this were true of all Christians, and especially preachers!

Let me say, I think it is most hindering to the cause of Christ and soul-winning efforts, for Christian leaders to fall out with each other over these matters of prophecy. Nobody has all the answers; the various men I have studied, on all sides, all contradict each other in some things; they do not agree, over and over again! So why should we "lesser" Bible students fail to have fellowship simply because we do not see eye-to-eye on these matters?

Please understand me when I say that this book (or any of my books) does not summarize the last word on what I feel the Bible teaches. I would hate to think I should never learn anything else new, nor anything different than I now understand to be true. Especially from 1980 to now, I have increasingly studied matters of eschatology and have been led step by step to see many new truths (to me) as I have so studied. I have continued to write what I have learned, even though some things differed from what I had previously understood and wrote. And there are some things which, when seen and understood, will never allow one to go back to what he once believed. But my learning has been progressive. As a result, so have been my writings. You can read any of my earlier writings as I was separating more and more from the modern pre-tribulation rapture teaching, millennialism, and futurism, and see this progression. To be sure, if I live and God lets me keep writing, there will yet be further developments of these truths to me, and some discarding of points here and there where improvement needs to be made. (Some of what was previously published in our smaller books on **Matthew 24** had to be revised before being published in this larger book. Not much, though.)

So don't fuss at me too much for what I believe and teach today; tomorrow there may be some improvement! I do not discount the possiblity of my being wrong on what I believe today. I do not believe

I have all the truth. What I am saying here is that I am not closing my mind to any new understanding of truth which God lets develop in my mind. But what I have learned may throw some light for you on these matters if you are seriously interested in studying what the Bible says.

James Russell Lowell said, "The foolish and the dead alone never change their opinions."

Bibliography

Many other books are available on the subject matter of this book other than those listed here. However, the books listed below are those from which direct quotations have been made in this book. They do not necessarily reflect the views of the author of this book. We have added the publisher's address if listed in the book.

ALFREE, John. *A World Destroyed by Fire.* Bible Study Publications, 1 Penrith Place, Mansfield, Nottinghamshire, NG19 6NE, England. 1994.

AMERICANA, Encyclopedia. Vol. 16. Grolier Incorporated, Danbury, Conn. 06816. 1986.

ALLIS, Oswald T. *Prophecy and the Church.* The Presbyterian and Reformed Publishing Company, Philadelphia, Pennsylvania. 1945, 1947.

ANTE-NICENE FATHERS, The. 10 vols. Wm. B. Eerdmans Publishing Co., Grand Rapids, Michigan. Reprint of October 1978.

APOCRYPHA, The. Destiny Publishers, Merrimac, Massachusetts. 1946.

AUGUSTINE, St. *The Nicene and Post-Nicene Fathers.* 28 vols. Wm. B. Eerdmans Pub. Co., Grand Rapids, Mich. Reprint of 1979.

AUBERLEN, Carl August. *The Prophecies of Daniel and The Revelation of St. John.* T. & T. Clark, 28, George Street, Edinburgh, Scotland. 1856.

AUNE, David E. *Prophecy in Early Christianity and the Ancient Mediterranean World.* William B. Eerdmans Publishing Company, Grand Rapids, Michigan. 1983.

BAHNSEN, Greg L. and Kenneth L. Gentry, Jr. *House Divided — The Break-Up of Dispensational Theology.* Institute for Christian Economics, P.O. Box 8000, Tyler, Texas 75711.

BALYEAT, Joseph R. *Babylon the Great City of Revelation.* Onward Press, P.O. Box 4690, Sevierville, Tenn. 37864. 1991.

BARNES, Albert. *Notes on the Old and the New Testament.* 27 vols. Baker Book House, Grand Rapids, Mich. 1949, 1953.

BARCLAY, William. *The Gospel of Matthew.* Vol. 2. Westminster Press, Philadelphia, Pennsylvania. Revised edition of 1975.

BEASLEY-MURRAY, George Raymond. *Jesus and the Future.* Macmillan and Co., London. 1954.

------------ *Jesus and the Kingdom of God.* Wm. B. Eerdmans Pub. Co., 225 Jefferson Ave. S.E., Grand Rapids, Mich 49503. 1986.

------------ *Jesus and the Last Days.* Hendrickson Publishers, Inc., P.O. Box 3473, Peabody, Mass. 01961. 1993.

BECKWITH, Isbon T. *The Apocalypse of John.* Baker Book House, Grand Rapids, Michigan. (1919). Paperback edition 1979.

BENGEL, John Albert. *Bengal's New Testament Commentary.* 2 vols. Kregel Publications, Grand Rapids, Mich. 49501. (1742). 1981.

BERKOUWER, G.C. *The Return of Christ.* Wm. B. Eerdmans Publishing Co., Grand Rapids, Mich. (1972) Reprinted August 1981 from the Dutch edition of 1961 and 1963.

BLOMBERG, Craig L. *The New American Commentary.* Broadman Press, Nashville, Tenn.

BOETTNER, Loraine. *The Millennium.* The Presbyterian and Reformed Publishing Company, Box 817, Phillipsburg, N.J. 08865. Revised edition 1984.

BOWMAN, George M. *Five Hours to a Better Eschatology.* Operation Balance, 190 Hespeler Rd., #1504, Cambridge, Ontario N1R 8B8, Canada. 1989.

BOYD, J.R. *The Berean Ambassador.* Box 232, Sudbury, Ont. P3E 4N5, Canada. Nov. 1990.

BRAY, John L. *Israel in Bible Prophecy.* John L. Bray Ministry, Inc., P.O. Box 90129, Lakeland, Florida 33804. 1983.

------------ *The Millennium — the Big Question.* John L. Bray Ministry, Inc., P.O. Box 90219, Lakeland, Florida 33804. 1984.

------------ *The Origin of the Pre-Tribulation Rapture Teaching.* John L. Bray Ministry, Inc., P.O. Box 90129, Lakeland, Florida 33804. 1982.

------------ *Morgan Edwards and the Pre-Tribulation Rapture Teaching (1788).* John L. Bray Ministry, Inc., P.O. Box 90129, Lakeland, Florida 33804. 1995.

BRITTANICA, Encyclopaedia. Vol. 12. 1973 ed.

BROADUS, John A. *An American Commentary on the New Testament.* The American Baptist Publication Society, 1701-1703 Chestnut St., Philadelphia, Pa. 1886. Vol. 1.

BROWN, David. *Christ's Second Coming: Will It Be Premillennial?* Reproduced and Distributed by The Old Paths Book Club, Box V, Rosemead, California. 1953.

BROWN, John. *Discourses and Sayings of Our Lord.* Vol. 1. The Banner of Truth Trust, Edinburgh, Scotland. 1852.

BRUCE, F. F. *Israel and the Nations.* Wm. B. Eerdmans Pub. Co., Grand Rapids, Michigan.

BUTLER'S Bible Readers Commentary. Funk & Wagnalls Publishers, 18 & 20 Astor Place, New York, New York. 1889.

CALVIN, John. *Calvin's Commentaries.* Reprinted 1984 by Baker Book House, Grand Rapids, Michigan 49506. 1847.

CAMP, Franklin. *The Work of the Holy Spirit in Redemption.* Roberts & Son, P.O. Box 1806, Birmingham, Alabama 35201. 1972.

CAMPBELL, Roderick. *Israel and the New Covenant.* Geneva Divinity School Press, Presbyterian and Reformed Pub. Co., Philadelphia, Pennsylvania. 1954.

CARINGOLA, Robert. *Seventy Weeks. The Historical Alternative.* Companion Press, P.O. Box 351, Shippensburg, Pennsylvania 17257. 1991.

CARROLL, B.H. *An Introduction of the English Bible.* Broadman Press, Nashville, Tennessee. 1947.

CARSON, D.A. *The Expositor's Bible Commentary.* Vol. 8. Zondervan Publishing House, Grand Rapids, Michigan. 1984.

CATHOLIC, *A Commentary on Holy Scripture.* Thomas Nelson & Sons, New York, New York. 1953.

CHILTON, David. *The Days of Vengeance.* Dominion Press, 7112 Burns Street, Fort Worth, Texas 76118. 1987.

------------ *The Great Tribulation.* Dominion Press, 7112 Burns Street, Fort Worth, Texas 76118. 1987.

------------ *Paradise Restored.* Reconstruction Press, P.O. Box 7999, Tyler, Texas 75711. 1985.

CLARKE, Adam. *Commentary on the New Testament.* Vol. 1. T. Mason &

G. Lane, New York, New York. 1837.
CLARK, David. *The Message from Patmos.* Baker Book House, Grand Rapids, Michigan 49516. Reprint of 1989.
CLEMENT of Alexandria. *The Ante-Nicene Fathers.* Vol. 2. William B. Eerdmans Publishing Co., Grand Rapids, Michigan. Reprint of 1979.
COLLIER'S Encyclopedia. Vol. 13. Macmillan Educational Corporation, New York. 1977.
COOPER, John W. *Body, Soul and Life Everlasting.* Wm. B. Eerdmans Pub. Co., 255 Jefferson Ave., S.E., Grand Rapids, Michigan 49503. 1989.
COWLES, Henry. *Matthew and Mark.* D. Appleton & Co., New York, New York. 1881.
COX, William E. *Biblical Studies in Final Things.* Presbyterian and Reformed Publishing Co., Phillipsburg, New Jersey. 1966.
CREWS, David. *Prophecy Fulfilled — God's Perfect Church.* New Light Publishing, P.O. Box 141635, Austin, Texas 78714. 1994.
DARBY, J.N. *The Collected Writings of J.N. Darby.* Bible Truth Publishers, 239 Harrison St., Oak Park, Illinois 60304. Reprint of 1971.
DAVIS, John Jefferson. *Christ's Victorious Kingdom.* Baker Book House, Grand Rapids, Michigan 49506. 1986.
DeMAR, Gary and Peter Leithart. *The Reduction of Christianity.* Dominion Press, Fort Worth, Texas (and) American Vision, P.O. Box 724088, Atlanta, Georgia 30339. 1988.
DESPRES, P.S. *The Apocalypse Fulfilled.* Brown, Green, and Longmans, London. 1854.
EDWARDS, Morgan. *Two Academical Exercises on Subjects Bearing the Following Titles; Millennium, and Last-Novelties.* Dobson and Lang, Second Street Between Market and Chesnut Street, Philadelphia, Pennsylvania. 1788.
ELLIOTT, E.B. *Horae Apocalypticae, or, A Commentary on the Apocalypse.* Vol. 4. Sealey's, London. 1851.
ELLICOTT, John. *Ellicott's Commentary on the Whole Bible.* Zondervan Publishing House, Grand Rapids, Michigan. 1981.
EUSEBIUS. *The History of the Church.* Dorset Press, New York. Edition of 1984. 1965.
------------ *The Nicene and Post-Nicene Fathers.* Second Series. Wm. B. Eerdmans Pub. Co., Grand Rapids, Michigan. Reprint 1979.
FARRAR, F. W. *The Early Days of Christianity.* Funk & Wagnalls, 10 & 12 Day Street, London. 1886.
FENTON, J.C. *Saint Matthew.* The Westminster Press, Philadelphia, Pennsylvania. 1963.
FORD, Desmond. *The Abomination of Desolation in Biblical Eschatology.* University Press of America, Inc., P.O. Box 19101, Washington, D.C. 20036. 1979.
FUDGE, Edward William. *The Fire That Consumes.* Providential Press, P.O. Box 21826, Houston, Texas 77218. 1982.
FUNK & WAGNALLS New Encyclopedia. Vols. 14, 25. Funk & Wagnalls, Inc., New York, New York.
GENTRY, Kenneth R., Jr. *The Beast of Revelation.* Institute for Christian Economics, P.O. Box 8000, Tyler, Texas 75711. 1989.
------------ *Before Jerusalem Fell.* Institute for Christian Economics, P.O. Box

8000, Tyler, Texas 75711.

------------ *He Shall Have Dominion.* Institute for Christian Economics, P.O. Box 8000, Tyler, Texas 75711.

GIBBON, Edward. *The Decline & Fall of the Roman Empire.* Vol. 1. Reprint by Random House, New York.

GILL, John. *An Exposition of the New Testament.* William Hill Collingridge, Long Lane, Aldersgate, London. 1852.

GOULD, Ezra P. *A Critical and Exegetical Commentary on the Gospel According to St. Mark.* Charles Scribner's Sons, New York, New York. 1896.

GRAYZEL, Solomon. *A History of the Jews.* Jewish Publication Society, Philadelphia, Pennsylvania. 1968.

HAMMOND, Henry. *A Paraphrase and Annotations upon all the books of the New Testament.* Oxford University Press, New York, New York. New edition 1845. First printing 1659.

HARRIS, John Tindall. *The Writings of the Apostle John.* Samuel Harris & Co., 5 Bishopgate Without, London. 1901.

HENRY, Matthew. *Commentary.* Fleming H. Revell Company, New York, New York. 1721. Reprint 1935.

HINDS, Samuel. *The Catechist's Manual and Family Lecturer.* B. Fellowes, Ludgate Street, London; and J. Parker, Oxford. 1829.

HOUSE, H. Wayne and Thomas D. Ice.*Dominion Theology, Blessing or Curse?* Multnomah Press, 8435 Northeast Glisan Street, Portland, Oregon 97220. 1988.

HUDSON, Henry T. *Echoes of the Ministries.* Vol. 11, No. 2. 8151 Stuhldreher N.W., Massillon, Ohio 44646.

HUGHES, Philip Edgcumbe. *The Book of Revelation.* Inter-varsity Press, 38 De Monfort Street, Leicester LE1 7GP, England, and Wm. B. Eerdmans Publishing Company, 255 Jefferson S.E., Grand Rapids, Michigan 49503. 1990.

ICE, Thomas. *Pre-Trib Perspectives.* Vol. 1, No. 3, Nov.-Dec. 1994. Pre-Trib Research Center, 370 L'Enfant Promenade, S.W., Suite 801, Washington, D.C. 20024.

INTERNATIONAL Bible Encyclopedia. Vol. 1. 1939.

INTERPRETER'S BIBLE, The. Vol. 11. Abingdon Press, Nashville, Tennessee. 1955.

KIK, J. Marcellus. *An Eschatology of Victory.* Presbyterian and Reformed Publishing Co., Phillipsburg, New Jersey. 1971.

KING, MAX R. *The Cross and the Parousia of Christ.* Parkman Road Church of Christ, 4705 Parkman Road, Warren, Ohio 44481. 1987.

IRONSIDE, Harry A. *The Great Parenthesis.* Zondervan Publishing House, Grand Rapids, Michigan. 1943.

JAMIESON, Fausset and Brown Commentary. Wm. B. Eerdmans Publishing Co., Grand Rapids, Michigan. Reprint 1984.

JEROME, The New, Biblical Commentary. Prentice Hall, Inc., Englewood Cliffs, New Jersey 07632. 1990.

JOSEPH, Raymond P. *Restoration of Our Theological Struction.* July-August 1991 edition, Vol. 3, No. 2, revised February 1992. South Reformed Presbyterian Church, 26580 Evergreen Road, Southfield, Michigan 48070.

JOSEPHUS, Flavius. *The Works of Flavius Josephus.* Vols. 1, 3. First published A.D. 93. Baker Book House, Grand Rapids, Michigan. 7th printing October 1980.

JUDAICA Jerusalem, Encyclopaedia. Vol. 3. Keter Publishing House Ltd., Jerusalem, Israel. 1971.

KEIL, C.F. *Commentary on the Old Testament.* Vol. 9. William B. Eerdmans Pub. Co., Grand Rapids, Michigan. Reprint of 1982.

KIK, J. Marcellus. *An Eschatology of Victory.* Presbyterian and Reformed Publishing Co., Philipsburg, N.J. 1971.

KIMBALL, William R. *The Rapture — A Question of Timing.* Baker Book House, Grand Rapids, Michigan 49506. 1985.

------------ *What the Bible Says About the Great Tribulation.* College Press Publishing Company, Joplin, Missouri. 1983.

KONIG, Adrio. *The Eclipse of Christ in Eschatology.* William B. Eerdmans Publishing Company, 255 Jefferson Ave. S.E., Grand Rapids, Michigan. 1989 (First published in England).

LACUNZA, Emmanuel. *The Coming of Messiah in Glory and Majesty.* L.B. Seely and Son, Fleet Street, London. 1827.

LADD, George Eldon. *The Blessed Hope.* Wm. B. Eerdmans Publishing Company, Grand Rapids, Michigan. 1956.

------------ *The Last Things.* Wm. B. Eerdmans Publishing Company, 255 Jefferson Ave., S.E., Grand Rapids, Michigan 49503. 1978.

LARDNER. *A Large Collection of Ancient Jewish and Heathen Testimonies To The Truth of Christ's Religion.* Vol. 1. London. 1764.

LEONARD, J.E. *Come Out of Her, My People.* Laudemont Press, 837 South Chestnut Ave., Arlington Heights, Illinois 60005. 1991.

LEONARD, Richard C. *The Promise of His Coming.* Laudemont Press, 834 South Chestnut Ave., Arlington Heights, Illinois 60005.

LIEFELD, Walter L. *Expositor's Bible Commentary.*

LIGHTFOOT, John. *A commentary on the New Testament from the Talmud and Hebraica.* Hendrickson Publishers, Peabody, Massachusetts 01961. Reprint of original edition of Oxford University Press 1859.

LINDSEY, Hal. *The Late Great Planet Earth.* Marshall, Morgan & Scott, 1 Bath Stree, London EC1V 9LB England. Reprint of 1971.

LINDSEY, Robert L. *Jesus, Rabbi and Lord.* Cornerstone Publishing, P.O. Box 311, Oak Creek, Wis. 53154. 1990.

LIVERMORE, Abriel Abbot. Vol. 1. James Munroe and Company, Boston, Massachusetts, and John Green, 121 Newgate Street, London. 1843.

MacRAE, Allan A. *The Prophecies of Daniel.* Christian Life Publishers, Tampines, P.O. Box 54, Singapore 9152. 1991.

MARGOLIS, Max L. and Alexander MARX. *A History of the Jewish People.* Published by Atheneum. Reprinted by arrangement with the Jewish Publication Society of America, Philadephia, Pennsylvania. 1927.

MAYHUE, Richard L. *Snatched Before the Storm.* BMH Books, P.O. Box 544, Winona Lake, Indiana 46590. 1980.

MELTON, J. Gordon. *The Encyclopedia of American Religions: Religious Creeds.* Gale Research Company, Book Tower, Detroit, Michigan 48226. 1988.

MEYER, Heinrich August Wilhelm. *Meyer's Commentary on the New Testament.* Hendrickson Publishers, Inc., Peabody, Massachusetts 09160. First completed in 1852. 1983 edition a reprint of the 6th edition of 1884..

MOODY, Dale. *The Word of Truth.* Wm. B. Eerdmans Publishing Co., 255 Jef-

ferson Ave. S.E., Grand Rapids, Michigan 49503.
MULLINS, Edgar Young. *The Christian Religion in its Doctrinal Expression.* Broadman Press, Nashville, Tennessee. 1917.
MURRAY, George L. *Millennial Studies.* Baker Book House, Grand Rapids, Michigan. 1948.
NEWPORT, John. *The Lion and the Lamb.* Broadman Press, Nashville, Tennessee. 1986.
NEWTON, Thomas. *Dissertations on the Prophecies.* B. Blake, 13, Bell Yard, Temple Bar., London. 1840. (Written 1754).
NICOLL, W. Robertson. *The Expositor's Greek Testament.* Vol. 1. William B. Eerdmans Publishing Company, Grand Rapids, Michigan. 1956.
NICENE, The, and Post-Nicene Fathers. Vol. 1. Wm. B. Eerdmans Publishing Company, Grand Rapids, Michigan. Reprint 1979.
NISBETT. *An Attempt to Illustrate Various important Passages in the Epistles, etc., of the New Testament, from Our Lord's Prophecies of the Destruction of Jerusalem, etc.,* London. 1787.
NORTH, Gary. *Rapture Fever.* Institute for Christian Economics, P.O. Box 8000, Tyler, Texas 75711. 1993.
OGDEN, Arthur M. *The Agenging of the Apostles and Prophets.* Ogden Publications, 212 Cherokee Trail, Somerset, Kentucky 42501. 2nd edition 1991.
OTTO, Randall E. *Coming in the Clouds — An Evangelical Case for the Invisibility of Christ at His Second Coming.* University Press of America, Inc., 4720 Boston Way, Lanham, Maryland 20706. 1994.
OWEN, John. *The Works of John Owen.* Johnstone and Hunter, London and Edinburgh. 1850-1953. Reprinted by The Banner of Truth Trust, P.O. Box 621, Carlisle, Pennsylvania 17013. 4th printing 1990.
PRESTON, Don K. *II Peter 3 — The Late Great Kingdom.* Don K. Preston, 421 Maxwell Ave., Ardmore, Oklahoma 73401. 1990.
------------ *Seal Up Vision & Prophecy.* Shawnee Printing Company, Shawnee, Oklahoma 74801.
(No author's name). *The Olivet Prophecy.* The Bible Way Publications, Ft. Lauderdale, Florida. Second ed. 1965.
RENAN, Joseph Ernest. *Renan's Antichrist.* Walter Scott, Ltd., Paternoster Square, London. 1899.
RIDDERBOS, Herman. *The Coming of the Kingdom.* The Presbyterian and Reformed Publishing Company, Philadelphia, Pennsylvania. 1962.
ROBINSON, Theodore. *The Gospel of Matthew.* Doubleday, Doran & Company, Inc., Garden City, New York. 1928.
RUSSELL, J. Stuart. *The Parousia.* Baker Book House, Grand Rapids, Michigan 49506. Written 1878. Reprint 1983 from the 1887 ed.
SANDERS, Cecil. *The Future: An Amillennial Perspective.* Randall House Publications, P.O. Box 17306, Nashville, Tennessee 37217. 1990.
SCHABOLIE, John Philip. *The Pilgrim Soul.* John Wilson, Pittsburgh. Translated from the Dutch to German, then to English. 1838.
SCHAFF, Philip. *The Creeds of Christendom.* 3 vols. Harper & Brothers Publishers, New York and London. 1877, 1905, 1919.
------------ *History of the Christian Church.* Vol. 1. Charles Scribner's Sons. Wm. B. Eerdmans Publishing Co., Grand Rapids, Michigan. Reprinted 1988.

SCHLECT, Chris. *"And It Came to Pass."* (Various authors). Canon Press, P.O. Box 8741, Moscow, Idaho 83843. 1993.

SCOFIELD, The, Reference Bible. 1917 ed. Oxford University Press, New York, New York.

SCOTT, Thomas. *Commentary on the New Testament.* Vol. 1. Samuel T. Armstrong, Theological Printer and Bookseller, No. 50, Cornhill. 1817.

SEVERUS, Sulpitius. *The Nicene and Post-Nicene Fathers.* 2nd series. Vol. 11. Wm B. Eerdmans Publishing Company, Grand Rapids, Michigan. Reprint 1978.

SPURGEON, Charles. *Metropolitan Tabernacle Pulpit.* Vol. 37. Banner of Truth Trust. Reprint 1970. First pub. in 1892.

STEVENS, William Arnold. *An American Commentary on the New Testament.* Commentary on the Epistles to the Thessalonians. American Baptist Publication Soceity, 1701-1703 Chestnut St., Philadelphia, Pennsylvania. 1887.

STUART, Moses. *Commentary on the Apocalypse.* Vol. 2. Morrill and Wardwell, Andover, 1845.

TACITUS. *The Annals of Imperial Rome.* Michael Grant Publications, Let. 1956, 1959, 1971.

TALMUD, The Babylonian. The Soncino ed. 18 Vol. Soncino Press, Oxford University Press, Oxford, England. 1918.

TASKER, R.V.G. *The Gospel According to St. Matthew.* Tyndale New Testament Commentaries. William B. Eerdmans Publishing Co., Grand Rapids, Michigan. 1961.

TERRY, Milton S. *Biblical Apocalyptics.* Baker Book House, Grand Rapids, Michigan. Reprint of 1988 from ed. of 1898.

------------ *Biblical Hermeneutics.* Zondervan Publishing House, Grand Rapids, Michigan 49506. Reprint of 1974 from 1898 ed.

TERTULLIAN. *The Ante-Nicene Fathers.* Vol. 4. William B. Eerdmans Pub. Co., Grand Rapids, Michigan. Reprint 1979.

VANDERWAAL, Cornelius. *Hal Lindsey and Biblical Prophecy.* Paidera Press, P.O. Box 1450, St. Catherines, Ont., Canada L2R 7J8. 1978.

VOS, Gerhardus. *The Pauline Eschatology.* Wm. B. Eerdmans Pub. Co., Grand Rapids, Michigan. 1953.

WALLACE, Foy E., Jr. *The Book of Revelation.* Foy E. Wallace, Jr., Publications, P.O. Box 7410, Fort Worth,Texas 76111. 1966.

WALVOORD, John F. *The Rapture Question.* Zondervan Publishing House, Grand Rapids, Michigan 49506. 1979.

WARFIELD, Benjamin. *Biblical and Theological Studies.* Presbyterian and Reformed Publishing Company, Philadelphia, Pennsylvania. 1968.

WELLS, H.G. *The Outline of History.* The MacMillan Company, New York, New York. 1927.

WHITEHEAD, Clyde F. *Israel versus Israel.* Covenant House Books, P.O. Box 4690, Sevierville, Tennessee 37864. 1993.

WILSON, Douglas. *"And It Came to Pass."* (Various authors). Canon Press, P.O. Box 8741, Moscow, Idaho 83843.

WILSON, Robert Dick. *Studies in the Book of Daniel.* Baker Book House, Grand Rapids, Michigan. Reprint 1979 from 1917 ed..

YOUNG, Edward J. *The Prophecy of Daniel, A Commentary.* Wm. B. Eerdmans Pub. Co., Grand Rapids, Michigan. 1953.

------------ *The Book of Isaiah.* Vol. 3. Wm. B. Eerdmans Publishing Co., Grand Rapids, Michigan. 1972.

ZARLEY, **Kermit.** *Palestine is Coming.* Hannibal Books, 921 Center St., Suite A, Hannibal, Missouri 63401. 1990.

This Book $15.00
(4 copies $30.00)
We pay postage.

PLEASE NOTE

Are you interested in reading other books on Prophecy, written by John L. Bray? Write us for an up-to-date price list and order blank.

Also ask us to place your name on our mailing list (free) to receive our newsletter telling of our Ministry activities and containing articles of interest on prophecy and Bible subjects. Those on our mailing list also receive a copy of our smaller books (also free) as each new title is published.

Write to:
JOHN L. BRAY MINISTRY, INC.
P.O. Box 90129
Lakeland, Florida 33804
(United States of America)

NOTES:

NOTES:

NOTES:

NOTES:

NOTES:

NOTES:

NOTES:

NOTES:

NOTES:

NOTES:

NOTES: